THE WORLD'S GREAT SERMONS

THE WORLD'S
GREAT
SERMONS

EDITED BY

S. E. FROST, JR., B.D., PH.D.

**Editor of *The Sacred Writings of the
World's Great Religions***

HALCYON HOUSE
Garden City, New York

Preface

THROUGHOUT THE AGES the sermon, in some form, has been an essential part of religion. The ancient prophets were great preachers. John the Baptist, the link between the prophets and Jesus, is known only for his preaching of the coming Messiah. Jesus delivered the greatest sermon of all times, the Sermon on the Mount. Paul, the first Christian missionary, went throughout the Mediterranean world preaching the gospel. Peter stood up among the Apostles at Pentecost and delivered one of the great sermons of the Christian tradition. And so on, down to our own day, we find the preacher standing in the pulpit proclaiming the word of God.

These sermons are found to be of many kinds. Some have sought to teach men and women about their religion and their God. Others are proclamations of right, justice, God's will, the path to be followed. Still others are clarion calls to duty, trumpet-like challenges to a wavering people. Then there are the sermons of consolation and comfort for those in distress. When the burdens of life become heavy and suffering sweeps o'er men like a flood, they turn to the preacher for words of hope and assurance. Indeed, whatever man's need the preacher is found proclaiming in a sermon religion's answer.

What are the great sermons of our religious tradition? Among the untold millions of sermons that have been preached since John the Baptist proclaimed the coming of the Lord, which ones are worthy of the title "Great"? This is the question we asked several hundred outstanding preachers, teachers, and laymen before beginning the compilation of this volume. Their answers were many and varied, but, from among all the sermons suggested there were certain ones which appeared time and again. These we have included in this volume.

One way of determining the greatness of a sermon is, of course, its literary value. Certain sermons are literary masterpieces composed by men whose fame has been won in the field of writing. However, we

71592

have taken the position that though literary value is important it should not be the major criterion of greatness as far as sermons are concerned. In our opinion, those sermons are truly great that more than others satisfy the fundamental cravings of mankind which are to be found among all men and in all ages. These cravings are the desire for knowledge, hope, comfort, challenge, constructive criticism, and pointed condemnation. From the saint to the sinner man must have all these from time to time if he is to live the good life. Especially in these times when the world that many have built seems to crumble about them, when the ideals of a generation are flaunted by another generation, when there are so many pressing temptations to renounce the God of our fathers and seek the easy road to worldly success, men and women need knowledge of the right, hope to live courageously in an at times hopeless world, comfort when sorrow o'erflows, challenge to exert their best, constructive criticism and pointed condemnation when they have taken the wrong road of life.

It is on this basis, then, that we have selected the one hundred and one great sermons constituting this book.

The arrangement of the sermons here is chronological. This will enable the reader to see the development of the sermon as a form of literary endeavor. It makes possible a clear view of the development of preaching as an art from the time of Jesus to our own day.

We are deeply grateful to those who took time to suggest sermons to be included. To the living ministers who have given us permission to use their sermons and to the publishers who have granted us the right to use sermons for which they hold the copyright, we express our sincerest appreciation. Then too, the teachers under whom we have worked during our student days at the Yale Divinity School and at the Union Theological Seminary and the ministers and devoted laymen with whom it has been our privilege to labor during the years of our ministry—each has made his contribution to this volume; and we are thankful to each of them.

S. E. FROST, JR.

Contents

THE WORLD'S GREAT SERMONS

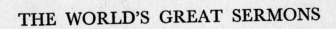

Jesus of Nazareth

[4 B.C.–30 A.D.]

The greatest of all preachers was Jesus of Nazareth. Born in a manger at Bethlehem, he was reared in the traditions of Judaism, and at an early age learned the Law and the Prophets. While still a child he confounded the scholars in the temple. As a young man of 30 he was baptized by John the Baptist and began a career of teaching and preaching which brought him in conflict with both the Jewish and Roman authorities of Palestine and led to his crucifixion. During the short period of his preaching he convinced a few faithful followers that he was the Messiah, the Christ, for which the world waited. This conviction grew after his death and resurrection until what began as a small Jewish sect became a world-conquering religion. The Sermon on the Mount (St. Matthew, Chapters 5–7) is Jesus' greatest sermon, and has become a Christian classic. In it is summed up all the teachings of Jesus. Many have affirmed that if the rest of the four gospels were lost and it alone remained, we would still have the essence of Christianity.

THE SERMON ON THE MOUNT

Blessed are the poor in spirit: for theirs is the kingdom of heaven.

Blessed are they that mourn: for they shall be comforted.

Blessed are the meek: for they shall inherit the earth.

Blessed are they which do hunger and thirst after righteousness: for they shall be filled.

Blessed are the merciful: for they shall obtain mercy.

Blessed are the pure in heart: for they shall see God.

Blessed are the peacemakers: for they shall be called the children of God.

Blessed are they which are persecuted for righteousness' sake: for theirs is the kingdom of heaven.

Blessed are ye, when men shall revile you, and persecute you, and shall say all manner of evil against you falsely, for my sake.

Rejoice, and be exceeding glad: for great is your reward in heaven: for so persecuted they the prophets which were before you.

Ye are the salt of the earth: but if the salt have lost his savour, wherewith shall it be salted? it is thenceforth good for nothing, but to be cast out, and to be trodden under foot of men.

Ye are the light of the world. A city that is set on an hill cannot be hid.

Neither do men light a candle, and put it under a bushel, but on a candlestick; and it giveth light unto all that are in the house.

Let your light so shine before men, that they may see your good works, and glorify your Father which is in heaven.

Think not that I am come to destroy the law, or the prophets: I am not come to destroy, but to fulfil.

For verily I say unto you, Till heaven and earth pass, one jot or one tittle shall in no wise pass from the law, till all be fulfilled.

Whosoever therefore shall break one of these least commandments, and shall teach men so, he shall be called the least in the kingdom of heaven: but whosoever shall do and teach them, the same shall be called great in the kingdom of heaven.

For I say unto you, That except your righteousness shall exceed the righteousness of the scribes and Pharisees, ye shall in no case enter into the kingdom of heaven.

Ye have heard that it was said by them of old time, Thou shalt not kill; and whosoever shall kill shall be in danger of the judgment:

But I say unto you, That whosoever is angry with his brother without a cause shall be in danger of the judgment: and whosoever shall say to his brother, Raca, shall be in danger of the council: but whosoever shall say, Thou fool, shall be in danger of hell fire.

Therefore if thou bring thy gift to the altar, and there rememberest that thy brother hath ought against thee;

Leave there thy gift before the altar, and go thy way; first be reconciled to thy brother, and then come and offer thy gift.

Agree with thine adversary quickly, whiles thou art in the way with him; lest at any time the adversary deliver thee to the judge, and the judge deliver thee to the officer, and thou be cast into prison.

Verily I say unto thee, Thou shalt by no means come out thence, till thou hast paid the uttermost farthing.

Ye have heard that it was said by them of old time, Thou shalt not commit adultery:

But I say unto you, That whosoever looketh on a woman to lust after her hath committed adultery with her already in his heart.

And if thy right eye offend thee, pluck it out, and cast it from thee: for it is profitable for thee that one of thy members should perish, and not that thy whole body should be cast into hell.

And if thy right hand offend thee, cut it off, and cast it from thee: for it is profitable for thee that one of thy members should perish, and not that thy whole body should be cast into hell.

It hath been said, Whosoever shall put away his wife, let him give her a writing of divorcement:

But I say unto you, That whosoever shall put away his wife, saving for the cause of fornication, causeth her to commit adultery: and whosoever shall marry her that is divorced committeth adultery.

Again, ye have heard that it hath been said by them of old time, Thou shalt not forswear thyself, but shalt perform unto the Lord thine oaths:

But I say unto you, Swear not at all; neither by heaven; for it is God's throne:

Nor by the earth; for it is his footstool: neither by Jerusalem; for it is the city of the great King.

Neither shalt thou swear by thy head, because thou canst not make one hair white or black.

But let your communication be, Yea, yea; Nay, nay: for whatsoever is more than these cometh of evil.

Ye have heard that it hath been said, An eye for an eye, and a tooth for a tooth:

But I say unto you, That ye resist not evil: but whosoever shall smite thee on thy right cheek, turn to him the other also.

And if any man will sue thee at the law, and take away thy coat, let him have thy cloke also.

And whosoever shall compel thee to go a mile, go with him twain.

Give to him that asketh thee, and from him that would borrow of thee turn not thou away.

Ye have heard that it hath been said, Thou shalt love thy neighbour, and hate thine enemy.

But I say unto you, Love your enemies, bless them that curse you, do good to them that hate you, and pray for them which despitefully use you, and persecute you;

That ye may be the children of your Father which is in heaven: for he maketh his sun to rise on the evil and on the good, and sendeth rain on the just and on the unjust.

For if ye love them which love you, what reward have ye? do not even the publicans the same?

And if ye salute your brethren only, what do ye more than others? do not even the publicans so?

Be ye therefore perfect, even as your Father which is in heaven is perfect.

Take heed that ye do not your alms before men, to be seen of them: otherwise ye have no reward of your Father which is in heaven.

Therefore when thou doest thine alms, do not sound a trumpet before thee, as the hypocrites do in the synagogues and in the streets, that they may have glory of men. Verily I say unto you, They have their reward.

But when thou doest alms, let not thy left hand know what thy right hand doeth:

That thine alms may be in secret: and thy Father which seeth in secret himself shall reward thee openly.

And when thou prayest, thou shalt not be as the hypocrites are: for they love to pray standing in the synagogues and in the corners of the streets, that they may be seen of men. Verily I say unto you, They have their reward.

But thou, when thou prayest, enter into thy closet, and when thou hast shut thy door, pray to thy Father which is in secret; and thy Father which seeth in secret shall reward thee openly.

But when ye pray, use not vain repetitions, as the heathen do: for they think that they shall be heard for their much speaking.

Be not ye therefore like unto them: for your Father knoweth what things ye have need of, before ye ask him.

After this manner therefore pray ye: Our Father which art in heaven, Hallowed be thy name.

Thy kingdom come. Thy will be done in earth, as it is in heaven.

Give us this day our daily bread.

And forgive us our debts, as we forgive our debtors.

And lead us not into temptation, but deliver us from evil: For thine is the kingdom, and the power, and the glory, for ever. Amen.

For if ye forgive men their trespasses, your heavenly Father will also forgive you:

But if ye forgive not men their trespasses, neither will your Father forgive your trespasses.

Moreover when ye fast, be not, as the hypocrites, of a sad countenance: for they disfigure their faces, that they may appear unto men to fast. Verily I say unto you, They have their reward.

But thou, when thou fastest, anoint thine head, and wash thy face;

That thou appear not unto men to fast, but unto thy Father which is in secret: and thy Father, which seeth in secret, shall reward thee openly.

Lay not up for yourselves treasures upon earth, where moth and rust doth corrupt, and where thieves break through and steal:

But lay up for yourselves treasures in heaven, where neither moth nor rust doth corrupt, and where thieves do not break through nor steal:

For where your treasure is, there will your heart be also.

The light of the body is the eye: if therefore thine eye be single, thy whole body shall be full of light.

But if thine eye be evil, thy whole body shall be full of darkness. If therefore the light that is in thee be darkness, how great is that darkness!

No man can serve two masters: for either he will hate the one, and love the other; or else he will hold to the one, and despise the other. Ye cannot serve God and mammon.

Therefore I say unto you, Take no thought for your life, what ye shall eat, or what ye shall drink; nor yet for your body, what ye shall put on. Is not the life more than meat, and the body than raiment?

Behold the fowls of the air: for they sow not, neither do they reap, nor gather into barns; yet your heavenly Father feedeth them. Are ye not much better than they?

Which of you by taking thought can add one cubit unto his stature?

And why take ye thought for raiment? Consider the lilies of the field, how they grow; they toil not, neither do they spin:

And yet I say unto you, That even Solomon in all his glory was not arrayed like one of these.

Wherefore, if God so clothe the grass of the field, which to day is, and to morrow is cast into the oven, shall he not much more clothe you, O ye of little faith?

Therefore take no thought, saying, What shall we eat? or, What shall we drink? or, Wherewithal shall we be clothed?

(For after all these things do the Gentiles seek:) for your heavenly Father knoweth that ye have need of all these things.

But seek ye first the kingdom of God, and his righteousness; and all these things shall be added unto you.

Take therefore no thought for the morrow: for the morrow shall take thought for the things of itself. Sufficient unto the day is the evil thereof.

Judge not, that ye be not judged.

For with what judgment ye judge, ye shall be judged: and with what measure ye mete, it shall be measured to you again.

And why beholdest thou the mote that is in thy brother's eye, but considerest not the beam that is in thine own eye?

Or how wilt thou say to thy brother, Let me pull out the mote out of thine eye; and, behold, a beam is in thine own eye?

Thou hypocrite, first cast out the beam out of thine own eye; and then shalt thou see clearly to cast out the mote out of thy brother's eye.

Give not that which is holy unto the dogs, neither cast ye your pearls before swine, lest they trample them under their feet, and turn again and rend you.

Ask, and it shall be given you; seek, and ye shall find; knock, and it shall be opened unto you:

For every one that asketh receiveth; and he that seeketh findeth; and to him that knocketh it shall be opened.

Or what man is there of you, whom if his son ask bread, will he give him a stone?

Or if he ask a fish, will he give him a serpent?

If ye then, being evil, know how to give good gifts unto your children, how much more shall your Father which is in heaven give good things to them that ask him?

Therefore all things whatsoever ye would that men should do to you, do ye even so to them: for this is the law and the prophets.

Enter ye in at the strait gate: for wide is the gate, and broad is the way, that leadeth to destruction, and many there be which go in thereat:

Because strait is the gate, and narrow is the way, which leadeth unto life, and few there be that find it.

Beware of false prophets, which come to you in sheep's clothing, but inwardly they are ravening wolves.

Ye shall know them by their fruits. Do men gather grapes of thorns, or figs of thistles?

Even so every good tree bringeth forth good fruit; but a corrupt tree bringeth forth evil fruit.

A good tree cannot bring forth evil fruit, neither can a corrupt tree bring forth good fruit.

Every tree that bringeth not forth good fruit is hewn down, and cast into the fire.

Wherefore by their fruits ye shall know them.

Not every one that saith unto me, Lord, Lord, shall enter into the kingdom of heaven; but he that doeth the will of my Father which is in heaven.

Many will say to me in that day, Lord, Lord, have we not prophesied in thy name? and in thy name have cast out devils? and in thy name done many wonderful works?

And then will I profess unto them, I never knew you: depart from me, ye that work iniquity.

Therefore whosoever heareth these sayings of mine, and doeth them, I will liken him unto a wise man, which built his house upon a rock:

And the rain descended, and the floods came, and the winds blew, and beat upon that house; and it fell not: for it was founded upon a rock.

And every one that heareth these sayings of mine, and doeth them not, shall be likened unto a foolish man, which built his house upon the sand:

And the rain descended, and the floods came, and the winds blew, and beat upon that house; and it fell: and great was the fall of it.

Saint Peter

[First Century]

Saint Peter was the first apostle of Jesus. His name was Simon, son of John, until Jesus changed it to Peter, from the Greek "petros," meaning "rock." A fisherman living near Capernaum, he was noted for his vacillating character. At times he was Jesus' most ardent disciple, and at others he denied his Master. But after Jesus' death he became a true "rock" of the early church, finally suffering martyrdom in Rome. This sermon, delivered at the time of Pentecost in Jerusalem, is one of the masterpieces of the New Testament. It links Jesus with the prophecies of the Jews and affirms His divinity through His resurrection.

SERMON AT PENTECOST

Ye men of Judæa, and all ye that dwell at Jerusalem, be this known unto you, and hearken to my words:

For these are not drunken, as ye suppose, seeing it is but the third houɪ of the day.

But this is that which was spoken by the prophet Joel;

And it shall come to pass in the last days, saith God, I will pour out of my Spirit upon all flesh: and your sons and your daughters shall prophesy, and your young men shall see visions, and your old men shall dream dreams:

And on my servants and on my handmaidens I will pour out in those days of my Spirit; and they shall prophesy:

And I will shew wonders in heaven above, and signs in the earth beneath; blood, and fire, and vapour of smoke:

The sun shall be turned into darkness, and the moon into blood, before that great and notable day of the Lord come:

And it shall come to pass, that whosoever shall call on the name of the Lord shall be saved.

Ye men of Israel, hear these words; Jesus of Nazareth, a man approved of God among you by miracles and wonders and signs, which God did by him in the midst of you, as ye yourselves also know:

Him, being delivered by the determinate counsel and foreknowledge of God, ye have taken, and by wicked hands have crucified and slain:

Whom God hath raised up, having loosed the pains of death: because it was not possible that he should be holden of it.

For David speaketh concerning him, I foresaw the Lord always before my face, for he is on my right hand, that I should not be moved:

Therefore did my heart rejoice, and my tongue was glad; moreover also my flesh shall rest in hope:

Because thou wilt not leave my soul in hell, neither wilt thou suffer thine Holy One to see corruption.

Thou hast made known to me the ways of life; thou shalt make me full of joy with thy countenance.

Men and brethren, let me freely speak unto you of the patriarch David, that he is both dead and buried, and his sepulchre is with us unto this day.

Therefore being a prophet, and knowing that God had sworn with an oath to him, that of the fruit of his loins, according to the flesh, he would raise up Christ to sit on his throne;

He seeing this before spake of the resurrection of Christ, that his soul was not left in hell, neither his flesh did see corruption.

This Jesus hath God raised up, whereof we all are witnesses.

Therefore being by the right hand of God exalted, and having received of the Father the promise of the Holy Ghost, he hath shed forth this, which ye now see and hear.

For David is not ascended into the heavens: but he saith himself, The Lord said unto my Lord, Sit thou on my right hand,

Until I make thy foes thy footstool.

Therefore let all the house of Israel know assuredly, that God hath made that same Jesus, whom ye have crucified, both Lord and Christ.

Saint Paul

[?-67]

The son of a Hebrew father who possessed the right of Roman citizenship, Paul of Tarsus was educated by the great Jewish scholar, Gamaliel. His early life was spent in the strictest Jewish tradition and was marked by his energetic persecution of the Christians. After his conversion to Christianity, he became the first missionary preacher and organizer of this despised sect. Mainly through his efforts Christianity grew from a small Jewish sect to a world religion, and thriving churches were organized throughout the Roman world. Paul's sermon on Mars Hill is typical of his style and power of expression. It states the Christian point of view as it was preached to the non-Christian world of that day, and affirms the divinity and eternal nature of Jesus.

SERMON ON MARS HILL

Ye men of Athens, I perceive that in all things ye are too superstitious.

For as I passed by, and beheld your devotions, I found an altar with this inscription, TO THE UNKNOWN GOD. Whom therefore ye ignorantly worship, him declare I unto you.

God that made the world and all things therein, seeing that he is Lord of heaven and earth, dwelleth not in temples made with hands;

Neither is worshiped with men's hands, as though he needed any thing, seeing he giveth to all life, and breath, and all things;

And hath made of one blood all nations of men for to dwell on all the face of the earth, and hath determined the times before appointed, and the bounds of their habitation;

That they should seek the Lord, if haply they might feel after him, and find him, though he be not far from every one of us:

For in him we live, and move, and have our being; as certain also cf your own poets have said, For we are also his offspring.

Forasmuch then as we are the offspring of God, we ought not to think that the Godhead is like unto gold, or silver, or stone, graven by art and man's device.

And the times of this ignorance God winked at; but now commandeth all men every where to repent:

Because he hath appointed a day, in the which he will judge the world in righteousness by that man whom he hath ordained; whereof he hath given assurance unto all men, in that he hath raised him from the dead.

Tertullian

[160–230]

Quintus Septimius Florens Tertullianus was born at Carthage. His father, a pagan, was a centurion in the service of the proconsul of that city. As a young man he was interested in law and rhetoric. However, as he grew older he became a Christian, rose to the office of presbyter, and throughout the rest of his life exerted a profound influence upon the theological opinion of his time. The sermon given here, usually known as De Patientia, has always been regarded as "the most exquisite of all the author's writings." Neander refers to it as "Tertullian's beautiful treatise." It is also important in the history of ethics as the first discussion we have of a cardinal Christian virtue and an exposition of the then little understood Christian theology.

THE DUTY AND BENEFITS OF PATIENCE

But let patience have her perfect work, that ye may be perfect and entire, wanting nothing. JAMES 1:4.

THE GOOD HEALTH of faith and soundness in the Lord's religion do not easily result to any one, unless patience sit at his side. Such an object is it made to the things of God, that no one, who is a stranger to patience, can obey any commandment or do any work pleasing to the Lord. Its good quality, even they who live blindly, honor with the title of the highest virtue.

To us it is no human affection of cynical indifference, schooled by a stupid apathy, which giveth authority for the exercise of patience, but the divine ordering of a lively and heavenly rule, setting forth God Himself as the example of patience; first as the Being who scattereth the dew of His light over *the just and the unjust* equally, who suffereth the offices of the seasons, the services of the elements, the tributes of the whole creation, to come alike to the worthy and the unworthy; bearing with those most unthankful nations who worship the follies of their own craft, and the works of their own hands, and persecute His name, His household; bearing with covetousness, with iniquity, with wantonness, with the maliciousness which daily waxeth insolent, so that by His own patience He robbeth Himself; seeing that the greater part believe not in the Lord for this reason, because that for so long a time they have not known that He is wroth with the world.

And this instance indeed of Divine patience being, as it were, afar off, may perchance be reckoned among those things which be too high for us. But what shall we say of that which hath in a manner been *handled* among men openly in the world? God suffereth Himself to be conceived in the womb of a mother, and abideth the time; and being born, waiteth to grow up; and being grown up, is not eager to be acknowledged, but putteth a further slight upon Himself, and is baptized by his own serv- ant, and repelleth the attacks of the tempter by words only. When from the Lord He became the Master, teaching man to escape death, having well learned, for salvation's sake, the forgiving spirit of offended patience, He *strove* not; He *cried* not; neither did *any hear His voice in the streets; the shattered reed* did *He not break, the smoking flax He* did *not quench.* For there was no lying voice in the Prophet, yea rather in the testimony of God Himself, who put His own Spirit in His Son, with perfection of patience. None that desired to cleave unto Him did He not receive; no man's table or house did He despise; yea, Himself ministered to the washing of His disciples' feet. He scorned not the sinners nor the publi- cans. He was not angry even with that city which would not receive Him; when even His disciples would have desired that fires from Heaven should presently appear against a town so scornful. He healed the un- thankful; He gave place to those that laid snares for Him. This were but little, if He had not had in His own company even His own betrayer, and yet did not determinately make him known. But when He is de- livered up, when *He is led as a sheep to the slaughter,* for *so He openeth not His mouth* more than *the lamb,* when in the power of *his shearer.* He at whose side, if He had desired it, *legions of angels* from Heaven would at one word have been present, approved not the avenging sword of even a single disciple. In Malchus the patience of the Lord was wounded. Wherefore also He cursed the works of the sword forever after, and by the restoration of soundness to him whom He had not Himself hurt, He made satisfaction through patience, the mother of mercy. I pass in silence the Crucifixion, for it was for that that He had come into the world; yet was there need of insults also, that He might undergo death? But being about to depart, He desired to be filled to the full with the pleasure of patience. He is spit upon, is beaten, is mocked, is foully clothed, still more foully crowned. Wondrous constancy in patience! He who had purposed to hide Himself in the form of man, followed none of the example of man's impatience! In this especially ought ye, O Pharisees, to have acknowledged the Lord; none among men could have worked patience such as this. Such and so great proofs—whose greatness is with the nations indeed a diminishing, but with us is the cause and building up of faith—manifest clearly enough to those to whom it is given to believe, not only by the discourses of the Lord in teaching, but by His sufferings in enduring, that patience is the nature of God, the effect and excellency of a sort of innate property.

If the mind be disturbed by the loss of property, it is warned in almost every place in the Scriptures of the Lord to despise the world nor is there added any more powerful exhortation to despise money than the fact that the Lord Himself is found with no riches: He ever justifieth the poor and condemneth beforehand the rich. Thus did contempt of riches foreminister unto patience of losses, showing by the rejection of wealth that the damage of it also ought not to be regarded. That therefore which we have no manner of need to seek after, because the Lord also sought not after it, we ought to bear the diminution of, or even its privation, without disquiet. The Spirit of the Lord hath declared by the Apostle, that covetousness is *the root of all evil*. This let us understand as consisting not in the desire of that only which is another's, for even that which seemeth to be our own is another's; for nothing is our own, since all things are God's. Whose also are we ourselves. Wherefore if, when we suffer loss, we take it impatiently, we shall be found, in grieving for a loss in that which is not ours, to border upon covetousness. We covet that which is another's. He that is disturbed by impatience under loss, by preferring earthly to heavenly things, sinneth immediately against God: for he disturbeth that spirit which he hath received from God for the sake of a thing of this world. Let us therefore willingly lose the things of earth, and keep the things of Heaven. Let the whole world perish so that I gain patience. Now I know not whether the man who hath not determined to bear with firmness the loss of any of his goods either by theft, or by violence, or even by slothfulness, could, easily or with his whole heart, himself lay hands on his goods for the sake of alms-giving. For who that can not at all bear to be cut by another, applieth the steel himself to his own body? Patience under losses is an exercise in the act of giving and communicating. He is not unwilling to give, who feareth not to lose. Besides how shall he *that hath two coats impart* one of them *to him that hath none,* unless he be also one, who if a man *take away his coat,* can offer unto him *his cloak also?* How shall we *make to ourselves friends of Mammon,* if we love him so much that we can not bear to lose him? With the loss of him we shall be lost also. Why in this world do we *find* where we ought to *lose?*

In this world we carry about us our very souls and bodies exposed to injury from all men, and under this injury we submit to be patient. Shall we be grieved by taking thought for things of lesser moment? Away with such defilement from the servant of Christ, that his patience, made ready for greater temptations, should fall away in trifling ones. If any shall try to provoke thee by open violence, the admonition of the Lord is at hand: *To him that smiteth thee on the face,* saith He, *turn the other cheek also.* Let his wickedness be wearied out by thy patience. Be the blow what it may, bound up with pain and insult, he will suffer a heavier one from the Lord. Thou beatest that wicked man the more by bearing with him, for he shall be beaten by Him, for whose sake thou bearest with him. If the bitterness of the tongue should break out in cursing or railing, reflect on that which hath been said: *Rejoice when men shall curse you.* The Lord Himself was cursed under the Law, and yet is the only Blessed. Wherefore let us His servants follow our Lord, and let us take cursing patiently, that we may be able to be blessed. If I hear not with unruffled mind any wanton or naughty word spoken against me, I must needs myself also render bitter speech in my turn, or I shall be tortured by silent impatience. When therefore I have smitten another with evil speaking, how shall I be found to have followed the teaching of the Lord, wherein it is delivered unto us that a man is *defiled* not by the pollutions of *vessels,* but of *those things which proceed out of* the mouth?

Nor is even that kind of impatience excused, which is felt on the loss of our friends, when a certain claim of grief pleadeth in its behalf. For the consideration of the Apostle's warning must be preferred, who saith, *Sorrow not* for the *sleep* of any one, *even as* the Gentiles which have no hope. And with good cause. *For if we believe that Christ rose again,* we believe also in our own resurrection, for whose sakes He *both died and rose again.* Wherefore since the resurrection of the dead is certain, grief for death is idle, and impatience in that grief is idle also. For why shouldst thou grieve, if thou believest not that he hath perished? Why shouldst thou take impatiently that he is withdrawn for a time, who thou believest will return again? That which thou thinkest to be death is but a departing on a journey. He that goeth before us is not to be mourned, but altogether to be longed for; and even this longing must be tempered with patience. For why shouldst thou not bear with moderation that he hath departed, when thou shalt presently follow? But impatience in such a matter augureth ill for our hope, and is a double-dealing with our faith. Besides, we injure Christ, when, as each is called away by Him, we bear it impatiently as though they were to be pitied.

As respecteth the rule of that peace, which is so pleasing unto God, who is there at all, that is of his own nature impatient, who will *forgive his brother* even once, not to say *seven times,* and still less *seventy times seven?* Who *whiles he is in the way* with his adversary *to the judge,* will end the matter by *agreeing with him,* except he first sever from himself that vexation, that harshness, that bitterness, which are in fact the venom of impatience? How wilt thou *forgive and it shall be forgiven* thee, if, for lack of patience thou be retentive of an injury? No man divided in spirit against his brother will *offer his gift upon the altar,* except first by being *reconciled with his brother,* he return to patience? If *the sun go down upon our wrath* we are in danger. We may not continue for even one day without patience. And since it directeth every kind of wholesome discipline, what wonder if it administer also to repentance, which is wont to come to the succor of the fallen! When, in a separation between man and wife (for some cause, that is, for which it is lawful either for a man or a woman to persevere in continuing in a state of widowhood), this patience waiteth for, desireth, urgeth, their salvation, as for those who will one day begin to repent. How much good doth it confer on both? The one it hindereth from adultery, the other it amendeth. In the same manner it is present also in those holy examples of patience in the Lord's parables. It is the patience of the shepherd which seeketh and findeth the sheep which was gone astray; for impatience might easily despise that *one sheep.* But through patience he undertaketh the labor of the search, yea, and moreover carrieth on his shoulders the deserted offender, a patient bearer of his burden. Again, it is the patience of the father which both receiveth and clotheth, and feedeth the prodigal son, and excuseth him to the impatience of his *angry* brother. He, therefore, which *had been lost* is saved, because he began to repent. His repentance is not lost, because it meeteth with patience. For by whose rules, save those of patience, is charity instructed, that chief mystery of the faith, that treasure of the Christian name which the apostle commendeth with all the power of the Holy Spirit? *Charity,* saith he, *suffereth long;* therefore, she useth patience. She *is kind.* Patience doeth no unkindness. She *envieth not:* this indeed properly belongs to patience. She *savoreth not of wantonness:* she hath derived her modesty from patience. She *is not puffed up, doth not insult,* for this belongeth not to patience. And she *seeketh not her own,* she beareth with her own, so she may profit another. Nor is she *easily provoked:* for otherwise what would she have left for impatience to do? Wherefore, saith he, *charity beareth all things, endureth all things:* that is, because she is patient. With good cause, therefore, she shall *never fail:* for all other things shall be cleared away, brought to a close. *Tongues, knowledge, prophecies* are exhausted. *Faith, hope, charity* abide. Faith, which the patience of Christ has produced; hope, which the patience of man waiteth for, charity, which patience accompanieth, God being its master.

Saint Cyprian

[200–258]

A native of Carthage, Thacius Caecilius Cyprian spent some years under the instruction of another great preacher of that city, Tertullian. This experience led him to become a teacher of rhetoric. He was converted to Christianity at the age of 46 and was so brilliant a preacher and leader that he was made bishop of his native city. He suffered persecution under Decius and was eventually banished to Churubis, where he was beheaded in 258. Cyprian was one of the most important leaders of the early church and did much to give form and character to the doctrine and practice of the Latin churches. Saint Augustine often referred to the following sermon, and Rettberg, in his biography of Cyprian, says of it, "In no work of Cyprian does the whole Christian character of the man speak out so distinctly as in this."

THE LORD'S PRAYER

Our Father, which art in heaven, hallowed be Thy name. Thy kingdom come; Thy will be done as in heaven, so in earth; give us this day our daily bread, and forgive us our debts, as we forgive our debtors; and lead us not into temptation, but deliver us from evil. Amen. Matthew 6:9–13.

First of all, the teacher of peace and master of unity would not have men pray singly and severally, since, when any prays, he is not to pray for himself only. For we say not, My Father which art in Heaven; nor, Give me this day my bread; nor does each individual pray that his own debt only should be forgiven, or ask for himself alone, not to be led into temptation, or to be delivered from evil. Our prayer is general, and for all; and when we pray, we pray not for one person, but for us all, because we all are one. God, the Master of peace and concord, so willed that one should pray for all, according as Himself in one did bear us all.

What sacraments, dearest brethren, are those of the Lord's Prayer! How numerous! How weighty! Gathered up in few words, but with such wealth of spiritual virtue, that not any thing, for prayer and petition of ours, is left unincluded in this comprehension of heavenly doctrine. *After this manner,* He saith, *pray ye: Our Father which art in Heaven.* The new man, born again, and restored to his God by His grace, first of all says, "Father," because he has now become a son.

Neither, dearest brethren, have we only to consider and observe that we speak of one in Heaven as a father, but we go further, and say, *Our Father*—Father, that is, of those who believe, of those who being sanctified by Him, and made again by a nativity of spiritual grace, have begun to be the sons of God. What indulgence is it of the Lord—what exuberance of condescension and goodness toward us, to permit us, when praying in God's presence, to address ourselves to God as a Father, and name ourselves sons of God, even as Christ is Son of God! A name which none of us in prayer would have dared to reach unto, had not He Himself allowed us thus to pray. We should, therefore, dearest brethren, recollect and feel, that when we call God a Father, we ought to act like sons of God, and if we have a comfort in regarding Him as our Father, let us cause that He may be comforted in us. Let us so walk as the temples of God, that it may be known that God dwelleth in us. Let our conduct not fall away from the Spirit, but let us, who have begun to be spiritual and heavenly, have only spiritual and heavenly thoughts and actions, for the Lord God Himself hath said, *They that honor Me I will honor; and he that despiseth Me shall be despised.* The blessed Apostle has likewise in his Epistle set forth: *Ye are not your own, with a great price ye are bought. Glorify and possess God in your body.*

After this we say, *Hallowed be Thy name;* not as wishing for God to be made holy by our prayers, but asking of Him, for His name to be kept holy in us. By whom indeed could God be sanctified, who Himself sanctifies? But seeing He Himself has said, *Be ye holy, for I also am holy,* it is this that we ask and request, that we who have been sanctified in baptism, may persevere such as we have begun. For this we daily make petition: since we need a daily sanctification, in order that we, who sin day by day, may cleanse afresh our offenses by a continual sanctification.

It follows in our prayer, *Thy kingdom come.* We here entreat that the kingdom of God may be manifested unto us, in the same way that we ask that His name may be hallowed in us. For when is God's kingdom not? or when begins with Him that which both ever has been, and will be ever? We pray for the coming of that our kingdom which has been promised to us by God, and was gained by the blood and passion of Christ; that we who have continued His subjects in the life below may afterward reign in Christ's kingdom, according to his own promise and word: *Come, ye blessed of My Father, inherit the kingdom prepared for you, from the beginning of the world.* The kingdom of God, dearest brethren, may stand for Christ Himself, whom we day by day wish to come, and for whose advent we pray, that it be quickly manifested to us. As He is our Resurrection, because in Him we rise again; so may He be called the kingdom of God, because we are to reign in Him. Rightly we ask for God's kingdom, that is, for the heavenly, because there is a kingdom of this earth besides. He, however, who has renounced the world, is superior to its honors and its kingdom; and hence he who dedicates himself to God and to Christ, longs not for the kingdom of earth, but for the kingdom of heaven.

We further go on to say, *Thy will be done, as in heaven so in earth:* not in order that God may do His own will, but that we may be enabled to do what He wills should be done by us. For who resists God, so that He can not do His own will? Yet since we are resisted by the Devil, so that our disposition and conduct does less submit itself to God in all points, we pray and desire that the will of God may be done in us; and that it may be done in us, we stand in need of that will, that is, of God's aid and protection; for no man is strong by his own strength, but is safe in the indulgence and pity of God. Furthermore the Lord, manifesting the infirmity of that human nature which He bare, says, *Father, if it be possible, let this cup pass from Me;* and yielding to His disciples the example of doing not their own will but that of God, He added, *Yet not My will but Thine be done.* And in another place He says, *I came down from heaven, not to do My own will, but the will of Him that sent Me.* If then the Son was obedient in doing His Father's will, how much more ought the servant to be obedient, in doing the will of his Lord; even as John also in his Epistle thus exhorts and instructs us; *Love not the world, neither the things that are in the world; if any man love the world, the love of the Father is not in him. For all that is in the world, is lust of the flesh, and lust of the eyes, and pride of life, which is not of the Father, but is of the lust of the world. And the world passeth away, and the lust thereof; but he that doeth the will of God, abideth forever, like as God also abideth forever.* Would we abide eternally, we must do the will of God who is eternal.

The will of God is what Christ has done and taught: it is humility in conduct, it is steadfastness in faith, scrupulousness in our words, rectitude in our deeds, mercy in our works, governance in our habits; it is innocence of injuriousness, and patience under it, preserving peace with the brethren, loving God with all our heart, loving Him as our Father, and fearing Him as our God; accounting Christ before all things, because He accounteth nothing before us, clinging inseparably to His love, being stationed with fortitude and faith at His cross; and when the battle comes for His name and honor, maintaining in words that constancy which makes confession, in torture that confidence which joins battle, and in death that patience which receives the crown. This it is, to endeavor to be co-heir with Christ; this it is to perform the commandment of God, and fulfill the will of the Father.

As the prayer proceeds, we offer request and say, *Give us this day our daily bread.* This may be understood both in the spiritual and in the simple meaning, seeing that either purport contains a divine aid, for the advancing of our salvation. For Christ is the bread of life, and this bread belongs not to all men, but to us; and as we say Our Father, because the Father of the understanding and believing, so we speak of our bread, because Christ is the bread of us, who appertain to His body. This bread we pray that it be given us day by day, lest we who are in Christ, and who daily receive the Eucharist for food of salvation, should by the admission of any grievous crime, and our being, therefore, shut out from communion, and forbidden the heavenly bread, be separated from the body of Christ, according as Himself preaches and forewarns: *I am the bread of life which came down from Heaven. If any man eat of My bread, he shall live forever. But the bread that I will give is My flesh, for the life of the world.* Seeing, therefore, that He says that if any man eat of His bread he shall live forever; it follows, that while it is manifest that those do thus live, who appertain to His body and receive the Eucharist by right of communication, so also is it matter both for our fears and prayers, that none of us by being forbidden communion be separated from the body of Christ, and so remain far from salvation, as Himself threatens and declares: *Unless ye eat the flesh of the Son of Man and drink His blood, ye shall have no life in you.* Hence, then, we pray that our bread, that is Christ, may be given to us day by day; that we who abide in Christ and live in Him, may not draw back from His sanctification and His body.

We next proceed to entreat for our sins, saying, *Forgive us our debts, as we forgive our debtors.* After supply of food, next pardon for sin is asked for; that he who is fed of God, may live in God, and not only the present and passing life be provided for, but the eternal also; whereunto we may come, if we receive the pardon of our sins, to which the Lord gives the name of debts, as in the gospel is expressed; *I forgave thee all that debt, because thou desiredst Me.* How well is it for our need, how provident and saving a thing, to be reminded that we are sinners, compelled to make petition for our offenses, so that in claiming God's indulgence, the mind is recalled to the recollection of its guilt. That no man may plume himself with the pretense of innocency, and perish more wretchedly through self-exaltation, he is instructed and taught that he commits sin every day, by being commanded to pray every day for his sins.

It is further agreeably to our need that the Lord instructs us to say in prayer, *And lead us not into temptation.* When we thus pray that we may not enter into temptation, we are cautioned by this prayer of our own infirmity and weakness, lest any presumptuously exalt himself, proudly and arrogantly placing aught to himself, and counting the praise of whether confession or passion to be his own, whereas the Lord Himself teaches humility, by saying, *Watch and pray, that ye enter not into temptation; the spirit indeed is willing, but the flesh is weak:* that while a humble and submissive confession comes first, and all is referred to God, whatever we suppliantly apply for, in the fear and reverence of God, may by His gracious favor be supplied.

After these things, at the conclusion of the prayer, comes a sentence comprising shortly and collectively the whole of our petitions and desires. We end by saying, *Deliver us from evil,* comprehending all adverse things which the enemy in this world devises against us; wherefrom we have a faithful and firm protection, if God deliver us, and grant His aid to our entreaties and complaints. But having said, *Deliver us from evil,* there remains nothing beyond for us to ask for, after petition made for God's protection from evil; for that gained, we stand secure and safe, against all things that the devil and the world work against us. What fear hath he from his life, who has God through life for his guardian? We need not wonder, dearest brethren, that this is God's prayer, seeing how His instruction comprises all our petitioning in one saving sentence.

Those who pray ought to come to God, not with unfruitful or naked prayers. Vainly we ask, when it is a barren petition that is given to God. For since *every tree, not bringing forth good fruit, is hewn down, and cast into the fire,* surely words also, which bring no fruit, must fail of favor with God, seeing they are joined with no productiveness in righteous deeds. Hence divine Scripture instructs us, saying, *Prayer is good, with fasting and alms.* For He who, in the day of judgment, will render to us a reward for our good works and alms, is now also a gracious listener to any that approaches Him in prayer, with the company of good works.

Saint Athanasius

[298–373]

Saint Athanasius was born in Alexandria. When but 21 years of age he was ordained, and at 28 he was elevated to the office of Bishop of Alexandria. His leadership of the orthodox party in the controversy with Arius and the Arians caused his banishment from Alexandria for a period of 20 years. However, he was eventually brought back to power. He died among his friends in the city which had been the seat of his devoted service. His greatest sermons are the controversial discourses usually published under the title of Orations and Discourses Against the Arians. *In them he championed the doctrine of the Trinity which has become orthodox in our day. The sermon below is taken from this group.*

CHRIST THE ETERNAL GOD

Thou lovest righteousness and hatest wickedness; therefore God, thy God, hath anointed thee with the oil of gladness above thy fellows.

All thy garments smell of myrrh, and aloes, and cassia, out of the ivory palaces, whereby they have made thee glad. PSALM 45:7, 8.

BEHOLD, O ye Arians, and acknowledge even hence the truth. The Psalmist speaks of us all as *fellows* or *partakers* of the Lord, but were He one of things which come out of nothing, and of things generate, He Himself had been one of those who partake. But, since he hymned Him as the eternal God, saying, *Thy throne, O God, is forever and ever,* and has declared that all other things partake of Him, what conclusion must we draw, but that he is distinct from generated things, and he only the Father's veritable Word, Radiance, and Wisdom, which all things generate partake, being sanctified by Him in the Spirit? And, therefore, He is here "anointed," not that He may become God, for He was so even before; nor that He may become king, for He had the kingdom eternally, existing as God's image, as the sacred oracle shows; but in our behalf is this written, as before. For the Israelitish kings, upon their being anointed, then became kings, not being so before, as David, as Ezekias, as Josias, and the rest; but the Saviour, on the contrary, being God, and ever ruling in the Father's kingdom, and being Himself the Dispenser of the Holy Ghost, nevertheless is here said to be anointed, that, as before, being said as man to be anointed with the Spirit, He might provide for us more, not only exaltation and resurrection, but the indwelling and intimacy of the Spirit. And signifying this, the Lord Himself hath said by His own mouth, in the Gospel according to John, *I have sent them into the world, and for their sakes do I sanctify Myself, that they may be sanctified in the truth.* In saying this, He has shown that He is not the sanctified, but the Sanctifier; for He is not sanctified by other, but Himself sanctifies Himself, that we may be sanctified in the truth. He who sanctifies Himself is Lord of sanctification. How, then, does this take place? What does he mean but this? "I, being the Father's Word, I give to Myself, when become man, the Spirit; and Myself, become man, do I sanctify in Him, that henceforth in Me, who am truth (for *Thy Word is Truth*), all may be sanctified."

If, then, for our sake, He sanctifies Himself, and does this when He becomes man, it is very plain that the Spirit's descent on Him in Jordan was a descent upon us, because of His bearing our body. And it did not take place for promotion to the Word, but again for our sanctification, that we might share His anointing, and of us it might be said, Know ye not that ye are God's temple, and the Spirit of God dwelleth in you? For when the Lord, as man, was washed in Jordan, it was we who were washed in Him and by Him. And when He received the Spirit, we it was who, by Him, were made recipients of it.

What advance, then, of promotion, and reward of virtue, or generally of conduct, is proved from this in our Lord's instance? For if He was not God, and then had become God—if, not being king, He was preferred to the kingdom, your reasoning would have had some faint plausibility. But if He is God, and the throne of His kingdom is everlasting, in what way could God advance? Or what was there wanting to Him who was sitting on His Father's throne? And if, as the Lord Himself has said, the Spirit is His, and takes of His, and He sends It, it is not the Word, considered as the Word and Wisdom, who is anointed with the Spirit, which He Himself gives, but the flesh assumed by Him, which is anointed in Him and by Him; that the sanctification coming to the Lord as man, may come to all men from Him. For, not of Itself, saith He, doth the Spirit speak, but the Word is He who gives It to the worthy. For this is like the passage considered above; for, as the Apostle hath written, *Who, existing in form of God, thought it not robbery to be equal with God, but humbled Himself, and took a servant's form,* so David celebrates the Lord, as the everlasting God and King, but sent to us, and assuming our body, which is mortal.

What advancement, then, was it to the Immortal, to have assumed the mortal? Or what promotion is it to the Everlasting to have put on the temporal? What reward can be great to the Everlasting God and King, in the bosom of the Father? See ye not, that this, too, was done and written because of us and for us, that us, who are mortal and temporal, the Lord, become man, might make immortal, and bring into the everlasting kingdom of heaven? Blush ye not, speaking lies against the divine oracles? For when our Lord Jesus Christ had been among us, we, indeed, were promoted, as rescued from sin; but He is the same: nor did He alter when He became man (to repeat what I have said), but, as has been written, *The Word of God abideth forever.*

Therefore *Jesus Christ is the same yesterday, to-day, and forever,* remaining unalterable, and at once gives and receives, giving as God's Word, receiving as man. It is not the Word then, viewed as the Word, that is promoted; for He had all things and has had them always; but men, who have in Him and through Him their origin of receiving them. For, when He is now said to be anointed in a human respect, we it is who in Him are anointed; since also, when He is baptized, we it is who in Him are baptized. But on all these things the Saviour throws much light, when He says to the Father, *And the glory which Thou gavest Me,*

I have given to them, that they may be one, even as We are one. Because of us, then, He asked for glory, and the words occur, *took* and *gave* and *highly exalted,* that we might take, and to us might be given, and we might be exalted, in Him; as also for us He sanctifies Himself, that we might be sanctified in Him.

The Spirit of the Lord is upon Me, because He hath anointed Me, in respect of His having become flesh, as John hath said; that it might be shown in both these particulars, that we are they who need the Spirit's grace in our sanctification, and again who are unable to cast out devils without the Spirit's power. Through whom then and from whom behooved it that the Spirit should be given but through the Son, whose also the Spirit is? and when were we enabled to receive It, except when the Word became man? and, as the passage of the Apostle shows, that we had not been redeemed and highly exalted, had not He who exists in form of God taken a servant's form, so David also shows, that no otherwise should we have partaken the Spirit and been sanctified, but that the giver of the Spirit, the Word Himself, had spoken of Himself as anointed with the Spirit for us. And therefore have we securely received it, He being said to be anointed in the flesh; for the flesh being first sanctified in Him, and He being said, as man, to have received for its sake, we have the sequel of the Spirit's grace, receiving *out of His fullness.*

Nor do the words, *Thou hast loved righteousness and hated iniquity,* which are added in the Psalm, show, as again you suppose, that the nature of the Word is alterable, but rather by their very force signify His unalterableness. For since of things generate the nature is alterable, and the one portion had transgressed and the other disobeyed, as has been said, and it is not certain how they will act, but it often happens that he who is now good afterward alters and becomes different, so that one who was but now righteous, soon is found unrighteous, wherefore, there was here also need of one unalterable, that men might have the immutability of the righteousness of the Word as an image and type for virtue. And this thought commends itself strongly to the right-minded. For since the first man Adam altered, and through sin death came into the world, therefore it became the second Adam to be unalterable; that, should the serpent again assault, even the serpent's deceit might be baffled, and, the Lord being unalterable and unchangeable, the serpent might become powerless in his assaults against all. For as when Adam had transgressed, his sin reached unto all men, so, when the Lord had become man and had overthrown the serpent, that so great strength of His is to extend through all men, so that each of us may say, *For we are not ignorant of his devices.* Good reason then that the Lord, who ever is in nature unalterable, loving righteousness and hating iniquity, should be anointed and Himself sent on mission, that He, being and remaining the same, by taking the alterable flesh, *might condemn sin in it,* and might secure its freedom, and its ability henceforth *to fulfill the righteousness of the law* in itself, so as to be able to say, *But we are not in the flesh, but in the Spirit, if so be that the Spirit of God dwelleth in us.*

Vainly then, here again, O Arians, have ye made this conjecture, and vainly alleged the words of Scripture; for God's Word is unalterable, and is ever in one state, not as it may happen, but as the Father is; since how is He like the Father, unless He be thus? or how is all that is the Father's the Son's also, if He has not the unalterableness and unchangeableness of the Father? Not as being subject to laws, and as influenced this way and that, does He love this and hate that, lest, if from fear of forfeiture He chooses the opposite, we admit in another way that He is alterable; but as being God and the Father's Word, He is a just judge and lover of virtue, or rather its dispenser. Therefore being just and holy by nature, on this account He is to love righteousness and to hate iniquity; as much as to say that He loves and takes to Him the virtuous, and rejects and hates the unrighteous. And divine Scripture says the same of the Father; *The righteous Lord loveth righteousness: Thou hatest all them that work iniquity;* and, *The Lord loveth the gates of Zion more than all the dwellings of Jacob;* and *Jacob have I loved, but Esau have I hated;* and in Esaias, there is the Voice of God again saying, *I the Lord love righteousness, and hate robbery of unrighteousness.* Let them then expound those former words as these latter; for the former also are written of the Image of God: else, misinterpreting these as those, they will conceive that the Father too is alterable. But since the very hearing others say this is not without peril, we do well to think that God is said to love righteousness and to hate robbery of unrighteousness, not as if influenced this way and that, and capable of the contrary, selecting one thing and not choosing another, for this belongs to things generated, but that as a judge He loves and takes to Him the righteous and withdraws from the bad. It follows then to think the same concerning the image of God also, that He loves and hates no otherwise than thus—for such must be the nature of the Image of Its Father, though the Arians in their blindness fail to see either that Image or any other truth of the divine oracles. For being forced from the conceptions or rather misconceptions of their own hearts, they fall back upon passages of divine Scripture, and here, too, from want of understanding, according to their wont, they discern not their meaning; but laying down their own irreligion as a sort of canon of interpretation, they wrest the whole of the divine oracles into accordance with it. And so on the bare mention of such doctrine, they deserve nothing but the reply, *Ye do err, not knowing the Scriptures nor the power of God;* and if they persist in it, they must be put to silence, by the words *Render to* man *the things that are* man's, *and to God the things that are God's.*

Saint Cyril

[315–386]

The life of Saint Cyril was marked by storm and conflict. He was ordained a presbyter of his native Jerusalem, and in 350 was made patriarch, or bishop, from which high position he was several times deposed. Although many of his teachings were later declared to be unorthodox, this early ecclesiastic has left us in his writings one of the most complete accounts known of the rites of the early church and of its theological position. The most important works of Cyril are 23 lectures which he delivered to new converts before their baptism and admission into full privileges of the church. The following is one of these lectures.

THE CREATOR SEEN IN THE CREATIONS

Who is this that darkeneth counsel by words without knowledge? Gird up now thy loins like a man: for I will demand of thee, and answer thou Me. JOB 38:2, 3.

WITH THE EYES of the flesh it is impossible to behold God; for the incorporeal can not be subject to fleshly sight, and the only-begotten Son of God Himself hath testified, saying, *No man hath seen God at any time.* Should, however, any one, from a passage in Ezekiel, understand that Ezekiel saw Him, let him inquire what that Scripture says. He saw *the likeness of the glory of the Lord,* not the Lord Himself; nay, the likeness of His glory, not the glory itself, as it is in truth; and beholding only the likeness of His glory, he fell to the earth with fear. But if the sight of the likeness of the glory, and not of the glory itself, wrought fear and distress in the prophets, any one who should attempt to behold God Himself, would to a certainty lose his life, according to the text, "There shall no man see Me and live." Wherefore, of His exceeding loving-kindness, God has spread out the heaven to be the vail of His proper Godhead, lest we perish. This is not my word, but the prophet's: "If thou shouldest open the heavens, trembling would take hold of the mountains from thee, and they would melt away." And what wonder if Ezekiel, seeing the similitude of the glory, fell down? since Daniel, when Gabriel, the servant of the Lord, appeared, straightway shuddered and fell on his face; and, prophet as he was, dared not answer him, until the angel turned himself into the likeness of a son of man. For if the sight of Gabriel wrought trembling in the prophets, had God Himself appeared according as He is, would they not all have perished?

The Divine nature, then, with the eyes of the flesh, we can not see; but from the Divine works we may obtain some idea of His power; according to the saying of Solomon, *For by the greatness and beauty of the creatures, proportionally the Maker of them is seen.* For he says not that from the creatures the Maker is seen, but hath added, "proportionally;" for so much the greater does God appear to each, as the man hath attained a large survey of the creatures; and when, by that large survey, his soul is raised aloft, he gains a more excellent conception of God.

What! is there not much to wonder at in the sun, which being small to look on, contains in it an intensity of power, appearing from the east, and shooting his light even to the west? The Psalmist describes his rising at dawn, when he says, *Which is as a bridegroom coming out of his chamber.* This is a description of his pleasant and comely array on first appearing to men; for when he rides at high noon we are wont to flee from his blaze; but at his rising he is welcome to all, as a bridegroom to look on. Behold also how he proceeds (or rather not he, but one who has by His bidding determined his course); how in summer time aloft in the heavens, he finishes off longer days, giving men due time for their works; while in winter he straightens his course, lest the day's cold last too long, and that the night's lengthening may conduce both to the rest of men, and to the fruitfulness of the earth's productions. And see likewise in what order the days correspond to each other, in summer increasing, in winter diminishing, but in spring and autumn affording one another a uniform length; and the night again in like manner. And as the Psalmist saith concerning them, *Day unto day uttereth speech, and night unto night showeth knowledge.*

No one must tolerate such as say that the Maker of light is different from the Maker of darkness; for let a man remember Isaiah's words, *I the Lord form the light and create darkness.* Why, O man, art thou offended with these? Why so annoyed at the time of rest given thee? The servant would not have gained it from his master, but for the darkness bringing a necessary respite. And often, after toiling in the day, how are we refreshed by night; and he who was yesterday amid labors, starts in the morning vigorous from a night's rest. And what more conduces to religious wisdom than the night, when oftentimes we bring before us the things of God, and read and contemplate the Divine Oracles? When too, is our mind more alive for psalmody and prayer than at night? When does a recollection oftener come over us of our sins than at night? Let us not then be perverse enough to entertain the notion that another beside

God is the Maker of darkness; for experience shows that darkness is good and most useful.

Those persons ought to have felt astonishment and admiration, not only at the sun and moon, but also at the well-ordered choirs of the stars, their unimpeded courses, their respective risings in due season; and how some are the signs of summer, others of winter, and how some mark the time of sowing, others introduce the season of sailing. And man, sitting in his ship, and sailing on the boundless waves, looks at the stars and steers his vessel. Well says Scripture concerning these bodies, *Let them be for signs and for seasons, and for days, and for years;* not for stargazing and vain tales of nativities. Observe, too, how considerately He imparts the daylight by a gradual growth; for the sun does not rise upon us, while we gaze, all at once, but a little light runs up before him, that by previous trial our eye-ball may bear his stronger ray: and again, how He has cheered the darkness of night by the gleam of moonlight.

Who is the father of rain: and who hath given birth to the drops of dew? Who hath condensed the air into clouds, and bid them carry the fluid mass of showers, at one time *bringing from the north golden clouds,* at another giving these a uniform appearance, and then again curling them up into festoons and other figures manifold? *Who can number the clouds in wisdom?* of which Job saith, *He knoweth the balancings of the clouds, and hath bent down the heaven to the earth; and, He who numbereth the clouds in wisdom; and, The cloud is not rent under them.* For though measures of water ever so many weigh upon the clouds, yet they are not rent; but with all order come down upon the earth. Who brings the winds out of His treasures? Who, as just now said, *hath given birth to the drops of dew? Out of whose womb cometh forth the ice,* watery in its substance, but like stone in its properties. And at one time the water becomes *snow like wool,* at another it ministers to Him *who scatters the hoar-frost like ashes;* at another it is changed into a stormy substance, since He fashions the waters as He will. Its nature is uniform, its properties manifold. Water in the vines is wine, *which maketh glad the heart of man;* and in the olives oil, *to make his face to shine;* and is further transformed into bread, *which strengtheneth man's heart,* and into all kinds of fruits.

And this great and wide sea, in it are things creeping innumerable. Who can tell the beauty of the fishes that are therein? Who can describe the greatness of the whales; and the nature of its amphibious animals? how they live both on dry land and in the waters? Who can tell the depth and breadth of the sea, or the force of its enormous waves? Yet it stays within its boundaries, because of Him who said, *Hitherto shalt thou come, and no further; and here shall thy proud waves be stayed.* And to show the decree imposed on it, when it runs upon the land, it leaves a plain line on the sands by its waves; declaring, as it were, to those who see it, that it has not passed its appointed bounds.

Who can understand the nature of the fowls of the air? how some have with them a voice of melody; and others have their wings enriched with all manner of painting, and others soaring on high, stay motionless in the midst of the sky, as the hawk. For by the Divine command, *the hawk, having spread out her wings, stays motionless, looking down* TOWARD THE SOUTH. Who of men can behold the eagle? But if thou canst not read the mystery of birds when soaring on high, how wouldest thou read the Maker of all things?

Who among men knows even the names of all wild beasts? or who can accurately classify their natures? But if we know not even their bare names, how should we comprehend their Maker? The command of God was but one, which said *Let the earth bring forth wild beasts, and cattle, and creeping things, after their kinds;* and distinct natures sprang from one voice, at one command—the gentle sheep and carnivorous lion—also the various instincts of irrational creatures, as representations of the various characters of men. The fox is an emblem of men's craftiness, and the snake of a friend's envenomed treachery, and the neighing horse of wanton young men, and that busy ant, to arouse the sluggish and the dull; for when a man passes his youth idly, then he is instructed by irrational creatures, being reproved by that Scripture which saith, *Go to the ant, thou sluggard; consider her ways, and be wise,* for when thou beholdest her in due season treasuring up food for herself, do thou copy her, and treasure up for thyself the fruits of good works for the world to come. And again, *Go to the bee, and learn how industrious she is;* how, hovering about all kinds of flowers, she culls the honey for thy use, that thou, also, ranging over Holy Scripture, mayest lay hold on thy salvation, and, being satisfied with it, mayest say, *How sweet are thy words unto my taste, yea, sweeter than honey and the honeycomb unto my mouth.*

Is not the Artificer, then, rather worthy to be glorified? For what, if thou know not the nature of every thing, are the things, therefore, which He has made, without their use? For canst thou know the efficacy of all herbs? or canst thou learn all the advantage which comes of every animal? Even from poisonous adders have come antidotes for the preservation of men. But thou wilt say to me, "The snake is terrible." Fear thou the Lord, and it shall not be able to hurt thee. "The scorpion stings." Fear thou the Lord, and it shall not sting thee. "The lion is blood-thirsty." Fear thou the Lord, and he shall lie down beside thee, as by Daniel. And, truly, there is whereat to wonder, in the power even of the creatures; how some, as the scorpion, have their weapon in a sting, while the power of others is in their teeth; and others, again, get the better by means of hoots, and the basilisk's might is his gaze. Thus, from this varied work-manship, think of the Artificer's power.

These things has my discourse dwelt on now, passing over many, yea, innumerable, other matters, and especially things incorporeal and invisible, that on the one hand thou mayest abhor those who blaspheme that good and wise Artificer; and that, on the other, from what has been spoken and read, and from what thou canst thyself find out or think of, thou mayest *proportionally see the Creator by the greatness and beauty of the creations:* and that bending the knee with godly reverence to the Maker of all things, things of sense and things of mind, visible and invisible, thou mayest, with an honest and holy tongue, and with unwearied lips and heart, sing praises to God, saying, *"O Lord, how manifold are Thy works! in wisdom hast Thou made them all;* for to thee belongeth honor, and glory, and greatness, both now and forever and ever. Amen."

Saint Gregory of Nazianzen

[325–389]

Saint Gregory of Nazianzen, in Cappadocia, has always been considered among the first preachers of ancient times. Before his birth he was consecrated to the Lord by his mother, and his parents saw to it that he received the best possible education. He studied at Cesarea in Cappadocia, Cesarea in Palestine, Alexandria, and finally at Athens. Several of his sermons were given in defense of the Nicene creed and show him to be a man "of sublime wit, subtle apprehension, clear judgment, and easy and ready elocution, and a great stock of human learning." Given here is part of a long funeral oration that reveals something of the preacher's eloquence and keen understanding.

ORATION OVER BASIL, BISHOP OF CESAREA

Their sound went into all the earth, and their words unto the end of the world. ROMANS 10:18.

WHO more than Basil honored virtue or punished vice? Who evinced more favor toward the right-doing, or more severity toward offenders—he whose very smile was often praise; whose silence, reproof, in the depths of conscience reaching and arousing the sense of guilt? Grant that he was no light prattler, no jester, no lounger in the markets. Grant that he did not ingratiate himself with the multitude by becoming all things to all, and courting their favor: what then? Should he not, with all the right judging, receive praise for this rather than condemnation? Is it deemed a fault in the lion that he has not the look of the ape; that his aspect is stern and regal; that his movements, even in sport, are majestic, and command at once wonder and delight? Or do we admire it as proof of courtesy and true benevolence in actors that they gratify the populace, and move them to laughter by mutual blows on the temple, and by boisterous merriment?

But, should we even pursue this inquiry, who, so far as my knowledge extends—and my acquaintance with him has been most intimate—who was so delightful as Basil in company? Who was more graceful in narration? Who more delicate in raillery? Who more tender in reproof, making neither his censure harshness, nor his mildness indulgence, but avoiding excess in both, and in both following the rule of Solomon, who assigns to every thing its season? But what is all this compared with his extraordinary eloquence and that resistless might of his doctrine which has made its own the extremities of the globe? We are still lingering about the base of the mountain, as at great distance from its summit. We still push our bark across the strait, leaving the broad and open sea. For assuredly, if there ever was, or ever shall be, a trumpet, sounding far out upon the air, or a voice of God encompassing the world, or some unheard-of and wondrous shaking of the earth, such was his voice, such his intellect, as far transcending that of his fellows as man excels the nature of the brute. Who more than he purified his spirit, and thus qualified himself to unfold the Divine oracles? Who, more brightly illuminated with the light of knowledge, has explored the dark things of the spirit, and with the aid of God surveyed the mysteries of God? And who has possessed a diction that was a more perfect interpreter of his thoughts? Not with him as with the majority, was there a failure, either of thought sustaining his diction, or of language keeping pace with thought: but alike distinguished in both, he showed himself as an orator throughout, self-consistent and complete. It is the prerogative of the spirit to search the deep things of God, not as ignorant, but as making the survey with infinite ease and delight. But all the mysteries of the spirit were profoundly investigated by Basil: and from these sources he trained and disciplined the characters of all, taught loftiness of speech, and, withdrawing men from the present, directed them to the future. The sun is praised by the Psalmist for his beauty and magnitude, for the swiftness and power of his course, resplendent as a bridegroom, mighty as a giant. His mighty circuit has power to light equally the opposite extremes of the globe, the extent of their diffusion lessens not the power of his beams. But the beauty of Basil was virtue; his greatness, theology; his course, perpetual activity, ever tending upward to God; his power, the sowing and distribution of the word. Thus I need not hesitate to apply to him the language which Paul, borrowing from David, applies to the Apostles, that *his sound went into all the earth, and the power of his words to the extremities of the world*. What other source of pleasure at the present day in our assemblies? What at our banquets? What in the forum? What in the churches? What constitutes the delight alike of magistrates and of private citizens, of monks and of those who mingle in society, of men of business, and of men of leisure, of the votaries of profane and of sacred science? The one all-pervading and highest source of enjoyment is the writings of Basil. Nay, even to writers, the sole material of their works, since he is found in his productions. The ancient commentaries on the Divine records cease to be heard: the new take their place: and he stands first in sacred eloquence who best knows *his* writing, and most frequently utters his language in our ears. A single man suffices as a substitute for all others to the training of the studious. I mention but this single instance. When I explore the pages or repeat the words of his Hexæmeron, I am brought into union with the Creator; I understand the laws of the creation; and, employing only the sense of sight as my teacher, I admire more than ever before the Creator. When I read his books against the heretics, I see the fires of Sodom, by which men of impious and lawless tongue are reduced to ashes, or the Tower of Babel, reared in wickedness and righteously overthrown. When I read his writings on the Spirit, I find the God whom I possess reveals Himself. I declare the truth with boldness, treading in the path of His Divine contemplations. When I meet with the other exhibitions of truth which, for those of dull intellect, he sets forth in a threefold way, impressing them on the solid tablets of his heart, I am persuaded to stay no longer with the letter, nor to rest my look merely on the surface; but to pass beyond, to go on from depth to depth, amid light still discovering light, till I reach the utmost limit of truth. When I read his praises of the martyrs, the noble combatants for the faith, I am borne away by his praises, and incited to the same glorious championship. When I read his ethical and practical discourses, I purify myself in soul and body, and seek to become a fitting temple of God, an instrument played upon by the Spirit, and hymning forth the divine power and glory. Thus am I corrected and disciplined, and through successive stages transformed with a Divine transformation.

And since I have spoken of Theology, and of his sublime mode of treating it, I wish yet to add the following. For it is eminently desirable that the multitude should not receive harm themselves by cherishing wrong sentiments respecting him. And my remarks are directed specially against those base persons who, by aspersing others, pander to their own depravity. For in defense of sound doctrine and the union and joint God-head of the Sacred Trinity—or by whatever still more direct and clearer term the doctrine may be designated—he was ready not merely to sacrifice places of power to which he never aspired, but to accept exile, death, and its preliminary tortures, not as evil, but as gain. Witness, in proof, what he has actually endured. When condemned to banishment for the truth, he merely bade one of his attendants take up his writing tablets and follow him. But following the counsel of David, he deemed it necessary to exercise prudence in the mere use of language, and thus, during the crisis of war and the reign of heresy, to forbear a little until the season of free and independent speech should be restored. They indeed aimed to assail the bare and naked declaration of the Godhead of the Spirit (a truth deemed impious by them and by their nefarious leader in impiety), in order that, banishing him and his religious teachings from the city, they might take possession of the Church, and making it the fortress and stronghold of their wickedness, thence, as from a citadel, overrun and devastate the whole field of truth. He, meanwhile, by other Scripture terms, and unambiguous testimonies having the same import, as well as by unanswerable reasonings, so swayed his opponents that they were impotent to assail him, and—which is the highest triumph of power and skill in argument—were held fast in the fetters of their own chosen expressions. Take in proof his discourse on the subject in which he moved his pen as under the very impulse of the Spirit. The specific term, nevertheless, he forbore for a time to use, guided by the Spirit himself, and begging his fellow-champions of the faith not to be displeased at his proceeding, nor, amid the temporary distractions of the faith, sacrifice all by tenacious adherence to a word. To them, he said, no harm would accrue by a slight change of terms, the same truth being conveyed in other language. For their safety did not lie in words rather than in things; nor would even the Jewish people have been rejected had they, substituting the term *anointed* for that of *Christ,* been willing to rank themselves among His followers. But to the whole Christian body it would be a source of infinite harm that the Church should be seized by heretics. Such were the grounds of his apparent temporizing. For that he held with the profoundest conviction to the divinity of the Spirit is clear, from his publicly proclaiming the doctrine on every occasion, and unhesitatingly avowing it when interrogated in private. And in his communications to me, from whom he concealed nothing, he has spoken yet more clearly, not only affirming it, but in an unwonted manner imprecating upon himself the fearful doom of being abandoned of the Spirit if he failed to worship Him as equal in essence and honor with the Father and the Son. It is not for the sake of defending his reputation that I have made these statements; for he is superior to all accusations. It is rather that none, regarding the terms employed by him as the law and limit of orthodoxy, may have their faith shaken; that none may pervert his mode of discussion, produced by stress of circumstances and with the sanction of the Spirit, to the strengthening of their own wickedness; but rather that, weighing the import and aim of his words, they may be drawn to the truth, and may seal the lips of the impious. To me and to all who are dear to me, may his doctrines be an inheritance. Such is my conviction of his purity in this matter, that in this as in other things, I would gladly unite my lot to his, and ask a common judgment alike from God and from all impartial men. None surely would affirm that the Evangelists conflict with each other, because some have dwelt upon the humanity of Christ, others attempted the heights of His divinity; some have taken their departure from His earthly, other from His heavenly origin. For by their varying representations they have met the wants of those whom they addressed, being informed and actuated by the Spirit that dwelt in them.

But now, there having arisen both in ancient and recent times, many men distinguished for piety, lawgivers, generals, prophets, teachers, valiant even to the shedding of their blood, let us compare our Basil with them, and thus learn better to estimate his virtues. Adam was deemed worthy of the fashioning hand of God, the delights of Paradise, and the first giving of the law. But to say nothing irreverent of our great ancestor, he failed to keep the commandment. But Basil both received and kept it, was unharmed by the tree of knowledge, and passing by the flaming sword, has, I am well assured, inherited Paradise. Enos first had confidence to call upon the Lord: Basil both himself invoked Him, and, what is yet more honorable, proclaimed Him to others. Enoch was translated as a reward for an imperfect piety (for his faith was yet amid shadows), and thus escaped the perils of after life: Basil's entire life was a translation, and he was proved to the end in a completed life. Noah was intrusted with the ark, and with the seeds of a new world, committed to a small vessel, and preserved amid the waters: Basil escaped a deluge of impiety, rendered his own city an ark of safety that floated lightly above the waves of heresy, and thus reclaimed the entire world. Abraham was illustrious, at once a Patriarch and the Priest of a new sacrifice, offering to Him who had bestowed it the child of promise, hastening, a ready and cheerful victim, to the altar. But not slight was the offering of Basil, who offered himself unto God, and that with no substitute interposed to prevent the sacred rite from being consummated. Isaac was promised before his birth: but Basil voluntarily proffered himself; and his bride, the Church, he wooed not from afar but near at hand, not through the ministry of servants, but confided to him by the immediate hand of God. Nor was he overreached in assigning the precedence to his children; but such awards as reason and the Spirit dictated he allotted to each according to their deserts. I commend the ladder of Jacob, the pillar which he anointed to God, and that wrestling with him which was but the confronting of human weakness with the Divine

Majesty, and whence he bears the tokens of a vanquished nature. I praise also his skillful continence with respect to the flocks of Laban, the twelve patriarchs his offspring, and the sublime prophetic foresight with which he bestowed on them his dying benediction. But in Basil I praise the ladder, not merely seen, but ascended by successive advances in virtue; the pillar which he did not anoint, but reared to God, a monument of the eternal infamy of the impious; his wrestling not against God but for Him, while he overthrew the doctrines of the heretics; the pastoral skill by which he gained over, as spiritual wealth, a large portion of his flock; the multitude of his children divinely begotten; and the blessing with which he established many.

Saint Basil the Great

[329–379]

Saint Basil the Great, so-called to distinguish him from the other Greek patriarch of the same name, is noteworthy for his resistance to the tyranny of the Emperor Valens and his fight for higher morals and better discipline among the clergy. He was born at Cesarea in Cappadocia, and studied at Athens where for a time he taught rhetoric and practiced law. He received his first religious instruction from his grandmother, Maerina, and soon turned to the rigid ascetic life of a monk. In 370 he became Bishop of Cesarea. The following example of his eloquence is a bitter rebuke of one who had renounced her vows of celibacy and married. Fénelon says of it: "There is nothing more eloquent; in my opinion, it is a masterpiece."

ADMONITION TO THE FALLEN

O that my head were waters, and mine eyes a fountain of tears, that I might weep for the slain of the daughter of my people! JEREMIAH 9:1.

FOR, although they are wrapped in profound silence, and lie quite stupefied by their calamity, and deprived, by their deadly wound, even of the very sense of suffering, yet it does not become us to withhold our tears over so sad a fall. For if Jeremiah deemed those worthy of countless lamentations who had received bodily wounds in battle, what shall we say when souls are involved in so great a calamity? "Thy wounded," says the prophet, "are not wounded with the sword, and thy dead are not the dead of war." But my lamentation is for grievous sin, the sting of the true death, and for the fiery darts of the wicked, which have cruelly kindled a flame in both body and soul. Well might the laws of God groan within themselves, beholding such pollution on earth, those laws which always utter their loud prohibition, saying in olden time, *Thou shalt not covet thy neighbor's wife;* and in the Gospels, *That whosoever looketh on a woman to lust after her, hath committed adultery with her already in his heart.* But now they behold the very bride of the Lord—her of whom Christ is the head—committing adultery without fear or shame. Yes, the very spirits of departed saints may well groan, the zealous Phineas, that it is not permitted to him now to snatch the spear and to punish the loathsome sin with a summary corporeal vengeance, and John the Baptist, that he can not now leave the celestial abodes, as he once left the wilderness, and hasten to rebuke the transgression, and if the sacrifice were called for, to lay down his head sooner than abate the severity of his reproof. Nay, let us rather say that, like blessed Abel, John *being dead yet speaketh,* and now lifts up his voice with a yet louder cry than in the case of Herodias, saying, *It is not lawful for thee to have her.* For, although the body of John, yielding to the inevitable sentence of God, has paid the debt of nature, and his tongue is silent, yet *the word of God is not bound.* And he who, when the marriage covenant had been violated in the case of a fellow servant, was faithful even unto death with his stern reproofs, what must he have felt if he had seen the holy bride-chamber of the Lord thus wantonly outraged?

But as for thee, O thou who hast thus cast off the yoke of that divine union, and deserted the undefiled chamber of the true King, and shamefully fallen into this disgraceful and impious defilement, since thou hast no way of evading this bitter charge, and no method or artifice can avail to conceal thy fearful crime, thou boldly hardenest thyself in guilt. And as he who has once fallen into the abyss of crime becomes henceforth an impious despiser, so thou deniest thy very covenant with the true bridegroom; alleging that thou wast not a virgin, and hadst never taken the vow, although thou hast both received and given many pledges of virginity. Remember the good confession which thou hast made before God, and angels, and men. Remember that venerable assembly, and the sacred choir of virgins, and the congregation of the Lord, and the Church of the saints. Remember thy aged grandmother in Christ, whose Christian virtues still flourish in the vigor of youth; and thy mother in the Lord, who vies with the former, and strives by new and unwonted endeavors to dissolve the bands of custom; and thy sister likewise, in some things their imitator, and in some aspiring to excel them, and to surpass in the merits of virginity the attainments of her progenitors, and both in word and deed diligently inviting thee, her sister, as is meet, to the same competition. Remember these, and the angelic company associated with them in the service of the Lord, and the spiritual life though yet in the flesh, and the heavenly converse upon earth. Remember the tranquil days and the luminous nights, and the spiritual songs, and the melodious psalmody, and the holy prayers, and the chaste and undefiled couch, and the progress in virginal purity, and the temperate diet so helpful in preserving thy virginity uncontaminated. And where is now that grave deportment, and that modest mien, and that plain attire which so becomes a virgin, and that beautiful blush of bashfulness, and that comely paleness—the delicate bloom of abstinence and vigils, that outshines every ruddier glow. How often in prayer that thou mightest keep unspotted thy virginal purity hast thou poured forth thy tears! How many letters hast thou indited to holy men, imploring their prayers, not that thou mightest obtain these human—nuptials, shall I call them? rather this dishonorable defilement—but that thou mightest not fall away from the Lord Jesus? How often hast thou received the gifts of the spouse! And why should I mention also the honors accorded for his sake by those who are his—the companionship of the virgins, journeyings with them, welcomes from them, encomiums of virginity, blessings bestowed by virgins, letters addressed to thee as to a virgin! But now, having been just breathed upon by the aerial spirit that worketh in the children of disobedience, thou hast denied all these, and hast bartered that precious and enviable possession for a brief pleasure, which is sweet to thy taste for a moment, but which afterward thou will find bitterer than gall.

For lo, thou hast been beguiled by the serpent more bitterly than Eve; for not only has thy mind become defiled, but with it thy very body also: and what is still more horrible—I dread to say it, but I can not suppress it; for it is as fire burning and blazing in my bones, and I am dissolving in every part and can not endure it—thou hast taken the members of Christ, and made them the members of a harlot. This is incomparably the greatest evil of all: this is a new crime in the world, to which we may apply the words of the prophet, "Pass over the isles of Chittim, and see; and send unto Kedar, and consider diligently, and see if there be such a thing. Hath a nation changed their gods, which are yet no gods?" For the virgin hath changed her glory, and now glories in her shame. The heavens are astonished at this, and the earth trembleth very exceedingly. Now also the Lord says, the virgin hath committed two evils, she hath forsaken me, the true and holy bridegroom of sanctified souls, and hath fled to an impious and lawless polluter of the body, and corrupter of the soul. She hath turned away from God her Saviour, and hath yielded her members servants to impurity and iniquity: she hath forgotten me, and gone after her lover, by whom she shall not profit.

It were better for him that a mill-stone were hanged about his neck, and he cast into the sea, than that he should cause one of the Lord's virgins to offend. What impudent servant ever carried his insane audacity so far as to fling himself upon the couch of his lord? Or what robber has ever become so madly hardened as to lay hands upon the very offerings devoted to God?—but here it is not inanimate vessels, but living bodies, inhabited by souls made in the image of God. Since the beginning of the world was any one ever heard of, who dared, in the midst of a great city, in broad mid-day, to deface the likeness of a king by inscribing upon it the forms of filthy swine? He that despises human nuptials dies without mercy under two or three witnesses; of how much sorer punishment, suppose ye, shall he be thought worthy who hath trodden under foot the Son of God, and defiled his espoused wife, and done despite to the spirit of virginity?

But after all this, *"shall they fall and not arise?* shall he turn away and not return?"* Why hath the virgin turned away in so shameless an apostasy?—and that too after having heard Christ the bridegroom, saying by Jeremiah, "And I said, after she had lewdly done all these things, turn thou unto me. But she returned not." "Is there no balm in Gilead? Is there no physician there? Why then, is not the health of the daughter of my people recovered?" Truly thou mightst find in the Divine Scriptures many remedies for such an evil—many medicines that recover from perdition and restore to life; mysterious words about death and resurrection, a dreadful judgment, and everlasting punishment; the doctrines of repentance and remission of sins; those innumerable examples of conversion—the piece of silver, the lost sheep, the son that had devoured his living with harlots, that was lost and found, that was dead and alive again. Let us use these remedies for the evil; with these let us heal our souls. Think, too, of thy last day (for thou art not to live always, more than others), of the distress, and the anguish, as the hour of death draws nearer, of the impending sentence of God, of the angels moving on rapid wing, of the soul fearfully agitated by all these things, and bitterly tormented with a guilty conscience, and clinging pitifully to the things here below, and still under the inevitable necessity of taking its departure. Picture to thy mind the final dissolution of all that belongs to our present life, when the Son of man shall come in his glory, with his holy angels: for He "shall come, and shall not keep silence," when he shall come to judge the living and the dead, and to render to every man according to his work: when the trumpet, with its loud and terrible echo, shall awaken those who have slept from the beginning of the world, and they shall come forth, they that have done good to the resurrection of the life, and they that have done evil to the resurrection of damnation. Remember the divine vision of Daniel, how he brings the judgment before our eyes. "I beheld," says he, "till the thrones were placed, and the Ancient of days did sit, whose garment was white as snow, and the hair of his head like the pure wool: his throne was like the fiery flame, and his wheels as burning fire. A fiery stream issued and came forth from before him: thousand thousands ministered unto him, and ten thousand times ten thousand stood before him: the judgment was set, and the books were opened," revealing all at once in the hearing of all men and all angels, all things whether good or bad, open or secret, deeds, words, thoughts. What effect must all these things have on those who have lived viciously? Where, then, shall the soul, thus suddenly revealed in all the fullness of its shame in the eyes of such a multitude of spectators—O, where shall it hide itself? In what body can it endure those unbounded and intolerable torments of the unquenchable fire, and the tortures of the undying worm, and the dark and frightful abyss of hell, and the bitter howlings, and woeful wailings, and weeping and gnashing of teeth; and all these dire woes without end. Deliverance from these after death there is none; neither is there any device, nor contrivance for escaping these bitter torments.

But now it is possible to escape them. Now then, while it is possible, let us recover ourselves from our fall, let us not despair of restoration, if we break loose from our vices. Jesus Christ came into the world to save sinners. "O, come let us worship and bow down," let us weep before him. His word, calling us to repentance, lifts up its voice and cries aloud, "Come unto me all ye that labor and are heavy laden, and I will give you rest." There is then a way to be saved, if we will. Death has prevailed and swallowed us up; but be assured, that God will wipe away every tear from the face of every penitent. The Lord is faithful in all His words. He does not lie, when he says, "Though your sins be as scarlet, they shall be as white as snow, though they be red like crimson, they shall be as wool." The great Physician of souls is ready to heal thy disease; He is the prompt Deliverer, not of thee alone, but of all who are in bondage to sin. These are His words—His sweet and life-giving lips pronounced them—"They that be whole need not a physician, but they that are sick. I am not come to call the righteous, but sinners to repentance." What excuse then remains to thee, or to any one else, when He utters such language as this? The Lord is willing to heal thy painful wound, and to enlighten thy darkness. The Good Shepherd leaves the sheep who have not strayed, to seek for thee. If thou give thyself up to Him, He will not delay, He in His mercy will not disdain to carry thee upon His own shoulders, rejoicing that He has found His sheep which was lost. The Father stands waiting thy return from thy wanderings. Only arise and come, and whilst thou art yet a great way off He will run and fall upon thy neck; and, purified at once by thy repentance, thou shalt be enfolded in the embraces of His friendship. He will put the best robe on thy soul, when it has put off the old man with his deeds: He will put a ring on thy hands when they have been washed from the blood of death: He will put shoes on thy feet, when they have turned from the evil way to the path of the gospel of peace; and He will proclaim a day of joy and gladness, to the whole family of both angels and men, and will celebrate thy salvation with every form of rejoicing. For He Himself says, "Verily I say unto you, that joy shall be in heaven before God over one sinner that repenteth." And if any of those that stand by should seem to find fault, because thou art so quickly received, the good Father Himself will plead for thee, saying, "It was meet that we should make merry and be glad; for this my daughter was dead, and is alive again; and was lost, and is found."

Saint Chrysostom

[347–407]

John, called Chrysostom (the golden-mouthed), is often referred to as "the Homer of orators." This "brightest ornament of the ancient Greek church" was born at Antioch, in Syria, and there spent most of his life. His pious mother, Anthusa, had full charge of his early education and religious instruction. He was trained for the law, studying for a time under the greatest legal mind of the times, Julian the Apostate. In his thirty-first year he entered the ministry and, because of his brilliant preaching, rose rapidly to a position of leadership in the church. He was made Patriarch of Constantinople in 398, but his strict life and his pointed preaching angered the leaders of that corrupt metropolis and led to his banishment and eventually to his death. This sermon is one of seven delivered by Chrysostom on Lazarus and is held to be one of his best.

EXCESSIVE GRIEF AT THE DEATH OF FRIENDS

But I would not have you to be ignorant, brethren, concerning them which are asleep, that ye sorrow not. I THESSALONIANS 4:13.

WE HAVE OCCUPIED four days in explaining to you the parable of Lazarus, bringing out the treasure that we found in a body covered with sores; a treasure, not of gold and silver and precious stones, but of wisdom and fortitude, of patience and endurance. For as in regard to visible treasures, while the surface of the ground shows only thorns and briars, and rough earth, yet, let a person dig deep, abundant wealth discovers itself; so it has proved in respect to Lazarus. Outwardly, wounds; but underneath these, unspeakable wealth; a body pined away, but a noble and wakeful spirit. We have also seen an illustration of that remark of the apostle's—as much as the outward man perishes, so much the inward man is renewed.

It would, indeed, be proper to address you to-day, also, on this same parable, and to enter the lists with those heretics who censure the Old Testament, bringing accusations against the patriarchs, and whetting their tongues against God, the Creator of the universe. But to avoid satiety, and reserving this controversy for another time, let us direct the discourse to another subject; for a table with only one sort of food produces satiety, while variety provokes the appetite. That it may be so in regard to our preaching, let us now, after a long period, turn to the blessed Paul; for very opportunely has a passage from the Apostle been read to-day, and the things which are to be spoken concerning it are harmonious with those that have lately been presented. Hear, then, Paul this day proclaiming—I would not have you to be ignorant concerning them which are asleep, that ye sorrow not even as others which have no hope. The parable of Lazarus is the evangelical chord; this passage is the apostolic note. And there is concord between them; for we have, on that parable, said much concerning the resurrection and the future judgment, and our discourse now recurs to that theme; so that, though it is on apostolic ground we are now toiling, we shall here find the same treasure. For in treating the parable, our aim was to teach the hearers this lesson, that they should regard all the splendors of the present life as nothing, but should look forward in their hopes, and daily reflect on the decisions which will be hereafter pronounced, and on that fearful judgment, and that Judge who can not be deceived. On these things Paul has counseled us to-day in the passages which have been read to us. Attend, however, to his own words—I would not have you to be ignorant, brethren, concerning them which are asleep, that ye sorrow not, even as others which have no hope. For if we believe that Jesus died and rose again, even so them also which sleep in Jesus will God bring with him.

Say not, a dead man hears not, nor speaks, nor sees, nor is conscious. It is just so with a sleeping person. If I may speak somewhat paradoxically, even the soul of a sleeping person is in some sort asleep; but not so the soul of a dead man; that is awake.

But you say, a dead man experiences corruption, and becomes dust and ashes. And what then, beloved hearers? For this very reason we ought to rejoice. For when a man is about to rebuild an old and tottering house, he first sends out its occupants, then tears it down, and rebuilds anew a more splendid one. This occasions no grief to the occupants, but rather joy; for they do not think of the demolition which they see, but of the house which is to come, though not yet seen. When God is about to do a similar work, he destroys our body, and removes the soul which was dwelling in it as from some house, that he may build it anew and more splendidly, and again bring the soul into it with greater glory. Let us not, therefore, regard the tearing down, but the splendor which is to succeed.

If, again, a man has a statue decayed by rust and age, and mutilated in many of its parts, he breaks it up and casts it into a furnace, and after the melting he receives it again in a more beautiful form. As then the dissolving in the furnace was not a destruction but a renewing of the statue, so the death of our bodies is not a destruction but a renovation. When, therefore, you see as in a furnace our flesh flowing away to corruption, dwell not on that sight, but wait for the recasting. And be not satisfied with the extent of this illustration, but advance in your thoughts to a still higher point; for the statuary, casting into the furnace a brazen image, does not furnish you in its place a golden and undecaying statue, but again makes a brazen one. God does not thus; but casting in a mortal body formed of clay, he returns to you a golden and immortal statue; for the earth, receiving a corruptible and decaying body, gives back the same, incorruptible and undecaying. Look not, therefore, on the corpse, lying with closed eyes and speechless lips, but on the man that is risen, that has received glory unspeakable and amazing, and direct your thoughts from the present sight to the future hope.

And how is it possible, you ask, not to grieve, since I am only a man? Nor do I say that you should not grieve: I do not condemn dejection, but the intensity of it. To be dejected is natural; but to be overcome by dejection is madness, and folly, and unmanly weakness. You may grieve and weep; but give not way to despondency, nor indulge in complaints. Give thanks to God, who has taken your friend, that you have the opportunity of honoring the departed one, and of dismissing him with becoming obsequies. If you sink under depression, you withhold honor from the departed, you displease God who has taken him, and you injure yourself; but if you are grateful, you pay respect to him, you glorify God, and you benefit yourself. Weep, as wept your master over Lazarus, observing the just limits of sorrow, which it is not proper to pass. Thus also said Paul—I would not have you to be ignorant concerning them which are asleep, that ye sorrow not as others who have no hope. Grieve, says he; but not as the Greek, who has no hope of a resurrection, who despairs of a future life.

For on what account, tell me, do you thus weep for one departed? Because he was a bad man? You ought on that very account to be thankful, since the occasions of wickedness are now cut off. Because he was good and kind? If so, you ought to rejoice; since he has been soon removed, before wickedness had corrupted him, and he has gone away to a world where he stands ever secure, and there is no room even to mistrust a change. Because he was a youth? For that, too, praise Him that has taken him, because He has speedily called him to a better lot. Because he was an aged man? On this account, also, give thanks and glorify Him that has taken him. Be ashamed of your manner of burial. The singing of psalms, the prayers, the assembling of the [spiritual] fathers and brethren—all this is not that you may weep, and lament, and afflict yourselves, but that you may render thanks to Him who has taken the departed. For as when men are called to some high office, multitudes with praises on their lips assemble to escort them at their departure to their stations, so do all with abundant praise join to send forward, as to greater honor, those of the pious who have departed. Death is rest, a deliverance from the exhausting labors and cares of this world. When, then, thou seest a relative departing, yield not to despondency; give thyself to reflection; examine thy conscience; cherish the thought that after a little while this end awaits thee also. Be more considerate; let another's death excite thee to salutary fear; shake off all indolence; examine your past deeds; quit your sins, and commence a happy change.

Consider to whom the departed has gone, and take comfort. He has gone where Paul is, and Peter, and the whole company of the saints. Consider how he shall arise, with what glory and splendor. Consider, that by mourning and lamenting thou canst not alter the event which has occurred, and that thou wilt in the end injure thyself. Consider whom you imitate by so doing, and shun this companionship in sin. For whom do you imitate and emulate? The unbelieving, those who have no hope; as Paul has said—That ye sorrow not, even as others who have no hope. And observe how carefully he expresses himself; for he does not say, Those who have not the hope of a resurrection, but simply, Those who have no hope. He that has no hope of a future retribution has no hope at all, nor does he know that there is a God, nor that God exercises a providential care over present occurrences, nor that divine justice looks on all things.

For I have now addressed you on this subject, though no one is in particular affliction, that when we shall fall into any such calamity, we may, from the remembrance of what has been said, obtain requisite consolation. As soldiers, even in peace, perform warlike exercises, so that when actually called to battle and the occasion makes a demand for skill, they may avail themselves of the art which they have cultivated in peace; so let us, in time of peace, furnish ourselves with weapons and remedies, that whenever there shall burst on us a war of unreasonable passions, or grief, or pain, or any such thing, we may, well armed and secure on all sides, repel the assaults of the evil one with all skill, and wall ourselves round with right contemplations, with the declarations of God, with the examples of good men, and with every possible defense. For so shall we be able to pass the present life with happiness, and to attain

to the kingdom of heaven, through Jesus Christ, to whom be glory and
dominion, together with the Father and the Holy Spirit, forever and
ever. Amen.

Saint Augustine

[354–430]

*Saint Augustine was a man of extremes. Born at Tagasta, in Numidia, he
was nurtured in the Christian faith by his mother. Although he became famous
as a teacher of grammar and rhetoric in Rome and Carthage, his personal life
was dissolute and crassly immoral. In 387 he was converted to Christianity and
became an ardent and zealous follower of the Christian life. For a while he
lived in seclusion and abject poverty. Then he turned to church leadership and
was raised to the high office of Bishop of Hippo, in North Africa. This eminent
father of the early church did much to make clear the doctrines and beliefs
of Christianity and to settle many dangerous controversies. His sermons show
"a sublime genius, an ardent love of truth, and an unflinching determination
to defend it, invincible patience, a subtle and lively wit, and sincere piety."
He is represented here by one of his most famous homilies on the New
Testament.*

THE RECOVERING OF SIGHT TO THE BLIND

Have mercy on us, O Lord, thou Son of David. MATTHEW 20:30.

YE KNOW, holy brethren, full well as we do, that our Lord and Saviour
Jesus Christ is the Physician of our eternal health; and that to this end
we task the weakness of our natures, that our weakness might not last
forever. For He assumed a mortal body, wherein to kill death. And,
though He was crucified through meekness, as the Apostle saith, *yet He
liveth by the power of God.* They are the words, too, of the same Apostle;
He dieth no more, and death shall have no more dominion over Him.
These things, I say, are well known to your faith. And there is also this
which follows from it, that we should know that all the miracles which
He did on the body, avail to our instruction, that we may from them
perceive that which is not to pass away, nor to have any end. He restored
to the blind those eyes which death was sure sometime to close; He raised
Lazarus to life who was to die again. And whatever He did for the
health of bodies, He did it not to this end that they should be forever;
whereas, at the last, He will give eternal health even to the body itself.
But because those things which were not seen, were not blieved; by

means of these temporal things which were seen, He built up faith in those things which were not seen.

These things, then, the Lord did to invite us to the faith. This faith reigneth now in the Church, which is spread throughout the whole world. And now, He worketh greater cures, on account of which He disdained not then to exhibit those lesser ones. For as the soul is better than the body, so is the saving health of the soul better than the health of the body. The blind body doth not now open its eyes by a miracle of the Lord, but the blinded heart openeth its eyes to the word of the Lord. The mortal corpse doth not now rise again, but the soul doth rise again which lay dead in a living body. The deaf ears of the body are not now opened; but how many have the ears of their heart closed, which yet fly open at the penetrating word of God, so that they believe who did not believe, and they live well who did live evilly, and they obey who did not obey; and we say, "such a man is become a believer;" and we wonder when we hear of them whom once we had known as hardened. Why, then, dost thou marvel at one who now believes, who is living innocently, and serving God; but because thou dost behold him seeing, whom thou hadst known to be blind; dost behold him living whom thou hadst known to be dead; dost behold him hearing whom thou hadst known to be deaf? For consider that there are who are dead in another than the ordinary sense, of whom the Lord spoke to a certain man who delayed to follow the Lord, because he wished to bury his father; *Let the dead,* said He, *bury their dead.* Surely these dead buriers are not dead in body; for if this were so, they could not bury dead bodies. Yet doth he call them dead; where but in the soul within? For as we may often see in a household, itself sound and well, the master of the same house lying dead; so in a sound body do many carry a dead soul within; and these the Apostle arouses thus, *Awake, thou that sleepest, and arise from the dead, and Christ shall give thee light.* It is the same who giveth sight to the blind that awakeneth the dead. For it is with His voice that the cry is made by the Apostle to the dead. *Awake thou that sleepest.* And the blind will be enlightened with light, when he shall have risen again. And how many deaf men did the Lord see before His eyes, when He said, *He that hath ears to hear let him hear.* For who was standing before Him without his bodily ears? What other ears, then, did He seek for, but those of the inner man?

Therefore, my brethren, since we too are born of him, and as the Apostle says, *In Adam all die;* for we were all at first two persons; if we were loth to obey the physician, that we might not be sick; let us obey him now, that we may be delivered from sickness. The physician gave us precepts, when we were whole; He gave us precepts that we might not need a physician. *They that are whole,* He saith, *need not a physician, but they that are sick.* When whole, we despised these precepts, and by experience have felt how to our own destruction we despised his precepts. Now we are sick, we are in distress, we are on the bed of weakness; yet let us not despair. For because we could not come to the Physician, He hath vouchsafed to come Himself to us. Though despised by man when he was whole, He did not despise him when he was stricken. He did not leave off to give other precepts to the weak, who would not keep the first precepts, that he might not be weak; as though He would say, "Assuredly thou hast by experience felt that I spoke the truth when I said, Touch not this. Be healed then now, at length, and recover the life thou hast lost. Lo, I am bearing thine infirmity; drink then the bitter cup. For thou hast of thine own self made those my so sweet precepts, which were given to thee when whole, so toilsome. They were despised, and so thy distress began; cured thou canst not be, except thou drink the bitter cup, the cup of temptations, wherein this life abounds, the cup of tribulation, anguish, and suffering. Drink then," He says, "drink, that thou mayest live." And that the sick man may not make answer, "I can not, I can not bear it, I will not drink;" the Physician, all whole though he be, drinketh first, that the sick man may not hesitate to drink. For what bitterness is there in this cup, which He hath not drunk? If it be contumely, he heard it first when he drove out the devils. *He hath a devil, and by Beelzebub he casteth out devils.* Whereupon, in order to comfort the sick, He saith, *If they have called the Master of the house Beelzebub, how much more shall they call them of His household?* If pains are this bitter cup, He was bound, and scourged, and crucified. If death be this bitter cup, He died also. If infirmity shrink with horror from any particular kind of death; none was at that time more ignominious than the death of the cross. For it was not in vain that the Apostle, when setting forth His obedience, added, *Made obedient unto death, even the death of the cross.*

But because He designed to honor His faithful ones at the end of the world, He hath first honored the cross in this world; in such wise that the princes of the earth who believe in Him have prohibited any criminal from being crucified; and that cross which the Jewish persecutors with great mockery prepared for the Lord, even kings, his servants at this day, bear with great confidence on their foreheads. Only the shameful nature of the death which our Lord vouchsafed to undergo for us is not now so apparent, Who, as the Apostle says, *was made a curse for us.* And when, as He hung, the blindness of the Jews mocked Him, surely He could have come down from the cross, Who, if He had not so willed, had not been on the cross; but it was a greater thing to rise from the grave than to come down from the cross. Our Lord, then, in doing these divine, and in suffering these human things, instructs us by his bodily miracles and bodily patience, that we may believe and be made whole to behold those things invisible which the eye of the body hath no knowledge of. With this intent, then, He cured those blind men of whom the account has just now been read in the Gospel. And consider what instruction He has by this cure conveyed to the man who is sick within.

Consider the issue of the thing, and the order of the circumstances. Those two blind men sitting by the wayside cried out, as the Lord passed by, that He would have mercy upon them. But they were restrained from crying out by the multitude which was with the Lord. Now do not suppose that this circumstance is left without a mysterious meaning. But they overcame the crowd who kept them back by the great perseverance of their cry, that their voice might reach the Lord's ears; as though he had not already anticipated their thoughts. So then the two blind men cried out that they might be heard by the Lord, and could not be restrained by the multitude. The Lord *was passing by,* and they cried out. The Lord *stood still,* and they were healed. For *the Lord Jesus stood still, and called them, and said, What will ye that I shall do unto you? They say unto Him, That our eyes may be opened.* The Lord did according to their faith, He recovered their eyes. If we have now understood by the sick, the deaf, the dead, the sick, and deaf, and dead within; let us look out in this place also for the blind within. The eyes of the heart are closed; *Jesus passeth by* that we may cry out. What is *Jesus passeth by?* Jesus is doing things which last but for a time. What is *Jesus passeth by?* Jesus doth things which pass by. Mark and see how many things of His have *passed by.* He was born of the Virgin Mary; is He being born always? As an infant He was suckled; is He suckled always? He ran through the successive ages of life until man's full estate; doth He grow in body always? Boyhood succeeded to infancy, to boyhood youth, to youth man's full stature in several passing successions. Even the very miracles which he did are *passed by;* they are read and believed. For because these miracles are written that so they might be read, they *passed by* when they were being done. In a word, not to dwell long on this, He was crucified; is He hanging on the cross always? He was buried, He rose again, He ascended into heaven, *now He dieth no more, Death shall no more have dominion over Him.* And His Divinity abideth ever, yea, the immortality of His body now shall never fail. But nevertheless all those things which were wrought by Him in time have *passed by;* and they are written to be read, and they are preached to be believed. In all these things, then, *Jesus passeth by.*

And what are *the two blind men by the wayside* but the two people to cure whom Jesus came? Let us show these two people in the Holy Scriptures. It is written in the Gospel, *Other sheep I have which are not of this fold; them also must I bring, that there may be one fold and one Shepherd.* Who then are the two people? One the people of the Jews, and the other of the Gentiles. *I am not sent,* He saith, *but unto the lost sheep of the house of Israel.* To whom did He say this? To the disciples; when that woman of Canaan who confessed herself to be a dog cried out that she might be found worthy of the crumbs from the Master's table. And because she was found worthy, now were the two people to whom He had come made manifest, the Jewish people, to wit, of whom He said, *I am not sent but unto the lost sheep of the house of Israel;* and the people of the Gentiles, whose type this woman exhibited, whom He had first rejected, saying, *It is not meet to cast the children's bread to the dogs;* and to whom, when she said, *Truth, Lord, yet the dogs eat of the crumbs which fall from their master's table,* He answered, *O woman, great is thy faith; be it unto thee even as thou wilt.* For of this people also was that centurion of whom the same Lord saith, *Verily I say unto you, I have not found so great faith, no, not in Israel.* Because he had said, *I am not worthy that Thou shouldest come under my roof, but speak the word only, and my servant shall be healed.* So then the Lord even before His passion and glorification pointed out two people, the one to whom he had come because of the promises to the Fathers, and the other whom for His mercy's sake He did not reject; that it might be fulfilled which had been promised to Abraham, *In thy seed shall all the nations be blessed.*

Attend, now, dearly beloved. The Lord was *passing by,* and the blind men *cried out.* What is, *was passing by?* As we have already said, He was doing works which *passed by.* Now upon these passing works is our faith built up. For we believe on the Son of God, not only in that He is the word of God, by whom all things were made; for if He had always continued *in the form of God, equal with God, and had not emptied Himself in taking the form of a servant;* the blind men would not even have perceived Him, that they might be able to cry out. But when He wrought passing works, that is, *when He humbled Himself, having become obedient unto death, even the death of the cross, the two blind men cried out, Have mercy on us, thou Son of David.* For this very thing that He, David's Lord and Creator, willed also to be David's son, He wrought in time, He wrought *passing by.*

For how are our eyes made whole? That as by faith we perceive Christ *passing by* in the temporal economy, so we may attain to the knowledge of Him as *standing still* in His unchangeable eternity. For there is the eye made whole when the knowledge of Christ's divinity is attained. Let your love apprehend this; attend ye to the great mystery which I am to speak of. All the things which were done by our Lord Jesus Christ in time, graft faith in us. We believe on the Son of God, not on the word only, *by which all things were made;* but on this very word, *made flesh that He might dwell among us.* Who was born of the Virgin Mary, and the rest which the Faith contains, and which are represented to us that Christ might *pass by,* and that the blind, hearing His footsteps as He *passeth by,* might by their works *cry out,* by their life exemplifying the profession of their faith. But now in order that they who cry out may be made whole, *Jesus standeth still.* For he saw Jesus now *standing still,* who says, *Though we have known Christ after the flesh, yet now henceforth know we Him no more.* For he saw Christ's divinity as far as in this life is possible. There is then in Christ the divinity, and the humanity. The divinity *standeth still,* the humanity *passeth by.* What means, the divinity *standeth still?* It changeth not, is not shaken, doth not depart away. For He did not so come to us as to depart from the father; nor did He so ascend as to change His place. When He assumed flesh, it changed place; but God assuming flesh, seeing He is not in place, doth not change His place. Let us then be touched by Christ *standing still,* and so our eyes be made whole. But whose eyes? The eyes of those who *cry out* when He is *passing by;* that is, who do good works through that faith which hath been dispersed in time, to instruct us in our infancy.

Peter Abélard

[1079–1142]

Peter Abélard was one of the great teachers of the Middle Ages. After marked success as a teacher at Melun, he went to Paris and there helped found the University of Paris. Though often at odds with the more conservative of his day, even being condemned for heresy in 1140, he was reconciled with his accusers and continued in a position of leadership. The story of his romance with Héloïse has become a classic. Typical of his style and power as a preacher is the following sermon.

THE DIVINE TRAGEDY

WHETHER, therefore, Christ is spoken of as about to be crowned or about to be crucified it is said that He "went forth"; to signify that the Jews, who were guilty of so great wickedness against Him, were given over to reprobation, and that His grace would now pass to the vast extent of the Gentiles, where the salvation of the Cross and His own exaltation by the gain of many peoples, in the place of the one nation of the Jews, has extended itself. Whence, also, to-day we rightly go forth to adore the Cross in the open plain, showing mystically that both glory and salvation had departed from the Jews and had spread themselves among the Gentiles. But in that we afterward returned [in procession] to the place whence we had set forth, we signify that in the end of the world the grace of God will return to the Jews; namely, when, by the preaching of Enoch and Elijah, they shall be converted to Him.

Whence the apostle: "I would not, brethren, that ye should be ignorant of this mystery, that blindness in part has fallen upon Israel, until the fulness of the Gentiles shall be come, and so all Israel shall be saved." Whence the place itself of Calvary, where the Lord was crucified, is now, as we know, contained in the city; whereas formerly it was without the walls. "The crown wherewith His Mother crowned Him in the day of His espousals, and in the day of the gladness of His Heart." For thus kings are wont to exhibit their glory when they betroth queens to themselves and celebrate the solemnities of their nuptials. Now the day of the Lord's crucifixion was, as it were, the day of His betrothal; because it was then that He associated the Church to Himself as His bride, and on the same day descended into Hell, and setting free the souls of faithful, accomplished in them that which He had promised to the thief: "Verily I say unto thee, to-day shalt thou be with me in Paradise."

"To-day," He says, of the gladness of His Heart, because in His body He suffered the torture of pain; but while the flesh inflicted on Him torments through the outward violence of men His soul was filled with joy on account of our salvation, which He thus brought to pass. Whence, also, when He went forth to His crucifixion He stilled the women that were lamenting Him and said, "Daughters of Jerusalem, weep not for me, but weep for yourselves and your children." As if He said, "Grieve not for me in these my sufferings, as if by their means I should fall into any real destruction; but rather lament for that heavy vengeance which hangs over you and your children because of that which they have committed against me."

So we, also, brethren, which rather weep for ourselves than for Him; and for the faults which we have committed, not for the punishments which He bore. Let us so rejoice with Him and for Him, as to grieve for our own offenses, and for that the guilty servant committed the transgression, while the innocent Lord bore the punishment. He taught us to weep who is never said to have wept for Himself, though He wept for Lazarus when about to raise him from the dead.

Saint Bernard

[1091–1153]

Saint Bernard, Abbot of Clairvaux, was born of a deeply religious mother and grew to manhood with an overwhelming love of the Bible and an all-possessing love for Christ. The high point of his life was his preaching of the second crusade before the Pope and King Louis VII at Vezelia in France. The people were stirred as never before, and vast throngs joined in the crusade. The following sermon is one of Saint Bernard's best. It is clear, imaginative, and full of the intensity that marked his preaching.

THE THREE SPIRITUAL PERFUMES

I HAVE NEITHER such depth of knowledge, nor such brilliancy of genius, as to discover of myself anything new. But the mouth of St. Paul is a great and unfailing fountain which is open to us. From him I draw what I am about to say on the subject of the bosom of the Bride, as indeed, I am accustomed frequently to do. Rejoice, he says, with them that do rejoice, and weep with them that weep. He here expresses, in a few words, the affections of a mother's heart, because little children cannot either be in pain and grief, or in health and gladness, without the close sympathy of their mother in either case, nor can she fail to feel with them. Thus, following the opinion of St. Paul, I shall assign those two affections to the breasts of the Bride—to the one compassion, to the other congratulation. If it were otherwise, if she had not these as yet—that is, if she had not learned to be quick in congratulating others, or to be ready to condole with them in their grief—she would be but a child, and not of a marriageable age. If a person of such character as this is taken to discharge the oversight of souls, or to preach, he does not profit others, and to himself he does very great harm. And if he should thrust himself into these ministries, what a shameless action is that!

But let us return to these thus typified, to the differences between them, and to the graces they yield. Congratulation pours forth the milk of exhortation, and compassion that of consolation.

Our spiritual mother feels her pious bosom abundantly supplied from above with both the one and the other of these as often as she is fulfilled with the love of God. You see her occupied in nourishing her little children out of her abundance; to one she gives consolation, to another exhortation, according as each seems to have need. For instance, if she sees that one of her children in the Gospel has been taken unawares by some violent temptation so that he is rendered troubled and sorrowful, doubting and fearful, and is no longer able to bear up against the force of the temptation, how she condoles with him and soothes him! How she sorrows for him and gives him comfort, and finds many a pious reason to enable him to rise out of his state of depression! If, on the contrary, she sees one active, energetic, and making good progress in the spiritual life she rejoices greatly, she plies him with beneficial advice, she animates him to advance still further, instructs him in that which is requisite to perseverance, and exhorts him so that he may go on from strength to strength. To all she adapts herself, in her own heart she reflects the feelings and the dispositions of all, and lastly, she allows herself the mother no less of the feeble and failing soul than of the strong and progressive.

How many are there at the present day—I mean of those who have taken upon them the cure of souls—who are animated by sentiments the very reverse of these? It is a fact not to be spoken of without groaning and tears; they forge, so to speak, in the furnace of avarice, and make merchandise of, the very instrument of Christ's Passion—the scourge, the spitting, the nails, the lance, and, in fine, the Cross and the Death of Christ. They squander all these things for the making of shameful gains; they hasten to huddle into their own pouches the price of the Redemption of the world. The only difference which distinguishes them from Judas Iscariot is that he, for the price of all these things, received but, comparatively speaking, a few pence; while they, with a greed much more insatiable, exact uncounted sums of money as their gains. They have for riches a thirst which is insatiable; well-nigh their sole fear is lest they may lose these; and if they should do so they grieve. Upon the love of them they look in satisfaction, if, perchance, there be a moment left free from the task of keeping what they have or of gaining more. As for the salvation of souls, or their loss, they think of it not at all. No maternal care for souls have they who, being too well nourished, have fattened and grown great upon the patrimony of the Crucified. They are not grieved for the affliction of Joseph. A true mother is unmistakably to be known; she is never void of nourishment for her children. She ceases not to rejoice with them that do rejoice, and to weep with them that weep; to press from her bosom the life-giving milk—from that of congratulation the milk of exhortation; from that of compassion, of consolation I need not say more of these, and of what they contain.

I have also to point out what are the perfumes with which the same are fragrant, provided that I am assisted by your prayers, so that by their means that which is given me to think may also be spoken worthily, and to the profit of my hearers. The perfumes of the Bride differ from those of the Bridegroom, as they are different the one from the other. What was to be said of those of the Bridegroom is contained in another discourse. Let us consider just now only the perfumes of the Bride; and that with the greater care, because Scripture commends them particularly to our attention in calling them not only good, but best of all. I mention several kinds, so that out of many those most befitting the Bride may be chosen. There is the perfume of contrition, the perfume of devotion, and that of piety. The first is pungent, and causes pain; the second is soothing, and relieves pain; the third is curative, and removes disease. Now we will speak of these separately.

There is, then, a perfume or unguent which the soul—that is, if it be ensnared and entangled with many crimes—compounds for itself, and if when it begins to reflect upon its ways, it collects, heaps together and pounds in the mortar of conscience its sins of many different kinds, and putting them into the caldron, as it were, of a heart that heaves and boils with distress, cooks them together over a kind of fire of grief and repentance, so that the man may be able to say, with the Psalmist: "My heart was hot within me; while I was musing the fire burned." Here, then, is one unguent which the sinful soul ought to prepare for itself at the commencement of its conversion, and to apply to its still fresh wounds; for the first sacrifice to be made to God is a troubled and contrite heart. Although the sinner is poor and needy, and therefore unable to compound for himself an unguent better and more valuable, yet let him not neglect to prepare this, though of poor materials and of no value, for a broken and contrite heart God will not despise; and it shall appear so much the less vile in the sight of God as by the remembrance of his sins it becomes the more so to the sinner himself.

Yet if we say that this invisible and spiritual unguent was designated in type by that visible ointment wherewith the feet of God manifest in the flesh were anointed by the woman who was a sinner, we shall not be able to regard it as altogether worthless. For what do we read of it in the Scripture? That the house was filled with the odor of the ointment. It was poured by the hands of a sinful woman, and poured upon the extremities of the body—that is, upon the feet; yet it was not so vile and so contemptible that the power and the sweetness of its perfume could not fill the whole house. And if we consider with what fragrance the Church is perfumed by the conversion of one sinner, and how powerful an odor of life unto life each penitent becomes if his repentance is perfect and public, we shall be able to pronounce, without the least doubt, that the house was filled with the odor of the ointment. Assuredly the odor of penitence extends even as far as the mansions of the blessed in heaven, so that as the Truth Himself declares, there is joy among the angels of God over one sinner that repented. Rejoice, O penitents; be strengthened, ye that are weak of heart. To you I speak who are but lately converted from the world and from your evil ways, who are feeling the bitterness and confusion of a mind touched with repentance, and in whom the excessive pain of wounds, as it were, yet recent, still throbs and torments. Your hands may with safety drop the bitterness of myrrh into this salutary ointment, for a broken and contrite heart God will not despise. Nor is such ointment as this to be despised or counted vile, of which the odor not only draws men to conversion but moves the angels to joy.

Yet there is a perfume as much more precious than this, as the materials of which it is composed are of more excellent kinds. For the materials of the former do not require to be sought from far; we find them without difficulty within ourselves, and in our own little garden plots gather them easily in great plenty, as often as necessity requires. For who is there who does not know himself to have sins and iniquities of his own, enough and too many, always at his hand, unless he desires to deceive himself upon this point? But these are, as you recognize, the materials of the former ointment, which I have described. But as for the sweet spices which compose the second, our earth does not produce them at all; we must seek them in a land very far off. For is not every good gift, and every perfect gift from above, and does it not come down from the Father of Lights? For this perfume is compounded which Divine goodness has bestowed upon the human race. Happy is he who with care and pains collects them for himself, and sets them before the eyes of his mind with acts of thanksgiving proportioned to their greatness. Assuredly when these shall have been bruised and pounded in the mortar of our breast, with the pestle of frequent meditation, then boiled together on the fire of holy desire, and finally enriched with the oil of joy, there will be as the result a perfume far more precious and more excellent than the former. Sufficient as proof of this is the testimony of Him who says: "Whoso offereth praise glorieth Me." Nor can we doubt that the remembrance of benefits is an excitement to praise of our benefactor.

Furthermore, while Scripture, when speaking of the former, testifies only that it is not despised by God, of this latter it is plain that it is the more commended, in that it is said to glorify God. Besides, the former is poured upon the Lord's feet; the latter upon His head. For if in Christ the head is to be referred to His Divinity, as St. Paul declares the head of Christ is God, then, without doubt, he anoints the head who renders thanks; for this is addressed to God, not to man. Not that He who is God is not Man also, for God and Man is one, Christ, but because every good gift, even that which is ministered through man, comes from

God, not from man. For it is the Spirit which quickeneth; the flesh profiteth nothing. And we know that cursed is the man that trusteth in man; although all our hope rests rightly upon Him who is the God-Man, yet this is not because He is Man, but because He is God. Therefore, the former perfume is poured upon His feet; but this upon His head, because the humiliation of a contrite heart is befitting to the humility of the flesh, but praise and glory to the Divine Majesty. See then of what a nature is this perfume which I have been describing to you, with which that head, so august even to the principalities and powers of heaven, does not disdain to be touched; nay, rather regards it as an honor to Him, as He Himself declares: "Whoso offereth praise glorifieth Me."

Wherefore it does not belong to him who is poor and needy and of small courage to compound such a perfume as this, inasmuch as it is confidence alone which commands the sweet spices which are its materials, but a confidence which is born of freedom of spirit and purity of heart. For the soul which is of small courage and of little faith is hampered by the consciousness of the little which it possesses; its poverty does not permit it to occupy itself in the praises of God, or in the contemplation of those benefits which produce the praises. And if ever it has the wish to rise to that point, immediately it is recalled to the consciousness of its cares and uneasiness about its necessities at home, and is straitened in itself by the miseries which press it hard. If you ask of me the cause of that misery, I reply that you are, or have been, conscious in your own selves of that which I refer to. It seems to me that this depression of mind and want of joyful trust usually comes from one of two causes. Either, that is to say, it is from newness of conversion, or especially, if the conversion is not recent, from lukewarmness of conduct. Both the one and the other cause humiliates and casts down the conscience, and throws it into trouble and inquietude, since it feels that its former passions are not yet dead in it, either because of the shortness of the time since its conversion or because of the feebleness and want of zeal in its efforts, and thus it is obliged to occupy itself entirely with rooting up from the garden of the heart the thorns of iniquity and briers of evil desires, nor is it able to divert any thoughts from itself. What then? How can one, who is wearily occupied in sighing and groaning over such a task as this, at the same time rejoice in the praises of God? How can thanksgiving and the voice of melody, to borrow from the phrase of the Prophet Isaiah, sound forth from the mouth of one that is groaning and lamenting? For, as the Wise Man teaches us, Music in mourning is a tale out of season. And the giving of thanks follows the benefit, not precedes it. But the soul that is still in sadness needs to receive the benefit, and does not rejoice in having obtained it. It has a great reason to offer its prayers, but not to offer its thanksgiving. How is it to acknowledge a blessing which it has not in fact received? It was correct, therefore, for me to say that it was not the privilege of a soul that is poor and needy and of small courage to compound this precious perfume, which requires to be composed of remembered benefits of God; nor is such one able to behold the light, as long as its gaze is fixed upon the darkness. For it is in bitterness—the sorrowful remembrance of past sins occupies it; nor can it admit any thought of joy. It is to such that the prophetic spirit bears testimony saying: "It is vain of you to rise up early;" as if he would remind them: It is in vain for you to rise up that you may behold bounties to be a delight to your soul, unless you have first received the light which shall comfort it with regard to the stains of sin which trouble it. This perfume, therefore, is not for the soul which is in a state of spiritual poverty.

But see who they are who may rightly take the glory of having it in abundance. The Apostles departed from the presence of the council, rejoicing that they were counted worthy to suffer shame for the name of Jesus. Assuredly these men were well filled with that unction of the Spirit, whose cheerfulness did not abandon them, I do not say, because of words, but even because of blows. They were indeed rich in charity, in whom it was exhausted by no spending, and who were enabled to offer themselves as a complete and worthy burnt sacrifice to God. Their hearts poured forth everywhere that holy unction with which they had been imbued in plenitude, when they spake in various tongues the wonderful works of God as the Spirit gave them utterance. Nor can it be doubted that they abounded in the same perfumes of whom the Apostle thus speaks: "I thank my God always on your behalf, for the grace of God which is given you by Jesus Christ: that in everything ye are enriched by Him in all utterance and in all knowledge; even as the testimony of Christ was confirmed in you, so that ye come behind in no gift." Would that I too might be able to render the same thanksgivings on your account, and to see you rich in virtue, ready and prompt to praise God, and superabounding in this spiritual fatness in Jesus Christ our Lord.

Saint Francis of Assisi

[1182–1226]

Saint Francis was born in Assisi, Italy. After a brief career as a soldier, he renounced all worldliness and devoted his life to the poor and oppressed and to religious worship. In 1209 he founded the monastic order which bears his name. He joined the crusaders at Damiatta in 1219. Believing in the brother-

hood of all men and all nature, Saint Francis preached the gospel to all—to rich and poor, to criminals and lepers, and even to the animals and birds.

SERMON TO THE BIRDS

My LITTLE SISTERS, the birds, much bounden are ye unto God, your Creator, and always in every place ought ye to praise Him, for that He hath given you liberty to fly about everywhere, and hath also given you double and triple raiment; moreover He preserved your seed in the ark of Noah, that your race might not perish out of the world; still more are ye beholden to Him for the element of the air which He hath appointed for you; beyond all this, ye sow not, neither do you reap; and God feedeth you, and giveth you the streams and fountains for your drink; the mountains and the valleys for your refuge and the high trees whereon to make your nests; and because ye know not how to spin or sew, God clotheth you, you and your children; wherefore your Creator loveth you much, seeing that He hath bestowed on you so many benefits; and therefore, my little sisters, beware of the sin of ingratitude, and study always to give praises unto God.

John Wycliffe

[1320–1384]

John Wycliffe, known as the father of the Reformation, was born in the village of Wycliffe near Richmond in Yorkshire, England. His early brilliance led to a career at the newly-founded Oxford University, where he became master of Balliol College, and later of Canterbury Hall. Because of his doctrines, he was tried for heresy three times. On the first two occasions he was acquitted, but on the third his beliefs were declared heretical. His followers were rounded up by the Church, and Wycliffe himself was saved from punishment by his death. Perhaps his most important work was his translation of the Bible into English. Wycliffe's sermons were largely expositions of passages from the Bible in terms of timely subjects. His method and style are exemplified in the sermon presented here, one of several issued under the general title of "Wycliffe's Wicket."

CHRIST'S REAL BODY NOT IN THE EUCHARIST

This is my body. MATTHEW 26:26.

Now UNDERSTAND ye the words of our Saviour Christ, as he spake them one after another—as Christ spake them. For he took bread and blessed, and yet what blessed he? The Scripture saith not that Christ took bread and blessed it, or that he blessed the bread which he had taken. Therefore it seemeth more that he blessed his disciples and apostles, whom he had ordained witnesses of his passion; and in them he left his blessed word, which is the bread of life, as it is written, Not only in bread liveth man, but in every word that proceedeth out of the mouth of God. Also Christ saith, I am the bread of life that came down from heaven. And Christ saith also in John, The words that I have spoken to you are spirit and life. Therefore it seemeth more that he blessed his disciples, and also his apostles, in whom the bread of life was left more than in material bread, for the material bread hath an end.

Furthermore, if they say that Christ made his body of bread, I ask, With what words made he it? Not with these words, *"Hoc est corpus meum";* that is to say in English, "This is my body," for they are the words of giving, and not of making, which he said after that he brake the bread; then parting it among his disciples and apostles. Therefore if Christ had made of that bread his body, [he] had made it in his blessing, or else in giving of thanks, and not in the words of giving; for if Christ had spoken of the material bread that he had in his hands when he said, *"Hoc est corpus meum,"* "This is my body," it was made before, or else the word had been a lie. For if I say, This is my hand, and if it be not a hand, then am I a liar; therefore seek carefully if ye can find two words of blessing, or of giving of thanks, wherewith Christ made his body and blood of the bread and wine. And that all the clerks of the earth know not, for if ye might find or know those words, then should ye wax great masters above Christ, and then ye might be givers of his substance, and as fathers and makers of him, and that he should worship you, as it is written, Thou shalt worship thy father and mother. Of such as desire such worship against God's law, speaketh St. Paul of the man of sin that enhanceth himself as if he were God. And he is worshiped over all things as God, and showeth himself as he were God. Where our clergy are guilty in this, judge ye or they that know most, for they say that when ye have said, *"Hoc est corpus meum,"* that is to say, "This is my body"; which ye call the words of consecration, or else of making; and when they are said over the bread, ye say that there is left no bread, but it is the body of the Lord. So that in the bread there remaineth nothing but a heap of accidents, as witness ruggedness, roundness, savor, touching, and tasting, and such other accidents. Then, if thou sayest that the flesh and blood of Christ, that is to say, his manhood, is made more, or increased by so much as the ministration of bread and wine is, the which ye minister—if ye say it is so—then thou must needs consent that the thing which is not God to-day shall be God to-morrow; yea, and that the thing which is without spirit of life, but groweth in the field by kind, shall be God at another time. And we all ought to believe that he was without beginning, and without ending; and not made, for if the manhood of Christ were increased every day by so much as the bread and wine draweth to that ye minister, he should increase more in one day by cart-loads than he did in thirty-two years when he was here in earth.

But now I shall ask you a word; answer ye me, Whether is the body of the Lord made at once or at twice? Is both the flesh and the blood in the host of the bread? or else is the flesh made at one time, and the blood made at other time; that is to say the wine in the chalice? If thou wilt say it is full and wholly the manhood of Christ in the host of bread, both flesh and blood, skin, hair, and bones, then makest thou us to worship a false god in the chalice, which is unconjured when ye worship the bread; and if ye say the flesh is in the bread, and the blood in the wine, then thou must grant, if thy craft be true, as it is not indeed, that the manhood of Christ is parted, and that he is made at two times. For first thou takest the host of bread, or a piece of bread, and makest it as ye say, and the innocent people worship it. And then thou takest to thee the chalice, and likewise marrest, makest, I would have said, the blood in it, and then they worship it also, and if it be so as I am sure that the flesh and blood of Christ ascended, then are ye false harlots to God and to us; for when we shall be houselled ye bring to us the dry flesh, and let the blood be away; for ye give us after the bread, wine and water, and sometimes clean water unblessed, or rather conjured, by the virtue of your craft; and yet ye say, under the host of bread is the full manhood of Christ. Then by your own confession must it needs be that we worship a false god in the chalice, which is unconjured when we worship the bread, and worship the one as the other; but where find ye that ever Christ or any of his disciples taught any man to worship this bread or wine?

Therefore, what shall we say of the apostles that were so much with Christ, and were called by the Holy Ghost; had they forgotten to set it in the creed when they made it, which is Christian men's belief? Or else we might say that they knew no such God, for they believe in no more gods but in him that was at the beginning, and made of naught all things visible and invisible, which Lord took flesh and blood, being in the Virgin, the same God. But ye have many false ways, to beguile the innocent people with sleights of the fiend.

Therefore all the sacraments that are left here in earth are but minds of the body of Christ, for a sacrament is no more to say but a sign or mind of a thing passed, or a thing to come; for when Jesus spake of the bread, and said to his disciples, As ye do this thing, do it in mind of me, it was set for a mind of good things passed of Christ's body; but when the angel showed to John the sacraments of the woman and of the beast that bare her, it was set for a mind of evil things to come on the face of the earth, and great destroying of the people of God. And in the old law there were many figures or minds of things to come. For before Christ, circumcision was commanded by a law; and he that kept not the law was slain. And yet St. Paul saith, And neither is it circumcision that is openly in the flesh, but he that is circumcised of heart in spirit, not the letter whose praising is not of men, but of God. Peter saith in the third chapter of his epistle, And so baptism of like form maketh not us safe, but the putting away of the filthiness of the flesh, and the having of good conscience in God by the again rising of our Lord Jesus Christ from death, that we should be made heirs of everlasting life, he went up into heaven, and angels, and powers, and virtues, are made subjects to him.

Have ye not read in John the second, when Christ came into the temple, they asked of him what token he would show, that they might believe him. And he answered them, Cast down this temple, and in three days I shall raise it again; which words were fulfilled in his rising again from death; but when he said, Undo this temple, in that he said this, they were in error, for they understood it fleshly, and had supposed that he had spoken of the temple of Jerusalem, because he stood in it. And therefore they accused him at his passion full falsely. For he spake of the temple of his blessed body, which rose again in the third day. And right so Christ spake of his holy body when he said, This is my body which shall be given for you, which was given to death, and to rising again to bliss, for all that shall be saved by him. But like as they accused him falsely of the temple of Jerusalem, so now-a-days they accuse falsely against Christ, and say that Christ spake of the bread that he brake among his apostles; for in that Christ said this, they are deceived, take it fleshly, and turn it to the material bread, as the Jews did to the temple; and on this false understanding they made abomination of discomfort, as is said by Daniel the prophet to be standing in the holy place; he that readeth let him understand.

Now, therefore, pray we heartily to God, that this evil may be made short for the chosen men, as he hath promised in his blessed Gospel. And the large and broad way that leadeth to perdition may be stopped, and the strait and narrow way that leadeth to bliss may be made open by Holy Scriptures, that we may know which is the will of God, to serve him in truth and holiness in the dread of God, that we may find by him a way of bliss everlasting. So be it.

Martin Luther

[1483–1546]

Martin Luther was born at Eisleben, in the electorate of Saxony, of a miner father and a deeply religious mother. His education was received at Magdeburg and Eisenach. While a teacher at the University of Wittenberg, he nailed the famous 95 theses against indulgences on the church door. This lighted the fires of the Reformation and made Luther the leader of the movement. His remaining years were spent in preaching and teaching the doctrines of the Reformation, in writing, and translating the Bible into German. Luther has been called "the most impressive preacher that the world has ever beheld." His pulpit power was unexcelled, and his use of idiomatic, virile, fiery German drew great crowds to hear him wherever he preached. Even in translation it is possible to grasp some idea of his eloquence.

THE METHOD AND FRUITS OF JUSTIFICATION

Now I say, that the heir, as long as he is a child, differeth nothing from a servant, though he be lord of all; but is under tutors and governors until the time appointed of the father. Even so we, when we were children, were in bondage under the elements of the world: but when the fullness of the time was come, God sent forth His Son, made of a woman, made under the law, to redeem them that were under the law, that we might receive the adoption of sons. And because ye are sons, God hath sent forth the Spirit of His Son into your hearts, crying, Abba, Father. Wherefore thou art no more a servant, but a son; and if a son, then an heir of God through Christ. GALATIANS 4:1–7.

THIS TEXT touches the very pith of Paul's chief doctrine. The cause why it is well understood but by few, is, not that it is so obscure and difficult, but because there is so little knowledge of faith left in the world; without which it is not possible to understand Paul, who every where treats of faith with such earnestness and force.

First, therefore, we must understand the doctrine in which good works are set forth, far different from that which treats of justification; as there is a great difference between the substance and its working; between man and his work. Justification pertains to man, and not to works; for man is either justified and saved, or judged and condemned, and not works. Neither is it a controversy among the godly, that man is not justified by works, but righteousness must come from some other source than from his own works.

From this it is plainly gathered that no work can be acceptable to God, unless he which worketh it was first accepted by Him: and again, that no work is disallowed of Him unless the author thereof be disallowed before. I think these remarks will be sufficient concerning this matter at present, by which it is easy to understand that there are two sorts of works, those before justification, and those after it; and that these last are good works indeed, but the former only appear to be good.

But here, perhaps, thou wilt say, what is needful to be done? by what means shall I become righteous and acceptable to God? how shall I attain to this perfect justification? The Gospel answers, teaching that it is necessary that thou hear Christ, and repose thyself wholly on Him, denying thyself and distrusting thine own strength; by this means thou shalt be changed from *Cain* to *Abel,* and being thyself acceptable, shalt offer acceptable gifts to the Lord. It is faith that justifies thee, thou being endued therewith, the Lord remitteth all thy sins by the mediation of Christ His Son, in whom this faith believeth and trusteth. Moreover, He giveth unto such a faith His Spirit, which changes the man and makes him anew, giving him another reason and another will. Such a one worketh nothing but good works. Wherefore nothing is required unto justification but to hear Jesus Christ our Saviour, and to believe in Him. Howbeit these are not the works of nature, but of grace.

He, therefore, that endeavors to attain to these things by works, shutteth the way to the Gospel, to faith, grace, Christ, God, and all things that help unto salvation. Again, nothing is necessary in order to accomplish good works but justification; and he that hath attained it performs good works, and not any other.

Every one by faith is certain of this salvation; but we ought to have care and fear that we stand and persevere, trusting in the Lord, and not in our own strength. When those of the race of Cain hear faith treated of in this manner, they marvel at our madness, as it seems to them. God turn us from this way, say they, that we should affirm ourselves holy and godly; far be this arrogance and rashness from us: we are miserable sinners; we should be mad, if we should arrogate holiness to ourselves. Thus they mock at true faith, and count such doctrine as this execrable error; and thus try to extinguish the Gospel. These are they that deny the faith of Christ, and persecute it throughout the whole world; of whom Paul speaks: "In the latter times many shall depart from the faith," etc., for we see by these means that true faith lies every where oppressed; it is not preached, but commonly disallowed and condemned.

Perhaps some godly man may think, If the matter be so, and our works do not save us, to what end are so many precepts given us, and why doth God require that they be obeyed? The present text of the Apostle will give a solution of this question, and upon this occasion we will give an exposition thereof. The Galatians being taught of Paul the faith of Christ, but afterward seduced by false apostles, thought that our salvation must be finished and made perfect by the works of the law; and that faith alone doth not suffice. These Paul calls back again from works unto faith with great diligence; plainly proving that the works of the law, which go before faith, make us only servants, and are of no importance toward godliness and salvation; but that faith makes us the sons of God, and from thence good works without constraint forthwith plentifully flow.

But here we must observe the words of the Apostle; he calls him a *servant* that is occupied in works without faith, of which we have already treated at large: but he calls him a *son* which is righteous by faith alone. The reason is this, although the servant apply himself to good works, yet he does it not with the same mind as doth the son; that is, with a mind free, willing, and certain that the inheritance and all the good things of the Father are his; but does it as he that is hired in another man's house, who hopes not that the inheritance shall come to him. The works indeed of the son and the servant are alike; and almost the same in outward appearance; but their minds differ exceedingly: as Christ saith, "The servant abideth not in the house forever, but the son abideth ever."

The Apostle endeavors here to prove that the law with all the works thereof makes us but mere servants, if we have not faith in Christ; for this alone makes us sons of God. It is the word of grace followed by the Holy Ghost, as is shown in many places, where we read of the Holy Ghost falling on Cornelius and his family, while hearing the preaching of Peter. Paul teaches that no man is justified before God by the works of the law; for sin only cometh by the law. He that trusts in works, condemns faith as the most pernicious arrogancy and error of all others. Here thou seest plainly that such a man is not righteous, being destitute of that faith and belief which is necessary to make him acceptable before God and His Son; yea, he is an enemy to this faith, and therefore to righteousness also. Thus it is easy to understand that which Paul saith, that no man is justified before God by the works of the law.

The *worker* must be justified before God, before he can work any good thing. Men judge the worker by the works; God judges the works by the worker. The first precept requires us to acknowledge and worship one God, that is, to trust Him alone, which is the true faith whereby we become the sons of God. Thou canst not be delivered from the evil of unbelief by thine own power, nor by the power of the law; wherefore all thy works which thou doest to satisfy the law, can be nothing but works of the law; of far less importance than to be able to justify thee before God, who counteth them righteous only who truly believe in Him; for they that acknowledge Him the true God are His sons, and do truly fulfill the law. If thou shouldst even kill thyself by working, thy heart can not obtain this faith thereby, for thy works are even a hinderance to it, and cause thee to persecute it.

He that studieth to fulfill the law without faith, is afflicted for the devil's sake; and continues a persecutor both of faith and the law, until he come to himself, and cease to trust in his own works; he then gives glory to God who justifies the ungodly, and acknowledges himself to be nothing, and sighs for the grace of God, of which he knows that he has need. Faith and grace now fill his empty mind, and satisfy his hunger; then follow works which are truly good; neither are they works of the law, but of the Spirit, of faith and grace; they are called in the Scripture, the works of God which He worketh in us.

Whatsoever we do of our own power and strength, that which is not wrought in us by His grace, without doubt is a work of the law, and avails nothing toward justification; but is displeasing to God, because of the unbelief wherein it is done. He that trusts in works does nothing freely and with a willing mind; he would do no good work at all if he were not compelled by the fear of hell, or allured by the hope of present good. Whereby it is plainly seen that they strive only for gain, or are moved with fear, showing that they rather hate the law from their hearts, and had rather there were no law at all. An evil heart can do nothing that is good. This evil propensity of the heart, and unwillingness to do good, the law betrays, when it teaches that God does not esteem the works of the hand, but those of the heart.

Philip Melancthon

[1497-1560]

Philip Melancthon's birthplace was Bretten, in the palatinate of the Rhine, and his original name was Schwartzerd (black earth). But later, becoming interested in Greek and Latin scholarship, he changed his name to its Greek equivalent, Melancthon. At 22 he was launched on a career of teaching at Wittenberg, where he met Martin Luther and worked with him constantly. While Luther was the firebrand of the Reformation, Melancthon gave the movement a sound basis of scholarship, and has been called the scholar of the Reformation. Melancthon's quiet, gentle spirit is revealed in this sermon, delivered in 1550.

THE SECURITY OF GOD'S CHILDREN

Neither shall any pluck them out of My hand. JOHN 10:28.

I HAVE IN THESE our assemblies often uttered partly admonitions and partly reproofs, which I hope the most of you will bear in mind. But since

I must presume that now the hearts of all are wrung with a new grief and a new pang by reason of the war in our neighborhood, this season seems to call for a word of consolation. And as we commonly say, "Where the pain is there one claps his hand," I could not in this so great affliction make up my mind to turn my discourse upon any other subject. I do not, indeed, doubt that you yourselves seek comfort in the Divine declarations, yet will I also bring before you some things collected therefrom, because always that on which we had ourselves thought becomes more precious to us when we hear that it proves itself salutary also to others. And because long discourses are burdensome in time of sorrow and mourning, I will without delay bring forward *that comfort* which is the most effectual.

Our pains are best assuaged when something good and beneficial, especially some help toward a happy issue, presents itself. All other topics of consolation, such as men borrow from the unavoidableness of suffering, and the examples of others, bring us no great alleviation. But the Son of God, our Lord Jesus Christ, who was crucified for us and raised again, and now sits at the right hand of the Father, offers us help and deliverance, and has manifested this disposition in many declarations. I will now speak of the words, "No man shall pluck My sheep out of My hand." This expression has often raised me up out of the deepest sorrow, and drawn me, as it were, out of hell.

The wisest men in all times have bewailed the great amount of human misery which we see with our eyes before we pass into eternity—diseases, death, want, our own errors by which we bring harm and punishment on ourselves, hostile men, unfaithfulness on the part of those with whom we are closely connected, banishment, abuse, desertion, miserable children, public and domestic strife, wars, murder and devastation. And since such things appear to befall good and bad without distinction, many wise men have inquired whether there were any Providence, or whether accident brings every thing to pass independently of a Divine purpose. But we in the Church know that the first and principal cause of human woe is this, that on account of sin man is made subject to death and other calamity, which is so much more vehement in the Church, because the devil, from hatred toward God, makes fearful assaults on the Church and strives to destroy it utterly. Therefore it is written, "I will put enmity between the serpent and the seed of the woman." And Peter says, "Your adversary, the devil, goeth about as a roaring lion and seeketh whom he may devour."

Not in vain, however, has God made known to us the causes of our misery. We should not only consider the greatness of our necessity but also discern the causes of it, and recognize His righteous anger against sin, to the end that we may, on the other hand, perceive the Redeemer and the greatness of His compassion; and as witnesses to these His declarations He adds the raising of dead men to life and other miracles.

Let us banish from our hearts, therefore, the unbelieving opinions which imagine that evils befall us by mere chance, or from physical causes.

But when thou considerest the wounds in thy own circle of relations, or dost cast a glance at the public disorders in the State, which again afflict the individual also (as Solon says, "The general corruption penetrates even to thy quiet habitation"), then think first of thy own and others' sins, and of the righteous wrath of God; and, secondly, weigh the rage of the devil, who lets loose his hate chiefly in the Church.

In all men, even the better class, great darkness reigns. We see not how great an evil sin is, and regard not ourselves as so shamefully defiled. We flatter ourselves, in particular, because we profess a better doctrine concerning God. Nevertheless, we resign ourselves to a careless slumber, pamper each one his own desires; our impurity, the disorders of the Church, the necessity of brethren, fills us not with pain; devotion is without fire and fervor; zeal for doctrine and discipline languishes, and not a few are my sins, and thine, and those of many others, by reason of which such punishments are heaped upon us.

Let us, therefore, apply our hearts to repentance, and direct our eyes to the Son of God, in respect to whom we have the assurance that, after the wonderful counsel of God, He is placed over the family of man, to be the protector and preserver of His Church.

We perceive not fully either our wretchedness or our dangers, or the fury of enemies, until after events of extraordinary sorrowfulness. Still we ought to reflect thus: there must exist great need and a fearful might and rage of enemies, since so powerful a Protector has been given to us, even God's Son. When He says, "No man shall pluck My sheep out of My hand," He indicates that He is no idle spectator of our woe, but that mighty and incessant strife is going on. The devil incites his tools to disturb the Church or the political commonwealth, that boundless confusion may enter, followed by heathenish desolation. But the Son of God, who holds in His hands, as it were, the congregation of those who call upon His name, hurls back the devils by His infinite power, conquers and chases them thence, and will one day shut them up in the prison of hell, and punish them to all eternity with fearful pains. This comfort we must hold fast in regard to the entire Church, as well as each in regard to himself.

If, in these distracted and warring times, we see states blaze up and fall into ruin, then look away to the Son of God, who stands in the secret counsel of the Godhead, and guards His little flock, and carries the weak lambs as it were in His own hands. Be persuaded that by Him thou also shalt be protected and upheld.

Here some, not rightly instructed, will exclaim, "Truly I could wish to commend myself to such a Keeper, but only *His* sheep does He preserve. Whether I also am counted in that flock, I know not." Against this doubt we must most strenuously contend. For the Lord Himself assures us in this very passage, that all who "hear and with faith receive the voice of the Gospel, are His sheep;" and He says expressly, "If a man love Me, he will keep My words, and My Father will love him, and We will come to him and make Our abode with him." These promises of the Son of God, which can not be shaken, we must confidently appropriate to ourselves. Nor shouldst thou, by thy doubts, exclude thyself from this blessed flock, which originates in the righteousness of the Gospel. They do not rightly distinguish between the law and the Gospel, who, because they are unworthy, reckon not themselves among the sheep. Rather is this consolation afforded us, that we are accepted "for the Son of God's sake," truly, without merit, not on account of our own righteousness, but through faith, because we are unworthy, and impure, and far from having fulfilled the law of God. That is, moreover, a universal promise, in which the Son of God saith, "Come unto Me, all ye that labor and are heavy laden, and I will give you rest."

The eternal Father earnestly commands that we should hear the Son, and it is the greatest of all transgressions if we despise Him, and do not approve His voice. *This* is what every one should often and diligently consider, and in this disposition of the Father, revealed through the Son, find grace.

Although, amid so great disturbances, many a sorrowful spectacle meets thine eye, and the Church is rent by discord and hate, and manifold and domestic public necessity is added thereto, still let not despair overcome thee, but know thou that thou hast the Son of God for a Keeper and Protector, who will not suffer either the Church, or thee, or thy family, to be plucked out of His hand by the fury of the devil.

With all my heart, therefore, do I supplicate the Son of God, our Lord Jesus Christ, who having been crucified for us, and raised again, sits at the right hand of the Father, to bless men with His gifts, and to Him I pray that He would protect and govern this little church and me therein. Other sure trust, in this great flame when the whole world is on fire, I discern nowhere. Each one has his separate hopes, and each one with his understanding seeks repose in something else; but however good that may all be, it is still a far better, and unquestionably a more effectual consolation to flee to the Son of God and expect help and deliverance from Him.

Such wishes will not be in vain. For to this end are we laden with such a crowd of dangers, that in events and occurrences which to human prudence are an inexplicable enigma, we may recognize the infinite goodness and presentness of God, in that He, for His Son's sake, and through His Son, affords us aid. God will be owned in such deliverance just as in the deliverance of your first parents, who, after the fall, when they were forsaken by all creatures, were upheld by the help of God alone. So was the family of Noah in the flood, so were the Israelites preserved when in the Red Sea they stood between the towering walls of waters. These glorious examples are held up before us, that we might know, in like manner, the Church, without the help of any created beings, is often preserved. Many in all times have experienced such Divine deliverance and support in their personal dangers, as David saith, "My father and my mother have forsaken me, but the Lord taketh me up," and in another place David saith, "He hath delivered the wretched who hath no helper." But in order that we may become partakers of these so great blessings, faith and devotion must be kindled within us, as it stands written, "Verily, I say unto you!" So likewise must our faith be exercised, that before deliverance we should pray for help and wait for it, resting in God with a certain cheerfulness of soul; and that we should not cherish continual doubt and melancholy murmuring in our hearts, but constantly set before our eyes the admonition of God, "The peace of God which is higher than all understanding keep your heart and mind;" which is to say, Be so comforted in God, in time of danger, that your hearts having been strengthened by confidence in the pity and presentness of God, may patiently wait for help and deliverance, and quietly maintain that peaceful serenity which is the beginning of eternal life, and without which there can be no true devotion.

Hugh Latimer

[1485–1555]

Hugh Latimer was a man of daring who preached as his conscience directed, regardless of personal danger. Born of humble parents at Thurcaston, in the county of Leicester, England, he rose to be one of the great martyr preachers of the Reformation. As pastor to King Henry VIII and Edward VI he incurred the enmity of the Catholic Church, and when Queen Mary I ascended to power in England, he was tried and burned at the stake. Both friend and foe admired his power as a preacher, a power which came from a lively style, a homely wit, and complete sincerity. His Sermon of the Plow was given in 1548 and shows how he used some immediate interest to catch and hold the attention of his hearers.

SERMON OF THE PLOW

For whatsoever things were written aforetime, were written for our learn-ing. ROMANS 15:4.

ALL THINGS that are written in God's book, in the Bible book, in the book of the Holy Scripture, are written to be our doctrine. I told you in my first sermon, honorable audience, that I proposed to declare unto you two things, the one, what seed should be sown in God's field, in God's plow-land; and the other, who should be the sowers.

That is to say, what doctrine is to be taught in Christ's Church and congregation, and what men should be the teachers and preachers of it. The first part I have told you in the three sermons past, in which I have assayed to set forth my plow, to prove what I could do. And now I shall tell you who are the plowers; for God's word is seed to be sown in God's field, that is, the faithful congregation, and the preacher is the sower. And it is said in the Gospel: "He that soweth, the husbandman, the plowman, went forth to sow his seed." So that a preacher is compared to a plowman, as it is in another place: "No man that putteth his hand to the plow, and looketh back, is apt for the kingdom of God." That is to say, let no preacher be negligent in doing his office.

Well may the preacher and the plowman be likened together; first, for their labor at all seasons of the year; for there is no time of the year in which the plowman has not some special work to do; as in my country in Leicestershire, the plowman has a time to set forth, and to assay his plow, and other times for other necessary works to be done. And they also may be likened together for the diversity of works, and variety of offices that they have to do. For as the plowman first sets forth his plow, and then tills the land, and breaks it in furrows, and sometimes ridges it up again; and at another time harrows it and clotteth it, and sometimes dungs it and hedges it, digs it and weeds it, and makes it clean; so the prelate, the preacher, has many diverse offices to do. He has first a busy work to bring his parishioners to a right faith, as Paul calleth it; and not a swerving faith, but to a faith that embraces Christ, and trusts to his merits; a lively faith, a justifying faith; a faith that makes a man righteous, without respect of works; as you have it very well declared and set forth in the homily. He has then a busy work, I say, to bring his flock to a right faith, and then to confirm them in the same faith. Now casting them down with the law, and with threatenings of God for sin; now ridging them up again with the Gospel, and with the promises of God's favor. Now weeding them, by telling them their faults, and making them forsake sin; now clotting them, by breaking their stony hearts, and by making them supple-hearted, and making them to have hearts of flesh;

that is, soft hearts, and apt for doctrine to enter in. Now teaching to know God rightly, and to know their duty to God and their neighbors. Now exhorting them when they know their duty, that they do it, and be diligent in it; so that they have a continual work to do. Great is their business, and therefore great should be their hire.

By this then it appears that a prelate, or any that has the cure of souls must diligently and substantially work and labor. Therefore, saith Paul to Timothy, "He that desireth to have the office of a bishop, or a prelate, that man desireth a good work." Then if it is a good work, it is work; you can make but a work of it. It is God's work, God's plow, and that plow God would have still going. Such then as loiter and live idly, are not good prelates, or ministers. And of such as do not preach and teach, and do their duties, God saith by his prophet Jeremy, "Cursed be the man that doth the work of God fraudulently, guilefully, or deceitfully; some books have it negligently or slackly." How many such prelates, how many such bishops, Lord, for Thy mercy, are there now in England? And what shall we in this case do? shall we company with them? O Lord, for Thy mercy! shall we not company with them? O Lord, whither shall we flee from them? But "Cursed be he that doth the work of God negligently or guilefully." A sore word for them that are negligent in discharging their office, or have done it fraudulently, for that is the thing which makes the people ill.

Now what shall we say of these rich citizens of London? what shall I say of them? Shall I call them proud men of London, malicious men of London, merciless men of London? No, no, I may not say so; they will be offended with me then. Yet must I speak. For is there not reigning in London as much pride, as much covetousness, as much cruelty, as much oppression, and as much superstition, as there was in Nebo? Yes, I think, and much more too. Therefore, I say, Repent, O London! repent, repent. Thou hearest thy faults told thee; amend them, amend them. I think, if Nebo had had the preaching that thou hast, they would have converted.

Oh London, London! repent, repent; for I think God is more displeased with London than ever he was with the city of Nebo. Repent, therefore; repent, London, and remember that the same God liveth now that punished Nebo, even the same God, and none other; and He will punish sin as well now as He did then: and He will punish the iniquity of London as well as He did them of Nebo. Amend, therefore. And you that are prelates, look well to your office; for right prelating is busy laboring, and not lording. Therefore preach and teach, and let your plow be going. Ye lords, I say, that live like loiterers, look well to your office— the plow is your office and charge. If you live idle and loiter, you do not your duty, you follow not your vocation; let your plow therefore be going, and not cease, that the ground may bring forth fruit.

But now methinks I hear one say unto me: "Wot ye what you say? Is it a work? Is it a labor? How then hath it happened that we have had for so many hundred years so many unpreaching prelates, lording loiterers, and idle ministers?" You would have me here to make answer, and to show the cause thereof. Nay, this land is not for me to plow, it is too stony, too thorny, too hard for me to plow. They have so many things that make for them, so many things to say for themselves, that it is not for my weak team to plow them. They have to say for themselves long customs, ceremonies, and authority, placing in Parliament, and many things more. And I fear this land is not yet ripe to be plowed; for, as the saying is, it lacketh weathering: it lacketh weathering, at least it is not for me to plow. For what shall I look for among thorns, but pricking and scratching? What among stones, but stumbling? What, I had almost said, among serpents, but stinging? But this much I dare say, that since lording and loitering hath come up, preaching hath come down, contrary to the apostles' time: for they preached and lorded not, and now they lord and preach not. For they that are lords will ill go to plow: it is no meet office for them; it is not seeming for their estate. Thus came up lording loiterers: thus crept in unpreaching prelates, and so have they long continued. For how many unlearned prelates have we now at this day! And no marvel; for if the plowmen that now are were made lords, they would give over plowing; they would leave off their labor, and fall to lording outright, and let the plow stand: and then both plows not walking, nothing should be in the commonweal but hunger. For ever since the prelates were made lords and nobles, their plow standeth, there is no work done, the people starve. They hawk, they hunt, they card, they dice, they pastime in their prelacies with gallant gentlemen, with their dancing minions, and with their fresh companions, so that plowing is set aside. And by the lording and loitering, preaching and plowing is clean gone. And thus, if the plowmen of the country were as negligent in their office as prelates are, we should not long live, for lack of sustenance. And as it is necessary to have this plowing for the sustentation of the body, so must we have also the other for the satisfaction of the soul, or else we can not live long spiritually. For as the body wastes and consumes away for lack of bodily meat, so the soul pines away for default of spiritual meat. But there are two kinds of inclosing, to hinder both these kinds of plowing; the one is an inclosing to hinder the bodily plowing, and the other to hinder the holy day plowing, the Church plowing.

But now for the fault of unpreaching prelates, methinks I could guess what might be said for excusing of them. They are so troubled with lordly living, they are so placed in palaces, couched in courts, ruffling in their rents, dancing in their dominions, burdened with embassages, pampering themselves like a monk that maketh his jubilee; and moiling in their gay manors and mansions, and so troubled with loitering in their lordships, that they can not attend it. They are otherwise occupied, some in the king's matters, some are embassadors, some of the privy council, some to furnish the court, some are lords of the Parliament, some are presidents, and some comptrollers of mints.

Well, well, is this their duty? Is this their office? Is this their calling? Should we have ministers of the Church to be comptrollers of the mints? Is this a meet office for a priest that hath cure of souls? Is this his charge?

The glory of God shall be spread abroad throughout all parts of the realm, if the prelates will diligently apply to their plow, and be preachers rather than lords. But our blanchers, who will be lords, and no laborers, when they are commanded to go and reside upon their cures, and preach in their benefices, they would say, Why? I have set a deputy there; I have a deputy that looks well to my flock, who shall discharge my duty. A deputy, quoth he, I looked for that word all this while. And what a deputy must he be, trow ye? Even one like himself; he must be a Canonist; that is to say, one that is brought up in the study of the Pope's laws and decrees; one that will set forth papistry as well as himself will do; and one that will maintain all superstition and idolatry; and one that will not at all, or else very weakly, resist the devil's plow; yea, happy it is if he take no part with the devil; and where he should be an enemy to him, it is well if he take not the devil's part against Christ. But in the mean time, the prelates take their pleasures. They are lords, and no laborers; but the devil is diligent at his plow. He is no unpreaching prelate; he is no lordly loiterer from his cure; but a busy plowman; he still applieth his business. Therefore, ye unpreaching prelates, learn of the devil; to be diligent in doing of your office, learn of the devil; and if you will not learn of God, nor good men, for shame learn of the devil; "I speak it for your shame;" if you will not learn of God, nor good men, to be diligent in your office, learn of the devil. Howbeit there is now very good hope that the king's majesty, being by the help of good governance of his most honorable counselors, trained and brought up in learning, and knowledge of God's word, will shortly provide a remedy, and set an order herein; which thing that it may so be, let us pray for him. Pray for him, good people; pray for him. You have great cause and need to pray for him.

John Knox

[1505-1572]

John Knox was comfortably established as a friar when he turned to Protestantism. This led to toil as a galley slave in France, to his persecution, and finally to leadership of the Protestant movement in Scotland. Knox was born in Haddington, near Edinburgh. He visited Geneva and was greatly influenced by the work of Calvin there. This sermon is the only one Knox ever issued himself, although two others were published after his death. On August 19, 1565, he preached to a public audience in Edinburgh and was arrested. While in prison he wrote the sermon so that others could read it and judge whether or not he was being rightfully persecuted.

THE SOURCE AND BOUNDS OF KINGLY POWER

O Lord our God, other lords besides Thee have had dominion over us; but by Thee only will we make mention of Thy name. They are dead, they shall not live; they are deceased, they shall not rise: therefore hast Thou visited and destroyed them, and made all their memory to perish. Thou hast increased the nation, O Lord, Thou hast increased the nation, Thou art glorified; Thou hast removed it far unto the ends of the earth. Lord, in trouble have they visited Thee, they poured out a prayer when Thy chastening was upon them. Isaiah 26:13-16.

These are the chief points of which, by the grace of God, we intend more largely at this present to speak:

First, The prophet saith, "O Lord our God, other lords besides Thee have ruled us."

For the better understanding of this complaint, and of the mind of the prophet, we must, *first,* observe from whence all authority flows; and *secondly,* to what end powers are appointed by God: which two points being discussed, we shall better understand what lords and what authority rule beside God, and who they are in whom God and His merciful presence rules.

The *first* is resolved to us by the words of the Apostle, saying, "There is no power but of God." David brings in the eternal God speaking to judges and rulers, saying, "I have said, ye are gods, and sons of the Most High." From which place it is evident that it is neither birth, influence of stars, election of people, force of arms, nor, finally, whatsoever can be comprehended under the power of nature, that makes the distinction betwixt the superior power and the inferior, or that establishes the royal throne of kings; but it is the only and perfect ordinance of God, who willeth His terror, power, and majesty, partly to shine in the thrones of kings, and in the faces of judges, and that for the profit and comfort of man. So that whosoever would study to deface the order of government that God has established, and allowed by His holy word, and bring in such a confusion that no difference should be betwixt the upper powers and the subjects, does nothing but avert and turn upside down the very throne of God, which He wills to be fixed here upon earth; as in the end and cause of this ordinance more plainly shall appear: which is the *second* point we have to observe, for the better understanding of the prophet's words and mind.

The end and cause then, why God imprints in the weak and feeble flesh of man this image of His own power and majesty, is not, to puff up flesh in opinion of itself; neither yet that the heart of him that is exalted above others should be lifted up by presumption and pride, and so despise others; but that he should consider he is appointed lieutenant to One, whose eyes continually watch upon him, to see and examine how he behaves himself in his office. St. Paul, in few words, declares the end wherefore the sword is committed to the powers, saying, "It is to the punishment of the wicked doers, and unto the praise of such as do well."

Of which words it is evident that the sword of God is not committed to the hand of man to use as it pleases him, but only to punish vice and maintain virtue, that men may live in such society as is acceptable before God. And this is the true and only cause why God has appointed powers in this earth.

For such is the furious rage of man's corrupt nature that, unless severe punishment were appointed and put in execution upon malefactors, better it were that man should live among brutes and wild beasts than among men. But at this present I dare not enter into the descriptions of this common-place; for so should I not satisfy the text, which by God's grace I purpose to explain. This only by the way—I would that such as are placed in authority should consider whether they reign and rule by God, so that God rules them; or if they rule without, besides, and against God, of whom our prophet here complains.

The *first* thing then that God requires of him who is called to the honor of a king, is, The knowledge of His will revealed in His word.

The *second* is, An upright and willing mind, to put in execution such things as God commands in His law, without declining to the right, or to the left hand.

Kings, then, have not an absolute power to do in their government what pleases them, but their power is limited by God's word; so that if they strike where God has not commanded, they are but murderers; and if they spare where God has commanded to strike, they and their throne are criminal and guilty of the wickedness which abounds upon the face of the earth, for lack of punishment.

Wouldst thou, O Scotland! have a king to reign over thee in justice, equity, and mercy? Subject thou thyself to the Lord thy God, obey His commandments, and magnify thou the Word that calleth unto thee, "This is the way, walk in it;" and if thou wilt not, flatter not thyself; the same justice remains this day in God to punish thee, Scotland, and thee Edinburgh especially, which before punished the land of Judah and the city of Jerusalem. Every realm or nation, saith the prophet Jeremiah, that likewise offendeth, shall be likewise punished, but if thou shalt see impiety placed in the seat of justice above thee, so that in the throne of God (as Solomon complains) reigns nothing but fraud and violence, accuse thine own ingratitude and rebellion against God; for that is the only cause why God takes away "the strong man and the man of war, the judge and the prophet, the prudent and the aged, the captain and the honorable, the counselor and the cunning artificer; and I will appoint, saith the Lord, children to be their princes, and babes shall rule over them. Children are extortioners of my people, and women have rule over them."

Hereof the tyrants have their admonition, and the afflicted Church inestimable comfort: the tyrants that oppress shall receive the same end which they did who have passed before: that is, they shall die and fall with shame, without hope of resurrection, as is aforesaid. Not that they shall not arise to their own confusion and just condemnation; but that they shall not recover power to trouble the servants of God; neither yet shall the wicked arise, as David saith, in the counsel of the just. Now the wicked have their counsels, their thrones, and finally handle (for the most part) all things that are upon the face of the earth; but the poor servants of God are reputed unworthy of men's presence, envied and mocked; yea, they are more vile before these proud tyrants than is the very dirt and mire which is trodden under foot. But in that glorious resurrection this state shall be changed; for then shall such as now, by their abominable living and cruelty, destroy the earth and molest God's children, see Him whom they have pierced; they shall see the glory of such as now they persecute, to their terror and everlasting confusion. The remembrance hereof ought to make us patient in the days of affliction, and so to comfort us that when we see tyrants in their blind rage tread under foot the saints of God, we despair not utterly, as if there were neither wisdom, justice, nor power above in the heavens to repress such tyrants, and to redress the dolors of the unjustly afflicted. No, brethren, let us be assured that the right hand of the Lord will change the state of things that are most desperate. In our God there is wisdom and power, in a moment to change the joy and mirth of our enemies into everlasting mourning, and our sorrows into joy and gladness that shall have no end.

Wherefore, dear brethren, we have no small consolation, if the state of all things be rightly considered. We see in what fury and rage the world, for the most part, is now raised, against the poor Church of Jesus Christ, unto which He has proclaimed liberty, after the fearful bondage of that spiritual Babylon, in which we have been holden captives longer space than Israel was prisoner in Babylon itself: for if we shall consider, upon the one part, the multitude of those that live wholly without Christ; and, upon the other part, the blind rage of the pestilent papists; what shall we think of the small number of them that profess Christ Jesus, but that they are as a poor sheep, already seized in the claws of the lion; yea, that they, and the true religion which they profess, shall in a moment be utterly consumed?

But against this fearful temptation, let us be armed with the promise of God, namely, that He will be the protector of His Church; yea, that He will multiply it, even when to man's judgment it appears utterly to be exterminated. This promise has our God performed, in the multiplication of Abraham's seed, in the preservation of it when Satan labored utterly to have destroyed it, and in deliverance of the same, as we have heard, from Babylon. He hath sent His Son Christ Jesus, clad in our flesh, who hath tasted of all our infirmities (sin excepted), who hath promised to be with us to the end of the world; He hath further kept promise in the publication, yea, in the restitution of His glorious Gospel. Shall we then think that He will leave His Church destitute in this most dangerous age? Only let us cleave to His truth, and study to conform our lives to the same, and He shall multiply His knowledge, and increase His people.

It behooves, therefore, that God Himself shall violently pull His children from these venomous breasts, that when they lack the liquor and poison of the world, they may visit Him, and learn to be nourished of Him. Oh if the eyes of worldly princes should be opened, that they might see with what humor and liquor their souls are fed, while their whole delight consists in pride, ambition, and the lusts of the corrupt flesh! We understand then how God doth visit men, as well by His severe judgments as by His merciful visitation of deliverance from trouble, or by bringing trouble upon His chosen for their humiliation; and now it remains to understand how man visits God. Man doth visit God when he appears in His presence, be it for the hearing of His word, or for the participation of His sacraments; as the people of Israel, besides the observation of their sabbaths and daily oblations, were commanded thrice a year to present themselves before the presence of the tabernacle; and as we do, and as often as we present ourselves to the hearing of the word.

For there is the footstool, yea, there is the face and throne of God Himself, wheresoever the Gospel of Jesus Christ is truly preached, and His sacraments rightly ministered.

Let us now humble ourselves in the presence of our God, and from the bottom of our hearts let us desire Him to assist us with the power of His Holy Spirit; that albeit, for our former negligence, God gives us over into the hands of others than such as rule in His fear; that yet He let us not forget His mercy, and the glorious name that hath been proclaimed among us; but that we may look through the dolorous storm of His present displeasure, and see as well what punishment He has appointed for the cruel tyrants, as what reward He has laid in store for such as continue in His fear to the end. That it would further please Him to assist, that albeit we see His Church so diminished, that it appears to be brought, as it were, to utter extermination, we may be assured that in our God there is great power and will, to increase the number of His chosen, until they are enlarged to the uttermost parts of the earth. Give us, O Lord! hearts to visit Thee in time of affliction; and albeit we see no end of our dolors, yet our faith and hope may conduct us to the assured hope of that joyful resurrection, in which we shall possess the fruit of that for which we now labor. In the mean time, grant unto us, O Lord! to repose ourselves in the sanctuary of Thy promise, that in Thee we may find comfort, till this Thy great indignation, begun among us, may pass over, and Thou Thyself appear to the comfort of Thine afflicted, and to the terror of Thine and our enemies.

Let us pray with heart and mouth,

Almighty God, and merciful Father, etc. Lord, unto Thy hands I commend my spirit; for the terrible roaring of guns, and the noise of armor, do so pierce my heart, that my soul thirsteth to depart.

John Calvin

[1509-1564]

John Calvin was born at Noyon, in Picardy. Although he evinced great religious zeal at an early age, he was for a time undecided between preaching and the law. Finally, however, he turned to the pulpit and became one of the leaders of the Reformation. His chief arena of work was Geneva, and from here his influence spread throughout the world. The following sermon is one published by Calvin in a group of four preached in 1552. Its purpose, according to Calvin, is "to exhort all believers to prize the honor and service of God more than their own life, and to strengthen them against all temptations."

ON BEARING PERSECUTION

Let us go forth out of the tents after Christ, bearing His reproach. HEBREWS 13:13.

As PERSECUTION is always harsh and bitter, let us consider *How and by what means Christians may be able to fortify themselves with patience, so as unflinchingly to expose their life for the truth of God.* The text which we have read out, when it is properly understood, is sufficient to induce us to do so. The Apostle says, "Let us go forth from the city after the Lord Jesus, bearing His reproach." In the first place, he reminds us, although the sword should not be drawn over us nor the fires kindled to burn us, that we can not be truly united to the Son of God while we are rooted in this world. Wherefore, a Christian, even in repose, must always have one foot lifted to march to battle, and not only so, but he must have his affections withdrawn from the world, although his body is dwelling in it. Grant that this at first sight seems to us hard, still we must be satisfied with the words of St. Paul, "We are called and appointed to suffer." As if he had said such is our condition as Christians; this is the road by which we must go, if we would follow Christ.

Meanwhile, to solace our infirmity and mitigate the vexation and sorrow which persecution might cause us, a good reward is held forth. In suffering for the cause of God, we are walking step by step after the Son of God, and have Him for our guide.

Now, in order that we may be more deeply moved, not only is it said that Jesus Christ walketh before us as our Captain, but that we are made conformable to His image; as St. Paul speaks in the eighth chapter to the Romans, "God hath ordained all those whom He hath adopted for His children, to be made conformable to Him who is the pattern and head of all."

Are we so delicate as to be unwilling to endure any thing? Then we must renounce the grace of God by which He has called us to the hope of salvation. For there are two things which can not be separated—to be members of Christ, and to be tried by many afflictions. We certainly ought to prize such a conformity to the Son of God much more than we do. It is true that in the world's judgment there is disgrace in suffering for the Gospel. But since we know that unbelievers are blind, ought we not to have better eyes than they? It is ignominy to suffer from those who occupy the seat of justice, but St. Paul shows us by his example that we have to glory in scourgings for Jesus Christ, as marks by which God recognizes and avows us for His own. And we know what St. Luke narrates of Peter and John, namely, that they rejoiced to have been "counted worthy to suffer infamy and reproach for the name of the Lord Jesus."

Many persons, however, can not refrain from pleading against God; or, at least, from complaining against Him for not better supporting their weakness. It is marvelously strange, they say, how God, after having chosen us for His children, allows us to be so trampled upon and tormented by the ungodly. I answer, even were it not apparent why He does so, He well might exercise His authority over us, and fix our lot at His pleasure. But when we see that Jesus Christ is our pattern, ought we not, without inquiring further, to esteem it great happiness that we are made like Him? God, however, makes it very apparent what the reasons are for which He is pleased that we should be persecuted. Had we nothing more than the consideration suggested by St. Peter, we were disdainful indeed not to acquiesce in it. He says, "Since gold and silver, which are only corruptible metals, are purified and tested by fire, it is but reasonable that our faith, which surpasses all the riches of the world, should be tried." It were easy, indeed, for God to crown us at once without requiring us to sustain any combats; but as it is His pleasure that until the end of the world Christ shall reign in the midst of His enemies, so it is also His pleasure that we, being placed in the midst of them, shall suffer their oppression and violence till He deliver us.

In ancient times vast numbers of people, to obtain a simple crown of leaves, refused no toil, no pain, no trouble; nay, it even cost them nothing to die, and yet every one of them fought for a peradventure, not knowing whether he was to gain or lose the prize. God holds forth to us the immortal crown by which we may become partakers of His glory. He does not mean to fight at hap-hazard, but all of us have a promise of the prize for which we strive. Have we any cause then to decline the struggle? Do we think it has been said in vain, "If we die with Jesus Christ we shall also live with Him?" Our triumph is prepared and yet we do all we can to shun the combat!

But it is said that "all we teach on this subject is repugnant to human judgment." I confess it. And hence when our Saviour declares, "Blessed are they who are persecuted for righteousness' sake," He gives utterance to a sentiment which is not easily received in the world. On the contrary, He wishes to account that as happiness, which in the judgment of sense is misery. We seem to ourselves miserable when God leaves us to be trampled upon by the tyranny and cruelty of our enemies; but the error is that we look not to the promises of God, which assure us that all will turn to our good. We are cast down when we see the wicked stronger than we, and planting their foot on our throat; "But such confusion should rather," as St. Paul says, "cause us to lift up our heads." Seeing we are too much disposed to amuse ourselves with present objects, God, in permitting the good to be maltreated and the wicked to have sway, shows by evident tokens that a day is coming on which all that is now in confusion will be reduced to order. If the period seems distant, let us run to the remedy, and not flatter ourselves in our sin; for it is certain that we have no faith if we can not carry our views forward to the coming of Jesus Christ.

It is vain for us to allege that pity should be shown us, inasmuch as our nature is so frail; for it is said, on the contrary, that Moses having looked to God by faith was fortified so as not to yield under any temptation. Wherefore, when we are thus soft and easy to bend, it is a manifest sign—I do not say that we have no zeal, no firmness—but that we know nothing either of God or His kingdom. When we are reminded that we ought to be united to our Head, it seems for us a fine pretext for corruption to say, that we are men! But what were those who have trodden the path before us? Indeed, had we nothing more than pure doctrine, all the excuses we could make would be frivolous; but having so many examples, which ought to supply us with the strongest proof, the more deserving are we of condemnation.

There are two points to be considered. The first is, that the whole body of the Church has always been, and to the end will be, liable to be afflicted by the wicked, as is said in Psalm 129:1: "From my youth up they have tormented me, and dragged the plow over me from one end to the other." The Holy Spirit there brings in the ancient Church, in order that we, having been much acquainted with her afflictions, may not regard it either as new or vexatious, when the like is done to ourselves in the present day. St. Paul, also, in quoting from another Psalm, a passage in which it is said, "We have been like sheep to the slaughter;" shows that that has not been for one age only, but is the ordinary condition of the Church, and shall be.

Therefore, in seeing how the Church of God is trampled upon in the present day by proud worldlings, how one barks, and another bites; how they torture, how they plot against her; how she is assailed incessantly by mad dogs, and savage beasts, let it remind us that the same thing was done in all the olden time.

I only touch on this article briefly, to come to the *second,* which is more to our purpose, viz.: *we ought to take advantage of the particular martyrs who have gone before us.*

These are not confined to two or three, but are, as the Apostle says, "a great and dense cloud." By this expression he intimates that the number is so great that it ought, as it were, completely to engross our sight. Not to be tedious, I will only mention the Jews, who were persecuted for the true religion, as well under the tyranny of King Antiochus as a little after his death. We can not allege that the number of sufferers was small, for it formed, as it were, a large army of martyrs. We can not say that it consisted of prophets, whom God had set apart from the common people; for women and young children formed part of the band. We can not say that they got off at a cheap rate, for they were tortured as cruelly as it was possible to be. Accordingly, we hear what the Apostle says: "Some were stretched out like drums, not caring to be delivered, that they might obtain a better resurrection; others were proved by mockery and blows, or bonds and prisons; others were stoned or sawn asunder; others traveled up and down, wandering among mountains and caves."

Let us now compare their case with ours. If they so endured for the truth, which was at that time so obscure, what ought we to do in the clear light which is now shining? God speaks to us with open voice; the great gate of the kingdom of heaven has been opened, and Jesus Christ calls us to Himself, after having come down to us, that we might have Him, as it were, present to our eyes. What a reproach would it be to us to have less zeal in suffering for the Gospel, than those had who only hailed the promises afar off, who had only a little wicket opened, whereby to come to the kingdom of God, and who had only some memorial and type of Christ! These things can not be expressed in words as they deserve, and therefore I leave each to ponder them for himself.

Let it be considered, then, as a fixed point among all Christians, that they ought not to hold their life more precious than the testimony to the truth, inasmuch as God wishes to be glorified thereby.

We see tyrants let loose: thereupon it seems to us that God no longer possesses any means of saving us, and we are tempted to provide for our own affairs as if nothing more were to be expected from Him. On the contrary, His providence, as He unfolds it, ought to be regarded by us as an impregnable fortress. Let us labor, then, to learn the full import of the expression that our bodies are in the hands of Him who created them. For this reason He has sometimes delivered His people in a miraculous manner, and beyond all human expectation, as Shadrach, Meshach, and Abednego, from the fiery furnace; Daniel from the den of lions; Peter from Herod's prison, where he was locked in, chained, and guarded so closely. By these examples He meant to testify that He holds our enemies in check, although it may not seem so, and has power to withdraw us from the midst of death when He pleases. Not that He always does it; but in reserving authority to Himself, to dispose of us for life and death, He would have us to feel fully assured that He has us under His charge; so that whatever tyrants attempt, and with whatever fury they may rush against us, it belongs to Him alone to order our life.

To be better assured that God does not leave us as it were forsaken in the hands of tyrants, let us remember the declaration of Jesus Christ, when He says that He Himself is persecuted in His members. God had indeed said before, by Zechariah, "He who touches you, toucheth the apple of Mine eye;" but here it is said much more expressly that if we suffer for the Gospel, it is as much as if the Son of God were suffering in person. Let us know, therefore, that Jesus Christ must forget Himself before He can cease to think of us when we are in prison, or in danger of death for His cause; and let us know that God will take to heart all the outrages which tyrants commit upon us, just as if they were committed on His own Son.

Jeremy Taylor

[1613–1667]

Born at Cambridge, England, the son of a barber, Jeremy Taylor was educated at Caius College and at All Souls' College, Oxford. His brilliance attracted the attention of Laud and, later, of Charles I. His opposition to the Republican government resulted in his imprisonment, but after the restoration he was made Bishop of Down and Conner. In addition to this appointment, he was made vice-chancellor of Trinity College, Dublin. The following sermon is one of his most celebrated, showing his keen imagination and decorative literary style.

THE FOOLISH EXCHANGE

For what shall a man be profited, if he gain the whole world and lose his own soul? or what shall a man give in exchange for his soul? MATTHEW 16:26.

WHEN THE SOUL is at stake, not for its temporal, but for its eternal interest, it is not good to be hasty in determining, without taking just measures of the exchange. Solomon had the good things of the world actually in possession; and he tried them at the touchstone of prudence and natural value, and found them alloyed with vanity and imperfection; and we that see them "weighed in the balance of the sanctuary," and tried by the touchstone of the Spirit, find them not only light and unprofitable, but pungent and dolorous. But now we are to consider what it is that men part with and lose, when, with passion and impotency, they get the world; and that will present the bargain to be an huge infelicity. And this I observe to be intimated in the word *lose*. For he that gives gold for cloth, or precious stones for bread, serves his needs of nature, and loses nothing by it; and the merchant that found a pearl of great price, and sold all that he had to make the purchase of it, made a good venture; he was no loser: but here the case is otherwise; when a man gains the whole world, and his soul goes in the exchange, he hath not done like a merchant, but like a child or prodigal; he hath given himself away, he hath lost all that can distinguish him from a slave or a miserable person, he loses his soul in the exchange.

If we consider what the soul is in its own capacity to happiness, we shall find it to be an excellency greater than the sun, of an angelical substance, sister to the cherubim, an image of the Divinity, and the great argument of that mercy whereby God did distinguish us from the lower form of beasts, and trees, and minerals.

A soul, in God's account, is valued at the price of the blood, and shame, and tortures of the Son of God; and yet we throw it away for the exchange of sins that a man is naturally ashamed to own; we lose it for the pleasure, the sottish, beastly pleasure of a night. I need not say, we lose our soul to save our lives; for, though that was our blessed Saviour's instance of the great unreasonableness of men, who by "saving their lives, lose them," that is, in the great account of doomsday; though this, I say, be extremely unreasonable, yet there is something to be pretended in the bargain; nothing to excuse him with God, but something in the accounts of timorous men; but to lose our souls with swearing, that unprofitable, dishonorable, and unpleasant vice; to lose our souls with disobedience, or rebellion, a vice that brings a curse and danger all the way in this life; to lose our souls with drunkenness, a vice which is painful and sickly in the very acting of it, which hastens our damnation by shortening our lives, are instances fit to be put in the stories of fools and madmen. And all vice is a degree of the same unreasonableness; the most splendid temptation being nothing but a pretty, well-weaved fallacy, a mere trick, a sophism, and a cheating and abusing the understanding. But that which I consider here is, that it is an affront and contradiction to the wisdom of God, that we should so slight and undervalue a soul in which our interest is so concerned; a soul which He who made it, and who delighted not to see it lost, did account a fit purchase to be made by the exchange of His Son, the eternal Son of God.

You take care, lest for the purchase of a little, trifling, inconsiderable portion of the world, you come into this place and state of torment. Although Homer was pleased to compliment the beauty of Helena to such a height, as to say, "it was a sufficient price for all the evils which the Greeks and Trojans suffered in ten years," yet it was a more reasonable conjecture of Herodotus, that, during the ten years' siege of Troy, Helena, for whom the Greeks fought, was in Egypt, not in the city; because it was unimaginable but the Trojans would have thrown her over the walls, rather than, for the sake of a trifle, have endured so great calamities. We are more sottish than the Trojans, if we retain our Helena, any one beloved lust, a painted devil, and sugared temptation with (not the hazard, but) the certainty of having such horrid miseries, such in-valuable losses. And certainly it is a strange stupidity of spirit that can sleep in the midst of such thunder; when God speaks from heaven with His loudest voice, and draws aside His curtain, and shows His arsenal and His armory, full of arrows steeled with wrath, headed and pointed, and hardened with vengeance, still to snatch at those arrows, if they came but in the retinue of a rich fortune or a vain mistress, if they wait but upon pleasure or profit, or in the rear of an ambitious design.

There is a sort of men, who, because they will be vicious and atheistical in their lives, have no way to go on with any plaisance and without huge disturbances, but by being also atheistical in their opinions; and to believe that the story of hell is but a bugbear to affright children and fools, easy-believing people, to make them soft and apt for government and designs of princes. And this is an opinion that befriends none but impure and vicious persons. Others there are, that believe God to be all mercy, that He forgets His justice; believing that none shall perish with so sad a ruin, if they do but at their death-bed ask God forgiveness, and say they are sorry, but yet continue their impiety till their house be ready to fall; being like the Circassians, whose gentlemen enter not in the Church till they be three-score years old, that is, in effect, till by their age they can not any longer use rapine; till then they hear service at their windows, dividing unequally their life between sin and devotion, dedicating their youth to robbery, and their old age to a repentance without restitution.

Our youth, and our manhood, and old age, are all of them due to God, and justice and mercy are to Him equally essential: and as this life is a time of the possibilities of mercy, so to them that neglect it, the next world shall be a state of pure and unmingled justice.

Remember the fatal and decretory sentence which God hath passed upon all mankind: "It is appointed to all men once to die, and after death comes judgment." And if any of us were certain to die next morning, with what earnestness should we pray! with what hatred should we remember our sins! with what scorn should we look upon the licentious pleasures of the world! Then nothing could be welcome unto us but a prayer-book, no company but a comforter and a guide of souls, no employment but repentance, no passions but in order to religion, no kindness for a lust that hath undone us. And if any of you have been arrested with arms of death, or been in hearty fear of its approach, remember what thoughts and designs then possessed you, how precious a soul was then in your account, and what then you would give that you had despised the world, and done your duty to God and man, and lived a holy life. It will come to that again; and we shall be in that condition in which we shall per-fectly understand, that all the things and pleasures of the world are vain, and unprofitable, and irksome, and that he only is a wise man who secures the interest of his soul, though it be with the loss of all this world, and his own life into the bargain. When we are to depart this life, to go to strange company and stranger places, and to an unknown condition, then a holy conscience will be the best security, the best possession; it will be a horror, that every friend we meet shall, with triumph, upbraid to us the sottishness of our folly: "Lo, this is the goodly change you have made! you had your good things in your lifetime, and how like you the portion that is reserved to you forever?"

Richard Baxter

[1615–1691]

This "English Demosthenes" was born at Rowton, in Shropshire, England. In 1638 he was admitted to orders in the Church of England, but he refused to take the oath of "Submission to Archbishops, Bishops, etc.," and became a non-conformist. In this role he held several influential pulpits and was under constant persecution, being twice imprisoned. His most important ministry was the 16-year period during which he was pastor of a church in Kidderminster. The sermon given here caused a sensation when it was preached at Kidderminster and, later, at London. It is illustrative of Baxter's vigor of intellect, keenness of logic, and mastery of language.

MAKING LIGHT OF CHRIST AND SALVATION

But they made light of it. MATTHEW 22:5.

IT IS the case of most sinners to think themselves freest from those sins that they are most enslaved to; and one reason why we can not reform them, is because we can not convince them of their guilt. It is the nature of sin so far to blind and befool the sinner, that he knoweth not what he doth, but thinketh he is free from it when it reigneth in him, or when he is committing it: it bringeth men to be so much unacquainted with themselves that they know not what they think, or what they mean and intend, nor what they love or hate, much less what they are habituated and disposed to. They are alive to sin, and dead to all the reason, consideration, and resolution that should recover them, as if it were only by their sinning that we must know they are alive. May I hope that you that hear me to-day are but willing to know the truth of your case, and then I shall be encouraged to proceed to an inquiry. God will judge impartially; why should not we do so? Let me, therefore, by these following questions, try whether none of you are slighters of Christ and your own salvation. And follow me, I beseech you, by putting them close to your own hearts, and faithfully answering them.

Things that men highly value will be remembered; they will be matter of their freest and sweetest thoughts. This is a known case.

Do not those then make light of Christ and salvation that think of them so seldom and coldly in comparison of other things? Follow thy own heart, man, and observe what it daily runneth after; and then judge whether it make not light of Christ.

We can not persuade men to one hour's sober consideration what they should do for an interest in Christ, or in thankfulness for His love, and yet they will not believe that they make light of Him.

Things that we highly value will be matter of our discourse; the judgment and heart will command the tongue. Freely and delightfully will our speech run after them. This also is a known case.

Do not those men make light of Christ and salvation that shun the mention of His name, unless it be in a vain or sinful use? Those that love not the company where Christ and salvation is much talked of, but think it troublesome, precise discourse: that had rather hear some merry jests, or idle tales, or talk of their riches or business in the world. When you may follow them from morning to night, and scarce have a savory word of Christ; but perhaps some slight and weary mention of Him sometimes; judge whether these make not light of Christ and salvation. How seriously do they talk of the world and speak vanity! but how heartlessly do they make mention of Christ and salvation!

The things that we highly value we would secure the possession of, and therefore would take any convenient course to have all doubts and fears about them well resolved. Do not those men then make light of Christ and salvation that have lived twenty or thirty years in uncertainty whether they have any part in these or not, and yet never seek out for the right resolution of their doubts? Are all that hear me this day certain they shall be saved? Oh that they were! Oh, had you not made light of salvation, you could not so easily bear such doubting of it; you could not rest till you had made it sure, or done your best to make it sure. Have you nobody to inquire of, that might help you in such a work? Why, you have ministers that are purposely appointed to that office. Have you gone to them, and told them the doubtfulness of your case, and asked their help in the judging of your condition? Alas, ministers may sit in their studies from one year to another, before ten persons among a thousand will come to them on such an errand! Do not these make light of Christ and salvation? When the Gospel pierceth the heart indeed, they cry out, "Men and brethren, what shall we do to be saved?" Trembling and astonished, Paul cries out, "Lord, what wilt Thou have me to do?" And so did the convinced Jews to Peter. But when hear we such questions?

The things that we value do deeply affect us, and some motions will be in the heart according to our estimation of them. O sirs, if men made not light of these things, what working would there be in the hearts of all our hearers! What strange affections would it raise in them to hear of the matters of the world to come! How would their hearts melt before the power of the Gospel! What sorrow would be wrought in the discovery of their sins! What astonishment at the consideration of their misery! What unspeakable joy at the glad tidings of salvation by the blood of Christ! What resolution would be raised in them upon the discovery of their duty! Oh what hearers should we have, if it were not for this sin! Whereas now we are liker to weary them, or preach them asleep with matters of this unspeakable moment. We talk to them of Christ and salvation till we make their heads ache: little would one think by their careless carriage that they heard and regarded what we said, or thought we spoke at all to them.

Our estimation of things will be seen in the diligence of our endeavors. That which we highliest value, we shall think no pains too great to obtain. Do not those men then make light of Christ and salvation that think all too much that they do for them; that murmur at His service, and think it too grievous for them to endure? that ask of His service as Judas of the ointment, What need this waste? Can not men be saved without so much ado? This is more ado than needs. For the world they will labor all the day, and all their lives; but for Christ and salvation they are afraid of doing too much. Let us preach to them as long as we will, we can not bring them to relish or resolve upon a life of holiness. Follow them to their houses, and you shall not hear them read a chapter, nor call upon God with their families once a day: nor will they allow Him that one day in seven which He hath separated to His service. But pleasure, or worldly business, or idleness, must have a part. And many of them are so far hardened as to reproach them that will not be as mad as themselves. And is not Christ worth the seeking? Is not everlasting salvation worth more than all this? Doth not that soul make light of all these that thinks his ease more worth than they? Let but common sense judge.

That which we most highly value, we think we can not buy too dear. Christ and salvation are freely given, and yet the most of men go without them because they can not enjoy the world and them together. They are called but to part with that which would hinder them from Christ, and they will not do it. They are called but to give God His own, and to resign all to His will, and let go the profits and pleasures of this world, when they must let go either Christ or them, and they will not. They think this too dear a bargain, and say they can not spare these things: they must hold their credit with men; they must look to their estates:

how shall they live else? They must have their pleasure, whatsoever becomes of Christ and salvation: as if they could live without Christ better than without these: as if they were afraid of being losers by Christ, or could make a saving match by losing their souls to gain the world. Christ hath told us over and over that if we will not forsake all for Him we can not be His disciples. Far are these men from forsaking all, and yet will needs think that they are His disciples indeed.

That which men highly esteem, they would help their friends to as well as themselves. Do not those men make light of Christ and salvation that can take so much care to leave their children portions in the world, and do so little to help them to heaven? that provide outward necessaries so carefully for their families, but do so little to the saving of their souls? Their neglected children and friends will witness that either Christ, or their children's souls, or both, were made light of.

That which men highly esteem, they will so diligently seek after that you may see it in the success, if it be a matter within their reach. You may see how many make light of Christ, by the little knowledge they have of Him, and the little communion with Him, and communication from Him; and the little, yea, none of His special grace in them. Alas! how many ministers can speak it to the sorrow of their hearts, that many of their people know almost nothing of Christ, though they hear of Him daily! Nor know they what they must do to be saved: if we ask them an account of these things, they answer as if they understood not what we say to them, and tell us they are no scholars, and therefore think they are excusable for their ignorance. Oh if these men had not made light of Christ and their salvation, but had bestowed but half as much pains to know and enjoy Him as they have done to understand the matters of their trades and callings in the world, they would not have been so ignorant as they are: they make light of these things, and therefore will not be at the pains to study or learn them. When men that can learn the hardest trade in a few years have not learned a catechism, nor how to understand their creed, under twenty or thirty years' preaching, nor can abide to be questioned about such things, doth not this show that they have slighted them in their hearts? How will these despisers of Christ and salvation be able one day to look Him in the face, and to give an account of these neglects?

The time is near when Christ and salvation will not be made light of as now they are. When God hath shaken those careless souls out of their bodies, and you must answer for all your sins in your own name, oh then what would you give for a saviour! When a thousand bills shall be brought in against you, and none to relieve you, then you will consider, Oh! Christ would now have stood between me and the wrath of God: had I not despised Him, He would have answered all. When you see the world hath left you, and your companions in sin have deceived themselves and you, and all your merry days are gone, then what would you give for that Christ and salvation that now you account not worth your labor! Do you think that when you see the judgment set, and you are doomed to everlasting perdition for your wickedness, that you should then make as light of Christ as now? Why will you not judge now as you know you shall judge then? Will He then be worth ten thousand worlds? and is He not now worth your highest estimation and dearest affection?

God will not only deny thee that salvation thou madest light of, but He will take from thee all that which thou didst value before it: he that most highly esteems Christ shall have Him, and the creatures, so far as they are good here, and Him without the creature hereafter, because the creature is not useful; and he that sets more by the creature than by Christ, shall have some of the creature without Christ here, and neither Christ nor it hereafter.

John Bunyan
[1628–1688]

John Bunyan, the "Shakespeare among divines," was born at Elstow in Bedfordshire, the son of a traveling tinker. Though a wild and dissipated youth, at the age of 25 he turned to religion and became one of the most popular preachers of his day. He had no formal education, learning from "nature and his own heart and the Bible." While in Bedford jail, during the persecutions of Charles II, he wrote the immortal Pilgrim's Progress. *His sermons are full of sparkling thoughts and are written in vigorous, racy English.*

THE BARREN FIG-TREE; OR, THE DOOM AND DOWNFALL OF THE FRUITLESS PROFESSOR

> And he answering, said unto him, Lord, let it alone this year also, till I shall dig about it, and dung it; and if it bear fruit, well; and if not, then after that, thou shalt cut it down. LUKE 13:8, 9.

THESE ARE the words of the Dresser of the vineyard, who, I told you, is Jesus Christ. And they contain a petition presented to offended justice, praying, that a little more time and patience might be exercised toward the barren cumber-ground fig-tree.

In this petition there are six things considerable. 1. That justice might be deferred. "O that justice might be deferred! Lord, let it alone, etc., a while longer." 2. Here is time prefixed, as a space to try if more means will cure a barren fig-tree. "Lord, let it alone this year also." 3. The means to help it are propounded; "till I shall dig about it, and dung it." 4. Here is also an insinuation of a supposition that by thus doing God's expectation may be answered: "and if it bear fruit, well." 5. Here is a supposition that the barren fig-tree may yet abide barren, when Christ has done what he will unto it: "and if it bear fruit," etc. 6. Here is at last a resolution, that if thou continue barren, hewing days will come upon thee: "and if it bear fruit, well; and if not, then after that, thou shalt cut it down."

But to proceed according to my former method, by way of exposition.

Lord, let it alone this year also. Here is astonishing grace indeed! Astonishing grace, I say, that the Lord Jesus should concern Himself with a barren fig-tree; that He should step in to stop the blow from a barren fig-tree! True, He stopped the blow but for a time: but why did He stop it at all? Why did He not fetch out the ax? Why did He not do execution? Why did He not cut it down? Barren fig-tree, it is well for thee that there is a Jesus at God's right hand, a Jesus of that largeness of bowels as to have compassion for a barren fig-tree; else justice had never let thee alone to cumber the ground as thou hast done. Barren fig-tree! dost thou hear? Thou knowest not how oft the hand of divine justice hath been up to strike, and how many years since thou hadst been cut down, had not Jesus caught hold of his Father's ax.

Lord, let it alone THIS YEAR. "Lord, a little longer! Let us not lose a soul for want of means. I will try. I will see if I can make it fruitful. I will not beg a long life, nor that it might still be barren, and so provoke Thee. I beg, for the sake of the soul, the immortal soul, Lord, spare it one year only, one year longer, this year also. If I do any good to it, it will be in little time. Thou shalt not be overwearied with waiting; one year, and then!"

Till I shall dig about it, and dung it. The Lord Jesus, by these words, supposeth two things as causes of the want of fruit in a barren fig-tree; and two things He proposeth as a remedy. The things that are a cause of the want of fruit, are, 1. It is earth-bound. "Lord, the fig-tree is earth-bound." 2. A want of warmer means, or fatter means.

Wherefore accordingly He propoundeth, 1. To loosen the earth, to dig about it. 2. And then to supply it with manure: to "dig about it, and dung it."

Lord, let it alone this year also, until I shall dig about it. I doubt it is too much earth-bound. The love of this world, and the deceitfulness of riches lie too close to the roots of the heart of this professor. The love of riches, the love of honors, the love of pleasures, are the thorns that choke the word.

Till I shall DIG *about it.*—"Lord, I will loosen his roots; I will dig up this earth, I will lay his roots bare. My hand shall be upon him by sickness, by disappointments, by cross providences. I will dig about him until he stands shaking and tottering, until he be ready to fall; then, if ever, he will seek to take faster hold." Thus, I say, deals the Lord Jesus ofttimes with the barren professor; He diggeth about him, He smiteth one blow at his heart, another blow at his lusts, a third at his pleasures, a fourth at his comforts, another at his self-conceitedness: thus He diggeth about him. This is the way to take bad earth from the roots, and to loosen his roots from the earth. Barren fig-tree! see here the care, the love, the labor, and way, which the Lord Jesus, the Dresser of the vineyard, is fair to take with thee, if haply thou mayest be made fruitful.

Till I shall dig about it, and DUNG *it.*—As the earth, by binding the roots too closely, may hinder the tree's being fruitful, so the want of better means may also be a cause thereof. And this is more than intimated by the Dresser of the vineyard; "till I shall dig about it and dung it." "I will supply it with a more fruitful ministry, with a warmer word. I will give them pastors after Mine own heart. I will dung them." You know dung is a more warm, more fat, more hearty and succoring matter, than is commonly the place in which trees are planted.

And if it bear fruit, well.—"And if the fruit of all My labor doth make this fig-tree fruitful, I shall count My time, My labor, and means, well bestowed upon it. And Thou also, O My God, shalt be therewith much delighted. For Thou are gracious and merciful, and repentest Thee of the evil which Thou threatenest to bring upon a people."

These words, therefore, inform us that if a barren fig-tree, a barren professor, shall now at last bring forth fruit to God, it shall go well with that professor, it shall go well with that poor soul. His former barrenness, his former tempting of God, his abuse of God's patience and long-suffering, his misspending year after year, shall now be all forgiven him.

And IF NOT, *then after that, Thou shalt cut it down.*—"And if not," etc. The Lord Jesus, by this *if*, giveth us to understand that there is a generation of professors in the world that are incurable, that will not, that can not repent, nor be profited by the means of grace. A generation, I say, that will retain a profession, but will not bring forth fruit; a generation that will wear out the patience of God, time and tide, threatenings and intercessions, judgments and mercies, and after all will be unfruitful.

And if not, AFTER THAT, *Thou shalt cut it down.* There is nothing more exasperating to the mind of a man than to find all his kindness and favor slighted. Neither is the Lord Jesus so provoked with any thing, as when sinners abuse His means of grace. "If it be barren and fruitless under My Gospel; if it turn My grace into wantonness; if after digging and dunging, and waiting, it yet remain unfruitful, I will let thee cut it down."

Gospel-means applied, is the last remedy for a barren professor. If the Gospel, if the grace of the Gospel will not do, there can be nothing expected, but "cut it down." "Then after that thou shalt cut it down."

After that, THOU SHALT CUT IT DOWN. When Christ giveth thee over, there is no intercessor or mediator, no more sacrifice for sin. All is gone but judgment, but the ax, but "a certain fearful looking-for of judgment, and fiery indignation, which shall devour the adversaries."

Now then, I will show you, by some signs, how you may know that the day of grace is ended, or near to ending with the barren professor. "And after that, thou shalt cut it down."

The day of grace is like to be past, *when a professor hath withstood, abused, and worn out God's patience.* Then he is in danger; this is a provocation; then God cries, "Cut it down." There are some men that steal into a profession, nobody knows how, even as this fig-tree was brought into the vineyard, by other hands than God's—and there they abide lifeless, graceless, careless, and without any good conscience to God at all. Perhaps they came in for the loaves, for a trade, for credit, for a blind; or it may be to stifle and choke the shocks and grinding pangs of an awakened and disquieted conscience. Now having obtained their purpose, like the sinners of Zion, they are at ease, secure; saying, like Agag, "Surely the bitterness of death is past"; in other words, "I am well, I shall be saved, and go to heaven." Thus in these vain conceits they spend a year, two or three; not remembering that at every season of grace, and at every opportunity of the Gospel, the Lord comes seeking fruit.

And now He begins to shake the fig-tree with His threatenings. "Fetch out the ax." Now the ax is death. Death, therefore, is called for. "Death, come, smite Me this fig-tree." And withal the Lord shakes this sinner, and whirls him upon a sick bed, saying, "Take him, Death. He hath abused My patience and forbearance, not remembering that it should have led him to repentance, and to the fruits thereof. Death, fetch away this fig-tree to the fire, fetch away this fig-tree to the fire, fetch this barren professor to hell!" At this Death comes, with grim looks into the chamber, yea, and Hell follows with him to the bed-side, and both stare this professor in the face, yea, begin to lay hands upon him, one smiting him with pains in his body, with head-ache, heart-ache, back-ache, shortness of breath, fainting qualms, trembling of joints, stopping at the chest, and almost all the symptoms of a man past all recovery. Now, while Death is thus tormenting the body, Hell is doing with the mind and conscience, striking them with its pains, casting sparks of fire in thither, wounding with sorrows and fears of everlasting damnation, the spirit of this poor creature.

These things proving ineffectual, God takes hold of His ax, sends death to a wife, to a child, to his cattle. "Your young men have I slain, and taken away your horses." "I will blast him, cross him, disappoint him, and cast him down, and will set Myself against him in all that he putteth his hand unto." At this the poor barren professor cries out again, "Lord, I have sinned; spare me once more, I beseech thee. O take not away the desire of mine eyes; spare my children, bless me in my labors, and I will mend and be better." "No," saith God, "you lied to me last time; I will trust you in this no longer." And withal He tumbleth his wife, the child, the estate, into a grave, and then returneth to His place, till this professor, more unfeignedly acknowledgeth his offense.

Yet again, the Lord will not leave this professor, but will take up His ax again, and will put him under a more heart-searching ministry; a ministry that shall search him and turn him over and over; a ministry that shall meet with him, as Elijah met with Ahab, in all his acts of wickedness. And now the ax is laid to the roots of the tree. Besides, this ministry does not only search the heart, but presenteth the sinner with the golden rays of the glorious Gospel. Now is Christ Jesus set forth evidently; now is grace displayed sweetly; now, now are the promises broken like boxes of ointment, to the perfuming of the whole room. But, alas! there is yet no fruit on this fig-tree. While his heart is searching, he wrangles; while the glorious grace of the Gospel is unvailing, this professor wags and is wanton; gathers up some scraps thereof; tastes the good word of God, and the powers of the world to come; drinketh in the rain that comes oft upon him, but bringeth not forth fruit meet for Him, whose Gospel it is, takes no heed to walk in the law of the Lord God of Israel with all his heart, but counteth that the glory of the Gospel consisteth in talk and show, and that our obedience thereto is a matter of speculation; that good works lie in good words; and if they can finely talk, they think they bravely please God. They think the kingdom of God consisteth only in word, not in power.

Well, now the ax begins to be heaved higher. For now, indeed, God is ready to smite the sinner; yet before He will strike the stroke, He will try one way more at last, and if that misseth, down goes the fig-tree. Now this last way is to tug and strive with this professor by the Spirit. Wherefore the Spirit of the Lord is now come to him, but not always to strive with man. Yet awhile He will strive with him; He will awaken, He will convince, He will call to remembrance former sins, former judgments, the breach of former vows and promises, the misspending of former days; He will also present persuasive arguments, encouraging promises, dreadful judgments, the shortness of time to repent in, and that there is hope if He come. Further, He will show him the certainty of death, and of the judgment to come; yea, He will pull and strive with this sinner. And behold, the mischief now lies here; here is tugging and striving on both sides! The Spirit convinces, the man turns a deaf ear to God; the Spirit saith, Receive My instruction and live, but the man pulls away his shoulder; the Spirit shows him whither he is going, but the man closeth his eyes against it; the Spirit offereth violence, the man strives and resists. They have "done despite unto the Spirit of grace." The Spirit parlieth a second time, and urgeth reasons of a new nature; but the sinner answereth, "No, I have loved strangers, and after them I will go." At this God's fury comes up into His face; now He comes out of His holy place, and is terrible; now He sweareth in His wrath, they shall never enter into His rest. "I exercised toward you My patience, yet you have not turned unto Me," saith the Lord. "I smote you in your person, in your relations, in your estate, yet you have not returned unto Me," saith the Lord. "In thy filthiness is lewdness. Because I have purged thee, and thou wast not purged, thou shalt not be purged from thy filthiness any more, till I have caused My fury to rest upon thee." Cut it down; why doth it cumber the ground?

James Bénigne Bossuet

[1627–1704]

James Bénigne Bossuet was one of the greatest of French orators; Voltaire referred to him as the only eloquent man of his day. Born at Dijon, in Burgundy, he was educated at the Jesuit College in Dijon and the College of Navarre in Paris. His first appearance in a pulpit in Paris created such a sensation that King Louis XIV called him to the Court to deliver the Lenten Sermons of 1662. This led to several important appointments and other high honors. Bossuet's best sermons were funeral orations, and this one is considered to be the best of all. It was delivered in the church of Notre Dame before a weeping crowd and served to immortalize his name.

FUNERAL ORATION FOR LOUIS BOURBON, PRINCE OF CONDÉ

The Lord is with thee, thou mighty man of valor. Go in this thy might. Surely I will be with thee. JUDGES 6:12–16.

AT THE MOMENT that I open my lips to celebrate the immortal glory of Louis Bourbon, Prince of Condé, I find myself equally overwhelmed by the greatness of the subject, and, if permitted to avow it, by the uselessness of the task. What part of the habitable world has not heard of the victories of the Prince of Condé, and the wonders of his life? Every where they are rehearsed. The Frenchman, in extolling them, can give no information to the stranger. And although I may remind you of them today, yet, always anticipated by your thoughts, I shall have to suffer your secret reproach for falling so far below them.

But here a greater object, and one more worthy of the pulpit, presents itself to my thoughts. God it is who makes warriors and conquerors. "Thou," said David, "hast taught my hands to war, and my fingers to fight." If He inspires courage He gives no less other great qualities, natural and supernatural, both of the mind and heart. Every thing comes from His powerful hand; from heaven He sends all generous sentiments, wise counsels, and good thoughts. But He would have us to distinguish between the gifts which He abandons to His enemies and those which He reserves for His servants. What distinguishes His friends from all others is piety; until that gift of Heaven is received, all others are not only useless, but aid the ruin of those whom they adorn. Without this inestimable gift of piety, what were the Prince of Condé, with all his great heart and lofty genius? No, my brethren, if piety had not consecrated his other virtues, neither these princes would have found any solace for their grief, nor that venerable prelate any confidence in his prayers, nor myself any support for the praises which are due to so great a man. Under the influence of such an example, let us lose sight of all human glory! Destroy the idol of the ambitious! Let it fall prostrate before these altars! On this occasion, group together—for we can do it with propriety—the highest qualities of an excellent nature, and to the glory of truth, exhibit in a Prince universally admired whatever constitutes the hero and carries the glory of the world to the loftiest eminence, valor, magnanimity, and natural goodness—qualities of the heart; vivacity and penetration, grandeur of thought, and sublimity of genius—qualities of the intellect; all would be nothing but an illusion if piety were not added—piety, which indeed is the whole of man! This it is, messieurs, which you see in the life, eternally memorable, of the high and illustrious Prince Louis Bourbon, Prince of Condé, Prince of the blood!

I have seen him (and do not imagine that I exaggerate here) deeply moved with the perils of his friends; I have seen him, simple and natural, change color at the recital of their misfortunes, entering into their minutest as well as most important affairs, reconciling contending parties, and calming angry spirits with a patience and gentleness which could never have been expected from a temper so sensitive, and a rank so high. Far from us be heroes without humanity! As in the case of all extraordinary things, they might force our respect and seduce our admiration, but they could never win our love. When God formed the heart of man He planted goodness there, as the proper characteristic of the Divine nature, and the mark of that beneficent hand from which we sprang. Goodness, then, ought to be the principal element of our character, and the great means of attracting the affection of others. Greatness, which supervenes upon this, so far from diminishing goodness, ought only to enable it, like a public fountain, to diffuse itself more extensively. This is the price of hearts! For the great, whose goodness is not diffusive, as a just punishment of their haughty indifference, remain forever deprived of the greatest good of life, the fellowship of kindred souls. Never did man enjoy this more than the Prince of whom we are speaking. Never did one less fear that familiarity would diminish respect.

What star shines more brilliantly in the firmament, than the Prince of Condé has done in Europe? Not war alone gave him renown; but his resplendent genius which embraced every thing, ancient as well as modern, history, philosophy, theology the most sublime, the arts and the sciences. None possessed a book which he had not read; no man of excellence existed, with whom he had not, in some speculation or in some work, conversed; all left him instructed by his penetrating questions or judicious reflections. His conversation too, had a charm, because he knew how to speak to every one according to his talents; not merely to warriors on their enterprises, to courtiers on their interests, to politicians on their negotiations, but even to curious travelers on their discoveries in nature, government or commerce; to the artisan on his inventions, and in fine to the learned of all sorts, on their productions. That gifts like these come from God, who can doubt? That they are worthy of admiration, who does not see? But to confound the human spirit which prides itself upon these gifts, God hesitates not to confer them upon His enemies.

The hour of God for our illustrious Prince is come; hour anticipated, hour desired, hour of mercy and of grace. Without being alarmed by disease, or pressed by time, He executes what He designed. A judicious ecclesiastic, whom he had expressly called, performs for him the offices of religion; he listens, humble Christian, to his instructions; indeed, no one ever doubted his good faith. From that time he is seen seriously occupied with the care of vanquishing himself; rising superior to his insupportable pains, making, by his submission, a constant sacrifice. God, whom he invoked by faith, gave him a relish for the Scriptures; and in that Divine Book, he found the substantial nurture of piety. His counsels were more and more regulated by justice; he solaced the widow and orphan, the poor approached him with confidence. A serious as well as an affectionate father, in the pleasant intercourse which he enjoyed with his children, he never ceased to inspire them with sentiments of true virtue; and that young prince, his grandchild, will forever feel himself indebted to his training. His entire household profited by his example.

The manner in which he began to acquit himself of his religious duties, deserves to be recounted throughout the world; not because it was particularly remarkable; but rather because it was, so to speak, not such;—for it seemed singular that a Prince so much under the eye of the world, should furnish so little to spectators. Do not then, expect those magniloquent words which serve to reveal, if not a concealed pride, at least an agitated soul, which combats or dissembles its secret trouble. The Prince of Condé knew not how to utter such pompous sentences; in death, as in life, truth ever formed his true grandeur. His confession was humble, full of penitence and trust. He required no long time to prepare it; the best preparation for such a confession is not to wait for it as a last resort. But give attention to what follows. At the sight of the holy Viaticum, which he so much desired, see how deeply he is affected. Then he remembers the irreverence with which, alas! he had sometimes dishonored that divine mystery.

Mourn then that great Captain, and weeping, say: "Here is the man that led us through all hazards, under whom were formed so many renowned captains, raised by his example, to the highest honors of war; his shadow might yet gain battles, and lo! in his silence, his very name animates us, and at the same time warns us, that to find, at death, some rest from our toils, and not arrive unprepared at our eternal dwelling, we must, with an earthly king, yet serve the King of Heaven." Serve then that immortal and ever merciful King, who will value a sigh or a cup of cold water, given in His name, more than all others will value the shedding of your blood. And begin to reckon the time of your useful services from the day on which you gave yourselves to so beneficent a Master. Will not ye too come, ye whom he honored by making you his friends? To whatever extent you enjoyed his confidence, come all of you, and surround this tomb. Mingle your prayers with your tears; and while admiring, in so great a Prince, a friendship so excellent, an intercourse so sweet, preserve the remembrance of a hero whose goodness equaled his courage. Thus may he ever prove your cherished instructor; thus may you profit by his virtues; and may his death, which you deplore, serve you at once for consolation and example. For myself, if permitted, after all others, to render the last offices at this tomb, O Prince, the worthy subject of our praises and regrets, thou wilt live forever in my memory. There will thy image be traced, but not with that bold aspect which promises victory. No, I would see in you nothing which death can efface. You will have in that image only immortal traits. I shall behold you such as you were in your last hours under the hand of God, when His glory began to dawn upon you. There shall I see you more triumphant than at Fribourg and at Rocroy; and ravished by so glorious a triumph,

I shall give thanks in the beautiful words of the well-beloved disciple, "This is the victory that overcometh the world, even our faith." Enjoy, O Prince, this victory, enjoy it forever, through the everlasting efficacy of that sacrifice. Accept these last efforts of a voice once familiar to you. With you these discourses shall end. Instead of deploring the death of others, great Prince, I would henceforth learn from you to render my own holy; happy, if reminded by these white locks of the account which I must give of my ministry; I reserve for the flock, which I have to feed with the word of life, the remnants of a voice which falters, and an ardor which is fading away.

François Fénelon

[1651–1715]

"The good Archbishop of Cambry" was born at Perigord, France. After his education at Cohoes and Paris, he served as tutor to the dukes of Burgundy, Anjou, and Berri, and was raised to the high seat of Archbishop of Cambry. His doctrine of Quietism angered many and brought him much persecution, especially by Bossuet, Bishop of Meaux. Only four of Fénelon's sermons are extant today. The following is considered his best and is believed to express the deepest convictions of the preacher.

PRAYER

Pray without ceasing. I THESSALONIANS 5:17.

OF ALL the duties enjoined by Christianity, none is more essential, and yet more neglected, than prayer. Most people consider this exercise a wearisome ceremony, which they are justified in abridging as much as possible. Even those whose profession or fears lead them to pray, do it with such languor and wanderings of mind, that their prayers, far from drawing down blessings, only increase their condemnation.

God alone can instruct us in our duty. The teachings of men, however wise and well disposed they may be, are still ineffectual, if God do not shed on the soul that light which opens the mind to truth. The imperfections of our fellow-creatures cast a shade over the truths that we learn from them. Such is our weakness that we do not receive, with sufficient docility, the instructions of those who are as imperfect as ourselves. A thousand suspicions, jealousies, fears, and prejudices prevent us from profiting, as we might, by what we hear from men; and though they announce the most serious truths, yet what they do weakens the effect of what they say. In a word, it is God alone who can perfectly teach us.

Do not think that it is necessary to pronounce many words. To pray is to say, Let Thy will be done. It is to form a good purpose; to raise your heart to God; to lament your weakness; to sigh at the recollection of your frequent disobedience. This prayer demands neither method, nor science, nor reasoning; it is not essential to quit one's employment; it is a simple movement of the heart toward its Creator, and a desire that whatever you are doing you may do it to His glory. The best of all prayers is to act with a pure intention, and with a continual reference to the will of God.

Were I to give all the proofs that the subject affords, I should describe every condition of life, that I might point out its dangers, and the necessity of recourse to God in prayer. But I will simply state that under all circumstances we have need of prayer. There is no situation in which it is possible to be placed, where we have not many virtues to acquire and many faults to correct. We find in our temperament, or in our habits, or in the peculiar character of our minds, qualities that do not suit our occupations, and that oppose our duties. One person is connected by marriage to another whose temper is so unequal that life becomes a perpetual warfare. Some, who are exposed to the contagious atmosphere of the world, find themselves so susceptible to the vanity which they inhale that all their pure desires vanish. Others have solemnly promised to renounce their resentments, to conquer their aversions, to suffer with patience certain crosses, and to repress their eagerness for wealth; but nature prevails, and they are vindictive, violent, impatient, and avaricious.

Whence comes it that these resolutions are so frail? that all these people wish to improve, desire to perform their duty toward God and man better, and yet fail? It is because our own strength and wisdom, alone, are not enough. We undertake to do every thing without God; therefore we do not succeed. It is at the foot of the altar that we must seek for counsel which will aid us. It is with God that we must lay our plan of virtue and usefulness; it is He alone that can render them successful. Without Him, all our designs, however good they may appear, are only temerity and delusion. Let us then pray; that we may learn what we are and what we ought to be.

Do not devote all your time to action, but reserve a certain portion of it for meditation upon eternity. We see Jesus Christ inviting His disciples to go apart, in a desert place, and rest awhile, after their return from the cities, where they had been to announce His religion. How much more necessary is it for us to approach the source of all virtue, that we may revive our declining faith and charity, when we return from the busy scenes of life, where men speak and act as if they had never known that there is a God! We should look upon prayer as the remedy for our weaknesses, the rectifier of our faults. He who was without sin, prayed constantly; how much more ought we, who are sinners, to be faithful in prayer!

We must *pray with attention*. God listens to the voice of the heart, not to that of the lips. Our whole heart must be engaged in prayer. It must fasten upon what it prays for; and every human object must disappear from our minds.

We must also *ask with faith;* a faith so firm that it never falters. He who prays without confidence can not hope that his prayer will be granted. Will not God love the heart that trusts in Him? Will He reject those who bring all their treasures to Him, and repose every thing upon His goodness? When we pray to God, says St. Cyprian, with entire assurance, it is Himself who has given us the spirit of our prayer. Then it is the Father listening to the words of His child; it is He who dwells in our hearts, teaching us to pray. But must we not confess that this filial confidence is wanting in all our prayers? Is not prayer our resource only when all others have failed us? If we look into our hearts, shall we not find that we ask of God as if we had never before received benefits from Him? Shall we not discover there a secret infidelity, that renders us unworthy of His goodness? Let us tremble, lest, when Jesus Christ shall judge us, He pronounces the same reproach that He did to Peter, "O thou of little faith, wherefore didst thou doubt?"

We must join *humility with trust*. Great God, said Daniel, when we prostrate ourselves at Thy feet, we do not place our hopes for the success of our prayers upon our righteousness, but upon Thy mercy. Without this disposition in our hearts, all others, however pious they may be, can not please God. Saint Augustine observes that the failure of Peter should not be attributed to insincerity in his zeal for Jesus Christ. He loved his Master in good faith; in good faith he would rather have died than have forsaken Him; but his fault lay in trusting to his own strength, to do what his own heart dictated.

It is not enough to possess a right spirit, an exact knowledge of duty, a sincere desire to perform it. We must continually renew this desire, and enkindle this flame within us, at the fountain of pure and eternal light.

It is the humble and contrite heart that God will not despise. Remark the difference which the Evangelist has pointed out between the prayer of the proud and presumptuous Pharisee, and the humble and penitent Publican. The one relates his virtues, the other deplores his sins. The good works of the one shall be set aside, while the penitence of the other shall be accepted.

We must *pray with love*. It is love, says St. Augustine, that asks, that seeks, that knocks, that finds, and that is faithful to what it finds. We cease to pray to God as soon as we cease to love Him, as soon as we cease to thirst for His perfections. The coldness of our love is the silence of our hearts toward God. Without this we may *pronounce* prayers, but we do not pray; for what shall lead us to meditate upon the laws of God, if it be not the love of Him who has made these laws? Let our hearts be full of love, then, and they will pray. Happy are they who think seriously of the truths of religion; but far more happy are they who feel and love them! We must ardently desire that God will grant us spiritual blessings; and the ardor of our wishes must render us fit to receive the blessings. For if we pray only from custom, from fear, in the time of tribulation—if we honor God only with our lips, while our hearts are far from Him—if we do not feel a strong desire for the success of our prayers—if we feel a chilling indifference in approaching Him who is a consuming fire—if we have no zeal for His glory—if we do not feel hatred for sin, and a thirst for perfection, we can not hope for a blessing upon such heartless prayers.

We must *pray with perseverance*. The perfect heart is never weary of seeking God. Ought we to complain if God sometimes leaves us to obscurity, and doubt, and temptation? Trials purify humble souls, and they serve to expiate the faults of the unfaithful. They confound those who, even in their prayers, have flattered their cowardice and pride. If an innocent soul, devoted to God, suffer from any secret disturbance, it should be humble, adore the designs of God, and redouble its prayers and its fervor. How often do we hear those who every day have to reproach themselves with unfaithfulness toward God, complain that He refuses to answer their prayers! Ought they not to acknowledge that it is their *sins* which have formed a thick cloud between Heaven and them, and that God has justly hidden Himself from them? How often has He recalled us from our wanderings! How often, ungrateful as we are, have we been deaf to His voice, and insensible to His goodness! He would make us feel that we are blind and miserable when we forsake Him. He would teach us, by privation, the value of the blessings that we have slighted. And shall we not bear our punishment with patience? Who can boast of having done all that he ought to have done; of having repaired all his past errors; of having purified his heart, so that he may claim as a right that God should listen to his prayer? Most truly, all our pride, great as it is, would not be sufficient to inspire such presumption! If then, the Almighty do not grant our petitions, let us adore His justice, let us be silent, let us humble ourselves, and let us pray without ceasing.

This humble perseverance will obtain from Him what we should never obtain by our own merit. It will make us pass happily from darkness to light; for know, says St. Augustine, that God is near to us even when He appears far from us.

We should pray *with a pure intention*. We should not mingle in our prayers what is false with what is real; what is perishable with what is eternal; low and temporal interests, with that which concerns our salvation. Do not seek to render God the protector of your self-love and ambition, but the promoter of your good desires. You ask for the gratification of your passions, or to be delivered from the cross, of which He knows you have need. Carry not to the foot of the altar irregular desires, and indiscreet prayers. Sigh not there for vain and fleeting pleasures. Open your heart to your Father in heaven, that His Spirit may enable you to ask for the true riches. How can He grant you, says St. Augustine, what you do not yourself desire to receive? You pray every day that His will may be done, and that His kingdom may come. How can you utter this prayer with sincerity when you prefer your own will to His, and make His law yield to the vain pretexts with which your self-love seeks to elude it? Can you make this prayer—you who disturb His reign in your heart by so many impure and vain desires?—you, in fine, who fear the coming of His reign, and do not desire that God should grant what you seem to pray for? No! if He, at this moment, were to offer to give you a new heart, and render you humble, and meek, and self-denying, and willing to bear the cross, your pride would revolt, and you would not accept the offer; or you would make a reservation in favor of your ruling passion, and try to accommodate your piety to your humor and fancies!

James Saurin

[1677–1730]

James Saurin was a native of Nîmes, France, but when the Edict of Nantes was repealed he went with his father into exile at Geneva. Here he studied until, at 17 years of age, he served as a cadet in the army. After a few years of army life he returned to his study of philosophy and divinity. In 1705 he was chosen pastor at The Hague, where he became famous as a preacher and teacher of theology. His sermons were brilliant discourses on matters of religion, philosophy, and psychology. This one places great emphasis on the relationship of psychology and religion, and through it the preacher seeks to instruct as well as help his congregation.

THE NATURE AND CONTROL OF THE PASSIONS

Dearly beloved, I beseech you as strangers and pilgrims, abstain from fleshly lusts, which war against the soul. I Peter 2:11.

THE PASSIONS produce in the mind a strong attention to whatever can justify and gratify them. The most odious objects may be so placed as to appear agreeable, and the most lovely objects so as to appear odious. There is no absurdity so palpable but it may be made to appear likely; and there is no truth so clear but it may be made to appear doubtful. A passionate man fixes all the attention of his mind on such sides of objects as favor his passion, and this is the source of innumerable false judgings, of which we are every day witnesses and authors.

Certainly the best advice that can be given to a man whose constitution inclines him to sin, is, that he avoid opportunities, and flee from such objects as affect and disconcert him. It does not depend on you to be unconcerned in the sight of an object fatal to your innocence: but it does depend on you to keep out of the way of seeing it. It does not depend on you to be animated at the sight of a gaming table: but it does depend on you to avoid such whimsical places, where sharping goes for merit. Let us not be presumptuous. Let us make diffidence a principle of virtue. Let us remember St. Peter; he was fired with zeal, he thought every thing possible to his love, his presumption was the cause of his fall, and many by following his example have yielded to temptation, and have found the truth of an apocryphal maxim, "he that loveth danger shall perish therein."

After all, that virtue which owes its firmness only to a want of an opportunity for vice is very feeble, and it argues very little attainment only to be able to resist our passions in the absence of temptation. I recollect a maxim of St. Paul, "I wrote unto you not to company with fornicators," but I did not mean that you should have no conversation "with fornicators of this world, for then must ye needs go out of the world." Literally, to avoid all objects dangerous to our passions, "we must go out of the world." Are there no remedies adapted to the necessity we are under of living among mankind? Is there no such thing as correcting, with the assistance of grace, the irregularities of our constitution, and freeing ourselves from its dominion, so that we may be able, if not to seek out temptation for the sake of the glory of subduing them, at least to resist them, and not suffer them to conquer us, when in spite of all our caution they will attack us? Three remedies are necessary to our success in this painful undertaking; to suspend acts—to flee idleness—to mortify sense.

We must *suspend acts.* Let us form a just idea of temperament or constitution. It consists in one of these two things, or in both together; in a disposition of organs in the nature of animal spirits. For example, a man is angry when the organs which serve that passion are more accessible than others, and when his animal spirits are easily heated. Hence it necessarily follows that two things must be done to correct constitutional anger; the one, the disposition of the organs must be changed; and the other, the nature of the spirits must be changed, so that on the one hand, the spirits no longer finding these organs disposed to give them passage, and on the other hand the spirits having lost a facility of taking fire, there will be within the man none of the revolutions of sense, which he could not resist when they were excited.

The second remedy is to *avoid idleness.* What is idleness? It is that situation of soul in which no effort is made to direct the course of the spirit this way rather than that. What must happen then? We have supposed that some organs of a man constitutionally irregular are more accessible than others. When we are idle, and make no efforts to direct the animal spirits, they naturally take the easiest way, and consequently direct their own course to those organs which passion has made easy of access. To avoid this disorder, we must be employed, and always employed.

The third remedy is *mortification of the senses,* a remedy which St. Paul always used, "I keep under my body, and bring it into subjection." Few people have such sound notions. Some casuists have stretched the subject beyond its due bounds so as to establish this principle, that sinful man can enjoy no pleasure without a crime, because sin having been his delight, pain ought to be forever his lot. This principle may perhaps be probably considered in regard to unregenerate men: but it can not be admitted in regard to true Christians.

The disorders produced by the passions in the imagination, and against which also we ought to furnish you with some remedies, are like those complicated disorders which require opposite remedies, because they are the effect of opposite causes, so that the means employed to diminish one part not unfrequently increase another. It should seem at first, that the best remedy which can be applied to disorders introduced by the passions into the imagination, is well to consider the nature of the objects of the passions, and thoroughly to know the world: and yet on the other hand, it may truly be said that the most certain way of succeeding would be to know nothing at all about the world.

But as in complicated disorders, to which we have compared them, a wise physician chiefly attends to the most dangerous complaint, and distributes his remedies so as to counteract those which are less fatal, we will observe the same method on this occasion. Doubtless the most dangerous way to obtain a contempt for the pleasures of the world, is to get an experimental knowledge of them, in order to detach ourselves more easily from them by the thorough sense we have of their vanity. We hazard a fall by approaching too near, and such very often is the ascendency of the world over us, that we can not detach ourselves from it though we are disgusted with it.

I would advise such a man, when his passions solicit him to sin, to call in the aid of some other idea to strike and affect his imagination. Let him make choice of that out of the truths of religion which seems most likely to impress his mind, and let him learn the art of instantly opposing impression against impression, and image against image; for example, let him often fix his attention on death, judgment, and hell; let him often say to himself, I must die soon, I must stand before a severe tribunal, and appear in the presence of an impartial judge; let him go down in thought into that gulf, where the wicked expiate in eternal torments their momentary pleasures; let him think he hears the sound of the piercing cries of the victims whom divine justice sacrifices in hell; let him often weigh in his mind the "chains of darkness" that load miserable creatures in hell; let him often approach the fire that consumes them; let him, so to speak, scent the smoke that rises up forever and ever; let him often think of eternity, and place himself in that awful moment in which "the angel will lift up his hand to heaven, and swear by him that liveth forever and ever, that there shall be time no longer;" and let the numerous reflections furnished by all these subjects be kept as *corps de reserve,* always ready to fly to his aid, when the enemy approaches to attack him.

In fine, to heal the disorders which the passions produce in the heart, two things must be done. First, the vanity of all the creatures must be observed; and this will free us from the desire of possessing and collecting the whole in order to fill up the void which single enjoyments leave. Secondly, we must ascend from creatures to the Creator, in order to get rid of the folly of attributing to the world the perfection and sufficiency of God.

Cotton Mather

[1663–1728]

Cotton Mather was known as a man of great learning. He published 382 works, the most voluminous being his seven-volume Ecclesiastical History of New England. *Born in Boston, he was graduated from Harvard College, and was ordained as minister of North Church. Boston, in 1684. The Joyful Sound* of Salvation *was given before the Commission for the Propagation of the Gospel Among the American Indians. It is a fine example of the preaching which Americans heard between the time of the founders of New England religious life and the great revivalist era.*

THE JOYFUL SOUND OF SALVATION

Blessed is the people that know the joyful sound. PSALM 89:15.

IN THE GOSPEL, and the ordinances of it, there is a joyful sound, which we are made partakers of. A true knowledge of this joyful sound, will render the people that have it, a *blessed people.*

Let us proceed more distinctly, in three propositions, to consider what we have before us.

First. There is a *joyful sound,* which is to be heard among the children of men, where the Gospel is published, and where the ordinances of it are established. The sound of the silver trumpets which entertained the ancient Israelites, in and for their solemn assemblies, was no less typical than musical.

There is a *sound* in the Gospel, and the ordinances thereof; and it is, first, a *great sound.* Oh! were we so much "in the spirit on the Lord's Day," as to hear, what is to be heard in the Gospel then brought unto us, we should be able to say, I heard a great voice as of a trumpet. There is a famous prophecy: "The great trumpet shall be blown, and they that were ready to perish, shall come and worship the Lord." Whatever other accomplishments this prophecy may have, it is very gloriously accomplished in the proclamation which our Saviour in His Gospel makes unto us. The Gospel, as with the sound of a trumpet, invites the sinners ready to perish, O come, and worship, and obey, and enjoy the Lord. And when this great trumpet is blown, *great, great* is the sound thereof. The sound of the trumpet is great in the *extent* of it. We read, "The sound goes into all the earth." In less than forty years, it reached unto the utmost bounds of the vast Roman Empire; and though Satan seduced numbers of miserables into America, that they might be out of its hearing, it has now reached hither also. The silver trumpets were at first but a couple, for the two sons of Aaron; but afterward, in Solomon's time, we find an hundred and twenty silver trumpets all sounding together. Before the incarnation of our Saviour, His Gospel was heard but a little way. Afterward, it sounded far and near, and the Gospel was *preached unto every creature:* it might be said, *it sounds in every place.* The sound of the trumpet is also *great* in the *effect* of it. A loud sound, indeed; so loud, as to awaken them that have a dead sleep upon them! So loud, as to convey life unto them that lie dead in trespasses and sins:

"The hour now is, when the dead hear the voice of the Son of God and live." The sound of this trumpet fetches back the lost souls of all the elect from the power of Satan unto God. They are not silver trumpets that are now sounding unto us; but they are *saving* trumpets! Faith comes, the love of God comes, the love of our neighbor comes, and the foretaste of heaven comes, by the hearing of them. What are they, but the power of God unto salvation.

Secondly. 'Tis a good sound as well as a great one. No trumpets can give so good, so grateful, so lovely a sound as the trumpets of the Gospel do. Fame often in her trumpet, has a sound, which may not be relied upon; but every trumpet of the Gospel gives a sound, of none but faithful sayings, and worthy of all acceptation. We are told: "As cold water to a thirsty soul, so is good news from a far country." In the trumpets of the Gospel, we have the sound of nothing but good news "from a far country." The sound which we hear in the trumpets of the Gospel, is what was once heard from the mouth of an angel: "Behold I bring you good tidings of great joy, that unto you there is born a Saviour." Wherever the Gospel comes, there is a sound of this tenor; good news for you who by your sins have the face of God hidden from you; there is a *Jesus,* who saves His people from their sins. Good news for you who have the wrath of God abiding on you. There is a *Jesus,* who delivers from the wrath to come. The joyful sound, which here distinguishes a blessed people, may carry some allusion to the trumpets of jubilee, heard once in fifty years among the Israelites. Once in fifty years, there was that custom observed; "Then shalt thou cause the trumpet of the jubilee to sound, and ye shall proclaim liberty throughout the land." Certainly, the trumpets of September, proclaiming the acceptable year of the Lord, made a very good sound unto the poor people that were now to see a release from various miseries: a good sound unto the servants, who were now to call for and to take up their indentures: a good sound unto the debtors, whose mortgages were now expired, and whose tenements returned unto them. Thus where the Gospel arrives, it brings a jubilee with it. It proclaims a liberty for the captives; a redemption for the miserable; a recovery of what we sinned away. 'Tis the Gospel of peace; the trumpets of the Gospel, are trumpets of peace. The sound of these trumpets is, a reconciliation with God obtained for sinners; the anger of God now turned away from those, whom He was once angry withal! The trumpets which gave the law, had a sound that was trembled at. The guilty sinner hearing those trumpets, may have it said of him, a dreadful sound is in his ears. The sound of those trumpets is, Cursed is he that continued not in all things to do them. The Gospel of our salvation, this is a much more pleasant sound than so. The sound of it is Grace! Grace! The grace that will pardon the penitent! The grace that will quicken the impotent! The grace that will heal them that languish under all sorts of maladies!

No wonder then if, *thirdly,* it be a glad sound, when we find it such a good one. A joyful sound! The souls that are effectually called by the sound of the Gospel, how joyful does it render them! The trumpets of the Gospel do to the soul, as the harps of David did unto Saul: they drive away the evil spirit of sorrow, of sadness, of despair. The Psalmist could say, "I was glad when they said unto me, Let us go into the house of the Lord." The trumpets which gave a joyful sound unto the blessed people, had this among other intentions of them, they were for the calling of the assembly. Glad, glad at heart, was that Israelite indeed, when he heard the trumpets give that call: "Come away to the sacrifices!" The trumpets of the Gospel call us to those appointments of God, wherein we are to glorify Him with the sacrifices of righteousness; and how glad will a sincere Christian be of such invitations! But then, in these appointments of God, what is it we meet withal? Enough to make us "rejoice with joy unspeakable, and full of glory!" The tenders of a Saviour, a powerful, a merciful, and only *Saviour,* are here made unto us. Oh, the joyful sound of such tenders! The promises of a most gracious Covenant are here brought unto us. These very great and precious promises; oh, the joyful sound of them. The sound of these promises is, Rejoice, O thou saved soul; God the Father is thy Friend; God the Son is thy Surety for good; God the Spirit is thy Conductor and Comforter; be of good cheer, thy sins are forgiven thee. The angels are thy guardians, thou art a temple of God. God will make all things work together for thy good. And there are the spiritual blessings of the heavenly places reserved for thee! Oh! joyful sound! How reviving! how ravishing! When the Gospel was preached with success: "There was great joy in the city." Well might there be so, on such a joyful sound! How joyful is the soldier when the trumpet invites him "to the spoil! to the spoil!" The joyful sound of the Gospel carries this in it: else it had not been said, "I rejoice at Thy word, as one that findeth great spoil." The blessings which the word of God lead us to, are matchless treasures. What a joyful sound must it be that leads us to them!

In order to blessedness, it is requisite, not only that we have, but also that we know the joyful sound, which is brought unto us in the Gospel, and in the ordinances of it. Indeed, in a larger sense, to have the joyful sound, is to know it. A people that have the Gospel, and know the joyful sound, in the external enjoyment of it, these do enjoy a rich favor of God. The places which enjoy the Scriptures and have the Church state, with the faith and order of the Gospel, are therein highly favored of the Lord.

The blessedness of the people who thus know this joyful sound, is a very glorious blessedness.

A most considerable article of the blessedness attending a people who hear the silver trumpets of the Gospel, and pay due regards unto them, is this: they shall walk, O Lord, in the light of Thy countenance. A gracious preference of the blessed God among a people accompanies the joyful sound. The silver trumpets are heard nowhere but where the King of heaven keeps His court. There are those whose office it is to blow in the silver trumpets. Unto those our Saviour has engaged himself, "Lo, I am with you always." Will health, and wealth, and rest among a people make a blessed people? 'Tis commonly thought so. But what will God have among a people? Oh, blessed that people whose God is the Lord, and who have a gracious preference of God among them. Even such are the people who know the joyful sound! Where the Gospel, with the ordinances of it, are well settled, maintained, respected, and the silver trumpets well sounded among a people, it may be said, as in Numbers 23:21, "The Lord their God is with them, and the shout of a king is among them." In one word the ordinances of the Gospel furnish us with opportunities for communion with God. "In them I will commune with you," saith the Lord. We may herein draw near to God, God will herein draw near to us. The voice of the silver trumpets is, Draw near to God, and He will draw near to you! Can any blessedness be more glorious?

But more particularly, *First,* In the joyful sound, we have the guide to blessedness. The silver trumpets put us into the way, unto the "rest that remaineth for the people of God." We are ignorant of the way to blessedness; and the way of peace we have not known. But where the trumpets of the Gospel sound, there is a fulfillment of that word: "Thine ears shall hear a word behind thee, saying, this is the way, walk in it." They reveal to us what we are to think, what we are to do, what we are to wish for; they lead us in the way wherein we should go.

Secondly. In the joyful sound we have the cause of blessedness. The silver trumpets are like the golden pipes in Zechariah, which convey the golden oil of grace into the souls of men. 'Tis by them that God fetches men out of the graves, in which they lie sinfully and woefully putrefying; and infuses a principle of piety into them; and inclines them to the things that are holy, and just, and good. That effectual calling which brings men into blessedness, 'tis in the trumpets of the Gospel that the spirit of God gives it unto His chosen ones; men hear the word of the Gospel and believe.

Joseph Butler

[1692–1752]

Joseph Butler was one of the great lights of the Church of England. He was born at Wantage, in Berkshire, and soon evinced unusual scholarly ability. His father placed him under the finest available tutelage, and the young man's ability attracted the attention of high church authorities. They secured his appointment to several noted churches, then to the Bishopric of Bristol and, finally, to the see of Durham. His famous work The Analogy of Religion *is a masterpiece of religious thought. The sermon given here is the first of a series which Bishop Butler gave entitled* Upon Human Nature. *It is typical of his profound reasoning on matters of doctrine.*

UPON THE SOCIAL NATURE OF MAN

For as we have many members in one body, and all members have not the same office; so we, being many, are one body in Christ, and every one members one of another. ROMANS 12:4, 5.

THE EPISTLES in the New Testament have all of them a particular reference to the condition and usages of the Christian world at the time they were written. Therefore as they cannot be thoroughly understood, unless that condition and those usages are known and attended to: so further, though they be known, yet if they be discontinued or changed; exhortations, precepts, and illustrations of things, which refer to such circumstances now ceased or altered, cannot at this time be urged in that manner, and with that force which they were to the primitive Christians. Thus the text now before us, in its first intent and design, relates to the decent management of those extraordinary gifts which were then in the church, but which are now totally ceased. And even as to the allusion that *we are one body in Christ;* though what the Apostle here intends is equally true of Christians in all circumstances; and the consideration of it is plainly still an additional motive, over and above moral considerations, to the discharge of the several duties and offices of a Christian: yet it is manifest this allusion must have appeared with much greater force to those, who, by the many difficulties they went through for the sake of their religion, were led to keep always in view the relation they stood in to their Saviour, who had undergone the same; to those, who, from the idolatries of all around them, and their ill-treatment, were taught to consider themselves as not of the world in which they lived, but as a distinct society of themselves; with laws and ends, and principles of life and action, quite contrary to those which the world professed themselves at that time influenced by. Hence the relation of a Christian was by them considered as nearer than that of affinity and blood; and they almost literally esteemed themselves as members one of another.

The relation which the several parts or members of the natural body have to each other and to the whole body, is here compared to the relation which each particular person in society has to other particular persons and to the whole society; and the latter is intended to be illustrated by the former. And if there be a likeness between these two relations, the consequence is obvious: that the latter shows us we were intended to do good to others, as the former shows us that the several members of the natural body were intended to be instruments of good to each other and to the whole body. But as there is scarce any ground for a comparison between society and the mere material body, this without the mind being a dead unactive thing; much less can the comparison be carried to any length. And since the Apostle speaks of the several members as having distinct offices, which implies the mind; it cannot be thought an unallowable liberty, instead of the *body* and *its members,* to substitute the *whole nature of man,* and *all the variety of internal principles which belong to it.* And then the comparison will be between the nature of man as respecting self, and tending to private good, his own preservation and happiness; and the nature of man as having respect to society, and tending to promote public good, the happiness of that society. These ends do indeed perfectly coincide; and to aim at public and private good are so far from being inconsistent, that they mutually promote each other: yet in the following discourse they must be considered as entirely distinct; otherwise the nature of man as tending to one, or as tending to the other, cannot be compared. There can no comparison be made, without considering the things compared as distinct and different.

From this review and comparison of the nature of man as respecting self, and as respecting society, it will plainly appear, that *there are as real and the same kind of indications in human nature, that we were made for society and to do good to our fellow-creatures; as that we were intended to take care of our own life and health and private good: and that the same objections lie against one of these assertions, as against the other.*

Mankind are by nature so closely united, there is such a correspondence between the inward sensations of one man and those of another, that disgrace is as much avoided as bodily pain, and to be the object of esteem and love as much desired as any external goods: and in many particular cases, persons are carried on to do good to others, as the end their affection tends to and rests in; and manifest that they find real satisfaction and enjoyment in this course of behaviour. There is such a natural principle of attraction in man towards man, that having trod the same tract of land, having breathed in the same climate, barely having been in the same artificial district or division, becomes the occasion of contracting acquaintances and familiarities many years after: for anything may serve the purpose. Thus relations merely nominal are sought and invented, not by governors, but by the lowest of the people; which are found sufficient to hold mankind together in little fraternities and copartnerships: weak ties indeed, and what may afford fund enough for ridicule, if they are absurdly considered as the real principles of that union: but they are in truth merely the occasions, as anything may be of anything, upon which our nature carries us on according to its own previous bent and bias; which occasions therefore would be nothing at all, were there not this prior disposition and bias of nature. Men are so much one body, that in a peculiar manner they feel for each other, shame, sudden danger, resentment, honour, prosperity, distress; one or another, or all of these, from the social nature in general, from benevolence, upon the occasion of natural relation, acquaintance, protection, dependence; each of these being distinct cements of society. And therefore to have no restraint from, no regard to others in our behaviour, is the speculative absurdity of considering ourselves as single and independent, as having nothing in our nature which has respect to our fellow-creatures, reduced to action and practice. And this is the same absurdity, as to suppose a hand, or any part, to have no natural respect to any other, or to the whole body.

But allowing all this, it may be asked, "Has not man dispositions and principles within, which lead him to do evil to others, as well as to do good? Whence come the many miseries else, which men are the authors and instruments of to each other?" These questions, so far as they relate to the foregoing discourse, may be answered by asking, Has not man also dispositions and principles within, which lead him to do evil to himself as well as good? Whence come the many miseries else, sickness, pain, and death, which men are instruments and authors of to themselves?

It may be thought more easy to answer one of these questions than the other, but the answer to both is really the same; that mankind have ungoverned passions which they will gratify at any rate, as well to the injury of others, as in contradiction to known private interest: but that as there is no such thing as self-hatred, so neither is there any such thing as ill-will in one man towards another, emulation and resentment being away; whereas there is plainly benevolence or good-will: there is no such thing as love of injustice, oppression, treachery, ingratitude; but only eager desires after such and such external goods: which, according to a very ancient observation, the most abandoned would choose to obtain by innocent means, if they were as easy, and as effectual to their end: that even emulation and resentment, by any one who will consider what these passions really are in nature, will be found nothing to the purpose of this objection: and that the principles and passions in the mind of man, which are distinct both from self-love and benevolence, primarily and most directly lead to right behaviour with regard to others as well as himself, and only secondarily and accidentally to what is evil. Thus, though men, to avoid the shame of one villainy, are sometimes guilty of a greater, yet it is easy to see, that the original tendency of shame is to prevent the doing of shameful actions; and its leading men to conceal such actions when done, is only in consequence of their being done; *i. e.,* of the passion's not having answered its first end.

If it be said, that there are persons in the world, who are in great measure without the natural affections towards their fellow-creatures: there are likewise instances of persons without the common natural affections to themselves; but the nature of man is not to be judged of by either of these, but by what appears in the common world, in the bulk of mankind.

I am afraid it would be thought very strange, if to confirm the truth of this account of human nature, and make out the justness of the foregoing comparison, it should be added, that, from what appears, men in fact as much and as often contradict that *part* of their nature which respects *self,* and which leads them to their *own private* good and happiness; as they contradict that *part* of it which respects *society,* and tends to *public* good: that there are as few persons who attain the greatest satisfaction and enjoyment which they might attain in the present world, as who do the greatest good to others which they might do; nay, that there are as few who can be said really and in earnest to aim at one, as at the other. Take a survey of mankind: the world in general, the good and bad, almost without exception, equally are agreed, that were religion out of the case, the happiness of the present life would consist in a manner wholly in riches, honours, sensual gratifications; insomuch that one scarce hears a reflection made upon prudence, life, conduct, but upon this supposition. Yet, on the contrary, that persons in the greatest affluence of fortune are no happier than such as have only a competency; that the cares and disappointments of ambition for the most part far exceed the satisfactions of it; as also the miserable intervals of intemperance and excess, and the many untimely deaths occasioned by a dissolute course of life: these things are all seen, acknowledged, by every one acknowledged; but are thought no objections against, though they expressly contradict, this universal principle, that the happiness of the present life consists in one or other of them.

Jonathan Edwards

[1703–1758]

Jonathan Edwards' career was from the beginning one of the most brilliant in American church history. Born at Windsor, Connecticut, the son of a minister, he early distinguished himself as a scholar and a preacher. He was graduated from Yale College before he was 17, preached for a few months in New York, then was appointed a tutor at Yale. He was ordained in 1727. In 1758 he accepted the presidency of Princeton College, but he died a few months after his appointment. The following sermon is his most celebrated. It was given at Enfield, Connecticut, on July 8, 1741, and had so marked an effect upon the audience that "the hearers groaned and shrieked convulsively; and their outcries of distress once drowned the preacher's voice, and compelled him to make a long pause." This sermon gave a powerful impulse to the great revival then in progress throughout New England.

SINNERS IN THE HANDS OF AN ANGRY GOD

Their foot shall slide in due time. DEUTERONOMY 32:35.

THE EXPRESSION that I have chosen for my text, "Their foot shall slide in due time," seems to imply the following things, relating to the punishment and destruction that these wicked Israelites were exposed to:

That they were always exposed to destruction; as one that stands or walks in slippery places is always exposed to fall.

It implies that they were always exposed to sudden, unexpected destruction.

Another thing implied is, that they are liable to fall of themselves, without being thrown down by the hand of another; as he that stands or walks on slippery ground needs nothing but his own weight to throw him down.

That the reason why they are not fallen already, and do not fall now, is only that God's appointed time is not come. For it is said that when that due time or appointed time comes, "their feet shall slide." Then they shall be left to fall, as they are inclined by their own weight. God will not hold them up in these slippery places any longer, but will let them go; and then, at that very instant, they shall fall into destruction; as he that stands on such slippery, declining ground, on the edge of a pit, that he can not stand alone, when he is let go he immediately falls and is lost.

There is nothing that keeps wicked men at any one moment out of hell but the mere pleasure of God.

By the mere pleasure of God I mean His sovereign pleasure, His arbitrary will, restrained by no obligation, hindered by no manner of difficulty, any more than if nothing else but God's mere will had in the least degree or in any respect whatever any hand in the preservation of wicked men one moment.

The truth of this observation may appear by the following considerations:

There is no want of power in God to cast wicked men into hell at any moment. Men's hands can not be strong when God rises up: the strongest have no power to resist Him, nor can any deliver out of His hands.

He is not only able to cast wicked men into hell, but He can most easily do it. Sometimes an earthly prince meets with a great deal of difficulty to subdue a rebel, that has found means to fortify himself, and has made himself strong by the number of his followers. But it is not so with God. There is no fortress that is any defense against the power of God.

They deserve to be cast into hell; so that Divine justice never stands in the way, it makes no objection against God's using His power at any moment to destroy them. Yea, on the contrary, justice calls aloud for an infinite punishment of their sins.

They are already under a sentence of condemnation to hell. They do not only justly deserve to be cast down thither, but the sentence of the law of God—that eternal and immutable rule of righteousness that God has fixed between Him and mankind—is gone out against them; and stands against them; so that they are bound over already to hell.

They are now the objects of that very same anger and wrath of God, that is expressed in the torments of hell; and the reason why they do not go down to hell at each moment, is not because God, in whose power they are, is not then very angry with them; as angry as He is with many of those miserable creatures that He is now tormenting in hell, and do there feel and bear the fierceness of His wrath. Yea, God is a great deal more angry with great numbers that are now on earth; yea, doubtless, with many that are now in this congregation, that, it may be, are at ease and quiet, than He is with many of those that are now in the flames of hell.

So that it is not because God is unmindful of their wickedness, and does not resent it, that He does not let loose His hand and cut them off. God is not altogether such a one as themselves, though they imagine Him to be so. The wrath of God burns against them; their damnation does not slumber; the pit is prepared; the fire is made ready; the furnace is now hot, ready to receive them; the flames do now rage and glow. The glittering sword is whet, and held over them, and the pit hath opened her mouth under them.

The devil stands ready to fall upon them, and seize them as his own, at what moment God shall permit him. They belong to him; he has their souls in his possession, and under his dominion. The Scripture represents them as his goods. The devils watch them; they are ever by them, at their right hand; they stand waiting for them, like greedy, hungry lions that see their prey, and expect to have it, but are for the present kept back; if God should withdraw His hand by which they are restrained, they would in one moment fly upon their poor souls. The old Serpent is gaping for them; hell opens its mouth wide to receive them; and if God should permit, they would be hastily swallowed up and lost.

There are in the souls of wicked men those hellish principles reigning, that would presently kindle and flame out in hell-fire, if it were not for God's restraints. There is laid in the very nature of carnal men, a foundation for the torments of hell: there are those corrupt principles, in reigning power in them, and in full possession of them, that are the beginnings of hell-fire.

It is no security to wicked men for one moment, that there are no visible means of death at hand. It is no security to a natural man, that he is now in health, and that he does not see which way he should now immediately go out of the world by any accident, and that there is no visible danger in any respect in his circumstances. The manifold and continual experience of the world in all ages, shows that this is no evidence that a man is not on the very brink of eternity, and that the next step will not be into another world. The unseen, unthought-of ways and means of persons going suddenly out of the world are innumerable and inconceivable. Unconverted men walk over the pit of hell on a rotten covering, and there are innumerable places in this covering, so weak that they will not bear their weight, and these places are not seen. The arrows of death fly unseen at noon-day; the sharpest sight can not discern them. God has so many different, unsearchable ways of taking wicked men out of the world and sending them to hell, that there is nothing to make it appear, that God had need to be at the expense of a miracle, or go out of the ordinary course of his Providence, to destroy any wicked man, at any moment.

Natural men's prudence and care to preserve their own lives, or the care of others to preserve them, do not secure them a moment. This, Divine providence and universal experience do also bear testimony to. There is this clear evidence that men's own wisdom is no security to them from death: that if it were otherwise we should see some difference between the wise and politic men of the world, and others, with regard to their liableness to early and unexpected death; but how is it in fact? "How dieth the wise man? As the fool."

God has laid Himself under no obligations, by any promise, to keep any natural man out of hell one moment: God certainly has made no promises either of eternal life, or of any deliverance or preservation from eternal death, but what are contained in the covenant of grace, the promises that are given in Christ, in whom all the promises are yea and amen. But surely they have no interest in the promises of the covenant of grace that are not the children of the covenant, and that do not believe in any of the promises of the covenant, and have no interest in the Mediator of the covenant.

So that thus it is, that natural men are held in the hand of God over the pit of hell; they have deserved the fiery pit, and are already sentenced to it; and God is dreadfully provoked, His anger is as great toward them as to those that are actually suffering the executions of the fierceness of His wrath in hell, and they have done nothing in the least to appease or abate that anger, neither is God in the least bound by any promise to hold them up one moment; the devil is waiting for them, hell is gaping for them, the flames gather and flash about them, and would fain lay hold on them and swallow them up; the fire pent up in their own hearts is struggling to break out; and they have no interest in any Mediator, there are no means within reach that can be any security to them. In short, they have no refuge, nothing to take hold of; all that preserves them every moment is the mere arbitrary will, and uncovenanted, unobliged forbearance of an incensed God.

The use may be of awakening to unconverted persons in this congregation. This that you have heard is the case of every one of you that are out of Christ. That world of misery, that lake of burning brimstone, is extended abroad under you. There is the dreadful pit of the glowing flames of the wrath of God; there is hell's wide gaping mouth open; and you have nothing to stand upon, nor any thing to take hold of. There is nothing between you and hell but the air; it is only the power and mere pleasure of God that holds you up.

The wrath of God is like great waters that are dammed for the present; they increase more and more, and rise higher and higher, till an outlet is given; and the longer the stream is stopped the more rapid and mighty is its course, when once it is let loose. It is true, that judgment against your evil work has not been executed hitherto; the floods of God's vengeance have been withheld; but your guilt in the mean time is constantly increasing, and you are every day treasuring up more wrath; the waters are continually rising, and waxing more and more mighty; and there is nothing but the mere pleasure of God that holds the waters back, that are unwilling to be stopped, and press hard to go forward. If God should only withdraw His hand from the flood-gate, it would immediately fly open, and the fiery floods of the fierceness and wrath of God would rush forth with inconceivable fury, and would come upon you with omnipotent power; and if your strength were ten thousand times greater than it is, yea, ten thousand times greater than the strength of the stoutest, sturdiest devil in hell, it would be nothing to withstand or endure it.

The bow of God's wrath is bent, and the arrow made ready on the string, and justice bends the arrow at your heart, and strains the bow, and it is nothing but the mere pleasure of God, and that of an angry God, without any promise or obligation at all, that keeps the arrow one moment from being made drunk with your blood.

The God that holds you over the pit of hell much as one holds a spider or some loathsome insect over the fire, abhors you, and is dreadfully provoked; His wrath toward you burns like fire; He looks upon you as worthy of nothing else but to be cast into the fire; He is of purer eyes than to bear you in His sight; you are ten thousand times as abominable in His eyes, as the most hateful and venomous serpent is in ours. You have offended Him infinitely more than ever a stubborn rebel did his prince; and yet it is nothing but His hand that holds you from falling into the fire every moment; it is ascribed to nothing else that you did not go to hell the last night that you were suffered to awake again in this world, after you closed your eyes to sleep; and there is no other reason to be given why you have not dropped into hell since you arose in the morning, but that God's hand has held you up; there is no other reason to be given why you have not gone to hell, since you have sat here in the house of God, provoking His pure eye by your sinful wicked manner of attending His solemn worship; yea, there is nothing else that is to be given as a reason why you do not this very moment drop down into hell.

O sinner! consider the fearful danger you are in: it is a great furnace of wrath, a wide and bottomless pit, full of the fire of wrath that you are held over in the hands of that God whose wrath is provoked and incensed as much against you as against many of the damned in hell; you hang by a slender thread, with the flames of Divine wrath flashing about it, and ready every moment to singe it, and burn it asunder; and you have no interest in any mediator, and nothing to lay hold of to save yourself, nothing to keep off the flames of wrath, nothing of your own, nothing that you have ever done, nothing that you can do to induce God to spare you one moment.

John Wesley

[1703–1791]

John Wesley was born at Epworth in Lincolnshire at a time when the English church was at its lowest ebb. After receiving a splendid education at Charterhouse and at Christ Church, Oxford, he was ordained in 1725. Although a religious man, he was not convinced of a clear conversion until 1738, when he experienced a definite emotional upheaval. From that time on he devoted himself to preaching and to organizing the body which has developed into the Methodist Church. A fine scholar, Wesley wrote much. In all his writings he shows familiarity with the best learning of his times. This sermon was given before Sir Edward Clive in St. Paul's Church, Bedford, March 10, 1758, upon the occasion of the assizes.

THE GREAT ASSIZE

We shall all stand before the judgment-seat of Christ. ROMANS 14:10.

How MANY circumstances concur to raise the awfulness of the present solemnity! The general *concourse* of people of every age, sex, rank, and condition of life, willingly or unwillingly gathered together, not only from the neighboring, but from distant parts; *criminals,* speedily to be brought forth, and having no way to escape; *officers,* waiting in their various posts, to execute the orders which shall be given; and the *representative* of our gracious *sovereign,* whom we so highly reverence and honor. The *occasion,* likewise, of this assembly, adds not a little to the solemnity of it: to hear and determine causes of every kind, some of which are of the most important nature; on which depends no less than life or death; death that uncovers the face of eternity! It was, doubtless, in order to increase the serious sense of these things, and not in the minds of the vulgar only, that the wisdom of our forefathers did not disdain to appoint even several minute circumstances of this solemnity. For these also, by means of the eye or ear, may more deeply affect the heart: and when viewed in this light, trumpets, staves, apparel, are no longer trifling or significant, but subservient, in their kind and degree, to the most valuable ends of society.

But, awful as this solemnity is, one far more awful is at hand. For yet a little while, and "we shall all stand before the judgment seat of Christ." "For, as I live, saith the Lord, every knee shall bow to Me, and every tongue shall confess to God." And in that day "every one of us shall give account of himself to God."

Had all men a deep sense of this, how effectually would it secure the interests of society! For what more forcible motive can be conceived to the practice of genuine morality, to a steady pursuit of solid virtue, and a uniform walking in justice, mercy, and truth? What could strengthen our hands in all that is good, and deter us from all that is evil, like a strong conviction of this, "The judge standeth at the door;" and we are shortly to stand before him?

"God will show signs in the earth beneath," particularly He will "arise to shake terribly the earth." "The earth shall reel to and fro like a drunkard, and shall be removed like a cottage." "There shall be earthquakes" (not in divers only, but) "in all places;" not in one only, or in a few, but in every part of the habitable world, even "such as were not since men were upon the earth, so mighty earthquakes and so great." In one of these "every island shall flee away, and the mountains will not be found."

At the same time, "the Son of man shall send forth His angels" over all the earth; "and they shall gather His elect from the four winds, from one end of heaven to the other." And the Lord Himself shall come with clouds, in His own glory, and the glory of His Father, with ten thousand of His saints, even myriads of angels, and shall sit upon the throne of His glory. "And before Him shall be gathered all nations, and He shall separate them one from another, and shall set the sheep (the good) on His right hand, and the goats (the wicked) upon the left." Concerning this general assembly it is that the beloved disciple speaks thus: "I saw the dead (all that had been dead), small and great, stand before God. And the books were opened, (a figurative expression, plainly referring to the manner of proceeding among men), and the dead were judged out of those things which were written in the books, according to their works."

The Person by whom God will judge the world is His only-begotten Son, whose "goings forth are from everlasting;" "who is God over all, blessed forever." Unto Him, being "the out-beaming of His Father's glory, the express image of His Person," the Father "hath committed all judgment, because He is the Son of man;" because, though He was "in the form of God, and thought it not robbery to be equal with God, yet He emptied Himself, taking upon Him the form of a servant, being made in the likeness of man;" yea, because, "being found in fashion as a man, He humbled Himself (yet further), becoming obedient unto death, even the death of the cross. Wherefore God hath highly exalted Him," even in His human nature, and "ordained Him," as man, to try the children of men, "to be the Judge both of the quick and dead;" both of those who shall be found alive at His coming and of those who were before gathered to their fathers.

And every man shall there "give an account of his own works;" yea, a full and true account of all that he ever did while in the body, whether it was good or evil.

Nor will all the actions alone of every child of man be then brought to open view, but all their words; seeing "every idle word which men shall speak, they shall give account thereof in the day of judgment;" so that "by thy words" as well as works, "thou shalt be justified; and by thy words thou shalt be condemned." Will not God then bring to light every circumstance also that accompanied every word or action, and if not altered the nature, yet lessened or increased the goodness or badness of them? And how easy is this to Him who is "about our bed, and about our path, and spieth out all our ways?" We know "the darkness is no darkness to Him, but the night shineth as the day."

"Then the King will say to them upon His right hand, Come ye, blessed of My Father. For I was hungry, and ye gave Me meat; thirsty, and ye gave Me drink; I was a stranger, and ye took Me in; naked, and ye clothed Me." In like manner, all the good they did upon earth will be recited before men and angels; whatsoever they had done either in word or deed, in the name or for the sake of the Lord Jesus. All their good desires, intentions, thoughts, all their holy dispositions, will also be then remembered; and it will appear that though they were unknown or forgotten among men, yet God noted them in His book. All their sufferings, likewise, for the name of Jesus, and for the testimony of a good conscience, will be displayed, unto their praise from the righteous Judge, their honor before saints and angels, and the increase of that "far more exceeding and eternal weight of glory."

After the righteous are judged, the King will turn to them upon His left hand, and they shall also be judged, every man according to his works. But not only their outward works will be brought into the account, but all the evil words which they have ever spoken, yea, all the evil desires, affections, tempers which have or have had a place in their souls, and all the evil thoughts or designs which were ever cherished in their hearts. The joyful sentence of acquittal will then be pronounced upon those upon the right hand, the dreadful sentence of condemnation upon those on the left, both of which must remain fixed and unmovable as the throne of God.

It remains only to apply the preceding considerations to all who are here before God. And are we not directly led so to do by the present solemnity; which so naturally points us to that day when the Lord will judge the world in righteousness? This, therefore, by reminding us of that more awful season, may furnish many lessons of instruction. May God write them on all our hearts!

How beautiful are the feet of all those who are sent by the wise and gracious providence of God, to execute justice on earth, to defend the injured and punish the wrong-doer! Are they not the ministers of God to us for good, the grand supporters of the public tranquillity, the patrons of innocence and virtue, the security of all our temporal blessings? And does not every one of these represent not only an earthly prince, but the Judge of the earth? Him, whose "name is written upon His thigh; King of kings, and Lord of lords?" Oh that all these sons of the right hand of the Most High, may be holy as He is holy! Wise with the wisdom that sitteth by His throne: like Him who is the eternal Wisdom of the Father! No respecter of persons, as He is none; but rendering to every man according to his works: like Him inflexibly; inexorably just, though pitiful and of tender-mercy! So shall they be terrible, indeed, to them that do evil, as not bearing the sword in vain. So shall the laws of our land have their full use and due honor, and the throne of our King be still established in righteousness.

George Whitefield

[1714–1770]

George Whitefield was born at Gloucester, England. He was a wild and dissolute youth, but developed into one of the most moving preachers of all times. He seemed to have an hypnotic power over his audiences, and it is said that at his first sermon fifteen persons went mad. He preached widely both in the British Isles and in America, and everywhere attracted great crowds, all equally moved by his eloquence. Most of Whitefield's sermons have come to us as mere notes. Here is one of the few exceptions, which shows us something of the power and penetration of the preacher.

THE KINGDOM OF GOD

For the kingdom of God is not meat and drink; but righteousness, and peace, and joy in the Holy Ghost. ROMANS 14:17.

WE ARE to take the kingdom of God in the text as signifying that inward work of grace, that kingdom which the Lord Jesus Christ sets up in the hearts of all that are truly brought home to God; so that when the Apostle tells us, "The kingdom of God is not meat and drink," it is the same as though he had said, "My dear friends, do not quarrel about outward things; for the kingdom of God, or true and undefiled religion, heart and soul religion, is not meat and drink."

By meat and drink, if we compare the text with the context, we are to understand no more than this, that the kingdom of God, or true religion, doth not consist in abstaining from a particular meat or drink. But I shall take the words in a more comprehensive sense, and shall endeavor to show you on this head that the kingdom of God, or true and undefiled religion, doth not consist in any, no, not in all outward things, put them altogether. And,

First, The kingdom of God, or true and undefiled religion, doth not consist in being of this or that particular sect or communion. Perhaps, my dear friends, were many of you asked what reason you can give for the hope that is in you, what title you have to call yourselves Christians— perhaps you could say no more for yourselves than this, namely, that you belong to such a Church, and worship God in the same way in which your fathers and mothers worshiped God before you; and perhaps, at the same time you are so narrow in your thoughts that you think none can worship God but those that worship God just in your way. It is certainly, my dear friends, a blessing to be born as you are, in a reformed Church; it is certainly a blessing to have the outward government and discipline of the Church exercised; but then, if you place religion merely in being of this or that sect—if you contend to monopolize or confine the grace of God to your particular party—if you rest in that, you place the kingdom of God in something in which it doth not consist—you had as good place it in meat and drink. There are certainly Christians among all sects and communions that have learned the truth as it is in Christ Jesus.

Again: as the kingdom of God doth not consist in being of this or that sect, so neither doth it consist in being baptized when you were young. Baptism is certainly an ordinance of the Lord Jesus Christ—it ought certainly to be administered; but then, my dear friends, take care that you do not make a Christ of your baptism, for there have been many baptized with water, as you were, who were never savingly baptized with the Holy Ghost.

But further: as the kingdom of God and true religion doth not consist in being baptized, neither doth it consist in being orthodox in our notions, or being able to talk fluently of the doctrines of the Gospel. There are a great many who can talk of free grace, of free justification, of final perseverance, of election, and God's everlasting love. All these are precious truths—they are all connected in a chain; take away one link and you spoil the whole chain of Gospel truths.

The kingdom of God is "righteousness." By righteousness we are here to understand the complete, perfect, and all-sufficient righteousness of our Lord Jesus Christ, as including both His active and His passive obedience. My dear friends, we have no righteousness of our own; our best righteousness, take them altogether, are but so many filthy rags; we can only be accepted for the sake of the righteousness of our Lord Jesus

Christ. This righteousness must be imputed and made over to us, and applied to our hearts; and till we get this righteousness brought home to our souls, we are in a state of death and damnation—the wrath of God abideth on us.

"The kingdom of God is righteousness and peace." By peace I do not understand that false peace, or rather carnal security, into which so many are fallen. There are thousands who speak peace to themselves when there is no peace. Thousands have got a peace of the devil's making; the strong man armed has got possession of their hearts, and therefore their goods are all in peace. But the peace here spoken of is a peace that follows after a great deal of soul trouble; it is like that calm which the Lord Jesus Christ spoke to the wind; "Peace, be still; and immediately there was a great calm;" it is like that peace which Christ spoke to His disciples, when He came and said, "Peace be unto you"—"My peace I leave with you." It is a peace of God's making, it is a peace of God's giving, it is a peace that the world can not give, it is a peace that can be felt, it is a peace that passeth human understanding—it is a peace that results from a sense of having Christ's righteousness brought home to the soul. For a poor soul before this is full of trouble; Christ makes application of His righteousness to his heart; and then the poor creature, being justified by faith, hath peace with God through our Lord Jesus Christ. My dear friends, I am now talking of heart-religion, of an inward work of God, an inward kingdom in your hearts, which you must have, or you shall never sit with Jesus Christ in His kingdom. The most of you may have peace, but for Christ's sake examine upon what this peace is founded—see if Christ be brought home to your souls, if you have had a feeling application of the merits of Christ brought home to your souls. Is God at peace with you? Did Jesus Christ ever say, "Peace be to you"— "Be of good cheer"—"Go thy way, thy sins are forgiven thee"—"My peace I leave with you, My peace I give unto you?" Did God ever bring a comfortable promise with power to your soul? And after you have been praying, and fearing you would be damned, did you ever feel peace flow in like a river upon your soul? so that you could say, Now I know that God is my friend, now I know that Jesus is my Saviour, now I can call Him "My Lord, and my God;" now I know that Christ hath not only died for others, but I know that Jesus hath died for me in particular. O my dear friends, it is impossible to tell you the comfort of this peace, and I am astonished (only man's heart is desperately wicked) how you can have peace one moment and yet not know that God is at peace with you. How can you go to bed this night without this peace? It is a blessed thing to know when sin is forgiven; would you not be glad if an angel were to come and tell you so this night?

But there is something more—there is "joy in the Holy Ghost." I have often thought that if the Apostle Paul were to come and preach now he would be reckoned one of the greatest enthusiasts on earth. He talked of the Holy Ghost, of feeling the Holy Ghost; and so we must all feel it, all experience it, all receive it, or we can never see a holy God with comfort. We are not to receive the Holy Ghost so as to enable us to work miracles; for, "Many will say in that day, We have cast out devils in Thy name, and in Thy name done many wonderful works." But we must receive the Holy Ghost to sanctify our nature, to purify our hearts, and make us meet for heaven. Unless we are born again, and have the Holy Ghost in our hearts, if we were in heaven we could take no pleasure there. The Apostle not only supposes we must have the Holy Ghost, but he supposes, as a necessary ingredient to make up the kingdom of God in a believer's heart, that he must have "joy in the Holy Ghost." There are a great many, I believe, who think religion is a poor melancholy thing, and they are afraid to be Christians. But, my dear friends, there is no true joy till you can joy in God and Christ. I know wicked men and men of pleasure will have a little laughter; but what is it, but like the crackling of a few thorns under a pot? it makes a blaze, and soon goes out. I know what it is to take pleasure in sin; but I always found the smart that followed was ten thousand times more hurtful than any gratification I could receive. But they who joy in God have a joy that strangers intermeddle not with—it is a joy that no man can take from them; it amounts to a full assurance of faith that the soul is reconciled to God through Christ, that Jesus dwells in the heart; and when the soul reflects on itself, it magnifies the Lord, and rejoices in God its Saviour. Thus we are told that "Zaccheus received Christ joyfully," that "the eunuch went on his way rejoicing," and that "the jailer rejoiced in God with all his house." O, my friends, what joy have they that know their sins are forgiven them! What a blessed thing is it for a man to look forward and see an endless eternity of happiness before him, knowing that every thing shall work together for his good!—it is joy unspeakable and full of glory. O may God make you all partakers of it!

Here, then, we will put the kingdom of God together. It is "righteousness," it is "peace," it is "joy in the Holy Ghost." When this is placed in the heart, God there reigns, God there dwells and walks—the creature is a son or daughter of the Almighty. But, my friends, how few are there here who have been made partakers of this kingdom! Perhaps the kingdom of the devil, instead of the kingdom of God, is in most of our hearts. This has been a place much favored of God; may I hope some of you can go along with me and say "Blessed be God we have got righteousness, peace, and joy in the Holy Ghost?" Have you so? Then you are kings, though beggars; you are happy above all men in the world—you have got heaven in your hearts; and when the crust of your bodies drops, your souls will meet with God, your souls will enter into the world of peace, and you shall be happy with God for evermore. I hope there is none of you who will fear death; fie for shame, if ye do! What! afraid to go to Jesus, to your Lord? You may cry out, "O death, where is thy sting? O grave, where is thy victory?" You may go on your way rejoicing, knowing that God is your friend; die when you will, angels will carry you safe to heaven.

Robert Hall

[1764–1831]

Robert Hall was a scholar almost from birth. At the age of nine he had read Bishop Butler's Analogy *and Edwards'* The Will, *and at sixteen he was an ordained minister. Hall was born in England, and was educated at Kings' College, Aberdeen, Scotland. He held several influential pulpits in England and greatly affected the religious thinking of the communities in which he worked. Though a man of small voice and weak physique, he was a master of pulpit oratory and held great congregations spellbound. His literary clarity was recognized by the men of letters of his day, and this sermon is one of his many distinguished discourses.*

MODERN INFIDELITY CONSIDERED

Without God in the world. EPHESIANS 2:12.

As THE Christian ministry is established for the instruction of men, throughout every age, in truth and holiness, it must adapt itself to the ever-shifting scenes of the moral world, and stand ready to repel the attacks of impiety and error, under whatever form they may appear. The Church and the world form two societies so distinct, and are governed by such opposite principles and maxims, that, as well from this contrariety as from the express warnings of Scripture, true Christians must look for a state of warfare, with this consoling assurance, that the Church, like the burning bush beheld by Moses in the land of Midian, may be encompassed with flames, but will never be consumed.

When she was delivered from the persecuting power of Rome, she only experienced a change of trials. The oppression of external violence was followed by the more dangerous and insidious attacks of internal enemies. The freedom and inquiry claimed and asserted at the Reformation degenerated, in the hands of men who professed the principles without possessing the spirit of the Reformers, into a fondness for speculative refinements; and, consequently, into a source of dispute, faction, and heresy. While Protestants attended more to the points on which they differed than to those on which they agreed—while more zeal was employed in settling ceremonies and defending subtleties than in enforcing plain revealed truths—the lovely fruits of peace and charity perished under the storms of controversy.

In this disjointed and disordered state of the Christian Church, they who never looked into the interior of Christianity were apt to suspect, that to a subject so fruitful in particular disputes must attach a general uncertainty; and that a religion founded on revelation could never have occasioned such discordancy of principle and practice among its disciples. Thus infidelity is the joint offspring of an irreligious temper and unholy speculation, employed, not in examining the evidences of Christianity, but in detecting the vices and imperfections of professing Christians. It has passed through various stages, each distinguished by higher gradations of impiety; for when men arrogantly abandon their guide, and willfully shut their eyes on the light of heaven, it is wisely ordained that their errors shall multiply at every step, until their extravagance confutes itself, and the mischief of their principles works its own antidote.

Animated by numbers and emboldened by success, the infidels of the present day have given a new direction to their efforts, and impressed a new character on the ever-growing mass of their impious speculations.

By uniting more closely with each other, by giving a sprinkling of irreligion to all their literary productions, they aim to engross the formation of the public mind; and, amid the warmest professions of attachment to virtue, to effect an entire disruption of morality from religion. Pretending to be the teachers of virtue and the guides of life, they propose to revolutionize the morals of mankind; to regenerate the world by a process entirely new; and to rear the temple of virtue, not merely without the aid of religion, but on the renunciation of its principles and the derision of its sanctions.

When we examine a watch, or any other piece of machinery, we instantly perceive marks of design. The arrangement of its several parts, and the adaptation of its movements to one result, show it to be a contrivance; nor do we ever imagine the faculty of contriving to be in the watch itself, but in a separate agent. If we turn from art to nature, we behold a vast magazine of contrivances: we see innumerable objects replete with the most exquisite design. The human eye, for example, is formed with admirable skill for the purpose of sight, the ear for the function of hearing. As in the productions of art we never think of ascribing the power of contrivance to the machine itself, so we are certain the skill displayed in the human structure is not a property of man, since he is very imperfectly acquainted with his own formation. If there be an inseparable relation between the ideas of a contrivance and a contriver, and it be evident in regard to the human structure, the designing agent is not man himself, there must undeniably be some separate invisible being, who is his former. This great Being we mean to indicate by the appellation of Deity.

To prove the unity of this great Being, in opposition to a plurality of gods, it is not necessary to have recourse to metaphysical abstractions. It is sufficient to observe that the notion of more than one author of nature is inconsistent with that harmony of design which pervades her works; that it explains no appearances, is supported by no evidence, and serves no purpose but to embarrass and perplex our conceptions.

But I proceed to the more immediate object of this discourse, which, as has been already intimated, is not so much to evince the falsehood of skepticism as a theory, as to display its mischievous effects, contrasted with those which result from the belief of a Deity and a future state. The subject, viewed in this light, may be considered under two aspects; the influence of the opposite systems on the principles of morals and on the formation of character. The first may be styled their direct, the latter their equally important, but indirect, consequence and tendency.

I. The skeptical or irreligious system subverts the whole foundation of morals. It may be assumed as a maxim that no person can be required to act contrary to his greatest good, or his highest interest, comprehensively viewed in relation to the whole duration of his being. It is often our duty to forego our own interest *partially,* to sacrifice a smaller pleasure for the sake of a greater, to incur a present evil in pursuit of a distant good of more consequence. In a word, to arbitrate among interfering claims of inclination is the moral arithmetic of human life. But to risk the happiness of the whole duration of our being in any case whatever, were it possible, would be foolish; because the sacrifice must, by the nature of it, be so great as to preclude the possibility of compensation.

The system of infidelity is not only incapable of arming virtue for great and trying occasions, but leaves it unsupported in the most ordinary occurrences. In vain will its advocates appeal to a moral sense, to benevolence and sympathy; for it is undeniable that these impulses may be overcome. In vain will they expatiate on the tranquillity and pleasure attendant on a virtuous course: for though you may remind the offender that in disregarding them he has violated his nature, and that a conduct consistent with them is productive of much internal satisfaction; yet if he reply that his taste is of a different sort, that there are other gratifications which he values more, and that every man must choose his own pleasures, the argument is at an end.

II. Hitherto we have considered the influence of skepticism on the principles of virtue; and have endeavored to show that it despoils it of its dignity, and lays its authority in the dust. Its influence on the formation of character remains to be examined. The actions of men are oftener determined by their character than their interest: their conduct takes its color more from their acquired taste, inclinations, and habits, than from a deliberate regard to their greatest good. It is only on great occasions the mind awakes to take an extended survey of her whole course, and that she suffers the dictates of reason to impress a new bias upon her movements. The actions of each day are, for the most part, links which follow each other in the chain of custom. Hence the great effort of practical wisdom is to imbue the mind with right tastes, affections, and habits; the elements of character, and masters of action.

The exclusion of a Supreme Being and of a superintending Providence tends directly to the destruction of moral taste. It robs the universe of all finished and consummate excellence even in idea. The admiration of perfect wisdom and goodness for which we are formed, and which kindles such unspeakable rapture in the soul, finding in the regions of skepticism nothing to which it corresponds, droops and languishes. In a world which presents a fair spectacle of order and beauty, of a vast family nourished and supported by an Almighty Parent—in a world which leads the devout mind, step by step, to the contemplation of the first fair and the first good, the skeptic is encompassed with nothing but obscurity, meanness, and disorder.

Modern infidelity not only tends to corrupt the moral taste, it also promotes the growth of those vices which are the most hostile to social happiness. Of all the vices incident to human nature, the most destructive to society are vanity, ferocity, and unbridled sensuality; and these are precisely the vices which infidelity is calculated to cherish.

That the love, fear, and habitual contemplation of a Being infinitely exalted, or, in other words, devotion, is adapted to promote a sober and moderate estimate of our own excellences, is incontestable; nor is it less evident that the exclusion of such sentiments must be favorable to pride. The criminality of pride will, perhaps, be less readily admitted; for though there is no vice so opposite to the spirit of Christianity, yet there is none which, even in the Christian world, has, under various pretenses, been treated with so much indulgence.

As we have already shown that pride hardens the heart, and that religion is the only effectual antidote, the connection between irreligion and inhumanity is in this view obvious. But there is another light in which this part of the subject may be viewed, in my humble opinion, much more important, though seldom adverted to. The supposition that man is a moral and accountable being, destined to survive the stroke of death, and to live in a future world in a never-ending state of happiness or misery, makes him a creature of incomparably more *consequence* than the opposite supposition. When we consider him as placed here by an Almighty Ruler in a state of probation, and that the present life is his period of trial, the first link in a vast and interminable chain which stretches into eternity, he assumes a dignified character in our eyes. Every thing which relates to him becomes interesting; and to trifle with his happiness is felt to be the most unpardonable levity. If such be the destination of man, it is evident that in the qualities which fit him for it his principal dignity consists; his moral greatness is his true greatness. Let the skeptical principles be admitted, which represent him, on the contrary, as the offspring of chance, connected with no superior power, and sinking into annihilation at death, and he is a contemptible creature, whose existence and happiness are insignificant. The characteristic difference is lost between him and the brute creation, from which he is no longer distinguished, except by the vividness and multiplicity of his perceptions.

Having already shown that the principles of infidelity facilitate the commission of crimes, by removing the restraints of fear; and that they foster the arrogance of the individual, while they inculcate the most despicable opinion of the species; the inevitable result is, that a haughty self-confidence, a contempt of mankind, together with a daring defiance of religious restraints, are the natural ingredients of the atheistical character; nor is it less evident that these are, of all others, the dispositions which most forcibly stimulate to violence and cruelty.

Settle it therefore in your minds, as a maxim never to be effaced or forgotten, that atheism is an inhuman, bloody, ferocious system, equally hostile to every useful restraint and to every virtuous affection; that, leaving nothing above us to excite awe, nor round us to awaken tenderness, it wages war with heaven and with earth: its first object is to dethrone God, its next to destroy man.

Friedrich Schleiermacher

[1768–1834]

Born at Breslau, Germany, of a family of preachers, Friedrich Schleiermacher was educated at the academy of the Moravian brethren at Niesky and at Halle. During his lifetime he worked both as a teacher and preacher, and attracted much attention in both fields of endeavor. His influence upon German theological thinking of the early nineteenth century was great. Although most of Schleiermacher's sermons and writings were designed for the academic and educated classes, some, of which this sermon is an example, were universally appealing.

CHRIST'S RESURRECTION A PATTERN OF OUR NEW LIFE

Therefore we are buried with Him by baptism into death, that like as Christ was raised up from the dead by the glory of the Father, even so we also should walk in a new life. But if we have been planted together with Him to a like death, we shall be also like the resurrection. Knowing this that our old man is crucified with Him, that the body of sin might be destroyed, that henceforth we should not serve sin. For he that is dead is justified from sin. But if we be dead with Christ we believe that we shall also live with Him. ROMANS 6:4-8.

MY DEVOUT FRIENDS, it is natural that the glorious feast of the resurrection of our Redeemer should allure the thoughts of believers into the remote distance, and that they should now be glad in anticipation of the time when they shall be with Him, who, after He had risen from the dead, returned to His Father and our Father, as our united song just now was occupied with this joyful prospect. But in the words of our text the Apostle calls us back out of the distance into that which is near, into the immediate present of our life here below. He seizes on that which lies nearest us, that in which we should now share a part, and which should already in this world form us into the likeness of our Lord's resurrection. We are buried, he says, "with Him into death, that as He was raised through the glory of the Father, we also should walk in a new life." And this new life is that which, as our Lord Himself saith, "all those who believe in Him as having passed through death unto life, even now possess." This the Apostle compares with those glorious days of the resurrection of our Lord; and how could we keep this feast—a feast in which, above all, the greater part of Christians are wont to derive renewed strength for that new life from the most intimate communion with our heavenly Head—how could we keep this feast more worthily, than while we endeavor to appropriate to ourselves this truth which lies on the face of the Apostle's words? Let us, therefore, after this introduction, contemplate *the Life of the resurrection of our Lord,* according to the representations of the Apostles, *as a glorious,* though it may be an unattainable *pattern of the new life* in which we ought all to walk through Him.

This new life resembles that of the risen Redeemer, first, in *the manner of its origin.* In order that He might appear to His disciples in that state of transfiguration which contained in itself already the traces of the eternal and deathless glory, He must needs undergo the pains of death. It was no light transformation. He must not indeed see corruption, but yet must He suffer the shadow of death to pass over Him. Friends and foes vied with each other to hold Him back in the power of the grave, friends rolling the stone before it that the beloved corpse might remain unmarred, while foes set the watch over it lest it should be taken away.

But when the hour came which the Father had prescribed to His power, the angel of the Lord appeared and rolled the stone away from the grave, and the watch fled, and at the call of the Almighty life returned anew into the inanimate frame.

When the Saviour first appeared to Mary, He said to her, as if His new life were yet timid and sensitive, Touch me not; I am not yet ascended to My God and your God. But after a few days He presented Himself to Thomas and called upon him to feel of Him thoroughly, to thrust his hand into his Maker's side and put his fingers into the prints which the nails of the cross had left, so that He shrank not from contact with even the most sensitive parts. Even on the first day, and as if thereby to become well strengthened, we see Him wander from Jerusalem toward Emmaus, and from Emmaus back to Jerusalem again, and afterward going before His disciples into Galilee, and leading them back again to Jerusalem, where He then went up before their eyes into heaven. And while He thus walked among them, living with them in all respects after the manner of man, and influencing them in a human way, His chief business with them was to speak to them of the kingdom of God, to rebuke and stir up the slowness of their hearts, and open the eyes of their minds.

Oh that we might set the risen Saviour more and more steadfastly before our eyes! Oh that we might copy from Him that beatific, heavenly breath, by which He communicated of His Spirit to His disciples! Oh that we might learn like Him to animate the stupid and drowsy hearts to a happy belief in the Divine promises, to active obedience to the will of their Lord and Master, and to the cheerful enjoyment and use of all the heavenly treasures which He has laid open to us! Oh that we spoke with ever-increasing strength to all around us of the kingdom of God and our inheritance therein, that they might see wherefore Christ must suffer, but also into what glory He has entered. So we wish, not with empty wishes! The vivifying Spirit which He has acquired for us, worketh all this in every one according to the measure which pleaseth Him; and when once the life from God is kindled in the soul of man, when once, as the Apostle says, we have become like His resurrection, oh then His powers also evince themselves, through the operations of His Spirit in us, more and more richly and gloriously for the general good.

Not at all as if we ought to practice a secret and exclusive way of life, and those only who have had quite similar experiences should form narrow circles by themselves, for even the days of the resurrection furnish us the example of diversified experiences and of an inner fellowship connected therewith. Not only so; for even those who have no experience at all of this life go not empty away. Only must they first of themselves become conscious, without our pressing it upon them, that here breathes a spirit to which they are strangers, that here a life is revealed of which they have known nothing. Then will we, as was done then, lead them by the word of our testimony to the ground of this new life, and as at that time, when the preached word pierced the heart, when to some the old man began to appear in his true light, and they felt the first pains which precede the death of the sinful man, as to them then arose the faith in the resurrection of Him whom they had crucified, so will it ever be with the recognition of the new life proceeding from Him who rose again. Therefore will we not be anxious; continually will the circle widen of those who perceive this life because they begin to share in it. And no sooner does the slightest suspicion of this arise in the soul of man, no sooner does the perishing and corrupt nature of this world cease to please and satisfy him, no sooner does his soul drink in the first beams of the heavenly light, than his eyes are opened and he feels what a different thing it is to serve righteousness from living in the bondage of sin.

But finally, my good friends, we can not thus feel all that is comfortable and glorious in the likeness of our new life to the resurrection of our Lord, without at the same time being touched with sadness at another aspect of this resemblance. For when we put together all which the evangelists and apostles of the Lord have preserved to us concerning the life of His resurrection, we still are not enabled to form from it the conception of a coherent, complete, and *thoroughly self-consistent existence.* There are separate moments and hours, particular conversations and transactions, when the risen One is lost to the inquiring gaze. In vain do we ask where He tarries, we must wait till He appears again. Not as if it had been so in itself, but for us, my good friends, it is so, and can not be otherwise, and we vainly strive to penetrate into the intervals of these scattered moments and hours. What then? Is not the case of the new life which resembles Christ's resurrection the same? Not at all as if it were limited to the glorious, surely, and beneficent, but still infrequent hours of public worship and devotion, for then we should have reason to fear that it was only a delusion; not as if it were limited to the few and scattered deeds, visible and tangible, so to speak, to the surrounding world, which we perform, each in his measure, through the gifts of the Spirit, for the kingdom of God, but in manifold other ways are we conscious of this new life, there is many a stiller and more secret moment when it acts powerfully, though deep within.

Still it remains true, and I think all, without exception, must confess that we are by no means conscious to ourselves of this new life as an entirely continuous existence. Too often it is lost to each of us, not only amid the joys, the distractions and cares, but also amid the commendable occupations of this world. This experience, however, my good friends.

humiliating though it be, should not make us unbelieving, as if perhaps the consciousness that we are a new creature in Christ Jesus were a deception, and what we have regarded as expressions of this life only morbid and extravagant excitement. As the Lord convinced His disciples that He had flesh and bones, so can we also convince, each one himself, and mutually convince each other, that this is a real, active life. If so, we must believe too, that even when hidden and unconscious, it still always exists, as the Lord always existed, and even at the time when He was lost to His disciples had neither returned into the grave, nor yet ascended to heaven.

But let us not overlook this difference. In Christ we do not conceive of it as something natural and necessary that during those forty days He should only lead a life in appearance so broken, while perhaps every one must understand that since the influences of this new life can only by degrees become perceptible in our outward conduct, it should often and for a length of time be quite hidden from us, and especially when we are occupied with our outward doings, and have our attention fixed on them. Still this remains an imperfection, and we should, as we go on, become more and more free from it. Let us, therefore, my good friends, ever anew resort to Him who is the fountain of this new spirit and life! Then shall we find it, though we find it not in ourselves; oh! we find it always with Him, and always afresh it streams forth from Him the Head, to us His members. If every moment in which we do not perceive it, is, when once we become conscious of its absence, a moment of longing, oh, so is it a moment in which the risen Saviour appears to our soul, and breathes on us anew with His quickening power. And thus while drawing only from Him, we ought to come where His heavenly gift in us may constantly grow to be a never-failing, an always-gushing and bubbling fountain of spiritual and eternal life. To this end is He risen from the dead, through the glory of the Father, that we may become like His resurrection. That ended in His return to the Father; our new life should ever more become His and the Father's return into the depths of our affections; there should they both make their abode; and evermore continuous, evermore active and powerful should the life from God in us become, that our life in the service of righteousness may even here, according to the promise of the Lord, be and remain an eternal life.

Thomas Chalmers

[1780–1847]

Thomas Chalmers was one of the founders of the Free Church of Scotland. He was born at Anstruthers, near St. Andrews, and while at the University of St. Andrews won honors in literature and science. Ordained when only 23, he soon became famous for his eloquence and profundity of thought. In 1824 he was called to the chair of Moral Philosophy at the University of St. Andrews, and four years later was made Professor of Theology at Edinburgh University. The following sermon has been pronounced by many as Chalmers' masterpiece. It reveals the beauty and strength of expression which characterize his best work.

THE EXPULSIVE POWER OF A NEW AFFECTION

Love not the world, neither the things that are in the world. If any man love the world, the love of the Father is not in him. I JOHN 2:15.

THERE ARE two ways in which a practical moralist may attempt to displace from the human heart its love of the world—either by a demonstration of the world's vanity, so as that the heart shall be prevailed upon simply to withdraw its regards from an object that is not worthy of it; or, by setting forth another object, even God, as more worthy of its attachment; so as that the heart shall be prevailed upon, not to resign an old affection which shall have nothing to succeed it, but to exchange an old affection for a new one. My purpose is to show, that from the constitution of our nature, the former method is altogether incompetent and ineffectual—and that the latter method will alone suffice for the rescue and recovery of the heart from the wrong affection that domineers over it. After having accomplished this purpose, I shall attempt a few practical observations.

Love may be regarded in two different conditions. The first is, when its object is at a distance, and then it becomes love in a state of desire. The second is, when its object is in possession, and then it becomes love in a state of indulgence. Under the impulse of desire, man feels himself urged onward in some path or pursuit of activity for its gratification. The faculties of his mind are put into busy exercise. In the steady direction of one great and engrossing interest, his attention is recalled from the many reveries into which it might otherwise have wandered; and the powers of his body are forced away from an indolence in which it else might have languished; and that time is crowded with occupation, which but for some object of keen and devoted ambition, might have driveled along in successive hours of weariness and distaste—and though hope does not always enliven, and success does not always crown this career of exertion, yet in the midst of this very variety, and with the alternations of occasional disappointment, is the machinery of the whole man kept in a sort of congenial play, and upholden in that tone and temper which are most agreeable to it.

The ascendant power of a second affection will do, what no exposition, however forcible, of the folly and worthlessness of the first, ever could effectuate. And it is the same in the great world. You never will be able to arrest any of its leading pursuits, by a naked demonstration of their vanity. It is quite in vain to think of stopping one of these pursuits in any way else, but by stimulating to another. In attempting to bring a worthy man, intent and busied with the prosecution of his objects, to a dead stand, you have not merely to encounter the charm which he annexes to these objects—but you have to encounter the pleasure which he feels in the very prosecution of them. It is not enough, then, that you dissipate the charm, by your moral, and eloquent, and affecting exposure of its illusiveness. You must address to the eye of his mind another object, with a charm powerful enough to dispossess the first of its influence, and to engage him in some other prosecution as full of interest, and hope, and congenial activity, as the former. It is this which stamps an impotency on all moral and pathetic declamation about the insignificance of the world.

These remarks apply not merely to love considered in its state of desire for an object not yet obtained. They apply also to love considered in its state of indulgence, or placid gratification, with an object already in possession. It is seldom that any of our tastes are made to disappear by a mere process of natural extinction. At least, it is very seldom that this is done through the instrumentality of reasoning. It may be done by excessive pampering—but it is almost never done by the mere force of mental determination. But what can not be thus destroyed, may be dispossessed—and one taste may be made to give way to another, and to lose its power entirely as the reigning affection of the mind.

It will now be seen, perhaps, why it is that the heart keeps by its present affections with so much tenacity—when the attempt is to do them away by a mere process of extirpation. It will not consent to be so desolated. The strong man, whose dwelling-place is there, may be compelled to give way to another occupier—but unless another stronger than he, has power to dispossess and to succeed him, he will keep his present lodgment inviolable. The heart would revolt against its own emptiness. It could not bear to be so left in a state of waste and cheerless insipidity. The moralist who tries such a process of dispossession as this upon the heart is thwarted at every step by the recoil of its own mechanism. You have all heard that Nature abhors a vacuum. Such at least is the nature of the heart, that though the room which is in it may change one inmate for another, it can not be left void without pain of most intolerable suffering. It is not enough then to argue the folly of an existing affection. It is not enough, in the terms of a forcible or an affecting demonstration, to make good the evanescence of its object. It may not even be enough to associate the threats and terrors of some coming vengeance, with the indulgence of it. The heart may still resist the every application, by obedience to which it would finally be conducted to a state so much at war with all its appetites as that of downright inanition. So to tear away an affection from the heart, as to leave it bare of all its regards, and of all its preferences, were a hard and hopeless undertaking—and it would appear as if the alone powerful engine of dispossession, were to bring the mastery of another affection to bear upon it.

The love of the world can not be expunged by a mere demonstration of the world's worthlessness. But may it not be supplanted by the love of that which is more worthy than itself? The heart can not be prevailed upon to part with the world, by a simple act of resignation. But may not the heart be prevailed upon to admit into its preference another, who shall subordinate the world, and bring it down from its wonted ascendency? If the throne which is placed there, must have an occupier, and the tyrant that now reigns has occupied it wrongfully, he may not leave a bosom which would rather detain him, than be left in desolation. But may he not give way to the lawful sovereign, appearing with every charm that can secure his willing admittance, and taking unto Himself His great power to subdue the moral nature of man, and to reign over it? In a word, if the way to disengage the heart from the positive love of one great and ascendant object, is to fasten it in positive love to another, then it is not by exposing the worthlessness of the former, but by addressing to the mental eye the worth and excellence of the latter, that all old things are to be done away, and all things are to become new.

This, we trust, will explain the operation of that charm which accompanies the effectual preaching of the Gospel. The love of God, and the love of the world, are two affections, not merely in a state of rivalship, but in a state of enmity—and that so irreconcilable, that they can not dwell together in the same bosom. We have already affirmed how impossible it were for the heart, by any innate elasticity of its own, to cast the world away from it, and thus reduce itself to a wilderness. The heart is not so constituted, and the only way to dispossess it of an old affection, is by the expulsive power of a new one. Nothing can exceed the magnitude of the required change in a man's character—

when bidden as he is in the New Testament, to love not the world; no, nor any of the things that are in the world—for this so comprehends all that is dear to him in existence, as to be equivalent to a command of self-annihilation. But the same revelation which dictates so mighty an obedience, places within our reach as mighty an instrument of obedience. It brings for admittance, to the very door of our heart, an affection which, once seated upon its throne, will either subordinate every previous inmate, or bid it away. Beside the world, it places before the eye of the mind, Him who made the world, and with this peculiarity, which is all its own—that in the Gospel do we so behold God, as that we may love God. It is there, and there only, where God stands revealed as an object of confidence to sinners—and where our desire after Him is not chilled into apathy, by that barrier of human guilt which intercepts every approach that is not made to Him through the appointed Mediator. It is the bringing in of this better hope, whereby we draw nigh unto God—and to live without hope, is to live without God, and if the heart be without God, the world will then have all the ascendency. It is God apprehended by the believer as God in Christ, who alone can dispost it from this ascendency. It is when He stands dismantled of the terrors which belong to Him as an offended lawgiver, and when we are enabled by faith, which is His own gift, to see His glory in the face of Jesus Christ, and to hear His beseeching voice, as it protests good-will to men, and entreats the return of all who will to a full pardon, and a gracious acceptance—it is then, that a love paramount to the love of the world, and at length expulsive of it, first arises in the regenerating bosom. It is when released from the spirit of bondage, with which love can not dwell, and when admitted into the number of God's children, through the faith that is in Christ Jesus, the spirit of adoption is poured upon us— it is then that the heart, brought under the mastery of one great and predominant affection, is delivered from the tyranny of its former desires, and in the only way in which deliverance is possible.

John Henry Newman

[1801–1890]

When it was known that John Henry Newman would preach at St. Mary's Church, the young men of Oxford crowded into its pews. Such was the power of the preacher over the students of that great university. In 1846, after spending his early ministry in the Anglican church, Newman left Oxford and entered the Roman Catholic Church, where he rose to the office of Cardinal. This Easter sermon reveals the simple excellence of Newman's style, the lack of rhetorical tricks, and the intense quality of his preaching.

THE THREE OFFICES OF CHRIST

Full of grace are Thy lips, because God hath blessed Thee for ever. Gird Thee with Thy sword upon Thy thigh, O Thou most mighty, according to Thy worship and renown. PSALM 45:2, 3.

OUR LORD is here spoken of in two distinct characters. As a teacher,—"Full of grace are Thy lips"; and as a conqueror,—"Gird Thee with Thy Sword upon Thy thigh"; or, in other words, as a Prophet and as a King. His third special office, which is brought before us prominently at this season, is that of a Priest, in that He offered Himself up to God the Father as a propitiation for our sins. These are the three chief views which are vouchsafed to us of His Mediatorial office; and it is often observed that none before Him has, even in type or resemblance, borne all three characters. Melchizedek, for instance, was a priest and a king, but not a prophet. David was prophet and king, but not a priest. Jeremiah was priest and prophet, but not a king. Christ was Prophet, Priest, and King.

He is spoken of as a prophet by Moses, as a prophet like, but superior, to himself.—"A Prophet shall the Lord your God raise up unto you of your brethren, like unto me; Him shall ye hear." And Jacob had already described Him as a king, when he said, "Unto Him shall the gathering of the people be." Balaam, too, speaks of Him as a conqueror and great sovereign—"There shall come a Star out of Jacob, and a sceptre shall rise out of Israel . . . Out of Jacob shall come He that shall have dominion." And David foretells Him as a priest, but not a priest like Aaron—"Thou art a Priest for ever after the order of Melchizedek"; that is, a royal priest, which Aaron was not. And again, the very first prophecy of all ran, "He shall bruise thy head (that is, the serpent's) and thou shalt bruise His heel." He was to conquer through suffering.

Christ exercised His prophetical office in teaching, and in foretelling the future;—in His sermon on the Mount, in His parables, in His prophecy of the destruction of Jerusalem. He performed the priest's service when He died on the Cross, as a sacrifice; and when He consecrated the bread and the cup to be a feast upon that sacrifice; and now that He intercedes for us at the right hand of God. And He showed Himself as a conqueror, and a king, in rising from the dead, in ascending into heaven, in sending down the Spirit of grace, in converting the nations, and in forming His Church to receive and to rule them.

Further, let it be observed, that these three offices seem to contain in them and to represent the three principal conditions of mankind; for one large class of men, or aspect of mankind, is that of sufferers,— such as slaves, the oppressed, the poor, the sick, the bereaved, the troubled in mind; another is, of those who work and toil, who are full of business and engagements, whether for themselves or for others; and a third is that of the studious, learned, and wise. Endurance, active life, thought,—these are the three perhaps principal states in which men find themselves. Christ undertook them all. On one occasion He said, with reference to His baptism in Jordan, "Thus it becometh us to fulfil all righteousness." Every holy rite of the law did He go through for our sakes. And so too did He live through all states of man's life up to a perfect man, infancy, childhood, boyhood, youth, maturity, that He might be a pattern of them all. And so too did He take man's perfect nature on Him, body, and soul, and reason, that He might sanctify it wholly. And in like manner did He unite in Himself, and renew, and give us back in Him, the principal lots or states in which we find ourselves,—suffering, that we might know how to suffer; labouring, that we might know how to labour; and teaching, that we might know how to teach.

Thus, when our Lord came on earth in our nature, He combined together offices and duties most dissimilar. He suffered, yet He triumphed. He thought and spoke, yet He acted. He was humble and despised, yet He was a teacher. He has at once a life of hardship like the shepherds, yet is wise and royal as the eastern sages who came to do honour to His birth.

And it will be observed, moreover, that in these offices He also represents to us the Holy Trinity; for in His own proper character He is a priest, and as to His kingdom He has it from the Father, and as to His prophetical office He exercises it by the Spirit. The Father is the King, the Son the Priest, and the Holy Ghost the Prophet.

And further this may be observed, that when Christ had thus given a pattern in Himself of such contrary modes of life, and their contrary excellences, all in one, He did not, on His going away, altogether withdraw the wonderful spectacle; but He left behind Him those who should take His place, a ministerial order, who are His representatives and instruments; and they, though earthen vessels, show forth according to their measure these three characters,—the prophetical, priestly, and regal, combining in themselves qualities and functions which, except under the Gospel, are almost incompatible the one with the other. He consecrated His Apostles to suffer, when He said, "Ye shall drink indeed of My cup, and be baptized with My Baptism"; to teach, when He said, "The Comforter, which is the Holy Ghost, He shall teach you all things"; and to rule, when He said to them, "I appoint unto you a kingdom, as My Father hath appointed unto Me; that ye may eat and drink at My table in My kingdom, and sit on thrones, judging the twelve tribes of Israel."

There is "a time to keep silence, and a time to speak." So in season He spoke, and then He was a Prophet. In season He opened His mouth and said, "Blessed are the poor in spirit"; and so with the other beatitudes upon the Mount. "In Him are hid all the treasures of wisdom and knowledge"; "Full of grace are His lips, because God hath blessed Him for ever." He not only commands, He persuades. He tempers His awful deeds, He explains His sufferings, by His soothing words. "The Lord hath given unto Him the tongue of the learned, that He may be able to speak a word in season to him that is weary." And when He began to teach, "all men marvelled at the gracious words which proceeded out of His mouth." He taught them "as one having authority." David, himself a prophet and king, a man of sacred song, though a man of blood, had shown beforehand what kind of ruler the promised Christ must be;—"He that ruleth over men must be just, ruling in the fear of God; and He shall be as the light of the morning." And Moses before him, another ruler of God's people: "My doctrine shall drop as the rain, my speech shall distil as the dew; as the small rain upon the tender herb, and as the showers upon the grass." And hence it was said of the Saviour to come, "He shall not strive nor cry, neither shall any hear His voice in the streets; a bruised reed shall He not break, and smoking flax shall He not quench, till He send forth judgment unto victory." Hence such stress is laid in the Prophets on His being a Just God and a Saviour; on "righteousness and peace kissing each other;" on "righteousness being the girdle of His loins, and faithfulness the girdle of His reins." Such is the Divine Prophet of the Church, the Interpreter of secrets, ruling not like conquerors of the earth, but by love; not by fear, not by strength of arm, but by wisdom of heart, convincing, persuading, enlightening, founding an empire upon faith, and ruling by a sovereignty over the conscience. And such, too, has been the rule of His servants after Him. They have been weak personally, without armies, without strongholds, naked, defenceless, yet sovereigns, because they were preachers and teachers, because they appealed to the reason and the conscience; and strange to say, though the arm of force seems as if it could do all things, this sovereignty of mind is higher, and the strong and the noble quail before it.

Christ came to make a new world. He came into the world to regenerate it in Himself, to make a new beginning, to be the beginning of the creation of God, to gather together in one, and recapitulate all things in Himself. The rays of His glory were scattered through the world; one state of life had some of them, another others. The world was like some fair mirror, broken in pieces, and giving back no one uniform image of its Maker. But He came to combine what was dissipated, to recast what was shattered in Himself. He began all excellence, and of His fulness have all we received. When He came, a Child was born, a Son given, and yet He was Wonderful, Counsellor, the Mighty God, the Everlasting Father, the Prince of Peace. Angels heralded a Saviour, a Christ, a Lord; but withal, He was "born in Bethehem," and was "lying in a manger." Eastern sages brought Him gold, for that He was a King, frankincense as to a God; but on the other hand myrrh also, in token of a coming death and burial. At the last, He "bore witness to the truth" before Pilate as a Prophet, suffered on the cross as our Priest, while He was also "Jesus of Nazareth, the King of the Jews."

And so His Apostles after Him, and in His likeness, were kings, yet without the pomp; soldiers, yet with no blood but their own; teachers, yet withal their own disciples, acting out in their own persons, and by their own labours, their own precepts.

And so, in aftertimes, those Saints and Fathers to whom we look up, have joined these three offices together. Great doctors they have been, but not mere philosophers or men of letters, but noble-minded rulers of the churches; nor only so, but preachers, missionaries, monastic brethren, confessors, and martyrs. This is the glory of the Church, to speak, to do, and to suffer, with that grace which Christ brought and diffused abroad. And it has run down even to the skirts of her clothing. Not the few and the conspicuous alone, but all her children, high and low, who walk worthy of her and her Divine Lord, will be shadows of Him. All of us are bound, according to our opportunities,—first to learn the truth; and moreover, we must not only know, but we must impart our knowledge. Nor only so, but next we must bear witness to the truth. We must not be afraid of the frowns or anger of the world, or mind its ridicule. If so be, we must be willing to suffer for the truth. This was that new thing that Christ brought into the world, a heavenly doctrine, a system of holy and supernatural truths, which are to be received and transmitted, for He is our Prophet, maintained even unto suffering after His pattern, who is our Priest, and obeyed, for He is our King.

Horace Bushnell

[1802–1876]

While still a student at Yale University, Horace Bushnell won a victory of faith over doubt. But he remained a true skeptic throughout his life, seeking a proof for everything. He spent his active ministry in a Congregational church in Hartford, Connecticut, where he exercised a tremendous influence upon the civic life of the community. A thinker first and foremost, the results of his thinking took the form of a simple, homespun religion. His sermons show an ability to use the vernacular of the people and to translate the great works of religion into language understandable to everyone. In this way he was able to make religion vital to the crowds which came to listen to him each Sunday.

EVERY MAN'S LIFE A PLAN OF GOD

I girded thee, though thou has not known me. ISAIAH 45:5.

CHRIST HIMSELF testifies to the girding of the Almighty, when He says,—"To this end was I born, and for this purpose came I into the world." Abraham was girded for a particular work and mission, in what is otherwise denominated his call. Joseph, in Egypt, distinguishes the girding of God's hand, when he comforts his guilty brothers in the assurance, —"So, it was not you that sent me hither, but God." Moses and Samuel were even called by name, and set to their great life-work, in the same manner. And what is Paul endeavoring, in all the stress and pressure of his mighty apostleship, but to perform the work for which God's Spirit girded him at his call, and to apprehend that for which he was apprehended of Christ Jesus. And yet these great master-spirits of the world are not so much distinguished, after all, by the acts they do, as by the sense itself of some mysterious girding of the Almighty upon them, whose behests they are set on to fulfill. And all men may have this; for the humblest and commonest have a place and a work assigned them, in the same manner, and have it for their privilege to be always ennobled in the same lofty consciousness. God is girding every man for a place and a calling, in which, taking it from Him, even though it be internally humble, he may be as consciously exalted as if he held the rule of a kingdom. The truth I propose then for your consideration is this,—

That God has a definite life-plan for every human person, girding him, visibly or invisibly, for some exact thing, which it will be the true significance and glory of his life to have accomplished.

The Holy Scriptures seem to be holding up the dignity of common life, and giving a meaning to its appointments, which the natural dullness and lowness of mere human opinion can not apprehend.

They not only show us explicitly, as we have seen, that God has a definite purpose in the lives of men already great, but they show us, how frequently, in the conditions of obscurity and depression, preparations of counsel going on, by which the commonest offices are to become the necessary first chapter of a great and powerful history.

Besides, what do the scriptures show us, but that God has a particular care for every man, a personal interest in him and a sympathy with him and his trials, watching for the uses of his one talent as attentively and kindly and approving him as heartily, in the right employment of it, as if He had given him ten; and, what is the giving out of the talents itself, but an exhibition of the fact that God has a definite purpose, charge and work, be it this or that, for every man?

They also make it the privilege of every man to live in the secret guidance of God; which is plainly nugatory, unless there is some chosen work, or sphere, into which he may be guided; for how shall God guide him, having nothing appointed or marked out for him to be guided into? no field opened for him, no course set down which is to be his wisdom?

God also professes in His Word to have purposes pre-arranged for all events; to govern by a plan which is from eternity even, and which, in some proper sense, comprehends every thing. And what is this but another way of conceiving that God has a definite place and plan adjusted for every human being? And, without such a plan, He could not even govern the world intelligently, or make a proper universe of the created system; for it becomes a universe only in the grand unity of reason, which includes it. Otherwise, it were only a jumble of fortuities, without counsel, end or law.

Turning, now, from the scriptures to the works of God, how constantly are we met here by the fact, everywhere visible, that ends and uses are the regulative reasons of all existing things. This we discover often, when we are least able to understand the speculative mystery of objects; for it is precisely the *uses* of things that are most palpable. These uses are to God, no doubt, as to us, the significance of His works. And they compose, taken together, a grand reciprocal system, in which part answers actively to part, constructing thus an all-comprehensive and glorious whole. And the system is, in fact, so perfect, that the loss or displacement of any member would fatally derange the general order.

There is, then, I conclude, a definite and proper end, or issue, for every man's existence; an end, which, to the heart of God, is the good intended for him, or for which he was intended; that which he is privileged to become, called to become, ought to become; that which God will assist him to become and which he can not miss, save by his own fault.

But there is, I must add, a single, but very important and even fearful qualification. Things all serve their uses, and never break out of their place. They have no power to do it. Not so with us. We are able, as free beings, to refuse the place and the duties God appoints; which, if we do, then we sink into something lower and less worthy of us.

That highest and best condition for which God designed us is no more possible. We are fallen out of it, and it can not be wholly recovered. And yet, as that was the best thing possible for us in the reach of God's original counsel, so there is a place designed for us now, which is the next best possible. God calls us now to the best thing left, and will do so till all good possibility is narrowed down and spent. And then, when He can not use us any more for our own good, He will use us for the good of others,—an example of the misery and horrible desperation to which any soul must come, when all the good ends, and all the holy callings of God's friendly and fatherly purpose are exhausted. Or it may be now that, remitting all other plans and purposes in our behalf, He will henceforth use us, wholly against our will, to be the demonstration of His justice and avenging power before the eyes of mankind; saying over us, as He did over Pharaoh in the day of his judgments, "Even for this same purpose have I raised thee up, that I might show My power in thee, and that My name might be declared throughout all the earth." Doubtless, He had other and more genial plans to serve in this bad man, if only he could have accepted such; but, knowing his certain rejection of these, God turned His mighty counsel in him wholly on the use to be made of him as a reprobate. How many Pharaohs in common life refuse every other use God will make of them, choosing only to figure, in their small way, as reprobates; and descending, in that manner, to a fate that painfully mimics his.

It follows, in the same way, that, as God, in fixing on our end or use, will choose the best end or use possible, so He will appoint for us the best manner possible of attaining it; for, as it is a part of God's perfection to choose the best things, and not things partially good, so it will be in all the methods He prescribes for their attainment. And so, as you pass on, stage by stage, in your courses of experience, it is made clear to you that, whatever you have laid upon you to do or to suffer, whatever to want, whatever to surrender or to conquer, is exactly best for you. Your life is a school, exactly adapted to your lesson, and that to the best, last end of your existence.

No room for a discouraged or depressed feeling, therefore, is left you. Enough that you exist for a purpose high enough to give meaning to life, and to support a genuine inspiration. If your sphere is outwardly humble, if it even appears to be quite insignificant, God understands it better than you do, and it is a part of His wisdom to bring out great sentiments in humble conditions, great principles in works that are outwardly trivial, great characters under great adversities and heavy loads of incumbrance. The tallest saints of God will often be those who walk in the deepest obscurity, and are even despised or quite overlooked by man.

The following sermon has been referred to as one of the best examples of preaching that America has produced. It is typical Bushnell, the scholar and the vigorous preacher. Here the spirit that was in the man burns brightly and his clear, timely insight is coupled with a penetrating understanding of the mainsprings of human action.

UNCONSCIOUS INFLUENCE

Then went in also that other disciple. JOHN 20:8.

IN THIS slight touch or turn of history, is opened to us, if we scan it closely, one of the most serious and fruitful chapters of Christian doctrine. Thus it is that men are ever touching unconsciously the springs of motion in each other; thus it is that one man, without thought or intention, or even a consciousness of the fact, is ever leading some other after him. Little does Peter think, as he comes up where his doubting brother is looking into the sepulchre, and goes straight in, after his peculiar manner, that he is drawing in his brother apostle after him. As little does John think, when he loses his misgivings, and goes into the sepulchre after Peter, that he is following his brother. And just so, unawares to himself, is every man, the whole race through, laying hold of his fellow-man, to lead him where otherwise he would not go. We overrun the boundaries of our personality—we flow together. A Peter leads a John, a John goes after a Peter, both of them unconscious of any influence exerted or received. And thus our life and conduct are ever propagating themselves, by a law of social contagion, throughout the circles and times in which we live.

There are, then, you will perceive, two sorts of influence belonging to man; that which is active or voluntary, and that which is unconscious;— that which we exert purposely or in the endeavor to sway another, as by teaching, by argument, by persuasion, by threatenings, by offers and promises,—and that which flows out from us, unawares to ourselves, the same which Peter had over John when he led him into the sepulchre. The importance of our efforts to do good, that is of our voluntary influence, and the sacred obligation we are under to exert ourselves in this way, are often and seriously insisted on. It is thus that Christianity has become, in the present age, a principle of so much greater activity than it has been for many centuries before; and we fervently hope that it will yet become far more active than it now is, nor cease to multiply its industry, till it is seen by all mankind to embody the beneficence and the living energy of Christ himself.

In the prosecution of my design, let me ask of you, first of all, to expel the common prejudice that there can be nothing of consequence in unconscious influences, because they make no report, and fall on the

world unobserved. Histories and biographies make little account of
the power men exert insensibly over each other. They tell how men
have led armies, established empires, enacted laws, gained causes, sung,
reasoned, and taught;—always occupied in setting forth what they do
with a purpose. But what they do without a purpose, the streams of influence that flow out from their persons unbidden on the world, they can
not trace or compute, and seldom even mention. So also the public laws
make men responsible only for what they do with a positive purpose,
and take no account of the mischiefs or benefits that are communicated,
by their noxious or healthful example. The same is true in the discipline
of families, churches, and schools; they make no account of the things
we do, except we will them. What we do insensibly passes for nothing,
because no human government can trace such influences with sufficient
certainty to make their authors responsible.

I call your attention, next, to the twofold powers of effect and expression by which man connects with his fellow man. If we distinguish
man as a creature of language, and thus qualified to communicate himself to others, there are in him two sets or kinds of language, one which
is voluntary in the use, and one that is involuntary; that of speech in
the literal sense, and that expression of the eye, the face, the look, the
gait, the motion, the tone or cadence, which is sometimes called the
natural language of the sentiments. This natural language, too, is greatly
enlarged by the conduct of life, that which, in business and society, reveals the principles and spirit of men. Speech, or voluntary language,
is a door to the soul, that we may open or shut at will; the other is
a door that stands open evermore, and reveals to others constantly and
often very clearly, the tempers, tastes, and motives of their hearts. Within,
as we may represent, is character, charging the common reservoir of
influence, and through these twofold gates of the soul, pouring itself
out on the world. Out of one it flows at choice, and whensoever we
purpose to do good or evil to men. Out of the other it flows each moment, as light from the sun, and propagates itself in all beholders.

Then if we go over to others, that is, to the subjects of influence,
we find every man endowed with two inlets of impression; the ear and
the understanding for the reception of speech, and the sympathetic
powers, the sensibilities or affections, for tinder to those sparks of
emotion revealed by looks, tones, manners, and general conduct. And
these sympathetic powers, though not immediately rational, are yet inlets,
open on all sides, to the understanding and character. They have a
certain wonderful capacity to receive impressions, and catch the meaning
of signs, and propagate in us whatsoever falls into their passive molds,
from others. The impressions they receive do not come through verbal
propositions, and are never received into verbal proposition, it may be,

in the mind, and therefore many think nothing of them. But precisely on this account are they the more powerful, because it is as if one heart were thus going directly into another, and carrying in its feelings with it. Beholding, as in a glass, the feelings of our neighbor, we are changed into the same image, by the assimilating power of sensibility and fellow-feeling. Many have gone so far, and not without show, at least, of reason, as to maintain that the look or expression, and even the very features of children, are often changed, by exclusive intercourse with nurses and attendants. Furthermore, if we carefully consider, we shall find it scarcely possible to doubt, that simply to look on bad and malignant faces, or those whose expressions have become infected by vice, to be with them and become familiarized to them, is enough permanently to affect the character of persons of mature age. I do not say that it must of necessity subvert their character, for the evil looked upon may never be loved or welcomed in practice; but it is something to have these bad images in the soul, giving out their expressions there, and diffusing their odor among the thoughts, as long as we live. How dangerous a thing is it, for example, for a man to become accustomed to sights of cruelty? What man, valuing the honor of his soul, would not shrink from yielding himself to such an influence? No more is it a thing of indifference to become accustomed to look on the manners, and receive the bad expression of any kind of sin.

The true philosophy or method of doing good is, first of all and principally, to be good—to have a character that will of itself communicate good. There must and will be active effort where there is goodness of principle; but the latter we should hold to be the principal thing, the root and life of all. Whether it is a mistake more sad or more ridiculous, to make mere stir synonymous with doing good, we need not inquire; enough, to be sure that one who has taken up such a notion of doing good, is for that reason a nuisance to the church. The Christian is called a light, not lightning. In order to act with effect on others, he must walk in the Spirit, and thus become the image of goodness: he must be so akin to God, and so filled with His dispositions, that he shall seem to surround himself with a hallowed atmosphere. It is folly to endeavor to make ourselves shine before we are luminous. If the sun without His beams should talk to the planets, and argue with them till the final day, it would not make them shine; there must be light in the sun itself, and then they will shine, of course. And this, my brethren, is what God intends for you all. It is the great idea of His gospel, and the work of His spirit, to make you lights in the world. His greatest joy is to give you character, to beautify your example, to exalt your principles, and make you each the depository of His own almighty grace. But in order to do this, some thing is necessary on your part—a full surrender of your mind to duty and to God, and a perpetual desire of this spiritual intimacy; having this, having a participation thus of the goodness of God, you will as naturally communicate good as the sun communicates his beams.

Have you not already felt, my brethren, the application to which I would bring you? We do not exonerate ourselves; we do not claim to be nearer to God or holier than you; but ah! you know not how easy it is to make a winter about us, or how cold it feels! Our endeavor is to preach the truth of Christ and His cross as clearly and as forcibly as we can. Sometimes it has a visible effect, and we are filled with joy; sometimes it has no effect, and then we struggle on, as we must, but under great oppression. Have we none among you that preach against us in your lives? If we show you the light of God's truth, does it never fall on banks of ice; which if the light shines through, the crystal masses are yet as cold as before? We do not accuse you; that we leave to God, and to those who may rise up in the last day to testify against you. If they shall come out of your own families; if they are the children that wear your names, the husband or wife of your affections; if they declare that you, by your example, kept them away from Christ's truth and mercy, we may have accusations to meet of our own and we leave you to acquit yourselves as best you may. I only warn you, here, of the guilt which our Lord Jesus Christ will impute to them that hinder his gospel.

Richard Chenevix Trench

[1807–1886]

Richard Chenevix Trench was born in Dublin, and was educated at Harrow, Trinity College, and at Cambridge. He was ordained a priest in 1835, and after a brilliant career as preacher in several noted parishes, he became Archbishop of Dublin. Trench was a scholar, writer, preacher, and one of the most noted church executives ever to occupy the famous see of Dublin. His art lay in a remarkable ability to use vivid images, as is evident in the following sermon. Here he takes a simple idea and draws from it lessons of the most profound import.

THE COATS OF SKINS

Unto Adam also and to his wife did the Lord God make coats of skins, and clothed them. Genesis 3:21.

Our first parents, so long as they stood in their original uprightness, were clothed with their own innocency as with a garment, and needed no other. But shame followed close on sin, and under the influence of this shame they proceeded to make *for themselves* such coverings as they could, yet such as they were conscious themselves to be slight and insufficient; and in proof that they felt them so, when they heard the voice of the Lord God calling them in the garden they were afraid, because, in Adam's own words, they were naked, and they went and hid themselves from Him. But now being drawn from their hiding-place, and having received from the mouth of their Judge at once the sentence of death and the sentence of life, the Lord God proceeds Himself to do for them what they had vainly attempted to do for themselves,—to make clothing for them, such as shall be indeed effectual, such as shall enable them to endure his else intolerable eye. This, however, He can only do at the cost of a life. Some harmless beast, which would never have died if they had not sinned, must perish, and perish by God's immediate decree and act, that they may be clothed; that its covering may henceforth be their covering, in which they may not be ashamed to appear before God.

Is not, I ask you, the whole mystery of our justification wrapped up in these most precious details? Have we not here a clear prophecy of the Lamb slain, to the end that the righteousness which was His might become ours? Trace it through all its steps. For, first, we have here the fact, as in a parable, that man is utterly impotent to bring to pass any satisfying righteousness of his own. He can see his shame, but he cannot effectually cover or conceal it. Adam and Eve, they could see and feel that they were guilty, miserable, naked—unfit for one another's company (for it is only the pardoned that have fellowship one with another), still more utterly unfit for the presence of God; but when they endeavored to help themselves, what profited all the cloaks and coverings of their shame which they devised for their own selves? No sooner did they hear the voice of the Lord God in the garden than they confessed in that act of hiding themselves their sense of the worthlessness of these.

And wherein, O my brethren, is any garment of our own righteousness which we devise for ourselves better than those aprons of fig-leaves of theirs? What is it but a garment narrower than we can wrap ourselves withal? It may seem to serve its purposes for a while, to constitute a sufficient protection for us; we may rest upon it, upon our decency of behavior, the absence of any gross vices from our lives, our diligence in the performance of the duties of our calling, our kindness to others, our forwardness in good works. Fig-leaves all! and we shall prove them such. Let God once call to us, let us once hear His voice singling out us in particular, let Him speak to us out of the whirlwind, show us a glimpse of His glory, and in His glory of our own shame, let it once come to this that we stand face to face with Him the Holy One, and we shall find how little all these devices of our own can do for us, we shall stand shivering, naked, and ashamed before Him. Like Job we may have washed ourselves with snow water, and made our hands never so clean; but He can plunge us in the ditch, so that our own clothes shall abhor us. And if we are only drawn out of our refuges of lies, if we only make this discovery of our nakedness and defilement, when it is too late to seek and to obtain any better covering, we may then cry to the rocks to cover us, and to the hills to hide us; but neither they, nor any other shelter, neither height nor depth, shall conceal us from those eyes of fire which shall at once look us through and consume us.

But while we thus learn that man cannot clothe himself, we learn also that God undertakes to clothe him. They were His hands which made the skins of beasts into garments for Adam and for Eve. What a blessed mystery is here! How much is contained for us in this gracious, this condescending act of God toward them whom just before He had judged! The bands which bind man to God have not been broken by man's sin—or rather, though broken once, they have been reunited again. He can yet devise a way by which His banished shall return home. As elsewhere He has said *in word,* "I am the Lord that *healeth* thee," so here He says *in act,* "I am the Lord that *clotheth* thee." He does not abhor man in his fallen estate, however that state may be one in itself sufficient to provoke abhorring. He beholds man, to use the image of Ezekiel, as a new-born infant cast out at the moment of its nativity to the loathing of its person, polluted in its own blood; and He spreads His skirt over it, and says unto it, Live. This is the second lesson of our history—that when man has, so to speak, unclothed himself, stripped himself bare of that righteousness with which he was arrayed at the first, God Himself undertakes to find garments for him, to the end that the shame of his nakedness may not appear.

But, thirdly, we note in this Scripture that the clothing which God found for Adam could only have been obtained at the cost of a life, and *that* the life of one unguilty, of one who had no share nor part in the sin which made the providing of it needful. So it must necessarily have been. A beast, one or more, must have been slain before these coats of skins could have been prepared; and it must have been slain by the act of God. I do not scruple to say that we have here the first institution of sacrifice; and what is more noticeable still, God Himself the institutor; not merely enjoining, commanding, but Himself ordaining, showing the way; and the central idea of sacrifice, as it afterwards unfolded itself in manifold rites, is wrapped up in this first sacrifice of Paradise. In proof that here we have nothing less than the first of that long series of sacrifices which were to follow, a type and shadow, a prelude and prophecy, of that crowning sacrifice on Calvary, in which all others were to find their consummation and their end, I ask you to note how close the similarity between that and this,—in what wonderful ways this points to and presignifies that. Already in Paradise there is not merely a prophecy of Christ in words, "The seed of the woman shall bruise the serpent's head," but a prophecy in act. A creature which has known no sin comes here notwithstanding, and by the will and act of God, under the law of death, under all the penal consequences of sin, dies, that so from man the sinner those same penal consequences of his sin may be turned away,—that man, who had stripped himself of the robe of his own innocency, may yet be clothed, though not now in anything of his own, but in a garment which is furnished him by another. What can all this point to but to Him, the Lamb of God, in whom was no sin, and who yet endured the penalty of our sin, died that we might live, and who thus died by the determinate counsel and foreknowledge of God,—God Himself putting Him to grief, bidding His sword to awake against the Man that was His fellow, and all for our sakes, that He might thus lay on our divine Substitute the iniquities of us all, that He might thus find a ransom for us, and One by whose stripes we should be healed, and by whose righteousness we should be clothed. O my brethren, we hear in the New Testament of the Lord our righteousness, of Christ our righteousness; He is *plainly* declared to us there: but He is not obscurely intimated in these words of Genesis, in this sacrament, for so we may call it, which was accomplished in Paradise, when to "Adam and to his wife did the Lord God make coats of skins, and clothed them."

And are not the lessons which we may draw from all this plain and palpable enough? As for instance, this first,—that there is no robe of our own righteousness which can cover us, which can conceal our shame. Those were poor miserable palliations of their dishonor which the guilty progenitors of our race invented and contrived for themselves; and ours, be sure, will be as poor, or poorer still. What! will you stand before God, before Him of the eyes of fire, before Him who charges His angels with folly, before Him in whose sight the heavens themselves are not pure, with nothing better to cover you than the rags of your own well-doings,—boasting, it may be, like that wretched Pharisee, that you are not as other men, adulterers, extortioners, and the like,—glorying in your virtues, your uprightness, your honesty, your almsdeeds, your diligence in good works, your constant attendance at God's house, your frequent participation in holy sacraments?—all of them good, all more or less indispensable for any who would see life, but yet constituting no part of the righteousness of a man in which he is to stand accepted and justified before God; and he is miserably mistaken if he so regard them.

But, secondly, that righteousness which we have not in ourselves we must be content, yea glad, yea thankful, to receive it at the hands of God. Pride may revolt at this; the old Adam may kick at this; but till a man is content to put his mouth in the dust, to give all glory to God, and to take all shame to himself, to renounce all trust in anything which he has wrought or ever will have wrought for himself, to place all trust in what God has wrought for him, he is not near to the kingdom of God. How gladly must our first parents have cast aside the poor, ineffectual makeshifts which they had sewn together for themselves, when God had supplied them with clothing sufficient for their utmost needs? With like gladness let us cast everything away which would hinder us from making our own that durable clothing, those garments at once of use and of beauty, which God has in Christ provided for us.

But, lastly, not Christ by His life, but by His life *and death,* and mainly by His death, supplies these garments for our spirits' need. It is not to the Lamb of God, but to the Lamb *slain,* that we must look. Those coats of skins of which we have been speaking today were so far dearly bought, that they were bought at the price of a life, and the very existence of them involved and implied a death. And so it was ever after in every sacrifice which followed. The sacrifice must die, if he on whose behalf it was offered was to have any profit by it. Without shedding of blood was no remission. It was so with Him who crowned and completed all the sacrifices which went before, to whom they had all pointed. It is His death which is our life. It is because He was stripped that we are clothed; because He hung naked upon his cross, therefore is it that the shame of our nakedness shall not appear;—that is, if indeed it shall not; for it is for us to determine whether it shall appear or no. If we would not have it appear, then let us buy of Him white raiment; let us seek to stand before God accepted in Him; His righteousness imputed to us, and all our sins covered by that ample robe. Yet even this is not all; as we must ever seek to preserve the due balance between one truth of God and another, I will therefore conclude with this warning word, namely, that to put on Christ is something more even than this. It is so to appropriate the righteousness of Christ that it becomes our righteousness, life of our life, woven into the web and tissue of our own moral and spiritual being; if in one sense a garment separable from us, yet in another as our own flesh and blood, having become part and parcel of our very selves; a Christ *for* us, who is a Christ *in* us as well. Let us as little dare to separate these two truths as to confound them.

Charles Kingsley

[1819–1875]

Charles Kingsley is remembered by most people today as the author of such famous novels as Westward Ho!, Hypatia, *and* Water-Babies. *But his career as a preacher was no less noted than that as a novelist. He was born at Dartmoor, Devon, and was educated at King's College, London, and Magdalene College, Cambridge. In 1842 he was ordained a minister in the Church of England. Most of his ministry was spent at Eversley in Hampshire. He served as chaplain to Queen Victoria and as professor of Modern History at Cambridge. In 1873 he became canon of Westminster. Throughout his life he was prominently identified with the movement known as Christian Socialism. The following sermon, which combines religion and patriotism, gives evidence of Kingsley's literary ability and high sense of England's great Christian mission.*

ENGLAND'S STRENGTH

I will defend this city, to save it, for mine own sake. II Kings 19:34.

The first lesson for this morning's service is of the grandest in the whole Old Testament; grander perhaps than all, except the story of the passage of the Red Sea, and the giving of the Law on Sinai. It follows out the story which you heard in the first lesson for last Sunday afternoon, of the invasion of Judea by the Assyrians. You heard then how this great Assyrian conqueror, Sennacherib, after taking all the fortified towns of Judah, and sweeping the whole country with fire and sword, sent three of his generals up to the very walls of Jerusalem, commanding King Hezekiah to surrender at discretion, and throw himself and his people on Sennacherib's mercy; how proudly and boastfully he taunted the Jews with their weakness; how he called in religion as the excuse for his conquests and robberies, saying, as if God's blessings were on them, "Am I now come up without the Lord against this place to destroy it? The Lord said to me, Go up against this place to destroy it"; while all the time what he really trusted in (as his own words showed) was their own strength and the number of their armies.

Jerusalem was thus in utter need and danger; the vast army of the Assyrians was encamped at Lachish, not more than ten miles off; and however strong the walls of Jerusalem might be, and however advantageously it might stand on its high hill, with lofty rocks and cliffs on three sides of it, yet Hezekiah knew well that no strength of his could stand more than a few days against Sennacherib's army. For these Assyrians had brought the art of war to a greater perfection than any nation of the old world: they lived for war, and studied, it seems, only how to conquer. And they have left behind them very remarkable proofs of what sort of men they were, of which I think it right to tell you all; for they are most instructive, not merely because they prove the truth of Isaiah's account, but because they explain it, and help us in many ways to understand his prophecies. There are a number of sculptures and paintings, representing Sennacherib, his army, and his different conquests, which were painted by his command, in his palace; and having been lately discovered there, among the ruins of Nineveh, have been brought to England, and are now in the British Museum, while copies of many of them are in the Crystal Palace. There we see these terrible Assyrian conquerors defeating their enemies, torturing and slaughtering their prisoners, swimming rivers, beating down castles, sweeping on from land to land like a devouring fire, while over their heads fly fierce spirits who protect and prosper their cruelties, and eagles who trail in their claws the entrails of the slain. The very expression of their faces is frightful for its fierceness; the countenances of a "bitter and hasty nation," as the Prophet calls them, whose feet were swift to shed blood. And as for the art of war, and their power of taking walled towns like Jerusalem, you may see them in these pictures battering down and undermining forts and castles, with instruments so well made and powerful, that all other nations who came after them for more than two thousand years, seem to have been content to copy from them, and hardly to have improved on the old Assyrian engines.

Such, and so terrible, they came up against Jerusalem: to attempt to fight them would have been useless madness; and Hezekiah had but one means of escaping from them; and that was, to cast himself and his people upon the boundless mercy, and faithfulness, and power of God.

And Hezekiah had his answer by Isaiah the prophet: and more than an answer. The Lord took the matter into His own Hand, and showed Sennacherib which was the stronger, his soldiers and horses and engines, or the Lord God; and so that terrible Assyrian army came utterly to naught, and vanished off the face of the earth.

Now, my friends, has this noble history no lesson in it for us? God forbid! It has a lesson which ought to come nearer to our hearts than to the hearts of any nation: for though we or our forefathers have never been, for nearly three hundred years, in such utter need and danger as Jerusalem was, yet be sure that we might have been so, again and again, had it not been for the mercy of the same God who delivered Jerusalem from the Assyrians. It is now three hundred years ago that the Lord delivered this country from as terrible an invader as Sennacherib himself; when He three times scattered by storms the fleets of the King of Spain, which were coming to lay waste this land with fire and sword; and since then no foreign foe has set foot on English soil, and we almost alone, of all the nations of Europe, have been preserved from those horrors of war, even to speak of which is dreadful. Oh, my friends! we know not half God's goodness to us!

And if you ask me, why God has so blest and favored this land, I can only answer, and I am not ashamed or afraid to answer—I believe it is on account of the Church of England; it is because God has put His name here in a peculiar way, as He did among the Jews of old, and that He is jealous for His Church, and for the special knowledge of His Gospel and His law, which He has given us in our Prayer-book and in our Church Catechism, lighting therein a candle in England which I believe will never be put out. It is not merely that we are a Protestant country—great blessing as that is,—it is, I believe, that there is something in the Church of England which there is not in Protestant countries abroad, unless perhaps Sweden: for every one of them (except Sweden and ourselves) have suffered, from time to time, invading armies, and the unspeakable horrors of war. In some of them the light of the Gospel has been quenched utterly, and in others it lingers like a candle flickering down into the socket. By horrible persecutions, and murder, and war, and pillage, have those nations been tormented from time to time; and who are we, that we should escape? Certainly from no righteousness of our own. Some may say, It is our great wealth which has made us strong. My friends, believe it not. Look at Spain, which was once the richest of all nations; and did her riches preserve her? Has she not dwindled down into the most miserable and helpless of all nations? Has not her very wealth vanished from her, because she sold herself to work all unrighteousness with greediness?

Some may say, It is our freedom which makes us strong. My friends, believe it not. Freedom is a vast blessing from God, but freedom alone will preserve no nation. How many free nations have fallen into every sort of misery, ay, into bitter slavery, in spite of all their freedom? How many free nations in Europe lie now in bondage, gnawing their tongues for pain, and weary with waiting for the deliverance which does not come? No, my friends, freedom is of little use without something else— and that is loyalty; reverence for law and obedience to the powers that be, because men believe those powers to be ordained of God; because men believe that Christ is their King, and they His ministers and stewards, and that He it is who appoints all orders and degrees of men in His Holy Church. True freedom can only live with true loyalty and obedience, such as our Prayer-book, our Catechism, our Church of England preaches to us. It is a Church meant for free men, who stand each face to face with their heavenly Father: but it is a Church meant also for loyal men, who look on the law as the ordinance of God, and on their rulers as the ministers of God; and if our freedom has had any thing to do (as no doubt it has) with our prosperity, I believe that we owe the greater part of our freedom to the teaching and the general tone of mind which our Prayer-book has given to us and to our forefathers for now three hundred years.

Not that we have listened to that teaching, or acted up to it: God knows, we have been but too like the Jews in Isaiah's time, who had the Law of God, and yet did every man what was right in his own eyes; we, like them, have been hypocritical; we, like them, have neglected the poor, and the widow, and the orphan; we, like them, have been too apt to pay tithe of mint and anise, and neglect the weightier matters of the law, justice, mercy, and judgment. When we read that awful first chapter of Isaiah, we may well tremble; for all the charges which he brings against the Jews of his time, would just as well apply to us: but yet we can trust in the Lord, as Isaiah did, and believe that He will be jealous for His land, and for His name's sake, and not suffer the nations to say of us, "Where is now their God"? We can trust Him, that if He turn His hand on us, as He did on the Jews of old, and bring us into danger and trouble, yet it will be in love and mercy, that He may purge away our dross, and take away all our alloy, and restore our rulers as at the first, and our counsellors as at the beginning, that we may be called, "The city of righteousness, the faithful city." True, we must not fancy that we have any righteousness of our own, that we merit God's favor above other people; our consciences ought to tell us that cannot be; our Bibles tell us that is an empty boast. Did we not hear this morning, "Bring forth fruits meet for repentance: and think not to say within yourselves, We have Abraham to our father; for God is able of these stones to raise up children to Abraham." But we may comfort ourselves with the thought, that there is one standing among us (though we see Him not) who will, ay, and does, "baptize us with the Holy Ghost and with fire, whose fan is in His hand, and He will thoroughly purge His floor, and gather the wheat into His garner," for the use of our children after us, and the generations yet unborn, while the chaff, all among us, which is empty, and light, and rotten, and useless, He will burn up (thanks be to His holy name) with fire unquenchable, which neither the falsehood and folly of man, nor the malice of the Devil, can put out, but which will purge this land of all its sins. This is our hope, and this is the cause of our thankfulness.

Frederick W. Robertson

[1816-1853]

The son and grandson of military men, Frederick W. Robertson's early ambition was to be a soldier. This desire clung to him throughout life. However, he entered the ministry and became, in the words of Dean Stanley "beyond question the greatest preacher of the nineteenth century." His pastorates included Cheltenham, Oxford, and Brighton, England. His work at Brighton made him famous, and he exercised an influence which continued long after his death. Among his followers was Tennyson, whose great religious poem In Memoriam *bears the impress of Robertson's thinking. This sermon, one of the few of Robertson's ever printed, was given on the first day of public mourning for the Queen Dowager Adelaide in 1894.*

THE ISRAELITE'S GRAVE IN A FOREIGN LAND

And Joseph said unto his brethren, I die: and God will surely visit you, and bring you out of this land unto the land which he sware to Abraham, to Isaac, and to Jacob. And Joseph took an oath of the children of Israel, saying, God will surely visit you, and ye shall carry up my bones from hence. So Joseph died, being an hundred and ten years old: and they embalmed him, and he was put in a coffin in Egypt. GENESIS 50:24, 26.

THE VERDICT of the Egyptian world was worth much. Joseph had gone to Egypt, some years before, a foreigner; had lived there in obscurity; had been exposed to calumny; by his quiet, consistent goodness, had risen, step by step, first to respect, then to trust, command, and veneration; was embalmed after death in the affections, as well as with the burial rights, of the Egyptians; and his honoured form reposed at last amidst the burial place of the Pharaohs.

The history of Joseph, as of every man, has two sides—its outward circumstances and its inner life.

The outward circumstances were chequered with misfortune. Severed from his home in very early years, sold into slavery, cast into prison—at first, grief seemed to have marked him for her own. And this is human life. Part of its lot is misery. Every son of man who would attain the true end of his being must be baptized with fire. It is the law of our humanity, as that of Christ, that we must be perfected through suffering. And he who has not discerned the Divine Sacredness of Sorrow, and the profound meaning which is concealed in pain, has yet to learn what life is. The Cross, manifested as the Necessity of the Highest Life, alone interprets it.

Besides this, obloquy was part of Joseph's portion. His brethren, even his father, counted him a vain dreamer, full of proud imaginings. He languished long in a dungeon with a stain upon his character. He was subjected to almost all the bitterness which changes the milk of kindly feelings into gall: to Potiphar's fickleness, to slander, to fraternal envy, to the ingratitude of friendship in the neglect of the chief butler who left his prison, and straightway forgot his benefactor. Out of all which a simple lesson arises, "Cease ye from man, whose breath is in his nostrils." Yet that may be over-stated. Nothing chills the heart like universal distrust. Nothing freezes the genial current of the soul so much as doubts of human nature. Human goodness is no dream. Surely we have met unselfishness, and love, and honour among men. Surely we have seen, and not in dreams, pure benevolence beaming from human countenances. Surely we have met with integrity that the world's wealth could not bribe; and attachment which might bear the test of any sacrifice. It is not so much the depravity as the frailty of men, that makes it impossible to count on them. Was it not excusable in Jacob, and even natural, if he attributed to vanity his son's relation of the dream in which the sun, and the moon, and the eleven stars, bowed down before him? Was it not excusable if Potiphar distrusted his tried servant's word, when his guilt appeared so indisputably substantiated? Was not even the chief butler's forgetfulness intelligible, when you remember his absorbing interest in his own danger, and the multiplied duties of his office? The world is not to be too severely blamed, if it misrepresents us. It is hard to reach the truth: very hard to sift a slander.

Success besides, marked the career of Joseph. Let us not take half views of men and things. The woof of life is dark; that we granted: but it is shot through a web of brightness. Accordingly, in Joseph's case, even in his worst days, you find a kind of balance, to be weighed against his sorrows. The doctrine of compensation is found through all. Amidst the schemings of his brothers' envy he had his father's love. In his slavery he had some recompense in feeling that he was gradually winning his master's confidence. In his dungeon he possessed the consciousness of innocence, and the grateful respect of his fellow-prisoners.

Now turn to the spirit of Joseph's inner life. First of all, that life was forgiveness. You cannot but have remarked that, conversant as his experience was with human treachery, no expressions of bitterness escape from him. No sentimental wailing over the cruelty of relations, the falseness of friendship, or the ingratitude of the world. No rancorous outburst of misanthropy: no sarcastic scepticism of man's integrity or woman's honour. He meets all bravely, with calm, meek, and dignified forbearance. If ever man had cause for such doubts, he had; yet his heart was never soured. At last, after his father's death, his brothers, apprehending his resentful recollections of their early cruelty, come to deprecate his revenge. Very touching is his reply. "Fear not: for am I in the place of God? But as for you, ye thought evil against me: but God meant it unto good, to bring to pass, as it is this day, to save much people alive. Now therefore, fear ye not: I will nourish you and your little ones."

One characteristic of Joseph's inner life remains—benevolence. It was manifested in the generosity with which he entertained his brethren, and in the discriminating tenderness with which he provided his best beloved brother's feast with extraordinary delicacies. These were traits of thoughtfulness. But farther still. The prophetic insight of Joseph enabled him to foresee the approach of famine. He took measures accordingly; and when the famine came, the royal storehouses were opened, and every man in Egypt owed his life to the benevolent providence of the Hebrew stranger.

The death of Joseph was in accordance with his life. The funeral was a homage paid to goodness. Little is said in the text of Joseph's funeral. To know what it was, we must turn to the earlier part of the chapter, where that of Jacob is mentioned. A mourning of seventy days; a funeral whose imposing greatness astonished the Canaanites. They said, "This is a grievous mourning to the Egyptians." Seventy days were the time, or nearly so, fixed by custom for a royal funeral; and Jacob was so honoured, not for his own sake, but because he was Joseph's father. We cannot suppose that Joseph's own obsequies were on a scale less grand.

Finally, in the last Will and Testament of Joseph, we find faith. He commanded his brethren, and through them, his nation, to carry his bones with them when they migrated to Canaan. In the Epistle to the Hebrews, that is reckoned an evidence of faith. "By faith Joseph gave commandment concerning his bones." How did he know that his people would ever quit Egypt? We reply, by faith. Not faith in a written word, for Joseph had no Bible; rather, faith in that conviction of his own heart, which is itself the substantial evidence of faith. For religious faith ever dreams of something higher, more beautiful, more perfect, than the state of things with which it feels itself surrounded. Ever, a day future lies before it: the evidence for which is its own hope.

And that is the evidence of immortality. When the coffin is lowered into the grave, and the dull, heavy sound of earth falling on it is heard, there are some to whom that sound seems but an echo of their worst anticipations; seems but to reverberate the idea of decay for ever, in the words, "Earth to earth, ashes to ashes, dust to dust." There are others, to whom it sounds pregnant with the expectations of immortality, the "sure and certain hope of a resurrection to eternal life." The difference between these two feelings is measured by the difference of lives. They whose life is low and earthly, how can they believe in aught beyond the grave, when nothing of that life which is eternal has yet stirred within them? They who have lived as Joseph lived, just in proportion to their purity and their unselfishness, must believe it. They cannot but believe it. The eternal existence is already pulsing in their veins; the life of trust and high hope, and sublime longings after perfection, with which the decay of the frame has nothing at all to do. That is gone—yes—but it was not that life in which they lived, and when it finished, what had that ruin to do with the destruction of the Immortal?

There is one to whom your thoughts must have reverted often during the history which we have been going through, suggesting a parallel, all the more delicately felt from the absence of direct allusion. That royal Lady, for whose loss the marvellous uniformity of the unbroken funeral hue which pervades this congregation, tells eloquently of general mourning, came to this land a few years ago, like Joseph, a foreigner. Like Joseph, the earlier years of her sojourn were spent in comparative obscurity. Like Joseph, she had her share of calumny, though in a different form. There are many here who can remember that in that year when our political feuds had attained the acme of rancour, the irreverent lip of party slander dared to breathe its rank venom upon the name of one of the gentlest that ever adorned a throne. There are some who know how that unpopularity was met: with meekness—with Christian forgiveness—with quiet dignity—with that composure which is the highest result and evidence of strength. Like Joseph, she passed through the temptations of a court with unsullied spotlessness—like Joseph, the domestic and social relationships were sustained with beautiful fidelity—like Joseph, she lived down opposition, outlived calumny—like Joseph, she used the noble income entrusted to her, in acts of almost unexampled munificence—like Joseph, her life was chequered with sorrow, and when the clouds of earlier difficulties had cleared away, the rainbow sign of peace, even in the midst of broken health, spanned the calmness of her evening years—like Joseph, she will have a regal burial, and her ashes will repose with the dust of England's princes, amidst the mourning of the nation in which she found a home.

The homage which is given to her is not the homage yielded to rank, or wealth, or genius. There will be silver on her coffin, and magnificence in the pageantry which attends her to the grave; but it is not in these that the glory of her funeral lies. These were the privileges of the most profligate of her ancestors as well as her. These are the world's rewards for those whom she delights to honour. There will be something in her funeral, beside which these things are mean. There is a grandeur in a nation's tears; and they will be shed in unfeigned reverence over the remains of all that was most queenly, and all that was most womanly. No political fervour mixes with her obsequies. She stood identified with no party politics. No peculiar religious party mourns its patroness. Of all our jarring religious sects, in the Church, and out of it, not one dares to claim her as its own. Her spirit soared above these things. It is known that she scarcely recognized them. All was lost in the sublimer name of Christian. It is a *Christian* who has passed from this earth away, to take her place in the general Assembly and Church of the first-born: to stand before God, the Judge of all, among the spirits of the just made perfect.

Henry Ward Beecher

[1813–1887]

Henry Ward Beecher began his ministry in the Congregational church in Indiana, but in 1847 he was called to the newly organized Plymouth Church in Brooklyn, New York. Almost immediately he rose to fame as a pulpit orator of power and brilliance. From this date until his death he was noted throughout the world as a great preacher, lecturer, writer, and reformer. He was a leader in public issues of historic import, and was recognized as a formidable agitator for good causes. This sermon shows Beecher's clear understanding of world problems.

WAR AND PEACE

And many people shall go and say, Come ye, and let us go up to the mountain of the Lord, to the house of the God of Jacob, and he will teach us of his ways, and we will walk in his paths; for out of Zion shall go forth the law, and the word of the Lord from Jerusalem. And he shall judge among the nations, and shall rebuke many people; and they shall beat their swords into ploughshares, and their spears into pruninghooks: nation shall not lift up sword against nation, neither shall they learn war any more. Isaiah 2:3, 4.

Does it not seem strange to you, when you look back upon the long line of nations, civilized or semi-civilized, and read their literature, their poetry, and their philosophies, and see on every side only a spirit of rivalry and of military glory,—does it not, then, seem strange that the one sweet voice that is lifted up like a chant or a hymn, through all the ages, was the voice of the old Hebrew people? They were themselves not unwarlike; they were a people of fierce passions, whom it required ages to discipline; and yet their prophets, instead of being the leaders of the people to believe that war was the favorite pastime of the gods, and that it was the mark of honor among men to be eminent in military skill and prowess, taught that when God should rule, the earth would be at peace; and that when the ways of God should be observed, and the law should go forth from Zion, it would be then the time when all people should turn from military occupations, and bestow themselves upon remunerative industrial and civil pursuits.

This passage which I have read is the exultant prediction that a day shall come to pass when the nations shall be governed by God's will. That is, national laws and national policies shall yet be controlled, not by the lowest passions of mankind as largely as hitherto, but by the highest moral sentiments. A day is coming when public sentiment shall demand that public men shall be nobler morally; when all public laws shall be couched and framed in the highest moral interest of the whole; and when the policy of nations shall conform to the beneficent policy of Divine providence. When that shall take place, there will be universal peace; and this peace will turn the resources of nations into wealth-producing channels.

The time has come, or at least is now near, when there shall be an organization of nations for the peace of the world. We have an organization in every town or village in this land by which no one man is allowed to let loose his passions as he pleases. The good of every citizen in the town requires that the lawless forces of men shall be regulated. The law undertakes to do for men what in a savage or barbarous condition they undertake to do for themselves. But the time is coming when nations shall organize for the same purposes that villages and towns do now, and when it shall be as unlawful for a nation to let loose its avaricious and vindictive desires in the community of nations, without their leave, as it is for a man to let loose his personal passions in the midst of civilized men, without law, and without the leave of a magistrate.

I do not believe that the use of physical force to maintain the great moral ends of justice, liberty and national life can yet be dispensed with. The time is coming when it can be dispensed with, but that time has not come yet. I agree with the most advanced men, that the ideal of Christianity is absolute peace; I believe that the ideal of Christianity is to suffer evil rather than inflict evil; but Christianity has not yet come to its ideal. You cannot bring communities up by the ears. You may say to the individual man, "You are bound to develop to the uttermost;" but he cannot develop thus all at once. Since God ordained that men and society should come up by growth, you cannot force them up. Growth, of necessity, requires time. The ideal of Christianity is final and universal peace, and it is the duty of nations to dispense with physical force as fast and as far as possible; but you cannot dispense with it suddenly, and disband all armies and police organizations, and leave the world to think that there is no government. To do that would be to leave the world to brutality, and make the tyrant more tyrannical, and the lawless more lawless. Until society is stronger in the direction of the social, intellectual and moral elements, we must use an inferior instrument. We must use the hand till the head and the heart are right. Christianity is so large that we are to grow into it gradually; but as fast as possible nations should take hold of its principles.

I take the ground that the time has come when by suitable efforts the war spirit may be abated, and men in the main set against it. The time has come when the forces of nations may be so combined as to reduce the temptations of war. Nations can be so organized as to prevent any unruly member from going to war, as rightfully as municipal bodies in towns and villages can prevent any citizen from going into a fight at the expense of the peace of the whole community. The peace of the world, in other words, is not to be subject to the whim or caprice of any single nation, any more than the peace of a nation is to be subject to the whim or caprice of any man or body of men in it.

We have seen dueling go out of practice almost entirely. It has been thought that two men might go out and settle their differences by the use of deadly weapons; but that idea is fast going out of date. It is thought that two nations have a right to fight national duels to settle their difficulties; but this sort of dueling is just as wrong as the other, and just as really and as easily vincible. There should be, therefore, such steps taken as, for instance, the organization of a national congress, for enacting international law, and administering that law between nation and nation. At present the law of nations is crude, and a large part of the ground between nation and nation is not covered by national enactments. But we have come to a time when I think we might begin, at last, to form a national congress, that shall enact laws which shall be for the good of all nations, and by which all nations alike shall be bound. There are some international laws, which pertain more largely to commerce than to anything else; but I think the time has come for a more thorough work through the organization of a national congress. There must be a determination to so educate the whole people that the current of public sentiment will run in that direction. If the people remain ignorant on the subject, or indifferent to it, it will be in vain to undertake to institute and carry out this reform; but if the people are instructed, and aroused to feel that their interests lie in peace, then *"Vox populi"* will be *"Vox Dei"* —a proverb which has been as little understood and as much abused as any proverb in the world. If by saying that the voice of the people is the voice of God, you mean that the people have the power to know a truth as God has power to know it, that is hideously false; for the vast mass of the common people have almost no power to comprehend the truth. But when the truth is found out and made known to the great mass of the common people, and they accept it, and lift up their voice, and give it power, then the voice of the people is indeed the voice of a heaven full of gods. And we must get the power of the people to enforce the laws which may be enacted by an international congress.

On the church of God rests, primarily, this work. I do not undertake to say, I am far from saying, that a church should turn aside from its work of individual evangelization, of preaching the Gospel from man to man, in the society where it exists; yet the church universal has a large sphere. It is bound to stand foremost in making reformatory laws, in tempering brutal penalties, and in infusing sympathy and love into men, instead of separating them by sharp theological prejudices. The church of God, as a representative of Christ, must go forth, not to preach will, nor even conscience, but a Gospel which shall employ that will and that conscience in the world as instruments by which to secure peace and harmony among nations, as well as individuals. God's church is hereafter to promote more widely and efficiently those institutions, and laws, and governments which shall diffuse through civil economy everywhere the essential spirit of humanity.

Alexander MacLaren

[1826–1910]

The preaching career of Alexander MacLaren was centered largely in Southampton and Manchester. His intensity and vigor made him recognized as one of England's outstanding preachers. He had a rare knowledge of the Bible and its background, and almost all his sermons consisted of a careful analysis of the text and a drawing of lessons from it. Christ's Touch *shows his great skill in using illustrations and making his points almost visual to his congregation.*

CHRIST'S TOUCH

Jesus put forth His hand and touched him. MARK 1:41.

"BEHOLD the servant of the Lord" might be the motto of this Gospel, and "He went about doing good, and healing," the summing up of its facts. We have in it comparatively few of our Lord's discourses, none of His longer, and not very many of His briefer, ones. It contains but four parables. This Evangelist gives no miraculous birth as in Matthew, no angels adoring there as in Luke, no gazing into the secrets of Eternity, where the Word, Who afterwards became flesh, dwelt in the bosom of the Father, as in John. He begins with a brief reference to the Forerunner, and then plunges into the story of Christ's life of service to man, and service for God.

In carrying out his conception the Evangelist omits many things found in the other Gospels, which involve the idea of dignity and dominion, while he adds to the incidents which he has in common with them not a few fine and subtle touches to heighten the impression of our Lord's toil and eagerness in His patient loving service. Perhaps it may be an instance of this that we find more prominence given to our Lord's touch as connected with His miracles than in the other Gospels, or perhaps it may merely be an instance of the vivid portraiture, the result of a keen eye for externals, which is so marked a characteristic of this Gospel. Whatever the reason, the fact is plain, that Mark delights to dwell on Christ's touch. The instances are these—first, He puts out His hand, and "lifts up" Peter's wife's mother, and immediately the fever left her, then, unrepelled by the foul disease, He lays His pure hand upon the leper, and the living mass of corruption is healed; again, He lays His hand on the clammy marble of the dead child's forehead, and she lives. Further, we have incidental statement that He was so hindered in His mighty works by unbelief that He could only lay His hands on a few sick folk and heal them. We find next two remarkable incidents, peculiar to Mark, both like each other and unlike our Lord's other miracles. One is the gradual healing of that deaf and dumb man whom Christ took apart from the crowd, laid His hands on him, thrust His fingers into his ears as if He would clear some impediment, touched his tongue with saliva, said to him, "Be opened"; and the man can hear. And the other is, the gradual healing of a blind man whom our Lord again leads apart from the crowd, takes by the hand, lays His own kind hands upon the poor sightless eyeballs, and with singular slowness of progress effects a cure, not by a leap and a bound as He generally does, but by steps and stages; tries it once and finds partial success, has to apply the curative process again and then the man can see. In addition to these instances there are two other incidents which may also be adduced. It is Mark alone who records for us the fact that He took little children in His arms, and blessed them. And it is Mark alone who records for us the fact that when He came down from the Mount of Transfiguration He laid His hand upon the demoniac boy, writhing in the grip of his tormentor, and lifted him up.

Whatever diviner and sacreder aspect there may be in these incidents, the first thing, and in some senses the most precious thing, in them is that they are the natural expression of a truly human tenderness and compassion.

Now we are so accustomed, and as I believe quite rightly, to look at all Christ's life down to its minutest events as intended to be a revelation of God, that we are sometimes apt to think about it as if His motive and purpose in everything was didactic. So an unreality creeps over our conceptions of Christ's life, and we need to be reminded that He was not always acting and speaking in order to convey instruction, but that words and deeds were drawn from Him by the play of simple human feelings. He pitied not only in order to teach us the heart of God, but because His own man's heart was touched with a feeling of men's infirmities. We are too apt to think of Him as posing before men with the intent of giving the great revelation of the Love of God. It is the love of Christ Himself, spontaneous, instinctive, without the thought of anything but the suffering it sees, which gushes out and leads Him to put forth His hand to the outcast beggars, the blind, the deaf, the lepers. That is the first great lesson we have to learn from this and other stories,—the swift human sympathy and heart of grace and tenderness which Jesus Christ had for all human suffering; and has to-day as truly as ever.

There is more than this instinctive sympathy taught by Christ's touch. But it is distinctly taught. How beautifully that comes out in the story of the leper! That wretched man had long dwelt in his isolation. The touch of a friend's hand or the kiss of loving lips had been long denied him. Christ looks on him, and before he reflects the spontaneous impulse of pity breaks through the barriers of legal prohibitions, and of natural repugnance, and leads Him to lay His holy and healing hand on his foulness.

True pity always instinctively leads us to seek to come near those who are its objects. A man tells his friend some sad story of his sufferings, and while he speaks, unconsciously his listener lays his hand on his arm and, by a silent pressure, tells his sympathy. So Christ did with these men— not only in order that He might reveal God to us, but because He was a man, and therefore felt ere He thought. Out flashed from His Heart the swift sympathy, followed by the tender pressure of the loving hand—a hand that tried through flesh to reach spirit and come near the sufferer that it might succour and remove the sorrow.

There is nothing to me more remarkable about the miracles of our Lord than the royal variety of His methods of healing. Sometimes He works at a distance, sometimes He requires, as it would appear for good reasons, the proximity of the person to be blessed. Sometimes He works by a simple word: "Lazarus come forth!" "Peace be still!" "Come out of him!"; sometimes by a word and a touch, as in the instances before us; sometimes by a touch without a word; sometimes by a word and a touch and a vehicle, as in the saliva that was put on the tongue, and in the ears of the deaf, and on the eyes of the blind; sometimes by a vehicle without a word, without a touch, without His presence, as when He said "Go wash in the pool of Siloam! and he washed and was clean." So the Divine Worker varies infinitely and at pleasure yet not arbitrarily but for profound, even if not alway discoverable, reasons, the methods of His miracle-working power, in order that we may learn by these varieties of ways that He is tied to no way; and that His hand, strong and almighty, uses methods and tosses aside methods according to His pleasure, the methods being vitalised when they are used by His will, and being nothing at all in themselves.

The very variety of His methods, then, teaches us that the true cause in every case is His own bare will. A simple word is the highest and most adequate expression of that will. His word is all powerful: and that is the very signature of divinity. Of Whom has it been true from of old that "He spake and it was done, He commanded and it stood fast?" Do you believe in a Christ Whose bare will, thrown among material things, makes them all plastic, as clay in the potter's hands, whose mouth rebukes the demons and they flee, rebukes death and it looses its grasp, rebukes the tempest and there is a calm, rebukes disease and there comes health?

But this use of Christ's touch as apparent means for conveying His miraculous power also serves as an illustration of a principle which is exemplified in all His revelation, namely, the employment in condescension to men's weakness, of outward means as the apparent vehicles of His spiritual power. Just as by the material vehicle sometimes employed for cure, He gave these poor sensebound natures a ladder by which their faith in His healing power might climb, so in the manner of His revelation and communication of His spiritual gifts, there is provision for the wants of us men, who ever need some body for spirit to make itself manifest by, some form for the ethereal reality, some "tabernacle" for the "sun." "Sacraments," outward ceremonies, forms of worship are vehicles which the Divine Spirit uses in order to bring His gifts to the hearts and the minds of men. They are like the touch of the Christ which heals, not by any virtue in itself, apart from His will which chooses to make it the apparent medium of healing.

No good is to be done by any man to his fellows except at the cost of true sympathy which leads to identification and contact. The literal touch of your hand would do more good to some poor outcasts than much solemn advice, or even much material help flung to them as from a height above them. A shake of the hand might be more of a means of grace than a sermon, and more comforting than ever so many free breakfasts and blankets given superciliously.

And, symbolically, we may say that we must be willing to take those by the hand whom we wish to help; that is to say, we must come down to their level, try to see with their eyes, and to think their thoughts, and let them feel that we do not think our purity too fine to come beside their filth, nor shrink from them with repugnance, however we may show disapproval and pity for their sin. Much work done by Christian people has no effect, nor ever will have, because it has peeping through it a poorly concealed "I am holier than thou." An instinctive movement of repugnance has ruined many a well-meant effort.

Christ has come down to us, and has taken all our nature upon Himself. If there is an outcast and abandoned soul on earth which may not feel that Jesus has laid a loving and healing touch on him, Jesus is not the Saviour for the world. He shrinks from none, He unites Himself with all, therefore He is able to save to the uttermost all who come unto God by Him.

His conduct is the pattern and the law for us. A Church is a poor affair if it be not a body of people whose experience of Christ's pity and gratitude for the life which has become theirs through His wondrous making Himself one with them, compel them to do the like in their degree for the sinful and the outcast. Thank God! there are many in every communion who know that constraint of the love of Christ! But the world will not be healed of its sickness till the great body of Christian people awakes to feel that the task and honour of each of them is to go forth bearing Christ's pity certified by their own.

Edward Everett Hale

[1822–1909]

Born at Boston, Massachusetts, and educated at Harvard University, Edward Everett Hale is best known as the author of The Man Without a Country. *He was a minister in the Congregational church, a writer of numerous works of importance, and a contributor to magazines and journals of his time. His* The Man Without a Country, *which appeared in the* Atlantic Monthly *in 1863, has become one of the most famous of American short stories. The sermon given here is one of four published in 1874 under the general title of* A Summer Vacation. *It is an excellent example of his simple, clear pulpit style, and explains his great popularity as a preacher.*

PILGRIMAGES

The Kingdom of God is within you. LUKE 17:21.

FIVE hundred men, women, and children, headed by the nobleman of oldest title in England, have made a pilgrimage since this month began, from the city of London to the sacred village in France where a sick girl saw the vision of the Sacred Heart, as if that place were more sacred than the palace or the hovel of their homes. Yet the Saviour, whom these people acknowledge, says to them, "The kingdom of God is within you."

And God's kingdom, remember, is God's home. God's home is within you! Yet, for all that, Christendom sees to-day a million discontented hearts, a million lives of men and women who are jealous, surly, all cast down, because they cannot come here and be happy, or go there and be happy. When I measure my place against any other man's place, jealous of the society or companionship which he enjoys, it is because I do not know, or do not understand that the kingdom of God is within me.

I can understand how it is that a savage, living in fight with hunger, with cold, or with savage men, should believe that the kingdom of God is far away from this earth, and that this earth is the kingdom of devils; of the fiends of war, of hunger, of cold, or of fire. I understand why he places Olympus, or the home of God, far beyond the clouds, where all is serene; or far beneath, in Elysium, where this clamor and havoc rouse no echo. And I have read enough of Mahomet's Bible, of the Koran, to know that there are descriptions, highly wrought indeed, of a certain heaven beyond this world, bright with jewels and flowers, where is enough to eat and drink, and that of the choicest; into which heaven the evils of this world do not enter. I can understand how a man whose religion has been forced upon him in the forms of that book, how an Islamite, thinks he must die out of this world to enter into the kingdom of God. But I find, nearer home, other men and women who believe, or say they believe, the same thing. I find the teachers and books of Christendom teaching the same thing. There are hymns in this hymn-book, which seem to mean nothing, unless they mean that God's special kingdom is somewhere outside this world, and that His control of this world is much more limited, as it were, spasmodic and secondary.

And this is no infrequent blunder in Christendom. To believe in God, or to rely on God, is the first necessity of life. Then to believe in God's kingdom; to see, were it only in the glory of midnight, or in the cadence of the sea, or in the perfume of flowers, that God rules; that all this wonderful symmetry and harmony and rhythm and order are His rule, and His kingdom: this also seems of course. One cannot, if he thinks, if he looks up or looks round, if he looks outside himself,—he cannot but know there is such a kingdom. Well! in the midst of passion, of lust unsatisfied, of wild desire ungratified, or of a boy's ambitions defeated, some child of God, just starting on his manhood, sees that God has such an order, such a kingdom. He sees that there are systems in which God is Ruler. And so, in some blessed reaction from lust; in some happy harmony of his being; in the luxurious omnipotence of youth, when every sense and pulse are in health and order, when every throb of the brain, and every thrill of the nerve, and every beat of the heart, are pure and right and in sympathy, he cries out within himself, because he is a child of God, "I also will live in God's kingdom." "I will serve devils no longer. I will serve lust no longer. I will worship myself no longer. I live with

God and for God. God's child am I? Then I seek my Father, and henceforth I am in allegiance." And then, because he is modest, because he supposes that older men know what he does not know, that centuries must have told something about God which he cannot see with a boy's insight, nor fathom with a boy's understanding; then he asks what he is to do, how he is to enrol himself in the army, how he is to be a fellow-laborer together with God, how he is to partake of God's nature, how he is to live in God's kingdom. And they tell him, that if he will believe thus and so, and worship here and there, and do this and that, that, by and by, when he is threescore and ten, or by reason of strength is fourscore, then, when he shall be lucky enough at last to die out of a world, which they tell him is a vale of misery and away from God,—

"Where storm after storm rises dark o'er the way,"

they tell him, that then, if the eager love of God which elevates him now has not all paled out in such black wading in the slough of despond which they call mortal life, that then, because he has bought the ticket, he *shall* enter the kingdom of heaven.

There was a young man, who was more fortunate. He had, it is true, been bred in this Jewish fancy, and he came running down the road one day, to ask the Master of Life, "What *shall* I do, that I may inherit eternal life." And the Master said to him what He says to you and me, that this kingdom is no kingdom of the future, but the kingdom of this moment. It is here. "If you will enter into life now," he said, "keep the commandments now. Follow Me now. Why,—'The kingdom of God is within you!'"

Do you remember the story of Rabia's pilgrimage to Mecca? Rabia joined in the caravan of pilgrims. She crossed the sea; she crossed the desert. Night brightened into day and day faded into night forty, fifty, sixty times; until at last they came, with crowds of other worshippers, to the sacred city. And there Rabia bent in worship at the shrine, to learn what the Samaritan woman learned beneath the shadow of Gerizim, "Neither in this city, nor yet at Jerusalem, shall ye worship the Father." And Rabia rose, and returned wiser to her home, saying,—

"Thou fool to tread the desert road,
    To toss upon the dreary sea,
To come so far to seek thy God,
    Who always was so near to thee."

I say all this now, because so many of us have come back from trying new experiments of life, and have just now to return to the old homes, and to see what new experiments we can try in them.

We expect to find heaven, or the kingdom of God, in another world after we die. Reverently I hope that we shall. I believe that we shall. We expect that, as the world advances after one millennium or more; after the killing out of this pestilence; after the abatement of that cruelty; after the unlearning, by hard remedies, of such habits as tyranny, and priestcraft and avarice, and the methods of demagogues, the reign of Christ will come over this world, and the kingdom of heaven will be here. Reverently and bravely let us hold to that hope, and do our best to make it good. But do not let us be satisfied with these hopes. When we pray "Thy kingdom come. Thy will be done on earth as it is in heaven," we are not to wait for any such millennium's end, or any such heaven after death, for the answer to our prayer. That prayer is answered in every happy and true home where two or three of us are together in a Saviour's spirit. Answered completely and brimful! Heaven has no nobler gift. It has no more perfect delights. It has no closer walk with God. You made your pilgrimage to Mecca. You fell on your face on the desert, morning, noon, and night. But never was God any nearer to you than when you took your little boy upon your knee, and heard his long story through from the beginning to the end, shared his baby triumph completely, and let him feel to the very bottom the glory and perfectness of a father's love. You went to the chapel of the Vatican, and you were lost in the exquisite raptures of the Miserere. But Vatican and Miserere have no raptures for you sweeter nor purer than the joy of uniting with your children, as young as they are, in their evening amusements, if you so join and inspirit them, that they are all glorified to them because you share them. And all this is no out-of-the-way accident. It is not the entertainment of a vacation week, or of a day or two. It is what it is: it renews itself with a charm never twice the same, because it is a part of God's kingdom, and not a plan of man's devising. It is love such as God's love. It is life, quickened and made abundant by the eternal elixir. So is it that it does not weary, that it is always new, because simply it is always a part of God's own eternal plan for His children. Or, more simply, say, because God is in the midst of you, enjoying your joy, and making your pleasure possible.

To learn that there is no place to God, or that in all places we may have his companionship, this is the first lesson of travel or of adventure. To come home, knowing what home is, His home as much as ours,—this, of such adventure, is the consecration; a consecration and a lesson, I think, not unneedful in the habits of our time. The care of business, or the demands of evening society, separate fathers and mothers from sons and daughters. A very foolish and provincial custom makes one party up of young people and another of old people. But good society, the most amusing and instructive society, only exists, as God made it, where the young and the old, the graver and the gayer, meet together. I say, I think the habits of separation which sent a man to his office every evening, which kept the children by themselves for fear they should disturb their father, all need to be consecrated and modified. A father is the best teacher to his girls. A mother is the best teacher to her boys. The boys and the girls are the best companions to their fathers and their mothers, and their fathers and mothers are the best companions to the boys and girls. Home, built up on the central principle which has disclosed these axioms, has capacities for amusement, for relaxation, for cheerfulness, for reasonable instruction which are nowhere else: it is indeed alive with the infinite Spirit, and glows with infinite love. Such homes, thus inspired, will give to us what we have not yet discovered in any circle of wealth, of fashion, or of culture,—what we rightly call "good society." For good society is the society where each lives in the other's life, gives to each, and gains from each. It is a part of the kingdom of heaven.

That kingdom is open to all of us, whether we live in a tenement on the seventh floor or in a palace. The rooms are nothing. The inmates are all in all. Let them be gathered, though there are only two or three, so that they dare say they meet "in a Saviour's name;" let them meet as he met with John, the beloved disciple, and in that pure companionship, lo the presence of the Father also; His inspiration, His strength; and courage and cheerfulness which He alone can give. The joy of abundant life is there: the heartiness of daily victory. For the kingdom of God is within you.

Thomas DeWitt Talmage

[1832–1902]

The great crowds that were attracted to the preaching of Thomas DeWitt Talmage in Brooklyn were rewarded with an experience they could not easily forget. This brilliant orator reached millions through his sermons which were printed each week in many newspapers. Talmage has been called a master of sensational rhetoric, "a scene-painter rather than an artist." The following sermon is one of his best. It shows his vital concern with political and social problems, and his conviction that the Christian must make his religion count in the political as well as the church environment.

THE CHRISTIAN AT THE BALLOT-BOX

Some therefore cried one thing, and some another: for the assembly was confused; and the more part knew not wherefore they were come together. And they drew Alexander out of the multitude, the Jews putting him forward. And Alexander beckoned with the hand, and would have made his defense unto the people. But when they knew that he was a Jew, all with one voice about the space of two hours cried out, Great is Diana of the Ephesians. ACTS 19:32–34.

EPHESUS was upside down. A manufacturer of silver boxes for holding heathen images had called his laborers together to discuss the behavior of one Paul, who had been in public places assaulting image-worship, and consequently very much damaging that particular business. There was great excitement in the city. People stood in knots along the streets, violently gesticulating, and calling each other hard names. Some of the people favored the policy of the silversmith; other people favored the policy of Paul. There were great moral questions involved; but these did not bother them at all. The only question about which they seemed to be interested was concerning the wages and the salaried positions. The silversmith and his compeers had put up factories at great expense for the making of these silver boxes; and now, if this new policy is to be inaugurated, the business will go down, the laborers will be thrown out of employment, and the whole city will suffer. Well, what is to be done? "Call a convention," says some one; for in all ages a convention has been a panacea for public evils. The convention is called, and, as they want the largest room in the city, they take the theatre. Having there assembled, they all want to get the floor, and they all want to talk at once. You know what excitement that always makes in a convention, where a great many people want to talk at once. Some cried one thing, some cried another. Some wanted to denounce, some wanted to resolve. After a while a prominent man gets the floor, and he begins to speak; but they very soon hiss him down, and then the confusion rises into worse uproar, and they begin to shout, all of them together, and they keep on until they are red in the face and hoarse in the throat, for two long hours crying out, "Great is Diana of the Ephesians! Great is Diana of the Ephesians!"

The whole scene reminds me of the excitement we have almost every autumn at the elections. While that goddess Diana has lost her worshipers, and her temples have gone into the dust, our American people want to set up a god in place of it, and they want us all to bow down before it; and that god is Political Party. Considering our superior civilization, I have to declare to you that the Ephesian idolatry was less offensive in the sight of God than is this all-absorbing American partisanship.

While there are honest men, true men, Christian men, who stand in both political parties, and who come into the autumnal elections resolving to serve their city or their State or the nation in the best possible way,

I have noticed also that with many it is a mere contest between the ins and the outs—those who are in trying to stay in and keep the outs out, and those who are out trying to get in and thrust the ins out. And one party cries, "Great is Diana of the Ephesians!" and the other party cries, "Great is Diana of the Ephesians!" neither of them honest enough to say, "Great is my pocket-book!"

Once or twice a year it is my custom to talk to the people about public affairs from what I call a Christian standpoint, and this morning I have chosen for that duty. I propose to tell the people very plainly what I consider to be their Christian duty at the ballot-box.

First, *set yourselves against all political falsehood.* The most monstrous lies ever told in this country are during the elections. I stop at the door of a Democratic meeting and listen, and hear that the Republicans are thieves. I stop at the door of a Republican meeting and listen, and hear that the Democrats are scoundrels. Our public men microscopized, and the truth distorted. Who believes a tenth part of what he reads or hears in the autumnal elections? Men who at other seasons of the year are very careful in their speech become peddlers of scandal.

In the Far East there is a place where, once a year, they let the people do as they please and say what they please, and the place is full of uproar, misrule, and wickedness, and they call it the "Devil's day." The nearest approximation to that in this country has been the first Tuesday in November. The community at such times seem to say, "Go to, now; let us have a good time at lying." Prominent candidates for office are denounced as renegade and inebriate. A small lie will start in the corner of a country newspaper, and keep on running until it has captured the printing-presses of the whole continent. What garbling of speeches! What misinterpretation of motives! What misrepresentation of individual antecedents! To capture the unwary you shall have a ticket with Democratic heading and Republican names following, and then a Republican heading with Democratic names following; and the poor man will stand at the polls bewildered, at last, perhaps, voting for those whom he has been three weeks vociferously denouncing. O Christian men! frown upon this political falsehood! Remember that a political lie is as black as any other kind of a lie. God has recorded all the falsehoods that have been told at the city, state, or national elections since the foundation of this Government; and, though the perpetrators and their victims may have gone into the dust, in the last day judgment will be awarded. The falsehoods that Aaron Burr breathed into the ear of Blennerhasset, the slanders that Lieutenant-general Gage proclaimed about George Washington, the misrepresentations in regard to James Monroe, are as fresh on God's book to-day as the lie that was printed last week about Samuel J. Tilden or

Governor Dix. "And all liars shall have their part in the lake which burneth with fire and brimstone: which is the second death."

Again, *I counsel you as Christian men to set yourselves against the misuse of money in political campaigns.* Of the tens of thousands of dollars already spent this autumn, how much of the amount do you suppose has been properly used? You have a right to spend money for the publishing of political tracts, for the establishment of organizations for the carrying-out of what you consider to be the best; you have a right to appeal to the reason of men by argument and statistics and by facts; but he who puts a bribe into the hand of a voter, or plies weak men with mercenary and corrupt motives, commits a sin against God and the nation. Bribery is one of the most appalling sins of this country. God says, "Fires shall consume the tabernacles of bribery." Have nothing to do with such a sin, O Christian man! Fling it from the ballot-box. Hand over to the police the man who attempts to tamper with your vote, and remember that elections that can not be carried without bribes ought never to be carried at all.

Again, *I ask you as Christian men to set yourselves against the dissipations that hover over the ballot-box.* Let me say that no man can afford to go into political life who is not a teetotaler. Hot political discussion somehow creates an unnatural thirst, and hundreds of thousands of men have gone down into drunkenness through political life. After an exciting canvass through the evening you must "take something;" and rising in the morning with less animation than usual, you must "take something;" and going off among your comrades through the forenoon, you meet political friends, and you must "take something;" and in the afternoon you meet other political friends, and you must "take something;" and before night has come something has taken you. There are but few cases where men have been able to stand up against the dissipations of political life. Joseph was a politician, but he maintained his integrity. Daniel was a politician, but he was a teetotaler to the last. Abraham was a politician, but he was always characterized as the father of the faithful. Moses was a politician, the grandest of them; but he honored God more than he did the Pharaohs. And there are hundreds of Christian men now in the political parties, maintaining their integrity, even when they are obliged to stand amidst the blasted, lecherous, and loathsome crew that sometimes surround the ballot-box; these Christian men doing their political duty, and then coming back to the prayer-meetings and Christian circles as pure as when they went out. But that is not the ordinary circumstance; that is the exception. How often you see men coming back from the political conflict, and their eye is glazed, and their cheek has an unnatural flush, and they talk louder than they usually do, and at the least provocation they will bet, and you say they are convivial, or they are exceedingly vivacious, or you apply some other sweet name to them; but God knows they are drunk! Some of you, a month or six weeks ago, had no more religion than you ought to have, and after the elections are over, to calculate how much religion you have left will be a sum in vulgar fractions. Oh, the pressure is tremendous!

Again, I counsel you that, when you go to the ballot-box at the city or the state or the national elections, *you recognize God, and appeal to Him for His blessing.* There is a power higher than the ballot-box, than the Gubernatorial chair, than the Presidential White House. It is high time that we put less confidence in political platforms and more confidence in God. See what a weak thing is human foresight. How little our wise men seem to know! See how, every autumn, thousands of men who are clambering up for higher positions are turned under. God upsets them. Every man, every party, every nation, has a mission to perform. Failing to perform it, down he goes.

God said to the House of Bourbon, "Remodel France, and establish equity." House of Bourbon would not do it. Down it went. God said to the House of Stuart, "Make the English people free, God-fearing, and happy." House of Stuart would not do it. Down it went. God said to the House of Hapsburg, "Rule Austria in righteousness, and open the prison-houses until the captives shall go free." House of Hapsburg refuses to do it. Down it goes. God says to the political parties in this day, "By the principles of Christianity remodel, govern, educate, save the people." Failing to do that, down they go, burying in their ruins their disciples and advocates. God can spare all the political intriguers of this day, and can raise up another generation who shall do justice and love mercy.

O Christian men! take out your Bible this afternoon, and in the light of that word make up your mind as to what is your duty as citizens. Remember that the highest kind of a patriot is a Christian patriot. Consecrate yourselves first to God, then you will know how to consecrate yourselves to your country. All these political excitements will be gone. Ballot-boxes and Gubernatorial chairs and continents will smoke in the final conflagration; but those who love God and do their best shall come to lustrous dominion after the stars have ceased their shining, and the ocean has heaved its last billow, and the closing thunder of the judgment-day shall toll at the funeral of a world! Oh, prepare for that day! Next Tuesday questions of the State will be settled; but there comes a day when the questions of eternity will be decided. You may vote right, and may get the victory at the ballot-box, and yet suffer eternal defeat. After you have cast your last vote, where will you go to? In this country there are two parties. You belong to the one or the other of them. Likewise in eternity there will be two parties, and only two. "These shall go away into everlasting punishment; but the righteous into life eternal." To which party will you belong? God grant that, while you look after the welfare of the land in which God has graciously cast your lot, you may not forget to look after your soul—blood-bought, judgment-bound, immortal! God save the people!

Charles Haddon Spurgeon
[1834–1892]

Charles Haddon Spurgeon was born in England, and rose quickly to fame. When only 22 years of age he was recognized as one of the most popular preachers in the world. His career, extending over almost two generations, was largely confined to his Tabernacle where he drew larger crowds than perhaps any other preacher of his time. This example of his sermons is typically evangelistic, and displays the vitality which characterized all of his pulpit utterances.

EVERYBODY'S SERMON

I have multiplied visions and used similitudes. HOSEA 12:10.

WHEN THE LORD would win His people Israel from their iniquities, He did not leave a stone unturned but gave them precept upon precept, line upon line, here a little and there a little. He taught them sometimes with a rod in His hand, at other times He sought to win them with bounties for He multiplied their corn and oil. But all the teachings of His providence were unavailing, and while His hand was stretched out still they continued to rebel against the Most High. Among God's agencies for striking their attention and their conscience, was the use of similitudes. The prophets were accustomed not only to preach but to be themselves as signs and wonders to the people.

On one occasion the Lord said unto Isaiah, "Go and loose the sackcloth from off thy loins and put off the shoe from thy foot." And he did so, walking naked and barefoot. And the Lord said, "Like as my servant, Isaiah, hath walked naked and barefoot three years for a sign and wonder, so shall the king of Assyria lead away captives young and old, naked and barefoot."

God is every day preaching to us by similitudes. When Christ was on earth He preached in parables. Providence is God's sermon. The things which we see about us are God's thoughts and God's words to us; and if we were but wise there is not a step that we take which we should not find to be full of mighty instruction. God warns you every day by His own word; He speaks to you by the lips of His servants, His ministers; but besides this by similitudes He addresses you. He leaves no stone unturned to bring His wandering children to Himself.

Your children gather around your table for the morning meal. If you have been wise God has been preaching to you by a similitude then. He seemed to say to you: "To whom should a child go but to his Father? And where should be his resort when he is hungry but to his Father's table?" And as you fed your children the Lord was speaking to you and saying, "How willingly would I feed you! How would I give you of the bread of heaven and cause you to eat angels' food! But thou hast spent thy money for that which is not bread. Hearken diligently unto me and eat ye that which is good and let thy soul delight itself in fatness." Did he not stand there as a Father and say, "Come, my child, come to my table for I love my children to be there and to feast upon the mercies I have provided."

And now it is time for thee to retire to thy rest. The door is bolted and thou hast fast closed it. Did not that remind thee of that saying, "When once the Master of the house is risen up and hath shut to the door and ye begin to stand without and to knock at the door saying, 'Lord, Lord, open unto us,' and He shall answer and say unto you, 'I know not whence you are.'" Did He not preach to thee by similitude?

It was but a little while ago that we were sowing the seeds in our garden and scattering the corn over the broad furrows. God had sent the seedtime to remind us that we too are like the ground and that He is scattering seeds in our hearts each day. And did He not say unto us, "Take heed, O man, lest thou shouldst be like the highway whereon the seed was scattered but the fowls of the air devoured it. But be thou like the good ground whereon the seed did fall and it brought forth fruit some twenty, some fifty and some a hundred fold."

In a very little while you will see the birds congregating on the housetops in great multitudes as if they were taking their last sight at old England, you will see them, with their leader in advance speed across the purple sea to live in sunnier climes. And doth not God seem to preach to you when the birds are taking their flight? Did you not remember how he himself puts it? "Yea, the stork in the heaven knoweth her appointed times; and the crane and the swallow observe the time of their coming; but my people know not the judgment of the Lord."

I remember well how once God preached to me by a similitude in the depth of winter. The earth had been black. On a sudden, God spake and unlocked the treasures of the snow and white flakes descended until there was no blackness to be seen and all was one sheet of dazzling whiteness. It was at the time that I was seeking the Saviour and it was then that I found Him and I remember well that sermon which I saw before me:

"Come now and let us reason together; though your sins be as scarlet they shall be as snow; though they be red like crimson they shall be whiter than wool." God's grace is like the white snow.

Are you busy in building all day long, laying the stone upon its fellow and the mortar in the crevice? Then remember thou art building for eternity. Oh that thou mayest thyself be built upon a good foundation. Oh that thou mayest build thereon, not wood, hay, stubble but gold and silver and precious stones and things that will abide. Jesus Christ saith to thee this day, "Oh that thou wouldst consider thy latter end!" He cries to thee today, "How often would I have gathered thee as a hen gathereth her chickens under her wings and ye would not." "Believe on the Lord Jesus Christ and thou shalt be saved."

Phillips Brooks

[1835–1893]

Phillips Brooks was born in Boston, where he spent the first years of his career as a teacher, not beginning his brilliant ministry until he moved to Philadelphia. Later he returned to his birthplace and passed the greater number of his preaching years at Trinity Church, which stands today as a memorial to his ministry. In the later years of his life he was Bishop of Massachusetts. Brooks had a vivid, powerful style as a preacher. The following sermon, preached on July 4, 1880, in Westminster Abbey, so moved Dean Stanley that he gave way to tears, saying that no sermon had ever affected him so deeply.

THE CANDLE OF THE LORD

The spirit of man is the candle of the Lord. PROVERBS 20:27.

THE essential connection between the life of God and the life of man is the great truth of the world; and that is the truth which Solomon sets forth in the striking words which I have chosen for my text this morning. The picture which the words suggest is very simple. An unlighted candle is standing in the darkness and some one comes to light it. A blazing bit of paper holds the fire at first, but it is vague and fitful. It flares and wavers and at any moment may go out. But the vague, uncertain, flaring blaze touches the candle, and the candle catches fire and at once you have a steady flame. It burns straight and clear and constant. The candle gives the fire a manifestation-point for all the room which is illuminated by it. The candle is glorified by the fire and the fire is manifested by the candle. The two bear witness that they were made for one another by the way in which they fulfil each other's life. That fulfilment comes by the way in which the inferior substance renders obedience to its superior. The candle obeys the fire. The docile wax acknowledges that the subtle flame is its master and it yields to his power; and so, like every faithful servant of a noble master, it at once gives its master's nobility the chance to utter itself, and its own substance is clothed with a glory which is not its own. The disobedient granite, if you try to burn it, neither gives the fire a chance to show its brightness nor gathers any splendor to itself. It only glows with sullen resistance, and, as the heat increases, splits and breaks but will not yield. But the candle obeys, and so in it the scattered fire finds a point of permanent and clear expression.

Can we not see, with such a picture clear before us, what must be meant when it is said that one being is the candle of another being? There is in a community a man of large, rich character, whose influence runs everywhere. You cannot talk with any man in all the city, but you get, shown in that man's own way, the thought, the feeling of that central man who teaches all the community to think, to feel. The very boys catch something of his power, and have something about them that would not be there if he were not living in the town. What better description could you give of all that, than to say that that man's life was fire and that all these men's lives were candles which he lighted, which gave to the rich, warm, live, fertile nature that was in him multiplied points of steady exhibition, so that he lighted the town through them?

And now, regarding all this lighting of life from life, two things are evident, the same two which appeared in the story of the candle and its flame: First, there must be a correspondency of nature between the two; and second, there must be a cordial obedience of the less to the greater. The nature which cannot feel the other nature's warmth, even if it is held close to it; and the nature which refuses to be held where the other nature's flame can reach it,—both of these must go unlighted, no matter how hotly the fire of the higher life may burn.

I think that we are ready now to turn to Solomon and read his words again and understand them. "The spirit of man is the candle of the Lord," he says. God is the fire of this world, its vital principle, a warm pervading presence everywhere. What thing of outward nature can so picture to us the mysterious, the subtle, the quick, live, productive and destructive thought, which has always lifted men's hearts and solemnized their faces when they have said the word GOD, as this strange thing, —so heavenly, so unearthly, so terrible, and yet so gracious; so full of creativeness, and yet so quick and fierce to sweep whatever opposes it out of its path,—this marvel, this beauty and glory and mystery of fire? Men have always felt the fitness of the figure; and the fire has always crowded, closest of all earthly elements, about the throne on which their conception of Deity was seated. And now of this fire the spirit of man is the candle. What does that mean? If, because man is of a nature which corresponds to the nature of God, and just so far as man is obedient to God, the life of God, which is spread throughout the universe, gathers itself into utterance; and men, aye, and all other beings, if such beings there are, capable of watching our humanity, see what God is, in gazing at the man whom He has kindled,—then is not the figure plain? It is a wondrous thought, but it is clear enough. Here is the universe, full of the diffused fire of divinity. Men feel it in the air, as they feel an intense heat which has not broken into a blaze. That is the meaning of a great deal of the unexplained, mysterious awfulness of life, of which they who are very much in its power are often only half aware. It is the sense of God, felt but unseen, like an atmosphere burdened with heat that does not burst out into fire. Now in the midst of this solemn, burdened world there stands up a man, pure, God-like, and perfectly obedient to God. In an instant it is as if the heated room had found some sensitive, inflammable point where it could kindle to a blaze. The vague oppressiveness of God's felt presence becomes clear and definite. The fitfulness of the impression of divinity is steadied into permanence. The mystery changes its character, and is a mystery of light and not of darkness. The fire of the Lord has found the candle of the Lord, and burns clear and steady, guiding and cheering instead of bewildering and frightening us, just as soon as a man who is obedient to God has begun to catch and manifest His nature.

This is the truth of which I wish to speak to you to-day, the perpetual revelation of God by human life. You must ask yourself first, what God is. You must see how at the very bottom of His existence, as you conceive of it, lie these two thoughts—purpose and righteousness; how absolutely impossible it is to give God any personality except as the fulfilment of these two qualities—the intelligence that plans in love, and the righteousness that lives in duty. Then ask yourself how any knowledge of these qualities—of what they are, of what kind of being they will make in their perfect combination—could exist upon the earth if there were not a human nature here in which they could be uttered, from which they could shine. Only a person can truly utter a person. Only from a character can a character be echoed. You might write it all over the skies that God was just, but it would not burn there. It would be, at best, only a bit of knowledge; never a Gospel; never something which it would gladden the hearts of men to know. That comes only when a human life, capable of a justice like God's, made just by God, glows with His justice in the eyes of men, a candle of the Lord.

I have just intimated one thing which we need to observe. Man's utterance of God is purely an utterance of quality. It can tell me nothing of the quantities which make up His perfect life. That God is just, and what it is to be just—those things I can learn from the just lives of the just men about me; but how just God is, to what unconceived perfection, to what unexpected developments of itself, that majestic quality of justice may extend in Him,—of that I can form no judgment, that is worth anything, from the justice that I see in fellow-man. This seems to me to widen at once the range of the truth which I am stating. If it be the quality of God which man is capable of uttering, then it must be the quality of manhood that is necessary for the utterance; the quality of manhood, but not any specific quantity, not any assignable degree of human greatness. Whoever has in him the human quality, whoever really has the spirit of man, may be a candle of the Lord. A larger measure of that spirit may make a brighter light; but there must be a light wherever any human being, in virtue of his humanness, by obedience becomes luminous with God.

I have tried to depict some of the difficulties which beset the full exhibition in the world of this great truth of Solomon, that "the spirit of man is the candle of the Lord." Man is selfish and disobedient, and will not let his life burn at all. Man is wilful and passionate, and kindles his life with ungodly fire. Man is narrow and bigoted, and makes the light of God shine with his own special color. But all these are accidents. All these are distortions of the true idea of man. How can we know that? Here is the perfect man, Christ Jesus! What a man He is! How nobly, beautifully, perfectly human! What hands, what feet, what an eye, what a heart! How genuinely, unmistakably a man! I bring the men of my experience or of my imagination into His presence, and behold, just when the worst or best of them falls short of Him, my human consciousness assures me that they fall short also of the best idea of what it is to be a man. Here is the spirit of man in its perfection. And what then? Is it not also the candle of the Lord? "I am come a light into the world," said Jesus. "He that hath seen Me hath seen the Father." "In Him was life and the life was the light of men." So wrote the man of all men who knew Him best. And in Him where are the difficulties that we saw? where for one moment is the dimness of selfishness? O, it seems to me a wonderful thing that the supremely rich human nature of Jesus never for an instant turned with self-indulgence in on its own richness, or was beguiled by that besetting danger of all opulent souls, the wish, in the deepest sense, just to enjoy himself. How fascinating that desire is. How it keeps many and many of the most abundant natures in the world from usefulness. Just to handle over and over their hidden treasures, and with a spiritual miserliness to think their thought for the pure joy of thinking, and turn emotion into the soft atmosphere of a life of gardened selfishness. Not one instant of that in Jesus. All the vast richness of His human nature only meant for Him more power to utter God to man.

Above all the pictures of life,—of what it means, of what may be made out of it,—there stands out this picture of a human spirit burning with the light of the God whom it obeys, and showing Him to other men. O, my young friends, the old men will tell you that the lower pictures of life and its purposes turn out to be cheats and mistakes. But this picture can never cheat the soul that tries to realize it. The man whose life is a struggle after such obedience, when at last his earthly task is over, may look forward from the borders of this life into the other, and humbly say, as his history of the life that is ended, and his prayer for the life that is to come, the words that Jesus said—"I have glorified Thee on the earth; now, O Father, glorify Me with Thyself forever."

Dwight L. Moody

[1837-1899]

Born in Northfield, Massachusetts, Dwight L. Moody founded a Bible school there which has become world famous and serves today as the training school for many ministers. He was one of the greatest evangelists in an era of evangelism. With Ira D. Sankey to lead the music, Moody traveled all over the English-speaking world, preaching to great throngs and piling up an almost unbelievable number of conversions. Good News is full of simple illustrations and instances drawn from Moody's personal experience. It appeals to his hearers to accept the Christian way of life, and admirably reveals his magnetic persuasive powers.

GOOD NEWS

The Gospel. I CORINTHIANS 15:1.

I DO not think there is a word in the English language so little understood as the word "gospel." We hear it every day, and we have heard it from our earliest childhood, yet there are many people, and even many Christians, who do not really know what it means. I believe I was a child of God a long time before I really knew. The word "gospel" means "God's spell," or good spell, or in other words, "good news." The gospel is good tidings of great joy. No better news ever came out of heaven than the gospel. No better news ever fell upon the ears of the family of man than the gospel. When the angels came down to proclaim the tidings, what did they say to those shepherds on the plains of Bethlehem? "Behold I bring you *sad* tidings?" No! "Behold, I bring you *bad* news?" No!

"Behold, I bring you *good* tidings of *great joy,* which shall be to all people; for unto you is born this day, in the city of David, a Saviour."

My mind very often rolls back twenty years ago, before I was converted, and I think how dark it used to seem, as I thought of the future. I well remember how I used to look on death as a terrible monster, how he used to throw his dark shadow across my path; how I trembled as I thought of the terrible hour when he should come for me; how I thought I should like to die of some lingering disease, such as consumption, so that I might know when he was coming. It was the custom in our village to toll from the old church bell the age of any one who died. Death never entered that village and tore away one of the inhabitants but I counted the tolling of the bell. Sometimes it was seventy, sometimes eighty; sometimes it would be away down among the teens; sometimes it would toll out the death of some one of my own age. It made a solemn impression upon me. I felt a coward then. I thought of the cold hand of death feeling for the cords of life. I thought of being launched forth to spend my eternity in an unknown land.

But that is all changed now. The grave has lost its terror. As I go on towards heaven I can shout, "O death! where is thy sting?" and I hear the answer rolling down from Calvary—"buried in the bosom of the Son of God." He took the sting right out of death for me, and received it into His own bosom. Take a hornet and pluck the sting out; you are not afraid of it after that any more than of a fly. So death has lost its sting. That last enemy has been overcome, and I can look on death as a crushed victim. All that death can get now is this old Adam, and I do not care how quickly I get rid of it. I shall get a glorified body, a resurrection body, a body much better than this. The gospel has made an enemy a friend. What a glorious thought, that when you die you but sink into the arms of Jesus, to be borne to the land of everlasting rest! "To die," the apostle says, "is gain."

Another terrible enemy that troubled me was *Sin*. What a terrible hour I thought it would be, when my sins from childhood, every secret thought, every evil desire, everything done in the dark, should be brought to the light, and spread out before an assembled universe! Thank God, these thoughts are gone. The gospel tells me my sins are all put away in Christ. Out of love to me He has taken all my sins and cast them behind His back. That is a safe place for them. God never turns back; He always marches on. He will never see your sins if they are behind His back—that is one of His own illustrations. Satan has to get behind God to find them. How far away are they, and can they ever come back again!

There is another enemy which used to trouble me a great deal—*Judgment*. I used to look forward to the terrible day when I should be summoned before God. I could not tell whether I should hear the voice of

Christ saying, "Depart from Me, ye cursed," or whether it would be, "Enter thou into the joy of thy Lord." And I thought that till he stood before the great white throne no man could tell whether he was to be on the right hand or the left. But the gospel tells me that is already settled: "There is now no condemnation to them which are in Christ Jesus." "Verily, verily"—and when you see that word in Scripture, you may know there is something very important coming—"Verily, verily, I say unto you, he that heareth my word, and believeth on Him that sent Me, *hath* everlasting life, and *shall not* come into condemnation, but *is passed* from death unto life." Well, now, *I* am not coming into judgment for sin. It is no open question. God's word has settled it. Christ was judged for me, and died in my stead, and I go free. He that believeth *hath*—h-a-t-h, hath. Is not that good news?

Sinner, would you be safe to-night? Would you be free from the condemnation of the sins that are past, from the power of the temptations that are to come? Then take your stand on the Rock of Ages. Let death, let the grave, let the judgment come, the victory is Christ's and yours through Him. Oh, will you not receive this gospel to-night—this wonderful message of His sacrifice for you?

It is a *free* gospel; any one may have it. You need not ask, "For whom is this good news?" It is for yourself. If you would like Christ's own word for it, come with me to that scene in Jerusalem where the disciples are bidding Him farewell. Calvary with all its horrors is behind Him; Gethsemane is over, and Pilate's judgment hall. He has passed the grave, and is about to take His place at the right hand of the Father. Around Him stands His little band of disciples, the little church He was to leave behind Him to be His witnesses. The hour of parting has come, and He has some "last words" for them. Is He thinking about Himself in these closing moments? Is He thinking about the throne that is waiting Him, and the Father's smile that will welcome Him to heaven? Is He going over in memory the scenes of the past; or is He thinking of the friends who have followed Him so far, who will miss Him so much when He is gone? No, He is thinking about *you*. You imagined He would think of those who loved Him? No, sinner, He thought of you then. He thought of His enemies, those who shunned Him, those who despised Him, those who killed Him—He thought what more He could do for them. He thought of those who would hate Him, of those who would have none of His gospel, of those who would say it was too good to be true, of those who would make excuse that He never died for *them*. And then turning to His disciples, His heart just bursting with compassion, He gives them His farewell charge, "Go ye into ALL the world and preach the gospel TO EVERY CREATURE." They are almost His last words, "to every creature."

I can imagine Peter saying, "Lord, do you really mean that we shall preach the gospel to *every* creature?" "Yes, Peter." "Shall we go back to Jerusalem and preach the gospel to those Jerusalem sinners who murdered you?" "Yes, Peter, go back and tarry there until you are endued with power from on high. Offer the gospel to them first. Go search out that man who spat in my face; tell him I forgive him; there is nothing in my heart but love for him. Go, search out the man who put that cruel crown of thorns on my brow; tell him I will have a crown ready for him in my kingdom, if he will accept salvation; there shall not be a thorn in it, and he shall wear it for ever and ever in the kingdom of his Redeemer. Find out that man who took the reed from my hand, and smote my head, driving the thorns deeper into my brow. If he will accept salvation as a gift, I will give him a sceptre, and he shall sway it over the nations of the earth. Yes, I will give him to sit with Me upon my throne. Go, seek that man who struck Me with the palm of his hand; find him and preach the gospel to him; tell him that the blood of Jesus Christ cleanseth from all sin, and my blood was shed for him freely." Yes, I can imagine Him saying, "Go, seek out that poor soldier who drove the spear into my side; tell him that there is a nearer way to my heart than that. Tell him that I forgive him freely; and tell him I will make him a soldier of the cross, and my banner over him shall be love."

I thank God that the gospel is to be preached to *every* creature. I thank God the commission is so free. There is no man so far gone, but the grace of God can reach him; no man so desperate or so black, but He can forgive him. Yes, I thank God I can preach the gospel to the man or the woman who is as black as hell itself. I thank God for the "whosoevers" of the invitations of Christ. "God so loved the world that He gave His only begotten Son, that *whosoever* believeth on Him should not perish, but have everlasting life," and *"Whosoever will,* let him take the water of life freely."

Washington Gladden

[1836–1918]

The voice of Washington Gladden will be remembered by many living today who were fortunate enough to hear him either from his own pulpit or from the lecture platform. He was born at Pottsgrove, Pennsylvania, and was educated at Williams College, the University of Wisconsin, and Notre Dame. In 1860 he was ordained in the Congregational ministry. Thus began a long and influential life of public service as preacher, lecturer, and writer which left a deep imprint upon the thinking of America. His poetic soul shone through all he wrote or preached and he ranks high both as a minister and as a literary figure.

THE GOSPEL IN THE GRASS

And he shall be as the light of the morning when the sun riseth, even a morning without clouds; as the tender grass springing out of the earth by clear shining after rain. II SAMUEL 23:4.

WE ARE STANDING once more among the glories of a new world. The heavens are old, they change not; by day the same soundless blue or the same somber curtaining of clouds; at night the same starry cope, upon whose arches the same constellations flash, in whose depths of gloom the same nebulæ are hiding; but the earth is new; we see

> "In all that meets the eyes
> The freshness of a glad surprise."

New color is in the meadows, new blooms are in the borders, new songs in the branches. Some of the old furniture of the earth is here—the houses in which we live, the pavements on which we walk; but the world itself is as new as it was when God first called the dry land earth and the gathering together of the waters seas—as new and a thousand times as beautiful. How do I know? I know partly by experience. Is there any knowledge more certain? The earth is a great deal more beautiful now than it was when I was a boy; the meadows are greener, the skies of May are sunnier, the blended colors and the mingled odors and the choiring voices of the world are fairer and sweeter every year. If the world has been going on in this way in my short day—from glory to glory—it is not unreasonable to suppose that it has always been going on in the same way; and that it was far less beautiful when it first began to be than it is to-day. There are other evidences, to other minds doubtless more convincing, but I will not go into them; that would lead us aside from the pleasant paths in which this morning we have chosen to go.

But the miracle of spring once more repeated before our eyes, the return of the birds and the blossoms, the reviving of life in the fields and the woods—this is not to be lightly noted, not to be passed by as commonplace, but to be studied with reverence and beheld with wonder and rejoiced in with ever increasing thankfulness.

Of all the things that come back to us from their long exile in the regions of winter, not the least pleasant, not the least welcome is the lowly grass. It was the last to leave us when the tribes of life took their departure. When the winter came in with his soft-footed frosts, and his careering blasts, and when, before his onset that grew deadlier, day by day, one after another of the green things growing failed and fled, the grass held its ground till all the rest had gone; bravely it covered the retreat of its kindred; its green pennants waved in the rear of the flying foliage and the departing bloom. The brave beauties that held their heads so high in the soft days of spring and the proud months of midsummer vanished long before the grass surrendered; the forests, after all their songs of battle, and their boastful notes of victory over winds and snows, had folded their splendid banners many a day when the grass was still keeping guard over the graves of the dead flowers. The last to depart it is the first to return.

The psalmist is speaking the language of science as well as of poetry when he says, "He causeth the grass to grow for the cattle and herb for the service of man." The word here translated "herb" in the original signifies those plants which are edible by man; the word translated grass, all those plants which furnish food mainly to animals. This is the chief economical use of the grass. It does not nourish our bodies directly; but it nourishes the lives of those creatures upon which we subsist. Is this ministry any the less beneficent because it is indirect? Are we any less indebted to the grass because the substance that its life organizes for us comes to us through other lives which it feeds and nourishes?

Here again we find a lesson that need not detain us long. Much of the good that we do will be done indirectly. Truth that we impart to those nearest us will be imparted by them in their turn to others. Impressions made upon the lives of those about us by our characters and conduct will be reflected from their lives to the lives of others. But this is not all. We must not forget that much indirect and preparatory work must needs be done in morals and in religion. It is not always possible for us to reach directly the ultimate and supreme results of character in our work for others. It is sometimes a question whether those results are in any way directly attainable. The ways of spiritual culture are sometimes long and circuitous; and there is no royal road to character any more than to knowledge. You would like to see the life of your friend and neighbor wholly transformed. He is now a gross, hard-natured, selfish man; you want to see him changed into a gentle, amiable, pure-minded man. That is a most benevolent wish. But perhaps if you should go to work to secure that great change by preaching to him immediate repentance and radical reformation, you might fail of your purpose. That is just what he ought to do, no doubt of that; but perhaps he is not yet ready for a moral revolution. It is sometimes necessary to take a character by siege; the attempt to take it by storm is not only futile but disastrous. A great many things can be done for this man that would tend indirectly, but very effectually, to bring about this result in his character. If you preached repentance to him he might turn you out of doors; but if you give him a kindly word as now and then you meet him; if you show yourself his friend sometimes at cost to yourself of time or toil or wounded sensibility; if you approve yourself to him as the servant of a better Master, by pureness, by long-suffering, by kindness, by the Holy Ghost, by love unfeigned, by the word of truth, by the power of God, by the armor of righteousness on the right hand and on the left, the Gospel as incarnated in you may make its impression on him, and though he would not receive your message when he heard it from your lips, he may be constrained to heed it when he sees it organized into your life.

We sometimes seek to reform men who have fallen into vice, and fail because we aim directly at the result, and are not ready to do the indirect and preparatory work which is necessary in order that the reform may have some sure ground to go upon. This man is a drunkard. You want him to sign the pledge. That may be well; but the danger is that he may not keep it. The man's habit of drinking is not an ultimate and isolated fact, out of all relation to other facts of his life and environment. There are reasons why he drinks; they are not good and sufficient reasons; they are bad and insufficient reasons; but they serve as motives to lead him into this evil course. You must get down to them, if you can, and remove them. Perhaps he is out of work, and low-spirited, and takes to drink in the hope of forgetting his anxieties. It is the device of a fool, of course; for the remedy only aggravates the disease; but this man is just such a fool as that, and there are many such. If you could help him to find work you might indirectly but very efficiently help him to reform. Perhaps he is lonely, and takes to the dram-shop for society. There ought to be places enough where he could find pleasanter society. If you will provide such places and bring him into them, and make him at home in them, you will indirectly aid him to break off his evil habit. Perhaps he is wretched for some unexplained cause, and foolishly seeks to forget his wretchedness in the momentary exhilaration of the cup. If so, by doing what you innocently can to make him happier you will take away a good part of his temptation.

My friends, this great evil of drunkenness is not merely the source of misery, it is a symptom of misery as well. People are not only miserable because they drink, they drink because they are miserable, and you will never get them to stop drinking, by the strongest laws that men can make and the strongest pledges men can frame, until you get at some of the causes of their vice and misery and remove them. The *indirect* work to be done in removing the evil of intemperance is measureless in its extent, and in its urgency, and the people who think they can cure it all by legislation or by preaching, either, have but childish notions of the real causes of it, or the depth to which its roots go down.

So, then, the parable of the grass has taught us once more not to despise the ministry that is indirect and mediate, that spends itself before its end is reached; the service that begins a long way from the reward and works toward it silently and patiently, content to merge itself in other lives, and to let the fruit of its sowing be reaped by other hands.

One of the commonest of the messages of the grass to men is the truth of our mortality: "As for man his days are as grass; as a flower of the field so he flourisheth; for the wind passeth over it and it is gone, and the place thereof knoweth it no more. In the morning they are like grass that groweth up. In the morning it flourisheth and groweth up. In the evening it is cut down and withereth." I need not emphasize the message. Even amid the fresh verdure of May you will not forget it. The tender grass springing out of the earth to-day will soon return to earth as it was, and so will you. "Whatsoever therefore thy hand now findeth to do, do it with thy might."

Henry Drummond

[1851–1897]

Henry Drummond was born at Stirling, Scotland, and early distinguished himself in religion and scholarship. He studied at Edinburgh University, and then at New College, Edinburgh, where he trained for the ministry of the Free Church. Though evangelical in his outlook, Drummond's keen interest in science and its relationship to religion led him to a lectureship on Natural Science in the Free Church College at Glasgow and the publication of a book, Natural Law in the Spiritual World. *This in turn led to a professorship in the college. He held this for the remainder of his life, lecturing on geology, botany, biology, and evolution. Although Drummond is popularly known for his little volume,* The Greatest Thing in the World, *the following sermon, written after the death of a friend, has been read by many and has proven a source of comfort and understanding. It is his answer to the question of death.*

GOING TO THE FATHER

I go to my Father. JOHN 14:12.

DID YOU ever notice Christ's favourite words? If you have, you must have been struck by two things—their simplicity and their fewness. Some half-dozen words embalm all His theology, and these are, without exception, humble, elementary, simple monosyllables. They are such words as these: world, life, trust, love.

But none of these was the greatest word of Christ. His great word was new to religion. There was no word there, when He came, rich enough to carry the new truth He was bringing to men. So He imported into religion one of the grandest words of human language, and transfigured it, and gave it back to the world illuminated and transformed, as the watchword of the new religion. That word was Father.

Now the thing which steadied Christ's life was the thought that He was going to His Father. This one thing gave it unity, and harmony, and success. During His whole life He never forgot His Word for a moment. There is no sermon of His where it does not occur; there is no prayer, however brief, where it is missed. In that first memorable sentence of His, which breaks the solemn spell of history and makes one word resound through thirty silent years, the one word is this; and all through the after years of toil and travail "the Great Name" was always hovering on His lips, or bursting out of His heart. In its beginning and in its end, from the early time when He spoke of His Father's business till He finished the work that was given Him to do, His life, disrobed of all circumtance, was simply this, "I go to My Father."

If we take this principle into our own lives, we shall find its influence tell upon us in three ways:

I. It explains Life.
II. It sustains Life.
III. It completes Life.

I. It explains Life. Few men, I suppose, do not feel that life needs explaining. We think we see through some things in it—partially; but most of it, even to the wisest mind, is enigmatic. Those who know it best are the most bewildered by it, and they who stand upon the mere rim of the vortex confess that even for them it is overspread with cloud and shadow. What is my life? whither do I go? whence do I come? these are the questions which are not worn down yet, although the whole world has handled them.

To these questions there are but three answers—one by the poet, the other by the atheist, the third by the Christian.

(a) The poet tells us, and philosophy says the same only less intelligibly, that life is a sleep, a dream, a shadow. It is a vapour that appeareth for a little and vanisheth away; a meteor hovering for a moment between two unknown eternities; bubbles, which form and burst upon the river of time. This philosophy explains nothing. It is a taking refuge in mystery. Whither am I going? Virtually the poet answers, "I am going to the Unknown."

(b) The atheist's answer is just the opposite. He knows no unknown. He understands all, for there is nothing more than we can see or feel. Life is what matter is; the soul is phosphorus. Whither am I going? "I go to dust," he says; "death ends all." And this explains nothing. It is worse than mystery. It is contradiction. It is utter darkness.

(c) But the Christian's answer explains something. Where is he going?

"I go to my Father." This is not a definition of his death—there is no death in Christianity; it is a definition of the Christian life. All the time it is a going to the Father. Some travel swiftly, some are long upon the road, some meet many pleasant adventures by the way, others pass through fire and peril; but though the path be short or winding, and though the pace be quick or slow, it is a going to the Father.

When we see Him, we must speak to Him. We have that language to learn. And that is perhaps why God makes us pray so much. Then we are to walk with Him in white. Our sanctification is a putting on this white. But there has to be much disrobing first; much putting off of filthy rags. This is why God makes man's beauty to consume away like the moth. He takes away the moth's wings, and gives the angel's, and man goes the quicker and the lovelier to the Father.

The other thing which this truth explains is why there is so much that is unexplained. After we have explained all, there is much left. All our knowledge, it is said, is but different degrees of darkness. But we know *why we do not know why*. It is because we are going to our Father. We are only going: we are not there yet. Therefore patience. "What I do thou knowest not now, but thou shalt know. Hereafter, thou shalt know." Hereafter, because the chief joy of life is to have something to look forward to. But, hereafter, for a deeper reason. Knowledge is only given for action. Knowing only exists for doing: and already nearly all men know to do more than they do do. So, till we do all that we know, God retains the balance till we can use it. In the larger life of the hereafter, more shall be given, proportionate to the vaster sphere and the more ardent energies.

Necessarily, therefore, much of life is still twilight. But our perfect refuge is to anticipate a little, and go in thought to our Father, and, like children tired out with efforts to put together the disturbed pieces of a puzzle, wait to take the fragments to our Father.

And yet, even that fails sometimes. He seems to hide from us and the way is lost indeed. The footsteps which went before us up till then cease, and we are left in the chill, dark night alone. If we could only see the road, we should know it went to the Father. But we cannot say we are going to the Father; we can only say *we would like to go*. "Lord," we cry, "we know not whither Thou goest, and how can we know the way?" "Whither I go," is the inexplicable answer, "ye know not now." Well is it for those who at such times are near enough to catch the rest: "But ye shall know hereafter."

II. Secondly, and in a few words, this sustains Life.

A year or two ago some of the greatest and choicest minds of this country laboured, in the pages of one of our magazines, to answer the question, "Is Life worth living?" It was a triumph for religion, some thought, that the keenest intellects of the nineteenth century should be stirred with themes like this. It was not so; it was the surest proof of the utter heathenism of our age. Is Life worth living? As well ask, Is air worth breathing? The real question is this—taking the definition of life here suggested—Is it worth while going to the Father?

There is nothing to sustain life but this thought. And it does sustain life. Take even an extreme case, and you will see how. Take the darkest, saddest, most pathetic life of the world's history. That was Jesus Christ's. See what this truth *practically* was to Him. It gave Him a life of absolute composure in a career of most tragic trials.

This is the Christian's only stay in life. It provides rest for his soul, work for his character, an object, an inconceivably sublime object, for his ambition. It does not stagger him to be a stranger here, to feel the world passing away. The Christian is like the pearl-diver, who is out of the sunshine for a little, spending his short day amid rocks and weeds and dangers at the bottom of the ocean. Does he desire to spend his life there? No, but his master does. Is his life there? No, his life is up above. A communication is open to the surface, and the fresh pure life comes down to him from God. Is he not wasting time there? He is gathering pearls for his Master's crown. Will he always stay there? When the last pearl is gathered, the "Come up higher" will beckon him away, and the weights which kept him down will become an exceeding weight of glory, and he will go, he and these he brings with him, to his Father.

III. Lastly, in a word, this completes life.

Life has been defined as a going to the Father. It is quite clear that there must come a time in the history of all those who live this life when they reach the Father. This is the most glorious moment of life. Angels attend at it. Those on the other side must hail the completing of another soul with ineffable rapture. When they are yet a great way off, the Father runs and falls on their neck and kisses them.

On this side we call that Death. It means reaching the Father. It is not departure, it is arrival; not sleep, but waking. For life to those who live like Christ is not a funeral procession. It is a triumphal march to the Father, and the entry at the last in God's own chariot in the last hour of all. No, as we watch a life which is going to the Father, we cannot think of night, of gloom, of dusk and sunset. It is life which is the night, and Death is sunrise.

"Pray moderately," says an old saint, "for the lives of Christ's people." *Pray moderately.* We may want them on our side, he means, but Christ may need them on His. He has seen them a great way off, and set His heart upon them, and asked the Father to make them come quickly. "I will," He says, "that such an one should be with Me where I am." So it is better that they should go to the Father.

These words have a different emphasis to different persons. There are three classes to whom they come home with a peculiar emphasis:—

1. They speak to those who are staying away from God. "I do not wonder at what men suffer," says Ruskin, "I wonder often at what they lose." My fellow pilgrim, you do not know what you are losing by not going to the Father. You live in an appalling mystery. You have nothing to explain your life nor to sustain it; no boundary line on the dim horizon to complete it. When life is done you are going to leap into the dark. You will cross the dark river and land on the further shore alone. No one will greet you. You and the Inhabitant of Eternity will be strangers. Will you not to-day arise and go to your Father?

2. They speak, next, to all God's people. Let *us* remember that we are going to the Father. Even now are we the sons of God. Oh let us live like it—more simple, uncomplaining, useful, separate, joyful as those who march with music, yet sober as those who are to company with Christ. The road is heavy, high road and low road, but we shall soon be home. God grant us a sure arrival in our Father's house.

3. And this voice whispers yet one more message to the mourning. Did Death end all? Is it well with the child? It is well. The last inn by the roadside has been passed—that is all, and a voice called to us, "Good-bye! I go to my Father."

Russell H. Conwell

[1843–1925]

One of the most remarkable lecturers ever to appear on the American platform was Russell H. Conwell. He was born at Worthington, Massachusetts, and was educated for the law at Yale University. But after practicing law for a time, he turned to newspaper work and became foreign correspondent for the New York Tribune *and the* Boston Traveler. *In 1879 he was ordained in the Baptist ministry, and went to Philadelphia. There he founded Temple University and served as its president for several years. His famous lecture* Acres of Diamonds *was heard by millions of Americans, and the proceeds from it were given to the University. The sermon given here is one of several delivered by Dr. Conwell in tribute to the great men of American history and tradition. It shows his wide historical knowledge and understanding, as well as his mastery of rhetorical style.*

ABRAHAM LINCOLN

That which my soul seeketh I find not; one man among a thousand have I found, but a woman among all those have I found not. Lo, this only have

I found, that God hath made man upright; but they have sought out many inventions. Ecclesiastes 7:28, 29.

It is a very interesting thing, and a very profitable thing to read what the great editors and the great authors of the country write concerning that singular character, Abraham Lincoln. But it is very confusing to see how they differ in their estimate of the man, or the reasons they give for the place he holds in the esteem of the American people.

It is an interesting thing to find that such a character, one who never joined the Church, who never made what people sometimes call an open profession of religion, should now be a hero of the Church, and his principles accepted as principles of genuine Christianity.

It appears to me that the one man in a thousand for whom the preacher was looking is found in Abraham Lincoln but not because he differs from other men. It would be very useless for me to turn your attention to this great man if it were not for the fact that the lesson can be very helpful.

What was it that made Abraham Lincoln great? He was great; his influence was great. We must all admit that. But what was it that made him great—without special intelligence, or money, without education, culture or friends? What was it that led him to become the central figure in our history, where he did certain deeds that impressed the ages? It is reasonable for us to discuss, in view of the Scriptural illustration, what it was that made him one great man.

Many a disciple of Christ has tried to find in Abraham Lincoln a proof of the truth of his own creed, and maybe prove the tenets of his own church. But nevertheless, the great fact remains, that Abraham Lincoln, while he was in the habit of attending church, and while he read the Bible, and while he read religious books, and while he gave religious advice, never allied himself in any close way with any one denomination of Christians. He kept himself aloof for the time. It does not seem to have been because of any choice on his part. It seems to have been a kind of modest under-estimation of himself, or a sense of his weakness, or lack of culture or money, that kept him from uniting with any Christian church. Yet as a Christian he was one of God's ideal men. He was nearer to it than any American ever known. He was an upright man; uprightness was the peculiar characteristic of Abraham Lincoln.

The ideal man, as God made him is upright, and the word uprightness, when we get back to the Hebrew, covers quite an extensive vocabulary. "Uprightness" means a man of a good heart. O, that's the foundation of human greatness, a great, loving, good heart. And that made Abraham Lincoln a great man, with the help of prayer to God. Abraham Lincoln was a man of prayer. Whether he went to church or not; or read often the Bible or not; whether he believed in this creed, or that or the other, one thing is sure that continually, like Washington, he was a man of prayer. He believed in prayer and felt that his prayers would be answered as well as other people's who went to church more than he did. He was a "good-hearted" man. O that means so much!

Milton could write the most wonderful poetry that was ever penned by man. But he had a weak character. Nelson could say, "England expects every man to do his duty," and that phrase rang all over the world, and yet he could be a libertine, and when we look at many of our great men, even our own Franklin, we see some things that we mention under our breath. We find in every great man who has done some great thing or invented some great thing, some great defect of character. It is said that every great man has some peculiar weakness, and that is true very largely. If you find any man prominent in one way he always has some weakness. But Abraham Lincoln's character was an all-around good character. You do not find any man to assault his motives for moral uprightness. You could not expect to find in the time that Abraham Lincoln lived any man who declared him to be dishonest. He was "Honest Old Abe," and he was a great man because he had a good heart, and he was strictly honest and honorable. He was an ideal man, then, in his heart, and being an ideal, Christian hearted man, believing in the teachings of Jesus and praying unto God for help in times of distress, he developed that all-around character, so that you may put up the moral statute of Abraham Lincoln upon the pedestal.

He was characterized by one other faculty, and that was wisdom; the wisdom that is mentioned in Proverbs; the wisdom that is mentioned by Jesus Christ; that broad, every-day application of common sense. That is real wisdom. Man may search into philosophy and go deep into all kinds of experiments; he may discover some; he may invent something and call the attention of men to himself, but real wisdom is wisdom like that of Abraham Lincoln, that sees every day some good in every man. He was a man who could recognize good in his enemies as well as in his friends; who ever exercised his every-day common sense; who showed us that we ought to be forgiving to those who despitefully use us. The ideal man is the man who makes no unnecessary enemies, and who, if he has an enemy, tries to look upon that man in the same way as he would upon a friend. Abraham Lincoln's life was a special exposition of that disposition of forgiveness and brotherly kindness. The kind position he took with reference to the people of the South was such as to bring down upon him the condemnation of those who supported Wendell Phillips. I knew him personally, and he often privately said bitter things against Abraham Lincoln because Mr. Lincoln spoke kindly of the South, and spoke of the people of the South as friends and never as enemies. In one of his great speeches he said, "They are not our enemies; they are our friends," and because he approached the slavery question with common sense he had both sides and both extremes often opposed to him. He proposed, before the war began, that the government should raise money and buy the slaves and set them free. The North considered that the greatest possible foolishness and oppression, forgetting how many millions might be spent in the war, how many would go to death, and how great would be the depression in all the after years. They did not exercise common sense. But Abraham Lincoln looked out upon the whole field, and regarded the Southern people as mistaken friends, and as friends who were mistaken he proceeded with his whole heart, and with a kindly spirit and determination, to do precisely right, in bringing about the triumph of the cause of the Union, and when he was assassinated by a foolish fanatic, there was put a martyr's crown upon his life, that called attention to it so distinctly that it impressed its mark upon the ages as nothing else could do. So martyrs are ever honored, almost worshipped. When Abraham Lincoln was murdered, with his good heart, his excellent intentions, his broad common sense, his statesmanship, his death put God's seal upon those characteristics of the man who brought about the return of the South to the Union, through a teaching which has made them a solid glorious and permanent part of this great nation.

Abraham Lincoln was an upright man such as cannot be made by clothing; such as cannot be made by money; but which is made only by building upon the foundation of Christian faith, upon a large and loving heart. That heart had been broken, and having been broken it is fair to assume that God made him suffer, in order that he might be a better instrument for bringing about peace and prosperity to this great nation, and the setting up of a great people whose ideal he should be. Abraham Lincoln's faith and broad common sense showed him that this nation should lead all the nations of the earth in bringing them all up to that standard of Christian fellowship and brotherly love, where each should do unto the other as he would have the other do to him.

These, then, are the great characteristics in the life of Abraham Lincoln, his every-day sound judgment; his great, loving soul; his prayers to God and his faith in the ultimate triumph of right. With malice toward none, but with love for all, Abraham Lincoln set his faith in God, believing that righteousness would prevail, and that at last truth would triumph. That makes a great character. A small character that lives within its own narrow limits, thinks that all is going to the bad, that evil is everywhere extant, that the good are ever crushed and the wicked are ever prosperous, takes a small, uncommonsense view of life. But Abraham Lincoln was a broad character, who, having faith that all things were working together for good in the sight of God, and that somehow evil would be crushed and righteousness would prevail, became the giant man that he was, and his great influence came, not from the fact that he was a great statesman, or a great soldier, or a great scientist, or a great scholar, or great in any one invention, but because of that all-pervading, permanent good character and broad common sense, that sublime purpose in life which goes with sincere faith in God.

George Angier Gordon

[1853–1929]

Born in Scotland and educated at Harvard University, Dr. George Angier Gordon became pastor of the Old South Church (Congregational) at Boston in 1884. From that pulpit his voice was heard throughout America. In addition to preaching, he lectured at Lowell Institute and at Yale University, and published many books of great merit. Dr. Gordon's pulpit style was unique for its literary beauty and poetic power, as well as for its deep scholarship and wide learning.

THE WORLD UNDER THE ASPECT OF TRAGEDY

Because his compassions fail not. LAMENTATIONS 3:22.

THERE are four things present in all great tragedy. Every one of the tragic persons is to blame for the fateful complication, and no one is altogether to blame; the magnitude of the experience is unmeasured, the sin, the mistake, the suffering, the woe; mystery, like starless midnight, broods upon all the confines of being and overhangs the whole field of action; and lastly, there is pity arising in the heart of the spectator of the awful tragic movements, pity that purifies his heart, that exalts his soul, that brings with it a strange peace and a great indefinable hope.

Look into the heart of one of the greatest of all tragedies and see if these statements are not true. There is King Lear. He is to blame for vanity, over-fondness for affection, and credulity. Cordelia, that rare and beautiful soul, is to blame for temper and want of tact. If these two tragic persons in the drama are to blame, all the others surely are. Each one is to blame, and no one wholly to blame. Then there is the extent of that tragic complication; persons, families, kingdoms are involved; sin, mistake, and suffering are there that no mind can measure. The last thing that the tragedy does for the one who beholds it is to melt his heart in compassion, and the compassion brings with it awe, exaltation, and a strange peace and hope.

The man of genius who wrote the text, a great deep-hearted patriot, looked at his nation under the aspect of tragedy. In 586 b.c. Jerusalem was laid waste by the Chaldeans, and the youth, the beauty, the promise, and the power of the people were carried away, and only the remnants remained of those not slain or not enslaved. His nation was a nation in ruin; thus he beheld it. Every one was to blame for the fateful complication, and no one was wholly to blame; the magnitude of the experience was evident, outrunning all possible measurement or comprehension; mystery was brooding over all like a thick cloud so that not even his prayers could pierce through. Then the resultant mood, "It is of the Lord's mercies that we are not consumed, because his compassions fail not."

There are many ways of regarding this world of ours, its tumult, its terrible processes of wickedness and of suffering. The text bids us look at it under the aspect of tragedy and behold the world-wide complication for which every living being is in part responsible and for which no single individual, however wicked, is wholly responsible. Again, it bids us look at the immeasurable extent of the experience, the sin, the sheer ignorance, the perversity, the suffering, the woe; and once more, it bids us look at the mystery that overhangs the whole, dark, as I have said, as starless midnight, impenetrable, utterly inscrutable, and finally it directs attention to our own hearts, if we are men of faith, men of patriotism, of humanity, to the fountain flowing there of pity, of compassion; it seems to whisper that we are on the great world's altar-stairs that slope through darkness up to God.

The first great attribute in compassion is the understanding mind. God knows His world from the inside. Sometimes during the summer I pass this church and look up at the windows scorched with heat, covered with dust, black, unmeaning, and then I come into the House of God, find the radiance of the summer sun flooding the building, and I see there the Good Samaritan still healing the sick, there the Apostles and the Prophets still holding forth the Word of Life, there the saintly and faithful ones silently running on their errands of grace; lastly my eye lights upon the Parable of the Sower. "Behold, a sower went forth to sow" in the minds and hearts and wills of men. Here, from the inside, is the promise of a new and glorious world. God, the compassionate Father of men, understands His world from the inside. He sees His prophets still with their visions and their dreams. He sees His apostles still declaring the message of His Mind and Character; His healers and His faithful ones are all at work unseen and silent, the music of whose feet only the angels hear. And He sees a sower going forth to sow in the tragedy of the world new and better thoughts in the minds of men, and in their hearts new and deeper feelings, and in their wills new and greater purposes. He beholds, from the inside, vast movements out of the depths of the tragic world, promising by and by a morning without clouds.

Two members of his family went out to meet the lost son on his return, the elder brother and the father. The elder brother looked from the outside and said, "This son of yours who wasted your substance with harlots, you have feasted him." This is the outside view; it was absolutely correct as far as it went. Did it comprehend that young man's life? Ah, no. The father went forth to meet him, moved with compassion; he read the whole secret tragedy of his son's life, his sin, the plot into which his sin threw him, his mistake, his suffering, his woe, and the emergence as from Erebus, of his soul seeking life. Which understood that son, the brother or the father? God understands His world from the inside and rests on the vision of the order that shall come forth out of the tragedy that now reigns.

The second great attribute of compassion is magnanimity. That is the Greek word for "great-mindedness." Greek tragedy, in one way, is unsurpassable, perhaps incomparable, in its simplicity, in its integrity, in its austere order and power. It has little or no humour in it, and herein it is surely surpassed by Shakespearian tragedy which composes in its own vast mind both the pathos and the humour of life. Look into your Hamlet again. Is there any scene anywhere of more piercing pathos or profounder tragedy than Ophelia, beautiful Ophelia, crazed with grief and yet undying in her loveliness, strewing flowers upon the new-made grave of her father who was slain by her lover. A little further on you find the grave-digging scene, with its pure, irresistible humour. The debate between the grave-diggers shakes one's soul with merriment; and there is the conversation of the callous, mirthful grave-digger with the sorrowful, awe-struck Hamlet. Here is humour, pure as the spirit that made it, coming from the very heart of humanity in this tragic world, and both the pathos and the humour are reconciled, composed, wrought into a whole by the great-minded poet. Is not this true of life?

And Jesus, the most tragic figure in all history, moves to His cross and on the way notes the irrationality and absurdity of the time in which He lives, and says, "This generation is like unto children sitting in the market-place who call unto their fellows and say, 'We piped unto you, and ye did not dance; we wailed, and ye did not mourn.'" The tragedy and the comedy, He saw them deep as life and broad as the world, and He composed them in His own magnanimity.

Does not this help us toward the vision of the magnanimous God, Who makes His sun to rise upon the evil and the good and Who sends His rain upon the just and the unjust, not because He is indifferent to moral distinctions, but because of His Eternal Magnanimity. Again, He rests on the vision of the issue of the tragic complication and waits in His Eternal Peace.

Finally, there is in compassion another vast attribute that touches every one of us, and that is recreative moral power. The classic example is the lost son. What changed him, what made him new forever? It was his father's compassion. What changed Peter after that triple denial, that terrific treason of his soul to the truth and to his Master? The Lord turned and looked upon Peter. It was that compassionate look; the look not of reproach, not of indignation, not of the cry of vengeance, but of sorrow, of purest, divinest compassion, that made Peter new, and new forever.

How far our Lord's prayer upon the cross has gone: "Father, forgive them; for they know not what they do." It has gone everywhere and been a source of moral hope to the despairing and recreative power to those crumbling into dust.

Every human being here this morning needs this gospel of the Eternal Compassion. Those who are morally successful need it, they are so much less successful than they should be. That those who are morally defeated need it, I do not need to say. They who have the prospect of long life before them need it; and we whose daily chant is, "We who are about to die salute thee," we need it. The whole race of men needs it. And when we come to our human world, what shall we say to it to-day, tempest-tossed and driven by the tides of its own wickedness and ignorance, what shall we say to it? Come back to the Eternal Compassion. Do not dwell simply on the guilt of all, the magnitude, the sin, and the woe, nor upon the mystery that like a pall overhangs the whole. Read it from the point of view of compassion, find its meaning there.

About the most tremendous words in the New Testament are those that I read to-day, the most tragic I think, in the literature of mankind:

"O Jerusalem, Jerusalem, that killeth the prophets, and stoneth them that are sent unto her! How often would I have gathered thy children together, even as a hen gathereth her brood under her wings, and ye would not!"

And yet the religion of Jesus is the religion of compassion, the religion of the Eternal Compassion that cannot finally be defeated.

Here is the gospel. Do not sit down and paint the blackness of the world. It knows how black it is. Tell it of the loving-kindness of the Lord and His unfailing compassion. Climb on the altar-stairway of the pity in your own heart up through the gloom and into the presence of God.

Newell Dwight Hillis

[1858–1929]

Newell Dwight Hillis was born at Magnolia, Iowa. His rise to popular fame began with his first pastorate, the Presbyterian Church at Evanston, Illinois. Later he went to Central Church, Chicago, and in 1899 he was called to Plymouth Church, Brooklyn, where he succeeded Henry Ward Beecher and Lyman Abbott. His many books are widely known, both in the United States and Britain. The sermons of Hillis were powerful pleas for the richness and fullness of the Christian life, and were couched in the finest of language. He was indeed "master of the pulpit art."

WHAT IF CHRIST WERE NOT?

And Jesus said to his disciples, Will ye also go away? And Peter answered,
To whom? John 6:67, 68.

SEVERAL authors, with varying skill, have written books on the condition of the world if Christ were not. Henry Rogers wrote a book called "The Eclipse of Faith," in which he imagines that some powerful hand has wiped the influence of Christ out of civilization, as some hand wipes the chalk writing from the blackboard of the schoolroom. This brilliant author represents himself as going into his library to discover that every vestige of Christ's life and words has wholly disappeared. He opens his law books upon the legal safeguards protecting children in the poorhouses, the orphans, the chimney sweeps, the boys in the coal mines, the poor in tenements, the slaves everywhere, and lo! all these laws have disappeared, leaving paragraphs blank in some law books, with here and there whole pages, and indeed, entire chapters, until what is left on the code is meaningless jargon. Alarmed, he turned to his histories of art, and where the Transfiguration had been he found a blank page, and to the galleries, but instead of the *Sistine Madonna* of Raphael and the *Ecce Homo,* by Guido Reni, and Rembrandt's *Prodigal Son,* with thousands of other masterpieces, he found only empty frames. Turning to the greatest poems of Dante and Milton, of Wordsworth and Tennyson and Browning, he found nothing but empty pages with the number of the page at the top. Having long loved architecture with a great passion, his thoughts flew to St. Peter's in Rome, to Milan and Cologne and Westminster Abbey, and lo, nothing remained there but great cellars, for when the cross went, the cathedrals fashioned in the form of that cross perished also. And then it was that Rogers realized that if Christ were not, the schools, the hospitals, the beautiful philanthropies, the missions, so beneficent in their influence at home and abroad, would all perish, as if shaken down by some cosmic earthquake, and this lawyer cried out that he would not want to live at all in a world where Christ was not.

And to-day we all have our vision of a revolution against Jesus in thought and life. What if in the stress of a great crisis representatives of the nations of the earth should meet together, ostensibly to destroy war and organize a universal peace. But when the chairman of the world's conference begins his opening address, every one should notice the cynical look upon his face and the bitter note that had crept into his voice. The burden of his argument has to do with the economic wastes of Christian sympathy. He makes a plea against the industrial losses incident to Christ's story of the Good Samaritan. He estimates that our generation would save fiften to twenty per cent by coming out boldly for the anarchistic principle of every fellow for himself and the devil take the hindmost. He urges that the weak have no right to survive and should go to the wall. And that it is an outrage for the strong to be made unhappy by carrying the burdens of the weak. "Look abroad over the world—everywhere this Galilean's baneful influence is found. Why should the poorly born not die to-day, since they must die to-morrow? Why should not this conference declare plainly that Jesus of Nazareth, with His doctrine of love, pity and self-sacrifice, has laid an unbearable burden upon men? The key-word in this crisis," he says, "is revolt. Let us return to Nature, and live as the beasts and birds in the forests live, and die as they die—namely, a natural death, having no regard for these petty dreams of Christian immorality——" and this man carries the delegates, and with one voice they shout aloud, "Away with this superstition! Down with these spires!" And in the midst of the noise and confusion the twilight falls, and suddenly in the darkness a still, small voice is heard, that in the silence of each heart turns to thunder, "What I have made shall be unmade."

It shall be as you have willed. "Henceforth the light that was given is withdrawn, and for angels' bread there shall be the apples of Sodom, and for the wine and the nectar of Paradise there shall be what you ask, the dropping of asps and the poison of serpents." But going into the streets, these apostates look with altered eyes upon an altered world. Lifted, now, all the restraints of law! Wild men who through fear and shame had restrained their appetites suddenly reveal themselves. It is as if harpies and assassins have leaped from every alleyway upon those delegates, when the mob spirit bursts loose. Then come the crashing of plate glass windows, the shrieks of night watchmen, the looting of splendid stores and shops, and in the suburbs from the flaming houses are heard the shrieks of women and the moans of little children, for the beast is let loose. In fact, there is no Christ to stand between the wicked man and his victims. The scene is as dreadful for that great city as if the bells of time have tolled the beginning of eternity, while the great serpent winds his coils about the earth to crush it into nothingness. That noise is the crash of falling domes, cathedrals and tumbling spires above gallery, and minister, with the sound of pictures falling from their places, and statues tumbling from their niches, when structures of art and literature and law and reform, manifest in architecture, come down in full ruin. It is as if the sun had tumbled from the sky, leaving a black socket.

If Christ were not, the human intellect loses its only rational explanation ever given of the problem of suffering and sorrow. To deny the existence of pain is as foolish as to deny an earthquake that destroyed those towns in Italy, or that tidal wave that destroyed Lisbon, or the war that cursed Belgium and France. Granted the existence of summer and the harvests, we must accept the winter also. Granted the garden, the palm trees and the fountains, we cannot deny the desert, and the occasional famine. Ours is a world over which, from time to time, troubles sweep like sheeted storms. No man can escape. Genius has sought out many inventions, discovered many secrets, but genius has never built a roof nor a door that can shut out trouble. Soon or late death robs us of our loved ones. At last comes the day when the grasshopper becomes a burden and desire fails. At last the messenger upon his errand of release and convoy comes, not for others this time, but for you yourself. And in the world of selfishness, and ignorance, and sin Jesus comes into collision with the Pharisees, and Roman governors, and slave owners, and the more unyielding His convictions and ideals, the fiercer the collision. Denial is not enough; mere denial of pain will cure no torture of the soul in its Gethsemane. And then Jesus enters the scene. His message is that sufferings are educatory; that when the summer fails to turn the acid of the grapes to sugar, or sweeten the nuts, the frost completes the transformation; that gold is tried in the fire, and acceptable men in the furnace of adversity; that the self-sacrifice of one hero, with his death, means life and happiness to those who come after; that the greatest souls have come out of great tribulation, from the days of Moses and Paul, with their martyrdom and unaccomplished aims, to the days of Lincoln and Livingstone; that the richness of the soil begins with the glaciers' ice plough; that granite boulders are melted by fire billows, and that slowly, from upheaval, come harvests and a soil fit for growing the tree of life.

But if the world were without Christ, men would lose the motive to service and heroism. It was Jesus who made the sum of religion to be service and kindness, its emblem a cup of cold water and its genius to be helpful. The soul is not self-propulsive. All sailing boats need winds for their sails. There is no locomotive that does not depend upon some exterior power named steam and coal. The human soul is dependent upon motives for its forward movement.

But if there were no Christ, then the immortal hope perishes with Him. One December day, Harriet Martineau wrote her friend, saying: "For England the summer has gone, and for me the everlasting winter has set in." And when James Mill gave up the Christ he said that, "the clouds had slowly closed in and choked all hope, and that death had become only a leap into the dark, over a chasm, whose sharp rocks held an unknown power for mangling." The philosophers argued. The poets have hoped for a meeting place of the dead. The lovers have cried out for the beloved one. The parents have sobbed, "Is death a door into another room? Or a fall into a black hole in the ground?" Then Jesus stood at the gate of the sepulchre, and His Message concerned the life immortal. What others talked about, He saw. His forehead grazed the stars, He looked over the top of the hill, named man's horizon, and saw afar off the sweet fields of living green in the land of pure delight. He plucked the fear out of men's souls as the husbandman plucks the tare out of the wheat, as the physician plucks the foul growth out of the fair body, and restores it to full health. He taught men that dying was home-going; that heaven was the Father's house, and that nothing could ever injure God's children, either here or there, either before death or after death. The sweetest music that ever fell over heaven's battlements are the words, "In my Father's house are many mansions." "Let not your heart be troubled, neither let it be afraid." And not until men prefer fog banks to wheat harvests, the will-o'-the-wisp light to the guiding star; not until they prefer candles flickering into the socket, to the summer-making sun, will they prefer these tawdry little superstitions before that Divine Teacher, whose music is sphere-music, and whose voice is the melody of the world.

Henry J. Van Dyke

[1852–1933]

Henry J. Van Dyke's life was full of variety. Besides being active as a minister, he was for many years a teacher of English literature at Princeton University, and at various periods served as United States Ambassador to the Netherlands and Luxemburg. He was born at Germantown, Pennsylvania. He received his education at Harvard and Princeton, and was ordained in the Presbyterian ministry in 1879. His writings have attracted world-wide attention. The following sermon bespeaks literary genius coupled with deep religious feeling.

THE LIVING CHRIST

I am He that liveth, and was dead; and behold I am alive for evermore, Amen; and have the keys of hell and of death. REVELATION 1:18.

THE world needs more than a Redeemer. It needs a Master, a Ruler, a living Lord.

When the guilt of sin has been taken away by the perfect sacrifice of the cross, when the inexorable law of righteousness has been satisfied and the barrier between man and God forever destroyed by the death of Jesus, the way of salvation is indeed made free and clear, but the work of salvation is not yet accomplished. There must be a continuous exercise of divine power upon the weakened and perverted hearts of men; there must be an uplifting, and quickening and guiding of the world by an ever-living and ever-present Saviour.

There must be the living Christ in our hearts. He must be raised again for our justification. The sepulchre must give Him back to us. The dark under-world, into which He descended for our sakes, must restore Him to our faith and fellowship. Yea, the heaven from which He came must receive Him, that He may be clothed once more with the glory which He laid aside at His birth, that He may no more be humbled to the narrow confines of a servant's form and a servant's life, but reigning in restored omniscience and omnipotence and omnipresence, may manifest throughout the world His wisdom and His power to save to the uttermost all that call upon Him.

You see, now, why the Church built upon this fact of the resurrection as the cornerstone of her faith. You see why she made it the great theme of her preaching to proclaim Jesus and the resurrection. You see why she chose not Friday, the day on which Christ died, but Sunday, the day on which He rose from the dead, as her holy-day of rest and gladness. Not because the resurrection is more sacred or more important than the crucifixion; but because, without the resurrection, the crucifixion would be an unutterable and irremediable loss, the disappearance of the most holy life and character that the world has ever seen, the vanishing forever from the earth of the most precious power that has ever entered it, yes, the seal of failure upon the work of Christ and the annihilation of all our hopes of immortality and heaven, for "if Christ be not raised your faith is vain; ye are yet in your sins." But if He be risen then our faith is sure. Then the triumph of love and life over sin and death is accomplished and secure. Then the dawning of every Lord's day that shines upon our darkened earth brings to us a bright and glad reminder of that eternal light which the grave itself could not quench,—that light which even now fills the heavens as it fills our hearts,—the light of the glory of God shining for evermore in the face of Christ Jesus.

Consider, in the first place, the glorious certainty of the fact that on the third day after His death, He left the grave and came forth alive into the living world. This fact I say is a glorious certainty. There is no event in history so well attested. If we can be sure of anything in the past we can be sure of this.

We know that Christ is risen because His sepulchre is empty. Where is He gone? What power has broken the imperial seal of Rome, and rolled away the ponderous stone from the mouth of the tomb? The feeble, scattered, trembling disciples who fled in terror when they saw Him condemned to die? Impossible. Physically impossible, that they should have braved and baffled and overcome the power of the world-empire as it was embodied in those stern and vigilant soldiers guarding the seal which it was death to touch.

We know it also by the testimony of many unimpeachable witnesses who saw Jesus in the flesh after He had risen,—men and women who were in no condition to see a vision of exalted fancy, for the dreadful gloom of the crucifixion, the strong impression of that visible and unmistakable death, still rested on their minds.

They tell us that they saw the risen Jesus. And mark the manner in which they saw Him. They do not tell us that Christ appeared to them in trances or midnight visions of ecstasy, but in the common walks of daily life, in the garden of the Arimathean Joseph, on the high-road to Emmäus, by the sea-shore where they were busy with their fishing. He talked with them, ate with them. They touched Him. They do not relate marvelous tales of garments rustling and features dimly gleaming in the shade of darkened rooms. In the cool hours of the early morning, under the searching sunlight, in the open air, Jesus comes to them. They do not tell us only of what was seen by solitary wanderers in their lonely hours; but they assure us that He was seen by more than five hundred brethren at one time, in the clear daylight. And this assurance was written, not long afterwards when all of the alleged beholders were dead, but within less than thirty years after the death of Christ, when many of the eyewitnesses still lived and could bear testimony to its truthfulness.

Consider, in the second place, the nature and evidences of this everlasting life which belongs to the risen Christ. Clearly it must be a reality, not a mere ideal or imaginary existence. And just as clearly it must be a mysterious and incomprehensible reality. We cannot look with our feeble and darkened eyes into the heavenly regions. We cannot discern or understand the manner of life in which the ascended Lord now dwells. We cannot tell how He looks, or in what glorious activities He is employed, or in what shining place His blessed throne is established.

"Jesus, these eyes have never seen
      That radiant form of Thine;
The veil of sense hangs dark between
      Thy blessed face and mine."

But one thing we do know, one thing we may be sure of:—the life of the risen Christ, reaching away out into the endless future, with all the power of sympathy and help won by His earthly experience, with all the might and glory of His victory over sin and death, abiding and growing through ages of ages,—this divine immortal life is for evermore a life for men, a life of succor and comfort, blessing and salvation, flowing out in heavenly grace and power into this sorrowful and sinful earth.

Here we touch the reality on its human side. Here we find that which we can know and understand. Here, in the moral and spiritual life of man, we behold the evidences of the living Christ, still dwelling and working in the world which He died to redeem.

Observe the bearing of this argument. We rely for the proof of the historical fact that Christ rose from the dead upon historical evidence. We rely for the proof of the spiritual fact that Christ is alive for evermore upon spiritual evidence. But the two facts correspond and are linked together. If Christ be not risen, then all the inward life of Christendom is a dream, a delusion, a lie. But if Christ be risen, then all the influences of purity and love and goodness that are working in the hearts of men, all the heavenly hopes and aspirations and endeavors of the world, are the proofs and revelations of His present and everlasting life.

Wherever human hearts are reaching up from the shadows of this mortal sphere to lay hold upon the eternal God, wherever the pure flowers of truth and peace and holiness are springing from the dull and barren soil of humanity, wherever men and women are suffering patiently, toiling nobly, giving themselves generously for the good of others, wherever the Holy Ghost is working, wherever faith is burning, wherever love is shining, *there is the living Christ*.

Finally, let us remember that this risen Christ, who liveth and was dead and is alive for evermore, is He who holds the keys of hell and of death.

Oh, that I could find the power to express the joy and comfort which dwell in this majestic truth!

There is one door which baffles us. Dark, cold, forbidding, it stands in the midst of this green and beautiful world,—the iron door of death. All the paths of mortal life lead thither; but there is none that returns from that mysterious portal. We see men and women and little children vanishing within its gloom; year by year, those that are nearest and dearest are passing away from us over that stern threshold; but not one of them comes back to us to tell us what is beyond. Our own footsteps are drawing near to it: we cannot shun or escape it: a heavy hand is on us pushing us forward. Through the flowers and sunshine, through the thorns and tempests, through every year and every day, we are moving toward that iron door.

We tremble. We are afraid. Our hearts are chilled and darkened by the awful mystery. Who will open this door for us? Who will show us the things which lie behind it? Who will unlock and disclose the mystery of death?

Behold the living Christ. He has passed through that shadowy portal, and has come back again. He holds the keys of the grave and of the under-world. He stands beside us in the hour of fear and grief. He touches the heavy door and it swings open. We see the inner side of it, and lo! *it is not of iron but of gold, for it is the door of the heavenly city.* Dark is the entrance of that gateway, but just within its shadow lies the world of light. Lonely is the brief passage to the eye of mortal sense, but the moment of parting is the moment of meeting with God, and Jesus, and the innumerable company of angels and ransomed saints.

Stoop down and look through that narrow opening, O mourning heart, and you shall see that those whom you bewail as lost are dwelling in peace and blessedness, and waiting for you to join them. Weep no more. Rejoice, be glad, and sing. The mystery of death is solved. The shadow of death is broken. For those who are in Christ, to be absent from the body is to be present with the Lord. This life of ours is no brief and transient stream, flowing turbidly through a few short years, and then sinking in the grave. It is immortal, glorious, blessed. Through the dark portal it passes instantly into light and peace.

Are the birds singing here with joyous melody? *Yonder the angels are singing forever about the throne.*

Are the flowers blooming here in fragrance and beauty? *Yonder the tree of life is blossoming beside the crystal waters.*

Is the sun shining here in majesty and glory? *Yonder the face of Christ is shining, and they need no candle, neither light of the sun, for the Lord God giveth them light, and they shall reign forever and ever.*

Felix Adler

[1851–1933]

Felix Adler was born in Alzey, Germany. His father, a Jewish rabbi, emigrated to the United States in 1857. Graduating from Columbia University, the son completed his studies at Berlin and Heidelberg. After a few years as writer, lecturer, and preacher in this country, he founded the Society for Ethical Culture and began to gather about him many outstanding liberals, both Jew and Gentile. At his death he left a flourishing movement which will long remain a memorial to his genius and faith. Adler is represented here by a collection of sermon-lecture notes expressing his fundamental convictions about life and its meaning.

THE MEANING OF LIFE

THERE are two kinds of light, the light on the hither side of the darkness and the light beyond the darkness. We must press on through the darkness and the terror of it if we would reach the holier light beyond.

We are here—no matter who put us here, or how we came here—to fulfil a task. We cannot afford to go of our own volition until the last item of our duty is discharged. We are here to make mind master of matter, soul of sense. We do so by overriding pain, not by weakly capitulating to it.

When we are smitten by the rod of affliction, do not let us sit still, but rather get to work as fast as we can. In action lies our salvation. But it must be remembered that only a great aim, one which remains valid, irrespective of our private griefs, is competent in the critical moments to put us into action and to sustain us in action.

The thought that extreme suffering is a key which unlocks life's deepest and truest meanings is the final rejoinder to the plea on behalf of suicide. It is a thought which, when fully apprehended, is calculated to give peace to every troubled soul.

The fact that there is a spiritual power in us, that is to say, a power which testifies to the unity of our life with the life of others, which impels us to regard others as other selves—this fact comes home to us even more forcibly in sorrow than in joy. It is thrown into clearest relief on the background of pain.

In the glow of achievement we are apt to be full of a false self-importance. But in moments of weakness we realise, through contrast, the infinitely superior strength of the power whose very humble organs and ministers we are. It is then we come to understand that, isolated from it, we are nothing; at one with it, identified with it, we participate in its eternal nature, in its resistless course.

There are two terms of the series of progress which we should always keep before us. The one is the starting-point, and the other the final goal. The former is the cave man; the latter is the divine man. We know in a measure what sort of being the cave man was. Instructed by anthropologists, we know how poor and mean were the beginnings of humanity on earth. But of that other term of progress—the goal of progress, the divine man of whom the cave man was the germ, the first rough draft—of the man who is to be, our notions are vague. He rises before us, indeed, in a vision of glory, but his shape is nebulous. And the result of progress is just this, that it makes us more and more able to define the outlines of that shape, to draw sharply and finely the noble lineaments of that face; that it makes us more and more able to see the divine, the perfect man, the only begotten son of all the spirits of the myriads of the generations of men—the man that is to be, the perfection of our imperfection.

The perfect man has never yet appeared on earth. The perfect man is an apparition of light and beauty rising in the boundless infinite, an ideal to be more and more clothed with particularity. The purpose for which we exist is to help to create the perfect man, to incarnate him more and more in ourselves and in others.

That the lofty form of man may be wholly disengaged from the encompassing clay, that the traces of our bestial ancestry may be wholly purged from our nature, that our spirits may stand erect as our bodies already do—this, I think, is the end for which we exist.

Every man, however humble, is worthy of reverence because, in his limited sphere, he can be a beneficent, forward-working agent, he can help a little to create the perfect man. Every child is a possible avatar of the more perfect man. On every child the whole past lays its burdens, and of the outcome of its life the whole future is expectant.

The way to overcome dejection is to energise our nature vigorously. An eminent physician is quoted as saying: "I firmly believe that one-half of the confirmed invalids could be cured of their maladies if they were compelled to live busy and active lives, and had no time to fret over their miseries. The will has a wonderfully strong and direct influence over the body. Good work is the safeguard of health. The way to live well is to work well." If this be true, even when the cause of the dejection is corporeal, how much more likely is it to be true where the cause is seated in the mind.

In cases of bereavement, what is it that can enable a man to weather the hurricane of grief which is apt to descend upon the soul immediately after a great loss; and what can enable him to live through the dead calm which is apt to succeed that first whirlwind of passionate desolation? It is the thought that the fight must still go on, because there are issues of infinite worth at stake; and that, though wounded and crippled, he must still bear his part in the fight until the end.

For singleness of purpose, I plead. This alone can give strength to our will, coherence to our life. Without it we drift; with it we steer. Let us have before us, whatever we do, a sovereign aim, but let us also make sure that it be a worthy aim, one that will purge the clay from our eyes, from our lips, from our brains, from our hearts.

A great man helps us by the standard which he erects. He never really is level with his own standard, and yet we do not therefore reject him. He helps us by what he earnestly tries for, and by what he suggests to us that we should try for; he helps us, not so much by what he achieves, as by what he reveals, by the insight which he gives us into the nature of good.

So far as the forward movement of the human race is concerned, it is the effort that counts, and not the attainment; the realm of time and space can never be the scene of complete realisation. The reward of the effort is the wider outlook upon the ultimate aim; the truer estimate of its character as infinite, and, along with this, the recognition of that infiniteness of our own nature which enables us to conceive of and aspire to such an aim.

Joy is a light which those who possess are bound to keep burning brightly for the sake of others as well as for their own sake. Every pure joy in the world is so much pure gain.

Cold and bare is youth without the glow of generous idealism. Contemptible is middle age without the sense of definite attachments and the willing acceptance of limitations. And ungracious and unlovely is old age if it be not illumined by the light of contemplation, if it be not fruitful in counsel.

Every vocation, even the lowliest, which we pursue in a spirit of entire sincerity, is a means of acquiring culture. The artisan may be, in his way, as truly a cultivated man as the artist or the scholar, for by culture I understand insight gained into all manner of activities through genuineness and thoroughness in one. To be cultivated is to see things in their relations.

Our daily avocation, whatever it be, if we cling to it closely enough, is sure to engender in us a new respect for reality, a new humility.

To put forth power in such a way as to be provocative of power in others is the ethical aim that should guide men in all vocations and in all their relations.

This fair earth, with its fir-clad hills, its snowy mountains, its sparkling seas, its azure vaults, and the holy light of the stars, is but a painted screen behind which lurks the true reality.

The beauty of this earth and all that is precious and great in this human life of ours is but a hint and a suggestion of an eternal fairness, an eternal rightness.

We need something of the virility of stoicism to grapple with the difficulties of life; we need to cultivate a large patience; an humble spirit that teaches us to be prepared for every loss, and to welcome every joy as an unlooked-for gain. There are a thousand pleasures in little things which we, with the petulance of children, daily spurn, because we cannot have all we ask for.

The question, Is life worth living, implies a species of blasphemy. The right question to ask is: Am I worthy of living? If I am not, I can make myself so. That is always in my power.

The divine in man is our sole ground for believing that there is anything divine in the universe outside of man. Man is the revealer of the divine.

At bottom, the world is to be interpreted in terms of joy, but of a joy that includes all the pain, includes it and transforms it and transcends it.

The Light of the World is a light that is saturated with the darkness which it has overcome and transfigured.

Charles Edward Jefferson

[1860–1937]

Charles Edward Jefferson was born at Cambridge, Ohio, and received his education at Ohio Wesleyan and Boston University. He was ordained in the Congregational ministry in 1887. In 1898 he was called to the pulpit of the Broadway Tabernacle Congregational Church, New York City, and became noted as a writer of religious books and as a leader in world religious affairs. This example of his sermons was delivered before the Copenhagen Peace Conference in 1922 and represents Jefferson's clear understanding of the problems of world religion and international affairs.

THE SPIRIT OF CHRIST

Now if any man have not the Spirit of Christ he is none of His. ROMANS 8:9.

So SAID the first great interpreter of the Christian religion. The statement is straightforward, emphatic and beautifully clear. Only fifteen words, and all but one of them monosyllables. One does not need a dictionary to read them. A child of six can take them in. It is a sentence without mist or fog. It has in it the note of finality. It is positive, dogmatic, solid as an axiom. It is in the style of Euclid. Paul is not setting forth a thesis for discussion. There are some things not open for debate. A few questions are closed. We say there are two sides to everything, but there are not two sides to this. You cannot say that if a man have not the Spirit of Christ it makes no difference. Everybody sees that if a man have not the Spirit of Christ he is none of His. There are axioms in religion as in mathematics. This is one of them. Like all axioms, this one is a basal truth, and therefore a truth to start with.

Sometimes we do not begin with Christ at all; we begin with the

Church, its forms of worship, its sacraments, its orders, its government, its creedal statements, its traditions. But the first great Christian preacher did not begin in his thinking with the Church; he began always with Christ. To him Christ is all. If we have the Spirit of Christ we have everything. If we have not His Spirit we have nothing. That was Paul's conviction. See what this means. A man may be baptized with water, but if he is not baptized into the Spirit of Christ he is none of His. A man may come to the sacrament of the Lord's Supper all through his life, but if he have not the Spirit of Christ he has no part with Him. A man may repeat the most orthodox of the creeds, but if he have not the Spirit of Christ he is not a believer.

What is the Spirit of Christ? Fortunately we are not left in the dark. There is much twilight in the New Testament, but not at this point. Many things which we want to know about Jesus the New Testament refuses to disclose. One thing it makes gloriously luminous—the Spirit of Christ. His soul stands out before us radiant, full-statured, clear-cut as a star. We are uncertain sometimes as to His words; we are never in doubt concerning the sort of man He was. We are always absolutely sure of His attitude, His disposition, His spirit. First of all, He was brotherly. His spirit was warmly fraternal. His heart was big and friendly. He was a brother to everybody. The crowd at once saw that. His brotherliness was amazing, unprecedented, even scandalous. He carried it too far, so thought the Scribes. He shocked the prudent by being too brotherly. He was the friend of publicans and sinners. That was the first indictment brought in against Him. To Jesus brotherliness is of the essence of true religion. Fellowship is cardinal and indispensable. In religion worship does not come first; brotherliness comes first. It is far easier to worship than to be brotherly. "If thou bring thy gift to the altar and there rememberest that thy brother hath aught against thee, leave there thy gift before the altar and go thy way—first be reconciled to thy brother and then come and offer thy gift." This is what He was always saying. His disciples could never forget it. One of them, when he was an old man, wrote: "He that loveth not his brother, whom he hath seen, how can he love God whom he hath not seen?" Brotherliness expresses itself in intercourse, communion, coöperation. The Christian who is zealous in worship and indifferent to fellowship does not know the A B C of Christianity. What foolery to make a great to-do about forms of worship and crucify the spirit of brotherliness! Church bigots and snobs, ecclesiastical autocrats and churls have no part with Christ. Paul is right—"If a man have not the Spirit of Christ he is none of his." Brotherliness is the first note of a genuinely Christian Church.

Brotherliness leads to service. Christ was a servant. No one questions that. He so glorified the word servant that His disciples could think of no higher title for themselves than "servants." "He went about doing good." That was Peter's description of Jesus' life when he held Jesus up before the Romans in the house of Cornelius in Cæsarea. Jesus loved to think of Himself as a servant. "The Son of man came not to be ministered unto, but to minister." "If any man will be great, let him become the servant of all." The man who rises highest is the man who serves most.

Brotherly service finds its climax in sacrifice. The Spirit of Jesus is the spirit of sacrifice. Does any one doubt it? The fundamental principle of Christianity is self-denial. When Paul urges men to have the mind that was in Christ he portrays the self-surrender of the man Jesus, obedient unto death, even the death of the Cross. Jesus was always laying down His life for others. "If any man will come after me, let him take up his Cross every day." The Church is right in making the Cross the symbol of the Christian faith.

If the Church has not the Spirit of Christ it is none of His. Let us stress that. Jesus of Nazareth walked boldly across national, racial and social lines, and He said, "Follow Me." Let us follow Him. It is the duty of the Church to walk unafraid across national frontiers. It is ordained to carry across national boundaries considerateness and helpfulness and forgiveness and sacrifice. It should do this audaciously. Men must learn to clasp hands across racial chasms. The Church must train them to do it. Men's hearts must touch one another through the barriers of nationality and race and tradition and prejudice. The intertwining of human sympathies and affections, to this mighty work the Church is called.

If a nation have not the Spirit of Christ it is none of His. Let us say that with authority, and let us say it often. Diplomacy must be baptized into the Spirit of Christ. This must be insisted on. The diplomat must obey the law of Christ. He must be brotherly. His ambition must be to help, and he must do his work within sight of the principle of sacrifice. The mailed fist must go—only the pierced hands can lift the world to new levels. Love is the mightiest force in the universe. Let us believe it and act upon it. Scientists are not ashamed of the law of gravitation. It is inexorable, unchangeable, and those who ignore it perish. Let us not apologize for the law of love. It also is unalterable, inflexible, and those who violate it are ground to powder. The world is in its present deplorable condition solely because of the long continued and outrageous trampling upon the law of love.

If a government have not the Spirit of Christ it is none of His. If it lack His Spirit it is doomed. Its wealth will not save it, nor its learning, nor its genius, nor its military power. If a nation have not the Spirit of Christ it must go down. Let us press this upon the mind and conscience of the world. Let us put it in the forefront of all our teaching. God has made of one flesh every nation of men to dwell on all the face of the earth, having determined their appointed seasons and the bounds of their habitations. Corporate life is ordained of God, and ruled by Him. National development is held in the grip of unchanging and irresistible law. God is love, and rulers and statesmen lead nations to the abyss if they refuse to obey the law of love. Nations, like individuals, live and move and have their being in God (*i.e.,* in love). No nation lives to itself. Every nation is vitally related to every other nation, and all nations are bound up in the life of the Lord of Love. A nation which refuses to do justly and love mercy and walk humbly with its neighbours in the path of brotherly service and good will is sooner or later dashed to pieces like a potter's vessel. Those who doubt this should read history.

It is in the international realm that the Church must, through the coming centuries, perform its most zealous and arduous labour. The world is sick and the Church must heal it. The world is torn by evil spirits, suspicion and fear, and greed, and injustice, and hate, and revenge, and all these must be cast out. The Church is commissioned to cast out demons. War is a demon. War must go. We must have a warless world if we are to have any world at all.

To bring the separated races together and to train alienated nations to love one another—this is our heavenly Father's business and we must be about it. There are many obstacles. We must travel the way of the Cross. The adversaries are not few. We must go by way of Golgotha. The discouragements and disappointments and defeats and delays make the heart sick—this is the cup which our Father has given us to drink. Shall we not drink it? If God is for us, who is against us? "He that spared not His own Son, but delivered Him up for us all, how shall He not also with Him freely give us all things." "If ye being evil know how to give good gifts unto your children, how much more shall your Father who is in heaven give the Holy Spirit to them that ask Him."

Let us open our Conference with a great wish, a mighty longing, a passionate prayer that the Spirit of Love may come upon us and direct us in all our ways. Then shall we have the Spirit of Christ and the Conference will be His.

John Henry Jowett

[1864–1923]

A native of Halifax, England, John Henry Jowett was educated at Oxford and at Edinburgh University. He was ordained in the Congregational ministry in 1890. From this date he held increasingly influential pulpits, among which was that of the Fifth Avenue Presbyterian Church, New York City. Dr. Jowett was recognized as a leader of Christian thought on both sides of the Atlantic and exerted an influence which did not cease with his death. This sermon, delivered at the Fifth Avenue Presbyterian Church on October 17, 1915, is a shining example of the preacher's paramount loyalty to Christ and His teaching.

THE LOVE THAT HONORS CHRIST

He that loveth father or mother more than me is not worthy of me; and he that loveth son or daughter more than me is not worthy of me. MATTHEW 10:37.

I KNOW no word in the New Testament scriptures which has given more needless distress to the hearts of gentle people than these. If the saying is to be interpreted by the letter it would seem to enshrine the very spirit of jealousy. Had it been used by you or me it would suggest the narrow peevish speech of a jealous husband or a jealous wife. It would denote a soul protesting in its pride against receiving the mere remnants of affection, the leavings of the table where one who was more beloved has sat at an ampler feast. If you or I had spoken the words we should have been regarded as ungraciously greedy for the first draught of love, and as bitterly resentful because the loving cup has been first handed to another. "He that loveth father or mother more than me is not worthy of me; and he that loveth son or daughter more than me is not worthy of me." But the words are spoken by our Saviour and no such shallow interpretation of the letter can express the grace and graciousness of our Lord. Nothing like jealousy ever found a moment's lodgment in the Master's heart. In His soul there was no nesting room for such a carnal bird. There was nothing in our Lord which offered even a pinch of hospitality to so foul and destructive a plague. It was the supreme purpose of Jesus to constrain us to love one another. If it were possible to name in a single word the end our Saviour sought through all His earthly ministry it might be expressed in the sovereign word "love." "This is my commandment that ye love one another." "The end of the commandment is love." Love is the spring blossom He came to quicken, the summer flower He came to train, the autumn fruit He came to mature; and if He sees the lovely grace growing in rich abundance in the orchard of anyone's soul, will He inflict the resentful judgment of condemnation? We must begin with questions like these in seeking to understand the word of the Lord. Christ is the heavenly gardener, and love is the fair flower He came to rear. We surely cannot be wrong in loving one another, for when we love one another our Lord sees of the travail of His soul and is satisfied.

Let us therefore read the words again, thoroughly uprooting every suggestion of jealousy from our minds. "He that loveth father or mother more than me is not worthy of me; and he that loveth son or daughter more than me is not worthy of me." Well, then, can we love anyone too much? Can parents lay too heavy a wealth of love on their little child? Can a husband and wife be wedded together in the bonds of an affection that is over-rich and over-done? Let me ask one or two searching questions which will bring us face to face with reality. Here is a young mother singing in the first wondering rapturous dawn of her motherhood, and bending over her first-born in the yearning, nestling, brooding warmth of ineffable affection. Do you think our Saviour would enter into that sacred temple and look with disapproval on that wistful, dreaming love, and utter the cold and chilling word, "over-done?" "He that loveth son or daughter more than me is not worthy of me."

Or, here again is a young heart in whom the early bird of newly-awakened love is pouring forth a perfect pæan of rapturous song, while she roams through fairy-worlds of radiant vision and dream. Do you think our Saviour would enter that bright, shadowless realm and silence the song in this young soul by some cold blast of sharp reproof? "Over-done! Over-done! She that loveth her lover more than she loves me is not worthy of me!" Does that sound like the Christ? Does it harmonize with all the rich and bewildering music of His grace? Does not the very assumption that this would be the freezing way of the Master awake immediate and instinctive resentment? Our Master Himself has declared that it is the thief who comes to steal, and to kill and to destroy. Christ came that we might have life and that we might have it more abundantly. Christ Jesus never comes to impoverish us. He would never blow out a single light. He always enriches our riches. He always enhances our joys, and whenever He comes to the wedding He turns water into wine.

No, we cannot love anybody too much. What, then, shall we say about His word? It is impossible to love too much, but it is possible to love unwisely. We cannot be wrong in loving, but we can love in the wrong way. Our love can never be too great, but our love can easily be too cheap. Our love can be like an inferior wine. Nay, it can be like a wine that has lost its life. For loves are of different vintages. They range from the love which is only a primitive animal instinct to the love which dwells in the sublime and burning spirits who shine in the immediate presence of God. And between these two extremes there is every shade of quality and re-finement. We cannot love too much, but our love can be of an inferior grade; our love can be unintelligent, unillumined, defiled, and it can be so unworthy as to be altogether unworthy of Christ, and an un-Christlike love crucifies the Christ afresh and puts Him to an open shame.

Crownless virtues are always unworthy of Christ. Take the virtue of patience. There is patience that wears a crown, and there is patience that goes about uncrowned. There is a form of patience which is in covenant with sin. A man's patience may be only cunning waiting, with selfishness and deviltry at the end. It is a patience which does not lead to anything noble and right. It is a patience which does not end in righteousness, and a patience which does not end in righteousness does not crown the Christ. There is nothing Christian about it. And such patience is unworthy of the Lord.

Or take the virtue of beneficence. A man's beneficence may be such a chivalrous creation of justice and gentleness, and tenderness, and grace that it manifestly wears the crown which crowns the Lord. But there is a beneficence which is loud and garish and self-advertising, strutting in the public way. And the aim and end of such beneficence is to exalt oneself and not to glorify the Lord. There is nothing Christian about it. It has no crown for Christ and it is therefore unworthy of Him.

Or take the virtue of hope. There is nothing more winsome and more attractive than the grace of hope in all the radiant circle of the graces. But even the shining genius of hope can degenerate into a quite common and crownless thing. Hope may be only the faculty of the speculator. It may be a mere commercial instrument. It may be merely an aptitude of the market and not a winged servant of the spirit. A business man may be a man of conspicuous hope, but his hope may be only the scout of moneyed opportunity, and never the unveiler of spiritual possibility, and the minister of heavenly vision and dream. There may be nothing Christian about our hope. It may wear no crown, and it will therefore be incompetent to crown the Lord and it is therefore altogether unworthy of Christ.

Or take again the virtue of courage. Courage may be only a rude, crude, animal passion; the daring temper of the bull-dog and not the fine unselfish prowess and chivalry of a blameless knight. A man may have a sort of courage but there may be nothing Christian about it. It may wear no crown, and therefore have nothing with which to crown the Lord.

Let me give you an example from Robert Browning, and let it be from his marvelous poem "Pippa Passes." A young, ardent soul, Luigi, feels the glow in his soul to be the foe of tyranny and to go forth on a grim and perilous crusade. Luigi has a mother who loves him. I do not doubt the reality and depth of her love, but it was a love of most unworthy grade. She would love him into the abandonment of his crusade. She would love him into an ignoble contentment and an immoral ease. She seeks by her love to quench the burning fire in his soul. She would love God out of him. She incites him to delay, if haply his holy fire may smoulder and die out.

> "Why go tonight? Morn's for Adventure.
> Jupiter is indeed a morning star."

She reminds him of the girl to whom his heart has gone out in the stirrings of early love and who is going to visit them later in the year.

> "In June: remember,
> Yourself appointed that month for her coming.
> She must be grown—with her blue eyes upturned
> As if life were one long and sweet surprise:
> In June she comes!"

His mother would have loved her son into moral apathy. By her love she
would have quenched the passion for his country's freedom; a passion
which was moving him to offer his life in willing, consecrated sacrifice.
She loved Luigi more than she loved the emancipation of the oppressed.
She loved her home and comfort more than she loved the freedom of
man. She loved Luigi more than she loved God, and "Whoso loveth son
or daughter more than me is not worthy of me."

And now, perhaps, we are able to state the teaching in a positive form.
All love that tends to purify, and ennoble, and elevate, and Christianize
the beloved is love that honors and crowns the Lord. If in my love for my
child I seek to love her into Christliness, then in a most deep and glorious
sense my love for my child is subordinate to my love for the Lord. If my
love for my child, or my love for my friend, or my love for anyone, is a
love that will never connive at sin, and never gloss over iniquity, and never
create a soft, humid atmosphere, in which all the moral resistances lose
their strength,—if I love with a passion for truth, a passion for holiness,
a passion to glorify Christ in the life of my beloved, then do I honour
Christ, then do I worship Christ, then do I crown Him Lord of all.

And, therefore, if the Saviour came to that young mother whom I mentioned, crooning over her babe, in the first wondering, rapturous dawn of
her motherhood, and saw that the supreme yearning of her love was that
her beloved should grow into His loveliness, He would surely say to her,
"Love on! Love yet more deeply! Love thy child into the image of thy
Lord!"

Do we love like that? And if we have not that love where are we going
to get the love that tends to make the loved one lovely, and in what way
is such a love to be sustained? What directions will you give me for
obtaining it? Do you know of any springs out in the world where a poor
pilgrim can find a plenteousness of crystal love? Do you know of any
springs in the fair realm of literature where we can find streams of love
which will make us royal ministers of purity and truth? Do you know
of any love-fountains in the attractive estates of music and art? Personally,
I confess to you I do not know anyone or anything or anywhere where
such unfailing springs of heavenly love can be found, and found both

night and day, in summer and in winter, but in the heart of the Lord
Jesus Christ. As our familiar hymn has it:

> "O Christ, He is the fountain,
> The deep, sweet well of love . . ."

And it is the blessed gospel of His grace that pilgrims like you and me
can dwell near those springs, and our souls may be every moment revived
and nourished by the wonderful love of Christ. And drinking at the
springs of His love our own love will be as a river of water of life, clear
as crystal; and on the banks of the river of our love shall be found the
tree of life, "bearing twelve manner of fruits, and the leaves of the tree
shall be for the healing of the nations."

Harold Marshall

[1866–1932]

*Born in New Hampshire and educated at Tufts College, Boston, Harold
Marshall was ordained in the Universalist Church in 1891 and began an
enviably successful ministry. In 1917 he was chosen manager of the Universalist
Publishing House, in which post he did much to effect better relations between
leaders of various churches and industry. His later years were devoted to the
religion of brotherhood and its application. The sermon given here is an expression of Marshall's deepest convictions. Its crisp, epigrammatic style and rich
tone of practical mysticism is illustrative of the sermons in which he argued
and proclaimed the truths of Christianity for more than a generation.*

THE RELIGION OF BROTHERHOOD

I am the way. JOHN 14:6.

THE great discovery of our age is not the universe within the atom but
the universe within the soul. This has enabled us to rediscover the religion
of Jesus, and we find that it was neither a church nor a creed but a way
of life by which we possess ourselves. The first and most dazzling result
of this discovery has been to give us back our long-lost spiritual freedom.

Paul and Augustine and Calvin are the trinity of misfortune that over-
bore Jesus' exultant, "You shall know the truth and the truth shall make
you free," and reduced it to a despairing cry, "O wretched man that I
am, who shall deliver me from the body of this death?" They have laid
upon lesser men The Great Fear. In terror whole generations have crawled
away from God and hidden under little creeds. Jesus was unafraid

of God. He did not prostrate himself before him; he laughed up into his face.

It is quite obvious that in the first flush of this rediscovered freedom liberty has run to license. Slavery does produce manners, if it cannot develop morals. It molds behavior into a counterfeit of character. It is obvious that some men and women, particularly young men and women, no longer afraid of the tabus of yesterday, are riotous if not wanton. The modern Sanhedrist, honestly believing that the only way to God is through His temple, raises anew the cry, "These young men and women eat with sinners. Away with them."

The priests and the Levites are right in realizing that between their religions about Jesus and this religion of Jesus it is a duel to the death. Christianity as the way of life is another Samson loosed among the pillars on which ecclesiasticism and dogmatism rest. It is this rediscovery of Christianity as the way of life that makes sectarianism a spent force, morally impotent and spiritually sterile.

But discovery that stops with discovery is useless. Columbus might as well have found a cloud as a continent at the end of his voyage if adventure and agriculture and industry had not followed him. As we begin to explore this rediscovered religion of Jesus, we find it to be a religion of brotherhood; that Christianity as the way of life means the way of brotherhood for all men, with all men. Love your enemy not because he is your enemy but because beneath his enmity is the eternal fact of brotherhood. Because there is one God and Father of us all, no child of God can be outside the pale of human brotherhood.

Our present problems, however, are not created by those who deny this but by those who seek to ignore it. When Jesus' disciples began to practice his religion of brotherhood, a good churchman of the day wrote that "they who have turned the world upside down are come hither."

Now what does the practice of brotherhood mean? You are invited to a beautiful home upon which generations have lavished wealth and taste. The possessor shows you its treasures and then takes you out into its great park. Presently, behind a screen of trees, you see some rotting hovels, and squalid men and women and filthy children. "My brothers and sisters," explains your host. "You see, I was grown up when father died and they were only children, so I took all his property." An explanation in terms of religion about Jesus, but not an answer in terms of the religion of Jesus. Nor would he see any difference in the situation if the children did not have the same earthly father, or if they lived in the next town or the next continent, or if their skins were black or yellow. "Have ye not all one Father and are ye not brethren one of another?"

But this does not imply anything so easy and futile as a division of the common heritage. "Henceforth I call you not servants but brethren," is a Magna Charta of the dispossessed, but it does not relieve possessors of responsibility. Brotherhood does not deal with ownership. That is as Cæsar decrees—so long as men are childish enough to need a Cæsar or foolish enough to endure one. Brotherhood deals with the deeper question of use, which alone gives meaning to possession. The practice of brotherhood means that we all have a right to find in the abundance of the Father's house satisfaction for our needs, but not indulgence of our greeds.

And the practice of brotherhood means the ordering of the world. Biology has long since confirmed Paul's discovery that God has made of one blood all the nations of the earth. Every civilization built on less than that has crashed or crumbled to ruin. Unless we can learn to practice brotherhood, our children's children must go back to the cave, perhaps to cannibalism.

Whether those who have discovered Christianity to be this way of the brotherly life can win the world to brotherhood depends on how far they themselves are ready to practice it. Across the centuries, with the emphasis of His cross upon it, comes Jesus' prayer "that they may be one." Yet he is still crucified wherever, in the name of Calvin or Luther, of Wesley or Murray, men build churchly walls against their brothers. For men and women to come together in churches and conventions and talk about Christianizing the world, without making a serious attempt to achieve a common fellowship of service for the need of the world, is merely to say, "Lord, Lord." The time has come when the churches must decide between Apollos and Christ. In conflicting and competitive sectarianism is the apostasy of our time.

Twelve men were together in one place. Humble and unlettered men, hated where they were not despised. Twelve men were together in one place—separate bodies, different minds, differing types. Twelve men were together in one place. Had that been all, they themselves would have outlived the memory of it. Twelve men were together in one place, in one spirit. So through walls of stone and walls of hate he who had made them one came in and abode with them. Other men having eyes to see saw him in their faces, having ears to hear heard his voice in their voices, and each understood in his own soul.

For nineteen hundred years his other disciples have missed days like that by calling the first one a miracle. Yet the memory of that day of fellowship with him and with each other has outlived the centuries, not because men would remember, but because they could not forget. Here and there those who have lived greatly and loved much have been filled with it as it filled the house in the long ago. Then they have gone in and out among their fellows revealing in their lives that which neither kings nor things can give—or take away. Here and there some group has had enough of his prayer fulfilled to realize what it might mean to be one with the Father, with him and with each other.

Can we repeat the Day of Pentecost today and every day? Yes, if we honestly seek it with all our hearts. Upon that depends our future. God was long before the churches. Will he be even longer after them? Yes! if we go on trying to evade or ignore the religion of Jesus as the way of life. No! if we set ourselves to walk in that way.

It will help us to do that if we realize that it is the way of Life, not merely a way of living. Living is one of the deceits of time from which Jesus could not wholly free himself—hence Gethsemane. But when he made himself a metaphor of life, he lifted himself out of time into the eternal, and saw that a spring morning for a violet, a century for a crystal, and an eon for men are alike in the processes of God.

To know this will help us to pass the final barrier, and from living enter into Life. It is by that way we go out and God comes in, until each of us can say, "I and my Father are one."

Samuel Parkes Cadman

[1864–1936]

Samuel Parkes Cadman was born in Shropshire, England, and graduated from Richmond College, London University, in 1889. A year later he came to the United States as pastor of Metropolitan Temple, New York City. He was subsequently called to the Central Congregational Church, Brooklyn, where he spent the remainder of his life. From both pulpit and lecture platform Dr. Cadman did much to strengthen the friendship between his native and his adopted countries. A humanist among American Congregational ministers, Dr. Cadman possessed a rare evangelical fervor coupled with profound learning. His sermons were masterpieces of eloquence and penetrating thought.

FAITH'S CORONATION

Now the end of the commandment (charge) is love out of a pure heart and of a good conscience and of faith unfeigned. I TIMOTHY 1:5.

THE charge which St. Paul commissioned St. Timothy to lay upon the Church at Ephesus was meant to veto those useless speculations and controversies which injured the fraternity of the sacred household. Fine spun allegories, fabulous recitals of the generation and gradation of the angelic hosts, the arithmetic of mysterious æons, and lurid predictions of apocalypses, then, as now, had a strange fascination for a certain type of believers. They were too preoccupied with vain debates upon inexplicable themes to give heed to the real ends of religion. Evangelical discretion was at the mercy of zealots, who identified divine truth with their distorted notions, making them the test of spiritual understanding. In order that the growing evil should be eliminated the Apostle defined the outstanding purpose of the New Testament gospel as a salvatory education. His language is axiomatic, precise, compressed; erroneous or perverse constructions find no opening in his closely woven arguments. Both matter and words express the wisdom of a profound religious experience. They rank as a classic utterance embodying the aims of Christian being and its obligations. According to them the heart's pure love begins and continues in faith unfeigned. The power that surpasses any other; the one power in this world and the world beyond which is superior to the creeds, or better still, behind them, is the love herein named. The love that gives and does not ask, and being denied, still loves with joy and gladness. In their deepest selves, men and women know that this love is the grand reality of life, infinitely more substantial and authoritative than all objects of sensory perception.

Yet neither this love nor any other ordination of Heaven can possess our souls without the royal faculty of faith. Believers can be and do nothing worthy of their calling apart from the vitalizing energy of faith as the gift of God. Where it is complete it hallows every profession of allegiance to our Lord and Redeemer; where it is defective, the development of the hidden man of the heart is arrested. Rectitude of conscience and of conduct is secured by faith unfeigned. The motives and thoughts which lie far and remote in human nature are regulated by it. They, too, own the sway of a divine and unfaltering faith. Affectation, pretense, caprice, deference to conventionality, and even superstition or hypocrisy cannot defile the heritage of an undivided faith fixed upon its giver. But once this faith languishes, the weaknesses which simulate it speedily appear, evoking religious disaster.

Such a disaster fell upon ancient Israel and wrecked her usefulness to mankind. The prophet was displaced by the pharisee, and the interpreter by the scribe. These ardent advocates of Judaism suffered, not from secular but from religious skepticism; from disproportionate emphasis and confusion of sign with substance. Their outward pieties were ostentatious and austere. They loved to offer their endless prayers before the public eye. But these devotions were symptomatic of spiritual degeneracy. Excessive ceremonialisms, fastings for which sour faces were the bulletins; almsgiving to the tune of the trumpet's blare, and slavish adherence to outworn traditions were the trappings of Judaism's death. Shallow egotism and self-complacent arrogance marked its predominant tribe of religionists. Nor is the tribe extinct to-day. It still troubles God's Commonwealth, parading the insignia which denote the bigot and the formalist who thank Heaven they are not as other men are; who would willingly surrender the spirit of the Evangel to its letter, and the essences of Christian doctrine to their rituals.

Some recent crusades in Protestantism assert that Christian faith is an epidemic which spreads from soul to soul by means of associations surcharged with surface excitement. Fellowship stimulates religious beliefs and interests. But it is the individual alone in his or her own personal contact with the Spirit of the Living God who receives vitalizing faith. The operations of the Spirit should not be discounted by the press of the multitude. He prefers to deal with the man, not the mass. Devices for capturing the one through the many are not sure of His approval. They may be legitimate or again, as not a few are, illegitimate. Meanwhile the modest God delights to dwell in the single heart and there He witnesses of sin, of righteousness, and of a judgment to come. He is the great companion of conscience, memory, and will, and none but He has the passkey to the throne room of the soul. He unveils the bliss, the burden, the rapture, and the affliction of that mind which was in Christ Jesus. Through Him the attributes of human nature are harmonized with the Divine will. If you ask for a token of His indwelling, its chief evidence is in your penitential attitude. Contrition is His hall-mark, and its painfulness is the birth pang of your regenerate being. Those who deem iniquity a trifle, retribution an open question, goodness a matter of environment or of education, and evil habits no more than a reaction from irrestrainable tendencies, may escape the Spirit's searching for a time, but they never escape beggary of soul and moral destitution.

Their ideas of life are altogether too meager for its necessities. Nothing of lasting significance pivots on them or on what they think. Their capacity for ever enlarging blessedness is nullified by their alliance with the perishable elements of existence. On the other hand, the faith which fosters in us the sense of immortality and constrains us to shape our course accordingly is inevitably triumphant. It is not a speculation, nor a theory, nor a concession to what is seemly. These, if they exist at all, are its accidents. At the core it is the throb in men of the heart of honour and of fire at the center of all things: the divine dynamic which drives life toward its ascertainable and best ends.

God's purpose is to educe in His children the spiritual abandonment of Christian love. Its chief limitation is imposed upon it by playing off the will against the affections and the intellect against the conscience. St. Paul forewarns us against the chaos in which one faculty hoodwinks another. Their harmony by faith's free, full exercise is the distinctive note of the text. When this is gained, the clouds disperse, the shadows flee; the whole man rejoices in a divine life and law to which every member of his being yields cheerful obedience.

Mere emotionalism is barred; intellectual effort subserves spiritual liberty, and charity, the lifeblood of creeds and churches, becomes the perfectness of faith. It is needless to remark that much called love is veneered selfishness, covert grossness, masked anarchy. But this love, of which St. Paul's soul was full to overflowing, comes from the nature which God has revealed in Christ. Currents of feeling that assume its title often carry in solution the taint of moral squalor, the subtle poison of spiritual death. It has to be defined by one's experience and demonstrated by one's deeds. These together aim to confer the best upon the worst by bringing all men and women whom that love can reach within its radius. Because it holds the sinner very dear to God it is not likely to be a smiling affability. Politic affinities and honeyed phrases which nourish desire at the cost of character do not become its ministry to mankind. The parading of what is convenient or practicable or materially profitable as Christian love will not mislead those who have bowed at the Cross and there tasted the grace of God. Unfeigned faith is its parent, conscience is its preceptor, a purified heart the center from which it issues to bless its surroundings. None of them is dispensable, and all their springs are in God. We are here dealing with the discerner of hearts who is intent upon our fitness for His fellowship. We speak of the love He had for us when He sent the Saviour of the world to Bethlehem and to Calvary. "Behold! what manner of love the Father hath toward us that we should be called the sons of God," exclaimed St. John. It should be as altruistic in us as it was in the Master. Then the souls of the believers and the soul of the Church Universal alike shall be as a sea of glass mingled with fire, embracing peace and power, replete of force without waste, and of tranquillity with fervour.

The scenes of earthly circumstance which belonged to the Roman Empire when St. Paul wrote these words have vanished forever. The chariots of gold and silver, the pomp, the warriors, the pageants, the millions of followers drunk with the cup of abominations, have become as though they had not been. Wantonness, insolence and pride have passed with that corrupted world. The avenging gates have closed on them. The Temple at Jerusalem has shared their doom. But the truth of this text continues as an everlasting testimony to the Gospel which ministers to our penitence and our hope. Let us cling to its simplicity as the life of God in the souls of men, made known by faith unfeigned, by intellectual honesty, by the warrant of a conscience void of offense toward God and man, by the love which is faith's coronation.

Frank C. Doan

[1877–1927]

Frank C. Doan was a leader of liberal thought in the United States; as preacher and writer he did much to make understandable the liberal's faith. He was born at Nelsonville, Ohio, and educated at Hiram College, Ohio State University, and Harvard University. He began his career as a teacher of psychology and education, but, ever attracted to religion, he turned to the teaching of theology and was ordained as a Unitarian minister in 1914. The following sermon seeks to interpret the Humanist movement. It casts aside all mystery and profundity of thought, and shows how the basic human attitudes are the most truly religious.

JUST BEING HUMAN

> Though I speak with the tongues of men and of angels; and though I bestow all my goods to feed the poor; and though I give my body to be burned; but have not love, I am nothing. . . . Love never faileth. I Corinthians 13:1, 3, 8.

Some years ago, at the time when the late Thomas Mott Osborne was trying out his daring experiments in prison-reform and getting his astonishing results, a certain New York editor went up to Sing Sing to see with his own eyes what things were toward there. His mind was frankly skeptical, not to say supercilious, in its attitude toward this whole business of prison-reform. He looked upon it as merely a passing fad. This at its best; and, at its worst, as an experiment very risky to try in the then state of human society. As for Osborne, the editor felt that this softhearted man was giving these hardened criminals a degree of freedom which might easily grow to be a menace to society at large.

In a word, this sophisticated editor went up to Sing Sing that day to scoff, but he remained to learn. And he returned to New York a convert to prison-reform and an ardent defendant of the Osborne methods. The story of his change of heart and mind, as nearly as I can now remember it in his own words, reads like this:

"I went up to Sing Sing just to find out what was going on within its forbidding walls. *I found out!* I discovered one thing that caused me to pause in open-mouthed wonder. The prison-atmosphere I had felt on a former visit was not there any more.

"I set about to discover, if I could, by what reforms, by what methods Osborne had accomplished this transformation of the old prison-atmosphere, this seemingly miraculous softening of the convict-heart. I found no explanation—no rationale. Finally, as a last resort, I stepped up to one of the men, the most case-hardened of them all,—by his looks evidently a 'sub-normal'—but in whose eyes I thought I saw the light of a secret understanding. And I said to him, 'Tell me, what in the world has this man Osborne done to you fellows anyway? He seems to have no method, no system, no secret even. And yet he has contrived to transform darkness into light before you. Is he a magician, a miracle-working god, or what then?' Well, after a moment's hesitation the old man turned to me,—I was surprised to see tears streaming down his wizened cheeks,—and said brokenly, 'Why, Osborne, he hasn't any secret. He isn't any wizard, any god, or anything of that kind. *He's just human,* that's all!' "

Just being human! In this simple but soul-searching phrase by which that old man explained, the best way he knew how, Osborne's greatness lies the secret of all human greatness. It consists in just being human in one's way of living this human life of ours.

After all is said and done, after all the philosophy books have been read, after all the lectures and sermons about life have been taken in and digested, that is what we all are, is it not,—just human beings together? Perplexed, all of us, by the same human problems. All of us alike seeking for some light upon the path of this human life,—light and strength and wisdom and things like that. Divided against each other by the same human passions,—greeds, envyings, animosities and things like that.

Yes, but uplifted, all of us in our better moments, by the same human hopes, aspirations, dreams. Generous, all of us, at times almost to a fault. Affectionate, all of us, ready to die for those we love, ready to bestow all our goods to feed the poor, ready to give our bodies, if need be, to be burned, a willing sacrifice in any great cause of justice.

In short, ready, all of us, and quick to respond to any and every appeal to our better impulses.

Is there a criminal-brother anywhere in this whole wide world, seeming as if a willing victim to all the lowering instincts and passions of his all-too-physical body? How like a beast! So we are apt to say yes; but, we are apt to forget that it is not his fault—not altogether. Some one, sometime, somewhere, has failed to treat that man like a human being. Some one has despitefully used him, kicked him when he was down. Sometime an injustice has crushed and taken the heart out of him. Somewhere along his way of life, the cup of cold water has been snatched away from his panting spirit. Some one has failed to lay a helping, healing hand upon him when his soul was sick, nigh unto death, within him. Some disease, it may be, inherited from his guilty father; some disease, it may be, caught from this present-day decadent body-politic; it is this that has unfitted him for a completer, nobler life. It is he who has been robbed;

cheated out of his rightful heritage from his own earthly father, or from "humanity," the mother-matrix in which we are all equally conceived and bred and born. Some one, somewhere, sometime has treated that man like the scum of the earth! Find that some one! Perhaps it was I, perhaps it was you? For, these things even the best of us, well-meaning but spiritually blind, do do, albeit unconsciously and with no idea what we do and with no intention of harming any human soul. Find that some one, I say, and you will find the guilty party—the man who once failed to treat another man like a human being!

How dark this shield, you say! Yes, dark enough. But there is a brighter, converse side to it. If you and I are responsible, at least partly, for whatsoever is ugly and evil in this "common humanity" of ours, we are not the less creditable for whatsoever is lovely and of good report. Is there a man in this whole wide world who is noble in all his ways, lofty in all his thoughts, generous, tolerant and understanding in his heart, living how like a god? Ah, yes there are thousands and thousands of this human kind in this up-looking, onward progressing generation! Unheralded, mute, inglorious, they are still the salt of the earth, the leaven which is slowly raising this whole lump of humanity, a light to lighten this darkened age, to lead the peoples of the earth through the present wilderness of appearances into the realities of their own soul.

Now, why have these rare souls become as the salt, the leaven, the hope of the world? It is not to their credit, not altogether. Take any such soul. Search long enough and understandingly enough, and you will find some one—perhaps it was you, perhaps it was I—who, somewhere, sometime, once treated that man like a human being! Believing all sorts of fine things about him, expecting all sorts of noble actions from him, hoping all manner of god-like things of him. Perhaps it was a father he fairly worshiped in the days of his youth. Perhaps it was some understanding teacher, the memory of whom has been with him through the years, and whose now "invisible presence" is still his stay. Perhaps at one time he caught, never to lose, the spirit of one of the truly human souls of the past—Socrates, Buddha, Jesus, Saint Francis, Tolstoi. Perhaps the present discomforted soul of humanity has itself touched his heart with its need of his strength, his wisdom, his love—even his. Who can say? But we can say with great assurance that some one, somewhere, sometime, has treated that man like a human being, like a child of the Most High. And, treated like a child of the Most High, he has become a child of the Most High!

Is any one looking for a philosophy of life, one which always "works," one which will bring him contentment of spirit, peace of mind, joy of heart? The secret is here. Just be human in your way of taking human nature—your own and that of your fellowmen. Human, I mean, in this

high degree in which all great souls have been and are: human in your
condemnation of all injustice, all self-righteousness, all hypocrisy, whether
in others or in yourself; gently human in your understanding of the
weaknesses, the follies, the sins of our common human nature, by the
alchemy of your own human spirit transmuting this common clay into
pure gold; and patient while about it, steadfastly patient with all men—
with others as well as with yourself, forgiving them all their debts, forgetting all human faults—theirs as well as your own, seeing through all
their and your own evil deeds, underneath all the surface scum of this
human life to the good which is surely present in every human soul! This
is what I love to call the Eternal Presence—a purifying Presence which,
though often concealed by impurities, is none the less deep-hidden within
this common humanity of ours. Do this, just being human about it, but
constant in your sense of this Presence within you of the Most High, and
you will find your own soul, your own unconquerable, imperishable soul.
You will discover the unconquerable, imperishable soul of your fellow-
men. Yea, you will feel within you, as a very Presence, the unconquerable,
imperishable soul of the Eternal—that Presence which no metaphysics
has yet succeeded in revealing, no systematic philosophy ever yet made
clear, no skepticism ever yet contrived to conceal from the sight of understanding souls.

Edwin D. Mouzon

[1869–1937]

*Edwin D. Mouzon was identified with the South from the beginning of his
career. He was born in Spartanburg, South Carolina. In 1889 he entered the
Southern Methodist ministry as a member of the Texas Conference, and in
1910 was elected Bishop of the Methodist Episcopal Church, South. He served
as Professor of Theology in Southwestern University, Georgetown, Texas, and
was a leader of the movement which resulted in the founding of Southern
Methodist University at Dallas, Texas. This sermon is a fine example of his
style and his liberal point of view, a position which he championed throughout
his career.*

THE SPIRIT OF CHRIST

Now if any man have not the Spirit of Christ, he is none of His. ROMANS 8:9.

EVERYTHING in the Bible must be brought to the judgment bar of Jesus
Christ. His voice is the one supreme voice that sounds down through the
ages. His character is the one character in the light of which all men must

be judged. We go, therefore, to the four gospels and ask: What is the spirit of Christ?

The spirit of Christ is the spirit of utmost loyalty to truth.

He himself was truth. What He seemed He was, and what He was He seemed. Jesus was real. I never call any man a hypocrite. I do not know what a man's inner life may be. But Jesus did use that cutting word. Said He, "Alas, for you scribes and Pharisees, hypocrites." The scribes and Pharisees, according to Jesus, were not genuine in their religious life; they were artificial. They were only playing at religion. And it must be admitted that there is much of the theatrical in many of us who are professed Christians. We love the footlights and we keep our eyes on the galleries. We are concerned too much about what men think of us and not enough about what the Searcher of Hearts knows us to be. Jesus was real.

Now there are two age-old enemies of the truth: the one is literalism and the other, traditionalism.

In bondage to the letter of Scripture, the Jews had lost their spiritual liberty. They carefully studied the Scriptures. They counted the very words in their manuscripts. They zealously guarded the letter of the law; and in the very act of doing this, they lost their knowledge of the truth. Jesus said, "Ye search the Scriptures because ye think that in them ye have eternal life; and these are they which bear witness of Me; and ye will not come unto Me, that ye may have life." They supposed that eternal life was to be found in the written page of the sacred writings. Jesus declared that life is not to be had in the knowledge of the Bible except only as the Bible leads men to Him. And this, indeed, is a truth that needs to be laid to heart to-day; for nowadays there are many earnest men who in their very defense of the Holy Scriptures have lost the spirit of Jesus. Literalism, I say, is the enemy of the truth.

The other foe of the truth is traditionalism. The traditionalist is bound hand and foot to the past. He erects the institution into greater importance than the human beings institutions were intended to serve. And, therefore, he becomes much more interested in preserving ancient institutions than he is in saving living men. To the traditionalists of his day Jesus declared, "The Sabbath was made for man, not man for the Sabbath." They had perverted the purpose of the Sabbath. They had taken the position that by all means and at any cost the institution of the Sabbath must be preserved. But Jesus insists that institutions are made for men, not men for institutions. And we should declare with all possible emphasis that no matter what the institution may be, our chief interest is never in the institution as an end in itself, but in the institution only as it serves humanity. Otherwise, traditionalism will block the way to the coming in of the truth that sets free.

The spirit of Christ is the spirit of passionate purity.

None was ever so pure as He; and His purity glowed with a burning passion. Very truly has it been said, "No heart is pure that is not passionate; no virtue is safe that is not enthusiastic."

In His teachings concerning moral purity Jesus fell heir to the teachings of the Old Testament, but He advanced far beyond them. He built upon the foundation of the prophets, but He breathed a new spirit into their writings. Jesus was not a *destroyer* but a *fulfiller.* Said He, "Think not that I came to destroy the law or the prophets: I came not to destroy but to fulfil." And we will best understand the meaning of that word fulfil if we turn its component parts about and make it read *"fill full."* Jesus came not to destroy, but to fill full. He fulfils the Old Testament teaching, as the day fulfils the dawn, as the fruit fulfils the flower. Take by way of illustration the Master's teaching concerning personal purity: "Ye have heard it was said by those of old time, Thou shalt not commit adultery, but I say unto you that whosoever looketh upon a woman to lust after her hath committed adultery with her already in his heart." The men of Jesus' day supposed that the sin was in the outward act. Jesus traces it back to its source and says that the heart itself must be clean.

Thus Jesus brought a new passion into the world, the passion for personal purity. The story of the New Testament Church and the history of early Christianity cannot be understood unless this be kept in mind.

Now I submit that nothing is more needed in the moral life of the people of America to-day than a revival of this passion that burned in the heart of Jesus, the passion for personal purity. We have fallen upon a time when the psychological doctrine of "self-expression" has about worked itself out to a *reductio ad absurdum.* Certainly no one can object to self-expression when there is a worth-while self to express. But self-expression has come to mean, in the thought of many, self-indulgence, and by self-indulgence is meant sensual self-indulgence. But strength of character and force of personality depend upon self-discipline and self-control; and purity alone opens the way to spiritual vision. "Blessed are the pure in heart for they shall see God." Which is to say, what a man sees depends upon what he is. Moral affinity is necessary to the knowledge of personality. If we are to know God we must be spiritually akin to Him. "The problems of a man sinful are the axioms of a man holy."

The spirit of Christ is the spirit of self-sacrificing service.

Nothing reveals the spirit of Christ as does the cross. And by the cross is meant much more than that instrument of wood on which Jesus died.

The cross of Christ was set in the sharpest possible contrast with the spirit of Roman civilization. Two things were characteristic of Roman civilization in the days of Jesus and Paul—the one was *love of power,* and the other, *love of pleasure.*

Into that pagan world came Jesus with his cross; and then everything began to change. Heine dreamed that he was at a supper of the gods; heavenly wine was brought, and they all drank it and lived at ease. But suddenly in the midst of the feast the door flew open, and in came a wan figure staggering under the weight of a great cross, which he threw down upon the banquet table. Then the faces of the gods turned pale, and one by one they vanished away. Into that Roman civilization came Jesus with His cross. In the presence of it, false ideals faded and false gods vanished out of sight. This principle of the cross marks the essential difference between Christianity and all pagan ethics, ancient or recent.

The spirit of Christ is the spirit of the broadest human sympathy.

Lying at the centre of the teachings of Jesus is His doctrine concerning the value of the human soul. With Him the soul is of greater value than all material things. "What shall it profit a man if he shall gain the whole world and lose his own soul?" The only thing of intrinsic value is human personality. Everything else is of value only as it relates to the soul.

And see how Jesus teaches respect for man as man. In the Sermon on the Mount He traces the sin of murder back to its secret springs in the heart. Not only is it wrong to kill; it is wrong also to have those feelings that lead to murder. And so the Master says, "Whosoever is angry with his brother is in danger of the judgment." For anger leads to murder. Again, "Whosoever shall say to his brother, Raca, shall be in danger of the council." "Raca" was just a word of contempt. And whosoever has in his heart feelings of contempt sins against his brother. Again the Master said, "Whosoever shall say, thou fool, shall be in danger of hell fire." All of which is to say in the most forcible manner that we must have charity toward all men and contempt for none. Contempt is wickedness. It violates fundamentally the truth of the divine fatherhood and the principle of human brotherhood.

The final test of all religion is to be found in the kind of men it produces. Said the Master, "Not everyone that sayeth unto me, Lord, Lord, shall enter into the Kingdom of Heaven but he that doeth the will of my Father which is in Heaven." The final test is the moral test. Not everyone who professes belief in an orthodox creed, not everyone who professes an emotional experience; but only those whose lives are in harmony with the will of the Father shall be counted citizens of the Kingdom of Heaven. "If any man have not the spirit of Christ, he is none of His."

William Ralph Inge

[1860–   ]

The preaching and writings of William Ralph Inge, known as "the Gloomy Dean," have had an effect on all parts of the Christian world. Dean Inge was born at Crayke, Yorkshire, and educated at King's College, Cambridge University; in 1911 he became Dean of St. Paul's Cathedral. While his utterances have been mainly in the pessimistic vein, his profound scholarship and deep understanding have given him a position unique among church leaders. Inge's sermons have a deep flavor of mysticism. Couched in the finest literary style, they are stimulating to read as well as to hear.

WILLING AND KNOWING

If any man willeth to do his will, he shall know of the doctrine. JOHN 7:17.

THESE WORDS of our Blessed Lord seem to me to point the way to the solution of a very old controversy, which still divides us. What is the nature of religious faith? Is it an act of trust, or is it conviction? Is it a working hypothesis, or the result of reasoning? Is it an attitude of the will, which selects for acceptance those ideas which help us to live as we desire to live, or is it an apprehension of absolute truth?

Faith is and must be a venture; we walk by faith, not by sight. Faith is the resolution to stand or fall by the noblest hypothesis. It must be a matter of the will rather than of the intellect, both because ultimate truth is beyond our reach, and because, whether consciously or unconsciously, our world is constructed out of those facts which interest us and bear upon our own needs. We do not and cannot see life steadily and see it whole; we see what lies in our path—the stepping-stones and stumbling-blocks which we have to use or avoid. We have to practice the difficult art of living in a world which we do not understand. Religion is the chief portion of this art. Truth is relative to our spiritual need; it has been said whatever helps our souls is true. From this point of view, religion is a kind of mind-cure; it is to be studied and practiced as a man learns an art or uses a remedy. If we wish to learn an art, we put ourselves under a training which experts tell us will make us proficient in it; we are content if this result follows. If we wish to remedy some physical defect in ourselves, the true remedy is that which cures us. For example, if our eyesight is bad, we buy a pair of spectacles which will help us to see like other people. We do not inquire whether the spectacles are true;

their value for us depends on their not being true for healthy eyes. We are told that those who do not understand that this is the function of religion, criticize the beliefs of their neighbours from a wrong point of view. Such books, for example, as Lord Morley's essay on Compromise, waste a great deal of virtuous indignation on the intellectual disingenuousness of religious people who he says profess to believe dogmas which they ought to know to be untrue. The assumption all through such books is that religious truth is a branch of scientific truth, whereas it is really a method of ordering the whole life with a view of the formation of character.

Those who think in this way set but a small value on the labours of critics and philosophers, unless they devote their talents to the advocacy of traditional dogmas. The Liberal Churchman seems to them to be a man who has taken up, perhaps almost by accident, the study of theology, and who treats it, in an abstract manner, like any other science, a method under which its religious value evaporates, and its therapeutic efficacy almost disappears. They can find many well-worn maxims ready at their hand, such as that "God has not willed to save His people by dialectic," and that the "heart has its reasons which the intellect knows not of."

Scholars and thinkers must admit the partial truth of this charge against them. They know how easily the logical intellect transforms vital interests into dialectical counters. They know how easy it is to personify their own opinions and those of their opponents, labelled probably with their names, and to forget, in the excitement of an intellectual tournament, that they are dealing with the mysteries of time and eternity, and with the struggle of overburdened men and women to find their way and to work out their own salvation with fear and trembling. The intellectual study of religion is an abstract science; so are all other sciences; and though the aim of philosophy is to coördinate and at last to rise above abstractions, no sane thinker counts himself to have apprehended.

And yet I cannot think that we ought to be content with a merely subjective and relative standard of truth in religion. The God who has made us for Himself, and who will not let our hearts rest till they find rest in Him, has not so hidden His face from us that we cannot know Him, however dimly and imperfectly, as He is. And we cannot really hold that there are for us two standards or two kinds of truths, one speculative or scientific, and the other practical. Our minds are not divided or divisible, and we cannot with impunity play tricks with our reason, either to stimulate our wills or to win inward peace. There is after all a sterling sincerity in the negations of the honest rationality which we miss in such utterances as this of Renan: "What a delight to the man who is weighed down by six days of toil, to come on the seventh to rest upon his knees, to contemplate tall columns, arches, and altar, to listen to the chanting, to hear moral and consoling words. It is the privilege of pure sentiment to be invulnerable and to play with poison without being hurt by it." This is no doubt a crude and half-contemptuous description of a very common attitude, which is familiar to us in the phrase "the consolations of religion," as if religion were a species of anodyne, a cure for soul-ache. There is surely a levity, an indifference to truth, or a deep scepticism, in those who can use such language. I prefer the harsh dictum of the rationalist, that every wish to believe, when it is dragged into the open, is a reason for doubt. There is an asceticism of the intellect, which though it may be carried too far, is itself a noble thing. There are men who are afraid to accept what their souls—their whole selves—bid them to believe, because they know that they long to believe it and because it cannot be proved. This kind of renunciation is an act of homage to truth as an absolute principle; I do not think that it injures the character, though it makes life less bright than it ought to be. But in those who indulge what is called the wish to believe; who fly under the wings of authority to escape the buffetings of doubt; who grasp at an inward peace which they have not earned; who make religion a matter of emotion or sentiment or æsthetic thrill, I have observed that not only the intellect but the moral sense loses its finer qualities. A faith that is procured ready-made gives but little guidance where no authoritative precepts can be had.

There is a kind of doubt, which does not attach to any particular doctrine, but to the existence of God Himself, and the spiritual world. It is not so much that any anti-theistic arguments seem to us to be cogent, as that the whole subject matter of religion seems to us to be unreal. As the French encyclopædist said: "The question of God lacks actuality." This is a very different thing from the other kind of doubt, and only a bigot will confound them. In dealing with this type of doubt, it is a pertinent and not an impertinent question to ask whether there is anything in the character of the doubter to account for his failure to see what to too many others are the most certain of all truths. Theologians have often misused a perfectly legitimate argument by hinting at secret sins, moral obliquities of some kind, as the probable source of want of faith. It is certainly true that only the pure in heart can see God, and we must extend the meaning of purity of heart to all unfaithfulness to the light that is in us. The double heart, it has been said, makes the double head. But it is not necessary to assume that irreligious persons are evil livers. My argument this morning has been that inattention and want of interest are quite enough to account for the feeling of unreality which for many of us surrounds the spiritual world, and that however real and important the truths of religion may be, we cannot expect to feel their reality and importance if we hardly ever think of them.

I know that most of the younger generation are disposed to think that there is something small and selfish about care for their own souls, and that it is enough for them to cherish, on the one side, what a recent writer has called loyalty to the beloved community, the Church, and on the other, ardour for social reform. A breezy, familiar, confident religion, with this dual basis, has been brought back from the battle-field of France. But believe me, you can serve both the Church and the country best by deepening your own personal faith. The reason why organized religion has lost nearly all its credit, is not that it is not sufficiently organized, but that it has no vision of the invisible; it does not hold up before the nation that standard of values which Christ revealed to us; it does not believe from its heart with that noble rebel Mazzini, that the cause of all our trouble is the gradual substitution of the worship of material interests for the adoration of holy ideas; and so it fluctuates between shallow and mischievous political agitation and an equally shallow and eclectic medievalism. You will do far more good in your generation by being devout and open-minded Christians, "adding to your faith knowledge" in the spirit of the words of Clement which I quoted to you, than by plunging into movements which are too superficial to add any real strength to the cause of religion. If we are to have a religious revival, it must be unmistakably a spiritual revival—it must flow from an outpouring of the Holy Spirit, with His gifts of wisdom and understanding of counsel and might, of knowledge and the fear of the Lord; it must point straight to the Cross of Christ, and to heaven into which He is ascended. Such a revival can begin only in hearts which have prepared themselves earnestly to receive the heavenly Guest; and where can we hope to find the first promise of it if not here [Oxford University], the home of young life and of ancient wisdom, the storehouse of things new and old—new things that were old before the world was, and old things which spring ever fresh from the fountains of the river of God? If any man willeth to do His will, he shall know of the doctrine. The way is not yet clear before us; many old things are passing away, and we do not know what is coming. It is a time for thought and prayer and self-discipline. "I will hearken what the Lord God will say concerning me." Things may be clearer ten years hence, when the seed sown in a million heroic graves has had time to grow. Meanwhile, remember St. Paul's words to Timothy, "Take heed to thyself, and to the doctrine"; and to thyself first.

In the following sermon Inge is revealed as a poet with a keen sense of the value of science, not as antagonistic to religion but, when rightly interpreted and used, a true revealer of the deep mysteries of religion at its best.

THE ETERNAL VALUES

When I consider Thy heavens, the work of Thy fingers, the moon and the stars, which Thou hast ordained; what is man, that Thou art mindful of him? and the son of man, that Thou visitest him? PSALM 8:3, 4.

THE contrast between the starry heavens and the puny dwellers on this earth is far more tremendous than the Psalmist knew it to be. His universe was a small one compared with that which we contemplate. And yet the disproportion seemed to him almost crushing. But not quite. For man is, after all, "the roof and crown of things," at least within our knowledge. "Thou hast made him to have dominion over the works of Thine hands; thou hast put all things in subjection under his feet." So the old Hebrew poet, like the philosopher Kant, finds two things in the world worthy of awe and wonder—the heavens above, and the moral nature of man within him.

This feeling of awe at the vast scale on which nature works, whether it be solemn joy and consolation, or a crushing sense of impotence, has been countered by some tart criticism. Do we really suppose that a star, because it is a very bulky body, must have a correspondingly large soul, or that the Creator sets more store by an enormous gas-bag than by the spirit of a saint or hero? And what does it really mean—this exhortation to worship the hypothetical Creator and sustainer of the starry heavens? Is it not the characteristic tendency of an industrial civilisation to think of everything in terms of *ownership*? Is it really a valid argument for theism to ask whether so eligible a property as the universe can possibly belong to nobody? Do we ever unconsciously argue that if we bow respectfully to a duke who owns a hundred thousand acres, we ought to pay infinitely greater respect to the largest of all landed proprietors, who possesses a million estates each a million miles in diameter, and whose title-deeds are billions of years old? Indian thought has never been impressed by this idea of ownership.

Natural science is the principal vehicle of revelation to us in the twentieth century. It has modified our whole way of looking at things. The idea of evolution has transformed our outlook in dealing with almost every subject, including history, politics, and theology. The belief in uniform natural laws has banished the old notion of two orders, the natural and the supernatural, dovetailed into each other on the same plane, a notion which greatly retarded the progress of knowledge. Moreover, the scientific *temper* is as great an asset to humanity as scientific discovery. Nowhere else do we find such disinterested devotion to truth, such unquenchable faith in the power and value of disciplined intellectual labour, such bold sweeps of imagination checked by such punctiliously accurate experiments. The air breathed by science is like that of mountain heights, thin, but pure and bracing.

Science has affected both theology and morality in many ways, and must affect them much farther. After four hundred years, the Church has still failed to adapt her cosmology to the discoveries of Galileo. Officially, we clergy still have to live in a pre-Copernican universe. Otherwise, certain dogmas on which the Church insists would have no meaning. The battle against the dead hand of authority is not yet won, but the issue is certain. The educated Christian has already succeeded in fitting his creed within the framework of the universe as he knows it to be; and as the people become better educated, there will be less resistance to a reconstruction of that part of the building which is obviously crumbling. When this necessary work is done, it will be found that religion is a great gainer.

In the second half of this address I wish to speak shortly of the relation of science to religious faith. Some have thought it possible to prove the existence of God by the methods of natural science. But, in my opinion, no argument which abstracts from the religious experience can ever lead to the God of religion.

It is often said that science gives us, or tries to give us, a world of facts without values, and that this is why it excludes those aspects of reality with which religion is concerned. This is, in my opinion, a complete mistake. You cannot separate judgments of fact and judgments of value in this manner. A fact without value is no fact; a value without fact is no value. Take any branch of science you like, and you will find that it is built throughout upon a valuation of experience. Take any form of religion you like, and you will find that it is built upon what are believed to be facts. The proposed delimitation of territory will not work; it would be equally fatal to both sides.

Perhaps I ought to say a few words in justification of my statement that all science is a valuation of experience. I will not lay stress on the fact that nearly all scientific literature is steeped in valuations—that men of science habitually talk of higher and lower forms of life; that they assume that health is better than disease; that parasitism is a kind of biological sin; and that the extinction of any form of life marks it as a failure and in a sort condemns it, which means that for them existence itself is a value. These value-judgments creep into their investigations because they are men, and even if they wish to keep them out they cannot do so. But besides these, they assume, to start with, that order is better than chaos, law better than accident, correct observation and calculation better than incorrect. In so doing, they base their life's work on the values of truth, harmony, orderly succession, universal law. They hope to end by establishing that these are facts; that is their reasonable faith; but unquestionably they begin by assuming that they are values.

For we also know the world qualitatively. We stamp things, persons, and events as good or bad, as beautiful or ugly, judging them by ideal standards which we find within us very much as the scientist finds within him an ideal standard of truth and conformity to law. And I wish to insist earnestly—for it is the foundation on which the whole philosophy of religion is built—that these qualitative judgments are the basis of all our religious, moral, and intellectual life; that they are our deepest convictions; and that they are impartial, objective judgments of fact, no less than the judgments of natural science. Judgments of fact, I dare to say, because I repeat that a value which is no fact is no value. The affirmations of the religious consciousness claim to be eternal truths, not unrealised ideals.

This claim to objectivity by the religious consciousness is not confined to the mystics. Even Aristotle recognises the capacity of the soul for apprehending the Absolute and Eternal, though it seems to make a breach in his psychology to do so; and Spinoza, forgetting, it would seem, his doctrine of parallelism, declares that "we feel and experience that we are immortal." The late F. H. Bradley, perhaps our greatest contemporary philosopher and no friend to orthodox Christianity, says impressively: "There is nothing more real than what comes in religion. To compare facts such as these with what comes to us in outward existence would be to trifle with the subject. The man who demands a reality more solid than that of the religious consciousness knows not what he seeks."

And what does the religious consciousness affirm? In its widest sense, it affirms as living principles and universal standards of value the triple star of idealism, Goodness, Truth, and Beauty, a threefold cord not quicky broken. It affirms that these are known to us as attributes of God, and therefore the most real things that we know. Thus we are able to ascend in heart and mind to a spiritual and eternal world in which abide the thoughts of God which energise in the creation as vital laws. It is in this eternal world that we find our immortality; it is because we are not cut off from this eternal world that we know, as Spinoza says, that we are immortal.

But this is not all. The religious consciousness affirms a personal God. A personal God does not mean a magnified and non-natural man. It means a Being with whom a human person can hold personal relations. That we can hold personal relations with the Author of our being is the conviction of all religious people. Their conviction is not based on *a priori* reasoning; it is based on experience. Partly we think that we can trace the wise and merciful care of God in the course of our lives, the rod and the staff of His fatherly hand; but chiefly we are sure that He hears our prayers.

Speak to Him thou, for He hears; and spirit with spirit can meet;
Closer is He than breathing, and nearer than hands and feet.

We conclude, then, that the outstanding differences between science and religion are mainly differences of emphasis in asserting the reality of the ultimate values. The nature of our work, and of our dominant interests, leads some of us to see God in the order of nature, others in moral goodness, others in beauty, whether of nature or art. These are all divine attributes, and God manifests Himself in all three. But we have all chosen to be onesided, because only by specialising can we do any good in the world.

We none of us see all round the truth. But by the goodness of God, those who follow the gleam wholeheartedly and disinterestedly in any one direction are not much cramped by this specialising. The work to which they have given themselves takes on a universal quality, so that the beauty and goodness in the world are not hidden from those who are searching out nature's laws, and the saint feels something of the awe and wonder of the visible creation.

There is more than one path up the hill of the Lord. It is only from the top, we may say in a figure, that the paths meet and the view is the same. But true men are all engaged upon the same quest.

Lawrence Pearsall Jacks

[1860–   ]

Educated at University School, Nottingham; the University of London; Manchester College; Göttingen; and Harvard University, Lawrence Pearsall Jacks entered the ministry in 1887 as assistant to the Reverend Stopford Brooke at Bedford Chapel. In 1903 he became professor of Philosophy at Manchester College, and in 1915 was made principal of that institution. Since the beginning of his career he distinguished himself as one of the great philosophic minds of England, founding in 1902 the Hibbert Journal *and serving as its editor for a generation. His writings and lectures on the problems of education have been profoundly influential in the development of English secondary schools. The following sermon has the subtitle "A Sermon to Boys on a Wet Day" and reveals the simple, clear, almost informal nature of much of Dr. Jacks' preaching. It shows his understanding of boys and is testimony to his skill in dealing with the young men at Manchester College.*

THE RIGHT TO BE HAPPY

Happy is the man that hath his quiver full. PSALMS 127:5.

NOBODY has the right to be happy always. Nobody can be. You can't be happy when people you are fond of *die*—and you have no right to be. You can't be happy when you see your friends in misfortune—and you have no right to be. Nobody was meant to be happy *always*. If you study the human body, the way it is built up, you will see at once that happiness is by no means the only thing it is made for. The human body is a wonderful instrument for doing things with, the difficult things too. The hands, the eyes, the brain, the bones, the muscles, all show that the human body has been built up not for pleasure but for action—for standing strains, for carrying burdens, for embarking on dangerous expeditions, for all kinds of skilful and delicate and heroic operations—quite as much for bearing pain as for enjoying pleasure.

There was an ancient philosopher who said that very clearly; you older boys will make his acquaintance when you go to the University if you have not done so already. His name was Aristotle. Aristotle had a good deal to say about happiness—though he didn't mean by the word what most people mean when they use it to-day. But he saw that man is cut out not so much for happiness as for action, for *work*, as we should say, for difficult, skilful, beautiful work. And the only way to get happiness is by doing the work you are fitted for in the best manner it admits of. That is what Aristotle said, and that is what I am going to repeat to you to-day.

Looking back on the happiness I have had in life—and I have had my fair share of it, and many kinds of it—I think I can say that the best of it has come from the work I have had to do, and from the people who have helped me in doing it. Unless a person is happy in his work you can't make him very happy in anything else, though perhaps he may think you can. Holidays and play are good—no one has enjoyed them more than I have—but holidays and play don't amount to much unless they have a background of enjoyable work behind them. Don't suppose for a moment that I'm out against play—nobody believes in it more than I do. But I can't agree with those people who make out that work and play are opposites one to the other. In all good work there's a certain element of play; and in all good play there's a certain element of work—as you find out whenever you play a football match against a team that's worth playing with. Those people make a big mistake who think that play is all happiness and work is all misery. There's a great difference between playing and fooling. There's a great difference between playing the game and playing the fool. I will tell you who the people are who know most both about work and about play. They are the *artists,* the people who create beautiful things, fine buildings, fine music, fine poetry, fine painting and sculpture.

The artists: I should like to say a word about them, because I think they are almost the most important people in the world—next to boys and schoolmasters! Sometimes you hear artists spoken of as though they were only the people who make ornaments, pretty things to hang on the wall or to put on the mantelpiece. Well, they wouldn't be very important if they only did that. If that was all they did we might manage to get on without them. But they do a great deal more than that. They do something that we cannot get on without. Art is only work excellently done, and the artists are the people who do their work better than the rest of us are doing ours. I don't care what you are doing—I don't care what your work is—it may be translating a piece of Cicero into good English, or it may be playing a football match, or making tables and chairs, or it may be running the finances of a bank—I say that you have only to do the job just as well as it can be done and you will make a work of art of it, and you will become an artist in that line.

As far as I can make it out, there are two main kinds of happiness: the first is the kind that is given to us by other people, and the second is the kind we create for ourselves. I've had both kinds in my life; and my experience is that the kind of happiness we make for ourselves is more real and more lasting, and on the whole more worth having, than the kind which other people make for us and give us for nothing—though that also is very good in its way. Of course we all know what a fine and noble thing it is to make other people happy—we ought to do it whenever we can. But for my part I don't want all my happiness to be made for me by other people. I don't want to be dependent on others for my happiness, however kind and good they may be. I don't want to get into the habit of calling upon other people to make me happy. I should like to be able to make the main part of my happiness for myself. In fact, I'm inclined to think that unless I make the greater part of my happiness for myself, what other people can do for me in that line won't amount to very much.

A person who is happy only when other people make him so is really a very miserable sort of person, and there are a lot of them about—people who expect to be made happy by the State, or by the Government, or by the social system, or by their friends and neighbours in general, and who go about complaining and whining because other people are not making them as happy as they think they have the right to be. I hope there are none of that kind in your school, though it's a highly exceptional school if there are not. Nobody enjoys an occasional treat given him by other people more than I do. But what kind of person is it who can only be happy when somebody else is giving him a treat? What kind of person is it who wants his life to be a kind of picnic to which other people are always inviting him? I will tell you. That person is a moral baby. He is not a boy and not a man.

I believe that nobody can be really happy in this world unless he makes the greater part of his happiness for himself. And I will tell you another thing about that. The people who can make happiness for themselves are generally the very ones who help to make others happy at the same time. Think of the artist I was just speaking about. Think what a lot of happiness he makes for himself by his work; and then think what a lot he makes for other people at the same time by those beautiful things that he creates—by his music, or his singing, or his poetry, or his painting, or whatever else it may be. If you will take a word of advice from an old fellow like me, let me offer you this. If you want to be really happy, learn to make the greater part of your happiness for yourselves and not to be dependent on treats given you by other people.

But how can you do that? Well, there is one word that answers the question. The word is "skill"—a word which ought to have a greater place in education than it has. I know that word won't satisfy everybody. They will want me to use another word—"kindness," for example; but kindness is only a rare sort of skill in dealing with other people. Or "goodness"; but goodness is only a rare kind of skill in doing right. I give the word "skill" without any apologies, and I give it a very wide meaning; there is skill of the heart, skill of the brain, skill of the voice, skill of the hand. And I say this, that without skill of one kind or another nobody can be really happy. By acquiring skill in one or other or all these ways we acquire the means of making our happiness for ourselves instead of being dependent for it on other people—as nobody ought to be. Skill in work that makes it a kind of beautiful play, skill in play that makes it a kind of beautiful work—that is the great source of happiness for everybody, old and young. I think that nobody's education is complete unless it leads him to acquiring some kind of skill—and there are a thousand kinds of it.

But what is skill? How shall we define it? Skill, I take it, is simply *wisdom in action;* knowledge completing itself by doing the thing that it knows. Until our knowledge has turned itself into skill of one kind or another, it is a half-grown thing; it will be forgotten, it will die without bearing any fruit. And the main fault I have to find with our educational system at the present day is that it imparts knowledge up to a point, and then stops short without turning it into skill, so that the pupil goes out into the world unequipped for any kind of socially valuable occupation, ready for nothing that would give him a sense of his personal usefulness to the world. The idea of vocational training has been overdone, or rather it has been narrowed down to the purely economic sense. But if you mean by it the kind of education which equips the pupil for a socially valuable occupation and so gives him the sense of his personal value to society, then I would say vocational training is right. Our object should be not so much to make education vocational, but to make vocations educational. It will be so in the Kingdom of Heaven. In the Kingdom of Heaven every man will put God (who is the Supreme Excellence) into his daily work, thereby converting his work into beautiful play and himself into the kind of person whom others can love.

To the young people who hear me to-day I would say this: When the time comes for choosing your vocation, choose one that challenges your skill; choose one that will put your mind, your whole personality, *on its mettle*: the happiness best worth having is to be found on those lines. Beware of soft jobs. Don't listen to the people who tell you that man was made for happiness. He wasn't. He was made for doing difficult, beautiful, heroic work, and the only happiness he is entitled to is the happiness that comes from doing it.

Alfred E. Garvie

[1861–   ]

One of the great scholars of the British pulpit, Dr. Alfred E. Garvie was educated at Glasgow and at Oxford. In both places he received high honors in theology. He became minister of Macduff Congregational Church in 1893, and in 1902 was made president of the Congregational Union of Scotland. He has had a long and brilliant career as a minister and teacher, and his numerous publications are widely read throughout the British Isles. As a preacher, Dr. Garvie reveals his scholarship and his fine sense of literary values. His sermons are as fine to read as they are to hear.

GLORYING IN THE CROSS

Far be it from me to glory, save in the cross of our Lord Jesus Christ, through which the world hath been crucified unto me, and I unto the world. GALATIANS 5:14.

THIS personal confession of Paul, which is interjected in a controversial passage about circumcision, and comes upon us like a bright flash of sunlight out of a dark cloud, contains a historical fact, a theological truth, and an individual experience. It is in the *experience* that the *fact* becomes the *truth;* because for Paul, more than for any other Christian thinker, his

personality was the channel of his theology; he could think as he did
because he had become what he was. Since he had been crucified and been
raised again with Christ experimentally, he could interpret, as no other
has done, the Crucifixion and the Resurrection doctrinally. It is in this
way, and this way alone, that theology can be made vital; and that in
preaching, truth may come through personality.

Had Jesus not lived, taught, and wrought among men as He did, His
death would not, and could not, have had the significance which it had
for the community which had been gathered in His earthly ministry.
While Paul truly describes the content of the apostolic preaching in the
words, "I delivered unto you first of all that which also I received, how
that Christ died for our sins according to the Scriptures; and that He
was buried; and that He hath been raised on the third day according
to the Scriptures" (I Cor. xv. 3, 4), it must be remembered that the
Apostles were companions of Jesus, and had the memory of Him still
vivid, as they confronted the problem of His death and sought its solution in the teaching of the Scriptures. We can understand and prize the
Cross to-day only as we learn to think, as Jesus has taught us, of God and
man, sin and salvation, duty and destiny.

Even so, yea, still more so, the Crucifixion must not be separated from
the Resurrection. Had Christ not been raised from the dead, the faith
inspired by the earthly ministry would probably not have survived the
shock of His death, and such a death! for the disciples as Jews a death
on which fell the curse of God (Gal. iii. 13). For Paul, who knew not the
earthly ministry, the Resurrection alone made the Crucifixion not only
tolerable, but supremely significant and valuable. It was only after the
Resurrection that the truth concealed in the fact of the Cross was disclosed. Because by the Resurrection He was "instituted Son of God with
power, according to the spirit of holiness," his death was recognised as
atoning, propitiatory, and reconciling. We must not then separate the
Cross from what led to it, and followed upon it.

The Cross is so central in history because the truth enshrined in the
fact is so essential to theology, the revelation of God which issues in the
redemption of man.

The description which Paul gives in the text of the Crucified, *our Lord
Jesus Christ,* records the ascent of Christian faith. To the personal name
Jesus, significant as that was, ascribing salvation to God, was added at
Cæsarea Philippi the official title *Messiah* (Christ), as the fulfilment of
God's promise of a deliverer was found in Him. After the Resurrection
the first Christian creed was, *Jesus Christ is Lord.*

While many feel that they need go no farther in their quest for the
meaning and worth of the Cross, others there are who are constrained
to ask, Why must the forgiveness of sin come from the love of God in

this way? Some have answered, Thus and only thus could man be sufficiently impressed with what sin is, and what God is, to repent of sin, and have faith in God's forgiveness. That this is the effect of the Cross, none can doubt; but is that the reason, and the only reason, for the Cross? Many Christian thinkers have answered No, and have sought a reason.

There is necessarily in God as holy love a reaction against sin; He cannot tolerate it, or make compromise with it; He must condemn it, and execute judgment upon it, as He does in the consequences which in the moral order of the world attach to sin. When as in Christ God offered to the sinful race free and full forgiveness, it was a necessity of His nature as holy love to execute judgment upon sin, not in leaving its consequences to fall on sinners, but in taking them upon Himself in the shame and scorn, sorrow and suffering, death and desolation, that sin inflicted on Christ and God in Him. My conscience at least cannot be satisfied with a forgiveness which does not carry with it a judgment as adequate as the forgiveness is. Such a conclusion cannot be logically demonstrated. As Jesus in Gethsemane recognised the inevitable necessity of His death, on His knees in prayer, so only can we.

Whatever doubt or difficulty there may be about the reason for the death of Christ, its effect on those who in penitence and faith receive the grace of God, which the sacrifice of the Son and the Father in Him conveys, is manifest.

It is the instrument of the creative act of God: old things pass away, all things become new, there is a new creation morally and religiously; the man is born from above by the Spirit of God, and lives no longer unto the flesh, but unto the Spirit; he dies unto sin and becomes alive unto God; he is crucified and raised again with Christ; he passes out of darkness into God's marvelous light; he rises out of death in sin into life in God; the world is crucified unto him, and he to the world. In all these ways can the change be described. What needs always to be emphasised is the greatness of the contrast between the life apart from Christ and the life in Christ; the life still unsaved through His sacrifice, and the life His sacrifice is saving.

We must not insist on suddenness of change as essential to the reality of the experience. Paul's conversion was sudden for his consciousness, although it was not unprepared in his previous experience. Because of this suddenness, he realised more vividly, and has expressed more forcibly (some who do not understand such an experience might even say violently), the contrast. With others there is a gradual development, in which the contrast is not so vividly realised, and could not with sincerity be as forcibly expressed. What matters is that the change should be experienced, whether it be swiftly or slowly.

Many Christians are so conformed to the world around them, that they show little evidence of being transformed by the renewing of their mind. Much as the Christian leaven may have pervaded the whole lump of human society in lands nominally Christian, yet the change is not so complete that there is never any occasion for the world to be crucified to the Christian, or for him to be crucified to the world. The customs, standards, and institutions around the Christian to-day have not yet been so transformed by the Spirit of God that he can afford to be conformed to them, if he desires to realise the Christian character. For instance, there is on the part of many Christian business men an acquiescence in methods which from a truly Christian standpoint must be condemned. Ruthless competition, the deliberate forcing of rivals out of the trade, the driving of workers at greater speed than their bodily strength allows—these are not Christian. The success of many men in business is an evidence of their failure as Christians. There are Christian women who conform to fashion in the costliness of their dress and the luxury of their homes to such a degree that it is difficult to believe that they can be successfully cultivating the Christ-like life. In politics men will do for party or country what they would hesitate to do in self-interest, what they certainly could not justify to a sensitive conscience.

The hope of human society being Christianised does not lie with the Christians who thus conform to the world around them; it lies with those who have been so transformed by the change which the Cross of Christ has effected in them, that they are indeed crucified unto the world, and the world unto them. Much which the world values the Christian cannot prize; what he values the world must despise. From the Cross of Christ there comes the challenge to the safe, easy, and comfortable Christianity of to-day, accepted and approved even in many Churches, to realise the antagonism, and necessary antagonism, of the world as it now is to all Christ is and is doing.

Such nonconformity means sacrifice; it may be outward, it certainly is inward. Still, very many things that the world counts gain must be reckoned loss for the excellency of the knowledge of Christ Jesus as Lord. Ambitions must be subordinated to aspirations. Human companionships must be given up for the closer communion with Christ. Hardship must take the place of comfort, and toil of ease, if the Cross is taken up, and Christ is followed. Accordingly the Cross must be no less central in practice than in experience, in morality than in religion. And so intimately related and mutually dependent is the one upon the other that the grace of the Cross cannot be apprehended unless the duty of the Cross is accepted, and the duty of the Cross cannot be done unless the grace of the Cross is gained; the free giving and the free receiving of the Cross as Divine grace and human duty go together. It was the love of Christ, as displayed in His Cross, which constrained Paul not to reckon himself as his own; and it is only as the Cross of Christ means to us and does for us what it meant and did for Paul that we, even as he was, will be crucified unto the world, and the world unto us. To glory in the Cross of Christ without this crucifixion in ourselves is a vain boast; only when this result follows from that cause can it become a personal confession, which God will approve and bless with the increase of His grace to the glory of His Name.

Charles Reynolds Brown

[1862–   ]

From 1911 to 1928 Dr. Charles Reynolds Brown held the distinguished chair of dean of the Yale Divinity School. In addition, from 1914 to 1927, he was pastor of the University Church at Yale, and preached several times each year to a congregation made up largely of Yale men. During this time he was repeatedly voted the most popular preacher at the University. Born on a farm in Bethany, West Virginia, he was educated at the University of Iowa and at Boston University, completing his formal education at Yale in 1911. This sermon is typical of the simple, terse, straightforward style which has captivated congregations and college audiences throughout the country for more than a generation.

RELIGIOUS QUITTERS

No man, having put his hand to the plough, and looking back, is fit for the kingdom of God. LUKE 9:62.

THE gospel is not all velvet—there are places where it feels more like sandpaper. The Master did not go about handing out soft words indiscriminately, no matter how men were faced. He would sometimes thrust in the sharp sword of rebuke until it hurt. He did say, "Come unto me and I will give you rest," but He said it only to those who had become "weary and heavy laden" to some purpose. He stood more often uttering a clarion call to awaken men from their spiritual sloth.

Here in the lesson were three men who were "religiously inclined," as we say in our soft phrase. They had "great respect for religion." They always spoke well of the church and the clergy. They regarded themselves as men of excellent sentiments and they liked to make impressive moral gestures. If anyone had spoken slightingly of religious faith in their presence they would have been grieved.

One of them said, "Lord, I will follow Thee." But the Master noticed a certain droop in the man's voice and He replied, "Foxes have holes and the birds of the air have nests, but the Son of Man has nowhere to lay his head." Following Him might mean sleeping out occasionally. He was calling men to a life of hardship and self-sacrifice. They might have to lunch occasionally on locusts and wild honey. That was too much for his friendly soul. He did not care to go any farther—he turned back and that was the last of him. He quit.

The second man heard the summons, "Follow me." It awakened a response in his heart and he started up with his face toward the light. But he made certain conditions. "Let me first bury my father."

There is nothing to indicate that his father was dead at that time. He wanted to wait until his father died and the property was divided up and the estate all settled. Then, he said, he might be willing to give some thought to the claims of Christian discipleship. He might be ready to do his bit of Christian service. When the Master declined that postponed allegiance, he, too, turned away and that was the last of him. He quit.

The third man heard the call and accepted it. "Lord, I will follow Thee whithersoever Thou goest." His words seemed to have the right ring. But before he let his voice fall, he added, "First, however, let me go and bid farewell to those who are at my house. Let me go around and visit all my relatives and tell them that I am about to become a Christian!"

They were all quitters. They had good impulses; they meant well; they had a kindly feeling toward Christ. If anyone had uttered a harsh word about Him, they would have resented it. They felt that it would be a good thing if the whole world could have a larger measure of His spirit.

But when the time came to stand up and be counted, they were not there. They were not willing to go the whole way of Christian discipleship. They were on the fence, without sufficient sand in their crops to get down on the side where they belonged and take hold with their fellow Christians. Jesus described them as "men who having put their hands to the plough, looked back" and then went back. In that way they ceased to have any value for the kingdom of God. He dismissed them all as "quitters."

Let me ask two questions: Who are the quitters in these days? What can be done to line them up again?

Who are the quitters? Some of them are young people, college students perhaps, who were brought up in Christian homes. They have a splendid Christian inheritance and background. The showing they make in decent living to-day is due mainly to the moral legacies they received from their parents rather than to any spiritual capital which they have amassed by their own efforts. When they were children they were taught to pray, to read the Bible, to go to church. They were expected to line up on the Christian side of it in their habits and aspirations. Many of them joined the church, made open declaration of their loyalty to Christ, and received of the sacrament of remembrance. They were named with the name of Christ.

Then as the years came and went they were given a larger measure of liberty and there came a change. They became careless and listless in their religious habits. They no longer swam up stream—they were spiritual driftwood, carried here and there by whatever current of influence happened to flow. They may not be doing anything wicked—their social traditions would hold them back from the coarser sins of the flesh. But they have ceased to count for the kingdom of God. The religion of Christ is no stronger in the circles where they move because they are there.

In their better moments, when they take stock, reckoning up the debits and credits, they feel that no other life can be compared for one moment to a genuinely Christian life. They would withhold their highest admiration from any life which was not thoroughly Christian. Yet there they are on the sidelines rather than in the game—they are quitters.

Some of these quitters are mature people. Once they were active, useful, devoted Christians. Their serene, radiant joy in living in fellowship with Him and in the unselfish service of their fellows was such that they raised the spiritual temperature of any room or of any group they entered. There was a certain healthy contagion about them which brought others out of darkness into light, out of spiritual deadness into newness of life.

But here also there came a change. The cares of this world and the fact that they had more money to spend, their indulgence in a wider range of amusement and their absorptions in second, third, and fourth rate interests, crowded out those values which stand first. All this brought about a lowering of spiritual tone. The song in the heart went unsung, the prayer was left unsaid, there was no more "grace before meat," their places in the house of worship were frequently vacant and then vacant altogether. That full, fine measure of consecration and of capacity for self-sacrifice was gone.

They are not wicked people—God forbid—oftentimes they are very respectable, likeable people. But they are religious quitters. They are not in a position to hand on to their children any such rich heritage of Christian interest and devotion as that which they received from their earnest, godly parents. When you reckon up the forces which really count for the coming of the kingdom, the sway and rule of the spirit which was in Christ, it is hardly worth while to enter their names. They have quit.

"When I became a man, I put away childish things." Every man does who grows and thinks. But some people do it by tossing their entire religious interest out of the window without taking the trouble to replace those childish conceptions with a more mature, reasonable, workable faith. They quit merely because they thought that it would be too much trouble to grow. They gave up because of the apparent difficulty involved in thinking their way through into the open.

The putting away of childish things cannot be done all at once or overnight. It is a long, patient process of readjustment and growth. Some of the quitters seem to think that the rest of us still believe those childish notions. Some of them write articles about religion for the newspapers and magazines. When we read what they write we find that all they know about religion was learned apparently long ago in some rural Sunday-school when they were ten-year-olds. Poor things, before they undertake to discuss the subject of religion they had better grow up and learn to shave. "Be no more children, tossed to and fro" by every shallow notion which comes along, "but, speaking the truth in love, grow up into Him in all things, who is the head, even Christ."

There is nothing attractive about the quitters. To be perfectly frank, they are merely moral cowards who have thrown off their share of responsibility upon those who show themselves more robust. We all recognize that the greatest need of the world is for a larger supply of sound, reliable character. The careless, the flippant, the cynical are of no more value for social progress than the chaff which the wind driveth away. When two men are carrying a log and one of them suddenly steps out, throwing his share of the burden entirely upon the other man, you know what you think of him.

You might suppose that the shame of their action would sting some of these quitters into a worthier attitude toward life. There came one day from a hard-fought field a company of soldiers, weary and dirty, broken and bloodstained. They saw standing at one side, well toward the rear, a group of deserters, all clean and comfortable. The soldiers called out to them, "Go hang yourselves! We fought the battle through and won it, and you were not there."

We do not win men to Christian life by toning it down. Nothing is gained by mincing matters. You cannot make Christian life easy for the simple reason that Jesus made it difficult. The glad hand and the bright smile which "never comes off" may have a certain value at the Rotary Club but they soon reach their limit. They do not open the eyes of the blind nor cause the lame to walk nor make the crooked straight. It takes the One who made the cross the symbol of His method to do that. His demands are thoroughgoing. "Seek first the kingdom of God." Put the rule of the divine spirit first! Take Jesus seriously!

"No man having put his hand to the plough and looking back is fit."
It is plough work to which we are called, not a picnic. The furrows are to
be laid open, not always in black loam, or in grassy lawns, but in fields
where there are stumps, roots, stones, where the soil itself may seem
as unyielding as a concrete sidewalk. Rough, hard, strenuous toil! When
any man undertakes to follow Him, putting down evil under his feet,
facing his duties without flinching, striving to furnish his full share of
action in making our social order Christian, he will find that he has "put
his hand to the plough."

D. L. Ritchie

[1864-   ]

*A native of Scotland and trained in Edinburgh University and the University
Divinity School for Theology, Dr. D. L. Ritchie was ordained in the Congregational ministry in 1890. After a six-year pastorate at Dumferline, Scotland,
he was called to St. James' Church at Newcastle-on-Tyne, England, to succeed
the eminent Dr. Jowett. In 1903 he became principal of Nottingham Theological College. After World War I he moved to Canada to work for church union,
and this eventually led to his appointment as dean of the United Theological
College, Montreal. His sermon* Can the Churches Unite? *preceded the union
of churches in Canada and is illustrative of the part Dr. Ritchie played in this
accomplishment. It expresses his deep conviction that religious men should
dwell together despite minor differences of creed and doctrine.*

CAN THE CHURCHES UNITE?

Till we all attain unto the unity of the faith, and of the knowledge of the
Son of God, unto the measure of the stature of the fullness of Christ.
EPHESIANS 4:13.

A CHURCH, or the divine society, is native to Christianity. Where the
Christian life is, we expect to find the Church as we expect to see
heather in Scotland, palms in Egypt, or maples in Canada; it is indigenous
to the soil.

First, Then, Note Clearly That the Christian Faith Implies a Church.
I am not unmindful that scholars have raised the question whether the
Lord ever used the word "church," or whether the thing itself ever came
within His purview. Certainly, it is not thinkable that any of our modern
ecclesiasticisms ever did. But for practical purposes, none of these things
matter. The divine society is contained in the seed of the Christian life,

and just as assuredly as human life means a social order of some kind, so a Christian personality presupposes a Christian fellowship—a Church—in some form or another. Society is necessary to personality. Moreover, the wealthier we would have a personality become, the richer in the true things of life must his society be. All these things are plainly written in our modern thought and may now be regarded as elementary truth.

Moreover, if our Lord did not use the word "church" or utter its commission as set forth in St. Matthew's narrative of the Cæsarea Philippi incident, he did something more significant; he called to himself a band of disciples and lived with them in holy fellowship that they might know and receive the divine life, and have wherewith to witness and communicate to others. That was one of our Lord's originalities. He chose a circle of companionship; He founded a Christian college; in short, He instituted a Christian society—a Church—so that He might do His work of bringing them, and, through them, other men, into the unity of the faith, to the knowledge of the Son of God, to be as one man in Himself. We must have done with playing with words and trifling with quibbles; we must handle the substance and abiding reality of Christian things. The main question here is not a matter of words spoken or written, but the vital question of the inevitable issues and the abiding authority of the Christian life and its facts. The Christian life carries in it the idea and power of a Church. The Church is an inevitable outgrowth of the Christian life.

In the Second Place, Consider St. Paul's Conception of the Christian Church. The Pauline conception of the Church is that of a body vitalized by Christ's spirit. It is an organism created and sustained by life; without life we cannot have it. Men work with organizations which they build and into which they put power; God works with organisms that have power inherent in them. We cannot know spirit apart from body; we do not know life except in, and through an organism that expresses it. We cannot even think of spirit, or life as disembodied. But a body may be diversity in unity; not a phantom-unity, invisible and unrealizable as some suppose when they speak of Christian Unity, for the New Testament knows nothing of a unity that is not realized and seen; it is unity in a body of which St. Paul speaks. True, it is not a uniformity, not even mere oneness, but a fellowship, an active relationship of divers members, seen working harmoniously as a corporate unity. To use St. Paul's own beautiful word the sound of which seems to carry with it its sense of a harmony in living relationships, it is a "koinonia." And surely, Paul's teaching here is a photograph of Christian experience. Wherever Christian life is energetically at work, the Christian Church is a corporate fellowship.

It has to be acknowledged that when St. Paul comes to the thought of the Church as the embodiment of the Spirit, he takes to himself eagle's wings and soars into the empyrean of spiritual truth, where with undazzled eye he sweeps vast horizons and gazes steadily at them in the white light of God. The great human unity already exists in Christ, he says; but it is growing and being enriched all the time. It is at once a fact and a prophecy, an existence and a process; a gift and a goal. But even now, it is the commonwealth of the redeemed that bears the true witness to the unity of all mankind. That will be completed only when the unity of the faith is realized in the knowledge of the Son of God, and the perfect man has come.

Mark Therefore the Contrast to St. Paul's Vision in Churches Today. In the light of all this, with its appealing truth and glowing vision, what about the divided Church of Christ in the world today; especially what about our Protestantism, shattered and dismembered into powerlessness with its gaping wounds crying aloud for healing? What about the sects which, in the blindness of spiritual and social arrogance, un-church one another as if God's sunshine took any notice of their barbed fences, or God's gracious rain was restricted to their exclusive ecclesiastical paddocks? In the light of New Testament teaching, and of vital Christian experience, and of the one thing that matters—the manifestation of Christian life among men—can there be anything more ridiculously futile, and, if it were not so calamitous, more utterly preposterous and laughable than the assumed superiority of the sectarian spirit even unto un-churching one another in the name of Christ. It is a comfort to think that He that sits in the heavens can laugh; otherwise, in impatience, He might destroy us all. His endless mercy is abundantly seen in that He bears with, and waits for, the repentance of his silly children. What we all need to learn is, that ecclesiastical posturing and strutting is not Christianity. It is not enough to say that it is at least conscientiously done, for men, especially Christians, are responsible for an enlightened conscience. "If men, being evil, know how to give gifts unto their children, how much more will the Heavenly Father give His Holy Spirit to them that ask Him." But our divisions and bickerings are proof of the absence of that Spirit of Christ. Born of human pride and ecclesiastical folly, they are evidences of human littleness, and only give occasion to the unsanctified to blaspheme and for the saints to mourn.

The tendency today as taught by the Spirit is manifestly away from the musty ecclesiologies inherited from the past and kept alive largely by traditional sentiment—to the central reality in Christ Jesus, in whom men find life and God through brotherhood. Men want the Gospel that quickens, sustains, and enriches personality and society with the divine life; not a creed to be argued about, but a reality that meets the needs of daily experience, and which is a living power in thought and life.

More and more, they refuse as Christian men to parade in the dead issues of yesterday. They want a Christian life and a Church that are the surest things they know and the greatest treasures they possess. So, that for them, the best Church—the Holy Church—is that which most worthily expresses that life and ministers that treasure.

Of course in this regard, there are other things to be taken into account: temperament, tradition, early religious training, social contacts, personal predilection for a type of building or service, or, even the attraction of a minister. These things determine for many people their attachment to a church; and the whole situation raises the question whether there can be a Comprehensive Church inclusive of a variety of Church "order" and services. Rome, with her usual skill, within her unity has much variety to meet the needs of her children. Why should not Quakers and Ritualists be able to live in the same church, if not in the same congregation? Both of them are ritualists in their own ways. Cannot Congregationalists and Episcopalians merge their differences to serve their Lord? If fixed on a common center—the Lord, the Life-giver—why cannot they permit differences like spokes from the hub of a wheel to run out to meet a variety of temperament and training in the one circle of truth and life? Such a proposal may be too much for human nature, especially for some types of Protestant nature, but is it too high for the Christian spirit? Is it not the duty of Christian men to come to the unity of the faith in an increasing knowledge of the Son of God? Dare they rest content with present conditions while so many are straying from the way and missing the gate of life? Whence comes our own impoverished life? From our divisions. Whence come our futilities in service? From our divisions. Whence comes our failure to win the world? From our divisions, rending Christ's body, so that the world cannot see and know him as Saviour. Why cannot we have the unity of the faith in a Comprehensive Church that excludes no one that calls Jesus "Lord"; so that we might give the purpose of God a chance in the world.

Edwin Holt Hughes

[1866–   ]

Edwin Holt Hughes has been active in educational work as trustee of the Carnegie Foundation, Northwestern University, De Pauw, Ohio Wesleyan, and Boston University. He was born in Moundsville, West Virginia, and received his education at Ohio Wesleyan and Boston University. After his ordination in the Methodist ministry, he served several important pastorates and then became president of De Pauw University. In 1908 Dr. Hughes was elected to the bishopric in the Methodist Church. The following sermon is taken from his many brilliant addresses and is typical of his poetic approach to preaching.

THE UNHIDDEN CHRIST

He could not be hid. MARK 7:24.

WE MAY BEGIN with the claim that Christ could not be hid even before He came to Bethlehem. He was so much needed by the world that long prior to His earthly birth that need expressed itself in prophecy. Many heralds went before the approaching monarch to cry out, "The King comes! Long live the King!" Some of these heralds walked so far ahead of his chariot that the distance between them and Him seems pathetically long. None the less they heard the far-off footsteps and caught brief glimpses of the oncoming glory. We do not now discuss the precise nature of their prophecy. We may not say how distinctly they realized the type of His kingdom. We do not know how accurately they beheld the form of His royal Person. Doubtless there has often been a tendency to exaggerate the element of foretelling and to find a meaning for uncertain details. But this we know surely: Christ could not be hidden before He came in the flesh. His forerunners had made the world's heart tremulous and expectant. As men watch for the rising of the sun at the end of the weary night, so did men look for Him.

At His coming to the Bethlehem manger, it was even so again—an illustration of the fact that the world cannot easily hide its own Sun. Taking the accounts much as they stand, and leaving to the critical the privilege of reducing the stories for themselves, the irreducible minimum contains its own marvel. The decree of the Emperor drives an expectant mother to a wee village, and crowds its inn until she is compelled to rest her weariness and meet her pain in the stable-cave. This King was born in no palace; but He could not be hid. The manger was unlike a throne; but He could not be hid. The swaddling clothes were not as royal purple; but He could not be hid. He gave the name of His birthplace to a star and hung that star in the perpetual sky. He took the song of the heavens and put it on the lips of a million earthly choirs. He pulled to Himself out of all pastoral lands the brooding shepherds of the fields. He persuaded toward Himself throngs of wise men only to make them wiser still. The evidences at His birth, however literally construed, are not so amazing as the countless evidences since His birth—evidences which tell of His coming into the ever-extending life of humanity.

Yet all this is in spite of the fact that the place and manner of His birth appeared like a drama of concealment. Can the world ever find

Him there amid the lowly beasts, lying upon the hay, covered by the coarse garments, sleeping upon the breast of the poor and humble mother? Can it hear the voice of a Babe amid the confusion of moving caravans and the boisterous calls of pilgrims? It did find, and it did hear. Bethlehem and the Stable were good hiding places, but they were not equal to hiding Him.

After Bethlehem, He could not be taken from the world's sight. Study the record again and discount it as you please, but deal faithfully with the residuum. The reckless Herod pronounced his decree of butchery. The wee children were hidden in their graves and thus became what Prudentius called the "blossoms of martyrdom." But there was one Babe that could not be placed in an unknown grave. Some kind of an angel said it and led the way into some kind of an Egypt. The country of the Nile had no waters that were deep enough to drown Him; no deserts that were vast enough to envelop Him; no siroccos turgid enough to smother Him; no Sphinx silent enough to keep His secret; no Pharaoh powerful enough to take the scepter from an infant's hand. Out of all kinds of Egypts God called His Son that the hiding of His glory should be made manifest in the whole earth.

The conspiracy of happenings for the secreting of Christ continued. If events could have gotten together to plan certainly for shutting Him from the world's eyes, how could they have done better? He was carried back into little and despised Nazareth. As it was not great David's town, perhaps it would succeed in doing what Bethlehem appeared unable to do—draw the curtains of obscurity about a Boy and bury Him in its own insignificance. Since the village had won for itself a proverb of contempt, "Can any good thing come out of Nazareth?" perhaps it could now redeem itself in the esteem of wicked silencers, if it saw to it that the Best Thing came not out at all! For twelve years the Sun it obscured. Then it flashes for a moment before the doctors in the Temple, but sinks down again behind the Galilean hills to remain in apparent eclipse for long years more. We call them "the hidden years," the years of obscurity. But the searching eye can see a carpenter shop; the listening ear can hear the sound of a hammer; the attentive heart can discern strange communings. Those voiceless years still tell their story—the story of the sacredness of filial obedience, of symmetrical growth, of honest toil. So it was that a derided town, and a poor cottage, and a rough shop, and a workman's garb that did not screen Him from the gaze of the world. The final herald came at last, a man who had one work to do, one message to give, one Person to proclaim—crying out insistently, "There cometh One after me." "The Kingdom of Heaven is at hand. Get ready for the King." Jesus came forth from Nazareth village to journey to Jerusalem and to make the capital of His people's hearts the center and joy of the whole earth.

So violence tried its power where silence failed. Social and institutional force sought to put Him out of the world's sight. Scribes and Pharisees brought their religious influence to bear upon the minds of the people and sought to entomb Him in their prejudices, and to conceal Him beneath their scorn. They turned verbal powers against Him, called Him names, identified His good deeds with evil spirits, charged Him with insanity, poured upon Him accusations of blasphemy. But He emerged the more through all their words, and they found that, in spite of the vocabularies of abuse, "He could not be hid."

They were driven finally to the last resource of the desperate. Since all else seemed to be failing they turned to physical violence. Without the walls of Jerusalem they erected a Cross. Upon rude beams of wood they placed His form. As if more surely to put Him beyond the gaze of men they put a thief on either side, even as they placed Roman soldiers in front. Yet the very men that were intended to hide Him began to reveal Him. The penitent thief called Him Lord. The centurion said, "Truly this was the Son of God." Some of the persecutors themselves became involuntary preachers and cried out the unintended but blessed truth, "He saved others." The hill upon which they placed their deadly tree began to lift itself, until it became the highest mountain peak in all the earth. The crowds had gone back to the city, saying, "Now we have thrust Him away, and men shall not see Him more." How mistaken they were! Calvary looked like the final hiding place! Instead, it became the final revealing place!

The effort of the Cross was supplemented by the effort of the Grave. Dead men tell no tales if only you can keep them buried. The tomb is often an effective hiding place. Scores of lives, unknown to us all, lie buried yonder; thousands of secrets are folded beneath the sod. They took the body of Christ away and laid it in the granite prison. Over the doorway they rolled a rock so vast that it needed no cement. Around about they stationed the Roman soldiers who dared not sleep on duty lest they themselves should sleep in quickly made graves. They looked at the triple security of that Arimathean cave and said: "Now we have hidden Him. How can men find one who is buried?" An unseen hand broke the seal of the tomb; an unseen form passed the diligent sentry; and the One who had been put beyond publicity in the very midnight of the earth came forth to stand in the glare of a world and to say, "I am he that liveth, and was dead; and, behold, I am alive for evermore, Amen; and have the keys of hell and death." It was not possible for Him to be holden or hidden of death. Born in a cave which could not conceal Him, He was buried in a cave which could not hide Him. Above a manger, and above a desert, and above a cottage, and above a shop, and above a village, and above a province, and above a Church, and above a State, and above a Cross, and above a Tomb, we write with growing emphasis, "He could not be hid."

It remains now to ask the question, Why has it been impossible to hide Christ? Why did all efforts fail—the proclamation of Cæsar, the decree of Herod, the manger cradle, the width of Egypt, the contempt of Nazareth, the obscurity of Judea, the scorn of the Pharisees, the hideousness of the cross, the depth of a tomb, the height of a sky, the martyrdom of his believers, the arguments of the skeptical, the authority of ecclesiasticisms, the superstitions of sacerdotalism—why did they all fail to hide Christ? Doubtless the incident that evoked the text tells us why. "He could not be hid" because He was needed. When He went into that house and closed the door and shut Himself into its secrecy, there was one in the throng who needed Him so much that she could not have defeat. "He could not be hid, for a certain woman, whose young daughter had an unclean spirit, heard of Him, and came and fell at His feet." Having learned of His sympathy and power, she penetrated to His hiding place, and the very room that was His hiding became His revealing. The world has moved on for nearly nineteen hundred years, but it has never found that the past, over which it claims its flattering improvement, has been able to conceal the Lord. The house in the North Coasts could not hide Him; neither can the modern world. Our need of Him is too great. We are weary, and He promises rest. We are sorrowful, and He promises consolation. We are transient, and He promises eternal life. We are sinful, and He promises strength. We need Him! We need Him; and because our souls know their own there is no hiding place for the Son of Man and the Son of God. And, as was the case there in the regions of Tyre and Sidon, our children need Him. The devils that threaten them can be conquered only by His power. Like that ancient parent, we will seek Him and find Him, that we may see the new generation, claimed by His sanity, His grace, His strength, His love. We change the tense of the text and say it in unwavering confidence, "He cannot be hid."

George W. Truett

[1867-   ]

Before he entered the Baptist ministry, George W. Truett was principal of the Hiawassee, Georgia, high school, and financial secretary of Baylor University. After his ordination, he served as student pastor in Waco, then was called to the First Baptist Church of Dallas, Texas, where he has remained to the present. He was born in Clay County, North Carolina, and educated at Baylor. Dr. Truett is recognized as one of the South's great preachers and his leadership in the Southern Baptist Church has come in large degree from his pulpit ability.

THE PRIVILEGE AND PERIL OF OPPORTUNITY

> For if thou altogether holdest thy peace at this time, then shall there enlargement and deliverance arise . . . from another place; but thou and thy father's house shall be destroyed: and who knoweth whether thou art come to the kingdom for such a time as this? ESTHER 4:14.

THE book of Esther is probably not widely read, and yet it is a story of surpassing interest and instructiveness. There is in it much to shock you, just as there probably would be in the history of any capital or any court of any country of the world. Superficial readers of the Bible sometimes start back at what they find in the Bible. The Bible tells the truth, the whole truth. There is no veneer about the Bible. It does not gloss over and seek to cover defects. The Bible pictures humanity just as it is. And in this old-time story that centers about Queen Esther, much as there is in it to shock us, yet there is very much in it to teach us and to inspire us for the highest and best.

First of all, Esther sought to be silent and shrank back. She was timid and unresponsive before the clarion call of duty. She said, "I must hold my peace; I must be silent; I am the queen. My condition is such that my situation, my present, my future, my happiness, my life, my all, are involved. Mordecai, I will have to be silent." She was tempted to be silent when duty called for courageous speech, tempted to shirk responsibility, tempted to evade the clear path of duty. Now, who has not been in that identical situation, time and time again? Duty clear as the sunlight has stood before us, its path was not at all bordered by flowers, and lions roared at every step of the way. Frowns were there, difficulties, mountains, all sorts of oppositions, and we shrank back and said, "I cannot face this situation." Who has not known such an experience?

There are sins of silence as well as sins of speech. Time and time again we have bitten deep into our tongues, because we have sinned with our tongues. We have talked when we ought not to have talked. There are sins of speech, but equally so there are sins of silence. There are times when men are silent when they had better die than be silent. There are times when they are evasive and servile when they had better die than be that.

Esther has just come to the throne, to the exalted place of queen. She is the first woman in all the proud kingdom of Persia. She is fawned upon and flattered by the people everywhere. To say to the king, "I am of that despised people whom your chief minister of state hounds with all the fury of some mad beast. I am one of them, their fate is mine, their

God is mine, their cause is mine, their present mine, their future mine, their death mine, if it is to be death——" to say that calls for the highest principle and courage known to the human heart. She shrank back. You do not blame her. You are not surprised. "Very well, Esther," said Mordecai, "I have another thing to say to you. You will not escape by neglecting your duty. God can go on without any of us, my child, and He will. Esther, you may sell your people out, and in this poignant crisis of their history, surpassingly pathetic through the exiles that have come to us, you may betray us, and leave us, and forget us, and sell us out; but Esther, deliverance and enlargement will come from another quarter. The Jew is not going to be buried and demolished and overwhelmed. Esther, I believe in the promises of God; I believe in the purposes of a righteous Jehovah; and though you may be time-serving and silent and cowardly, yet deliverance and enlargement for our people will come from some other source. God's covenant with the Jews will not fail. God's promises to His old-time Israel will not be broken."

Here was a faithful friend of God, this man Mordecai. He believed God's promises and clung to them with all the childlike faith that should ever characterize the friends of God. He was a Jew of the old time, of the highest quality. The Jew is the miracle of history. He is the standing miracle around this planet. This man, the Jew Mordecai, said, "I cannot bow down to that man Haman, because I am a Jew. I believe in God. I cannot put anything between my soul and God." And Mordecai rose up with all the calmness and confidence of the faith of the old Hebrews, and clung to the covenant of God and the purposes of God for Israel.

Mordecai was a Jew, and he said to beautiful Esther, his ward, "Deliverance will come, my child, and enlargement for our people, whether you do or do not do your duty." Now, isn't that a wonderful truth for us to think about for a moment? God can get on without us. He can get on without any of us. He can get on without a nation. He can get on without a religious denomination. He can get on without any of us if He be so minded. "Esther, you may be cowering and evasive and silent. God is not dependent on you. You hold the key to a vast opportunity to do a great service for the world. My child, you can fail, you can falter. God will somehow take care of His people. He will get on without you, if you are going to have it that way."

God chose the Israelitish nation of old for peculiar honor and exceptional favor, and laid upon such nation certain high duties and responsibilities which did not belong to other nations. He set apart such nation to preserve His laws and to execute His plans for the human race. By the mouths of His prophets, He rebuked that chosen nation for its sins, chastened it for its backslidings, and used even hostile nations as His messengers of chastisement. Surely, surely, in the face of the responsibilities and warnings written large in the history of nations, it behooves leaders of this great Western democracy to discern her high mission and summon all her people to the high task of fulfilling such mission.

Great voices have all along proclaimed the greatness of the mission of America. One of them has said, "Our whole history appears like a last appeal of divine Providence in behalf of the human race." Pungently has another said, "The American democracy is the result of all that is great in bygone times. All led up to it; it embodies all. Mt. Sinai is in it; Greece is in it; Egypt is in it; Rome is in it; England is in it; all the arts are in it, and all the reformations and all the discoveries." If we forget and are purblind to the purposes of God, this nation may not hope to escape the doom of the unfaithful nations of the past.

Retribution surely follows neglect of duty. "Esther, if you hold your peace at this time, deliverance will come from another source, but you and your father's house will perish." Why? Because whatsoever a man soweth, or a woman, or a family, or a church, or an organization, or a nation, the reaping shall be in like kind. Let duty be neglected anywhere, at any time, by anybody, and retribution like a mad Nemesis is on the heels of such neglect. You cannot neglect duty without the most fearful consequences. Retribution ever follows neglect of duty. O, if we would but remember that! Let a parent neglect his duty there in the home; let him be indifferent to the proper standards and ideals of such a home; let him put gold and the things of time and earth high over the rest; let him put into the background the deepest and most vital things of life, and he has a wrecked family on his hands, and his children after him will rise up to mock him for his defalcation in the day of his opportunity. A family that to-day neglects the highest things shall sadly pay for it to-morrow. If the cheap and gaudy things of earth are put in the ascendancy, there is inevitable heartbreak to-morrow. There is a pay-day to-morrow. Out from the fearful ashes of human life the black Nemesis of retribution will follow and present its product and say, "This is the product for neglecting duty." Duty neglected means retribution—let us realize it in time!

You are your brother's keeper, and if you ignore that brother the blood of that brother will cry unto God against you. Ignore the world's need, and the world's darkness, and the world's sickness, and the world's wounds, and the world's sin, and God will somehow carry forward His purposes; but retribution appalling will come to you. Your education is not given you that you may get off into some corner and chatter in polysyllables that people may say how smart you are. Your education is given you that you may fling off your coat and get into the big battle of life, to help the weak and needy and downtrodden, the ignorant and the beaten on the roadside, to help them up and on to happiness and noblest serviceableness. Your money is not given you that you may loll and dress and dawdle. The world needs it, and woe betide those who forget what money is for! The meaning of all opportunity always is service. It is not enough for a man to be clever. It is not enough for a man to be smart. It is not enough for a man to be a scholar. It is not enough for a man to be a moneymaker. The meaning of all strength is to serve the world. The correct life principle for all mankind is Paul's principle of debtorship to all. All power is under inexorable bonds to serve humanity.

Let us side with God, whatever it costs. "He always wins who sides with God. To him no cause is lost." Let us side with God. Let us side with Him in our families. Let us side with Him as citizens. Let us side with Him as moneymakers. Let us side with Him as teachers and students. Let us side with Him as individuals. Let us ever side with God; and if we have defaulted, if we have been untrue, if we have slipped and forgotten and failed, blessed be His grace, there is deliverance, and there is recovery, and there is forgiveness, and there is a divine power pledged to help us to-day, to-morrow, and forever, if we will faithfully side with God!

"And the world passeth away, and the lust thereof: but he that doeth the will of God abideth forever."

William Pierson Merrill

[1867-   ]

William Pierson Merrill was born in Orange, New Jersey. After studying at Rutgers University, Union Theological Seminary, New York University, and Columbia University, he was ordained in the Presbyterian Church. In 1911 he was called to the Brick Presbyterian Church, New York City, and remained in that pulpit until 1938, when he retired and became pastor emeritus. He has been active in the work of his denomination and has written widely. His books have exerted considerable influence upon the thinking of young people, and his commanding position in one of New York's leading churches has made him a leader of religious life in that city. Is Christ Divine? was delivered at the Brick Presbyterian Church and reveals why Dr. Merrill has been for so long one of the great voices in New York.

IS CHRIST DIVINE?

Who is the image of the invisible God, the first-born of all creation.
Colossians 1:15.

Is CHRIST DIVINE? The very statement of the theme is likely to make some people uneasy. They will answer with quick impatience, "Of course He is. Why raise the question?" But it is not being raised for those who have a natural and satisfying belief in the divinity of our Lord. Let them rejoice and be at peace. But for the sake of the Lord in Whom they believe, and for the sake of their brethren who need to believe in Him, let them also *hold* their peace when the question is frankly discussed for the benefit of those who need it.

What do we mean by the divinity of Christ? Putting it in simplest terms, thinking most of practical uses and values, we mean by it two things:—*first,* that we find and know God in Jesus as nowhere else; *second,* that we give to Jesus the loyalty of our hearts as to no one else. These sum up the practical meanings and values of faith in the divinity of Christ.

It means that we find God in Jesus as nowhere else. We find God everywhere, in a rich variety of revelation. But the most satisfying knowledge of Him, the simplest, the most real in its values, is in terms of Jesus. One of our modern theologians has put the matter in an admirable way when he says, "It is not that God is only in Jesus, but that God is always and everywhere like Jesus." To believe in the divinity of Christ is in part to believe that God so showed His essential nature and character in Jesus that we can confidently interpret all of God in the spirit of that life of Christ.

The second meaning of faith in the divinity of Christ is that we yield our souls to Him as to no other. History is rich in great names, noble personalities. Something of God is revealed in each of them. In many of them, when we get close to them, we find that which claims our love and loyalty. But with each of them there are limitations. In the case of every one of them, we love him for some one or more characteristics, we follow him in some one or more ways. But we feel something different and vastly more in Jesus. We lose ourselves and find ourselves in His spirit. Somehow we can say of Him as of no other figure in history, that He is one with us as well as that He is one with God.

Now how can God reveal Himself as personal, except through and in a person? Personality, as we know it, is in terms of human nature. Man is the highest and best expression of God. God is more like man than like anything else we know. Does it not follow irresistibly that if there should come the perfect man, the ideal man, He would be,—just in that fact,—the highest possible revelation of God? When we find one in whom dwells all the fulness of humanity, we find one also in whom is "all the fulness of the Godhead," all of God that is intelligible to a human mind.

> "Thou seemest human and divine,
> The highest, holiest manhood Thou."

It is natural, then, and reasonable, to expect that God will reveal Himself in terms of humanity. It is not unreasonable to expect Him to bring that revelation to a climax in one supremely beautiful and true human being.

What is there then in the character and personality of Jesus of Nazareth, which justifies us in calling Him *divine?*

Out of the many elements one would like to mention, let me give but two or three. The first is His sinlessness. Some one may challenge me at once, "How can you call this man sinless, when you have such scanty records of His life, records of only a few days, only a few hours, out of His human existence?" My answer is that I am not claiming the sort of sinlessness which can defend every moment against examination with a microscope. I am talking about an atmosphere, a sense that we have when we come into contact with that life. It is true that we have the record of only a few hours of his life, but is there anybody who ever read that story, who ever had any doubt what Jesus did in the unrecorded parts of His life? Is there anybody who can suspect Him of secret indulgence in something wrong or low, when the eye of man was not upon His acts? I mean by His sinlessness an impression He creates as we watch Him. There is not the least trace in Him of any consciousness that He has ever done wrong. Harnack tells us that Jesus is the only human being in whose life there is not a trace of any break with His past at any time. Most of us, the great scholar goes on to say, come to times when we burn what we had previously adored, and adore that which we had burned. There is no such place in the experience of Jesus. There is no consciousness of failure in Him.

Clearly marked is another quality, the absence in Christ of that sense of moral helplessness, and limitation, so painfully felt by the best of men. Read the biography of any truly great man. You find moments of a doubt which amounts to positive anguish. Jesus is always calmly confident that He is on the right way. You simply cannot imagine Him as looking at any ideal of character, any achievement of the spirit, and saying regretfully, "I wish I could be that." He simply is what He ought to be, and knows that He is.

Consider also the high claims that He makes. I am not thinking of any claim to outward honors, Messiah, Son of God, or any other title or dignity. But who is this man who can calmly say, "Heaven and earth shall pass away, but my words shall not pass away," and that though He takes no pains to write down any word whatever? Who is this, who dares say in one breath, "Do this for righteousness' sake," and in the next breath, "Do this for my sake," as if He and righteousness were one and the same thing? Think of any other character in history, even the great-souled merciful Lincoln, imagine him as stretching out his arms and saying, "Come unto me, all ye that labor and are heavy laden, and I will give you rest." We would laugh at any other man as an insane egoist, who should say such a thing. We love and honor Jesus for saying it.

There are also what we may speak of as broader elements in the appeal He makes to us. There is the way He fits into human history; He stands where He does like a perfectly placed lens, which gathers into itself all the light from the past, and throws it forward in a steady stream. There is a whole argument for the divinity of Christ in the simple question asked by Fairbairn, "if there be any meaning in history, any moral order in the universe, can it be that Jesus stands where He does by accident?"

Notice again the growth of His personal influence with the passing of years and centuries. It is not merely that the church, the institution which He left behind, has grown in influence. The marvellous fact is that thousands of people who decry the church, and have little use for it, in their hearts have only reverence for Him. Unlike physical bodies, His attraction seems to increase with the square of the distance. You remember what Charles Lamb said, "If Shakespeare should come into this room, we would all rise to honor him; but if Jesus came into this room, we would all fall down and worship Him." What shall we say of the unquestionable fact that today, nineteen centuries after the life and death of this man, there are literally thousands of people, perhaps it would not be too much to say millions, who love Him better than they love their own life, thousands of them who would die for Him rather than give Him up? What does it mean that this man can gain such a personal hold?

We believe in His divinity because of His saving power over man and over the life of humanity as a whole. It is one of the indisputable facts in history that, through the ages since He came, thousands and millions of men and women have come into His presence, felt His touch within their spirits, believed in Him, trusted Him, felt the power and influence of His life and death, and have been transformed and made new by the experience. Everywhere that is taking place today.

Nor is His saving influence over the common and co-operative life of humanity less striking. There is not a hospital, not an institution for the care of defectives and the unfortunate, not a free enlightened political order, anywhere on earth, save where Christ has come. It is He who is responsible for the bringing down to us of all that is left of "the glory that was Greece and the grandeur that was Rome." Modern science itself, the champions of which often forget or scorn Him, has flourished only where Christ has set free the souls of men. It is literal truth that no other name has appeared on the pages of history whereby we can be saved. What has given and still gives Him such power?

Consider also the universality of the appeal that He makes. There is no other great man in history of whom it can be said that he takes hold upon all sorts of people. Christ's appeal is equally strong to saints and sinners, philosophers and children, men and women, Anglo-Saxons and Orientals. Wherever He goes, He finds the hearts of men, and they find Him.

The truth about Jesus has been well-stated in these words:—"Jesus is the only human being in whose likeness we can conceive the unseen God without involving ourselves in intellectual or moral confusion."

> "If Jesus Christ is a man, and only a man, I say,
>   That of all mankind I will cleave to Him, and to Him will I
>   cleave alway;
> If Jesus Christ be God, and the only God, I swear,
> I will follow Him through heaven and hell, the earth, the sea,
>   and the air."

They are on the straightest and surest path to joy and peace and godly human living, who can say "For though there be gods many, and lords many, yet for us there is but one God, the Father, and one Lord, Jesus Christ," and he that hath seen Him, hath seen the Father.

Reginald John Campbell

[1867–   ]

Reginald John Campbell was born in London. He was a Nonconformist and entered the Congregational ministry in 1895. In 1916 he turned to the Church of England and very quickly became one of its outstanding preachers and leaders. Before joining the Church of England, he held the historic pulpit of City Temple, London, from 1903 to 1915. As a minister in the established church, Dr. Campbell has held some of the great pulpits of England. His books deal with many subjects bearing directly and indirectly upon religion. The following sermon illustrates the definitely mystic strain in the life and ministry of Dr. Campbell and is, in a fashion, an apologia of that position in theology.

THE SUPREME QUEST

Fight the good fight of faith, lay hold on eternal life, whereunto thou art also called. I TIMOTHY 6:12.

IT IS IMPOSSIBLE to apprehend the true bearing of this exhortation without reading in connection therewith the whole chapter of which it forms part. The recipient of this apostolic letter, a young man who has been placed in a position of some spiritual authority, is being bidden to avoid all worldly seductions and concentrate his desires upon the one great thing which constitutes his vocation. Thus: "But thou, O man of God, flee these things—that is, worldly things—and follow after righteousness, godliness, faith, love, patience, meekness. Fight the good fight of faith, lay hold on eternal life, whereunto thou art also called."

Then follows a solemn adjuration to be faithful to this commission until the second coming of Christ took place, whenever that might be. "I give thee charge in the sight of God, who quickeneth all things . . . that thou keep this commandment without spot, unrebukable, until the appearing of our Lord Jesus Christ; which in His times He shall shew, who is the blessed and only Potentate, the King of kings, and Lord of lords; who only hath immortality, dwelling in the light which no man can approach unto; whom no man hath seen, nor can see; to whom be honour and power everlasting. Amen."

It has been conjectured that this fine ringing succession of appellations —Blessed and only Potentate, King of kings, and Lord of lords, the sole possessor of immortality, dwelling in light unapproachable, whom mortal eye has never beheld—formed part of an early Christian hymn, sung in the regular assemblies of the Church for worship. As a description of the Supreme Being it may have been derived from contemporary Greek sources; Platonists could and did use this kind of language; it was common enough among the Gnostics. Does it here refer to God the Father only or to God as revealed in Christ? There is good reason to believe that it includes both. It is God in Christ who is the supreme object of the soul's quest, but remains ever hidden and remote except as self-communicated to the heart that seeks Him in humility, faith, and love.

There is therefore an intentional importance in what is here so earnestly urged upon a youthful servant of Christ. He is to maintain a warfare for his faith, to lay firm hold upon eternal life and let all lesser things go, to put away from himself everything that would hinder him from attaining to the one all-inclusive good that man can know in this or any other world.

We do no violence to the meaning of the counsel so impressively given in these terms if we say that the appearing or manifestation of Christ here alluded to as the Christian's dearest hope can be mystically as well as historically construed. There is plentiful justification for this statement, not only in the Pauline letters, but in the Johannine writings. That the primitive Church lived in the intense expectation of the visible return of Christ in glory is of course obvious to any reader of the New Testament; but it is equally true that that consummation was felt to be anticipated in the experience of those who had laid hold on eternal life. There is a revelation of Christ in the sanctified soul, a parousia, an unveiling of the divine majesty in the inmost shrine of our being, which is in itself salvation, or rather the realisation thereof, and is the most precious possession that any of us can either know or desire as long as we dwell in this our earthly tabernacle.

Permit me an aside here for a moment or two. The word "mysticism" is one of the most misused of our time. Many people claim to be mystics or talk about mysticism who know little of what the great Christian mystics of the past either were or taught. They confuse mysticism with agreeable religious emotion or even with psychic abnormalities such as visions, auditions, and ecstasies. This kind of dilettantism—occasionally verging upon eroticism—is as far as possible removed from the mysticism of, say, St. Catharine of Genoa or St. John of the Cross. We should not feel at all attracted to-day by the terrible self-inflicted austerities of these types, and they in their turn would reject with scorn any suggestion that supernatural visions and voices had necessarily anything to do with their main quest. The great mystics were great sufferers. What they sought was union with God, and they were convinced that this was only obtainable by being crucified to self and the world. It does not follow that we ought to imitate their methods; on the contrary, such unnatural macerations are to be deprecated; but we do need to be as wholehearted in our pursuit of the one thing needful. There is a mystical element in all Christian life, namely, immediate apprehension of the presence and the love of God. It matters little whether we use the name or not; this is an essential of all higher experience, and without this it is hard to see how spirituality, properly so-called, could exist.

One further point before we pass on to consider the main message of the text. What is here asserted of God, and the very terms employed in so doing, are quite definitely applied to Christ elsewhere in the New Testament. In the Apocalypse, by a daring conjunction of metaphors, we are told that one who is the lamb slain from before the foundation of the world is also King of kings and Lord of lords. In the Fourth Gospel we are told that He is the Light of the world; and in a fine Pauline phrase, that God, who commanded the light to shine out of darkness, has shined in our hearts, to give the light of knowledge of the glory of God in the face of Jesus Christ. The Fourth Gospel again, in its opening chapter, says of the apostolic Church, "We beheld His glory, glory as of the only begotten of the Father." And it is the same hand that, in the first of epistles which bear the name of St. John, says almost in the very words of my text "No man hath seen God at any time; if we love one another, God dwelleth in us, and His love is perfected in us." Nor should it be overlooked that this precise expression, "No man hath seen God at any time," has a prominent place in the prologue to the Fourth Gospel, where it completes itself in the explicit affirmation, "The only begotten Son, who is in the bosom of the Father, He hath declared Him."

The message of my text, then, is just this. The one fundamental reality behind all that we know about ourselves and the world in which we live is the being of God. It is a fact that has far more to do with us than any other fact that enters into our experience. But what do we positively know about God? At first hand nothing. "No man hath seen God at any time." He is at once the most unescapable fact in our lives and the most inscrutable. Yet if we could only know God as He is, if the veil were only taken away from before our eyes, or, to put the truth more accurately, if only our eyes could be opened to behold the invisible and eternal, we should have found that which would for ever make an end of all that has power to hurt us and hold us in bondage. All that oppresses and hinders us in our quest for satisfaction, all that makes us burdened, anxious, afraid, or sad at heart, all our delusions and misgivings, would disappear like shadows dancing on a cloud. If we could uncover, if only for a moment, that underlying, all-pervading, all-comprehending Divine life without which nothing is or could be, we should be utterly at rest about the problem of living in all its vast and various modes and meanings. These would have no more dominion over us; the darkness would be swallowed up in the light of God's own presence.

This is what sanctified souls, the adepts of the spiritual life, have always told us with united voice. But there are those among the voices of to-day, as in every previous age, who tell us something very different about the ultimate mystery of existence; and if they be right, it were surely better that we should know the truth, however unwelcome. We are all standing, as it were, before a drawn curtain, the curtain that veils from us the great secret, the knowledge of which would explain everything, including ourselves. What is on the other side of that curtain? I do not mean on the other side of death; I mean on the other side, the inner side, of all the knowledge we at present possess of what we are and whence we came.

There are those, of course, and they are not few, who do not want to know what is on the other side. They either shrink from it, or are indifferent to it, or take for granted that everything desirable is on this side, not on that. These are what we may rightly call materialists—not in theory, but in practice. Materialism as a theory is dead; no one really holds it now; but materialism in practice is very much alive. In fact, I should say that there never was a time in the history of our civilisation when men were so absorbed in the contemplation of the things of sense or so satisfied therewith, to the virtual exclusion of all interest in the things of the spirit. They do not want to look on the other side of the curtain or to know anything about what is there.

Let us be sure that my use of a figure of speech is not being misunderstood. I repeat that I am not speaking of the screen that interposes between this life and the next, between the world that now is and that wherein we shall find ourselves after death. That is not what is in my mind at all. I am speaking of the veil of mystery that hides from us the real meaning of the life that now is; by what is on the other side of that veil I mean the all-pervading, ever-present, yet hidden Divine life and power without which nothing that we know could exist for a moment. I mean that fundamental fact or force or substance, or whatever you like to call it, which no scientific instrument will ever touch, which neither telescope nor microscope will ever reveal, but from whose operation none of us can get away for a single instant, that in which we live and move and have our being, which comes far nearer to us than any outward things, and is the source of every breath we draw and of our very ability to know ourselves. It is this, I say, which so many people are content to ignore at the present day while engaged in the strenuous and engrossing pursuit of ends which hardly matter a jot. When the love of God lays hold of us, when we become conformed to the likeness of Christ, we are at the very heart of the mystery of existence. It is limitless life, love, power, and bliss all in one. This it is which was from the beginning, is now, and ever shall be, world without end. "And we all, with unveiled face beholding as in a glass the glory of the Lord, are changed into the same image from glory to glory, even as by the Spirit of the Lord."

Hugh Black

[1868–   ]

Dr. Hugh Black has for many years been known to American college students as a preacher of distinguished scholarship and keen humor. After graduating from Glasgow University and Free Church College in Glasgow, he served Sherwood Church, Paisley, and St. George's United Free Church, Edinburgh. In 1906 he came to the United States to take the chair of Practical Theology at Union Seminary. This sermon is an example of the clear logic and simple style with which he has brought the best of modern Christian thought to college congregations throughout America.

DOES RIGHTEOUSNESS PAY?

For the sceptre of wickedness shall not rest upon the lot of the righteous; lest the righteous put forth their hands unto iniquity. PSALM 125:3.

THE scene of the Psalm seems to be the exile, when it has dragged its weary length out for many years. It is at least some such situation as that, in which the sceptre of wickedness is resting on the lot of Israel. There is a temptation to apostasy, a temptation even to the faithful to lose heart. At the very beginning of the trial some of the lower-souled among them would make the best of their surroundings and think nothing of Israel and all that Israel stood for. There has been such long delay, such dreary, hopeless waiting, and the sceptre of wickedness has lain so heavy, that now the fear strikes the Psalmist lest even some of the true and faithful will ultimately give way.

The Psalmist has laid hold of the truth that no true man is tried above what he can bear. He declares that the exile will not last so long but that the righteous can hold out to the very end. Nay, lest the righteous should give way and put forth their hands also to iniquity, the heavy rod shall be lifted from their lot. So it is a song of hope. The time is at hand: let the righteous be righteous still. They must not give way to evil now. It is a song of hope because it is a song of faith. Much may be moved, but Mount Zion abideth forever and they that trust in the Lord are as Mount Zion. To trust God is to root faith in the world's stable centre. It is to be as a mountain, even the holy hill which cannot be moved.

There is something pathetic in the Psalmist's fear, lest the trial should last too long and good men be tempted to despair of goodness. It is all the more pathetic because the Old Testament saints did believe that Jehovah's favour meant temporal prosperity. It was the lot of the righteous to sway the sceptre. Failure was explained as punishment, and if evil seemed to succeed there arose the very natural temptation to put forth the hand to iniquity. We find another psalmist stating it as an argument why God should deliver him from his present distress, because if he is not delivered it will discourage others. If Israel, God's servant, is left to be a taunt to the scoffer, it will shame and confound all true believers. If relief never comes to the good man, if he is heaped forever with un-merited reproach, if there is no evidence that God is even interested in his fate, then, argues the Psalmist with holy boldness, the good will be discouraged and may even lose their faith. That is the argument why God should show men in clear fashion that the world is governed in a moral way, that He loves good and hates evil, lest the righteous put forth their hands unto iniquity.

It is a legitimate argument, and at least we understand this prayer that God should justify faith in Him, that He should own His own, and testify by patent palpable fact that the righteous were right in trusting Him. The Psalmist prays that the rod might now be lifted not merely for the righteous' sake, but for the sake of righteousness, almost as it were for God's sake. The Psalmist's argument with God to show favour to the good and enmity to evil is lest good men may be discouraged.

It may be too surface a view of the way in which the world is gov-erned, and by itself would certainly be an unspiritual conception of life; for if goodness is to be judged by outward prosperity it would often be as a flower which grows in a night and which the first breeze of adversity would wither. It would not be the highest motive to be good if we could only say about it that it brings prosperity. Still, so far as it goes the argument is cogent enough that men should see that it does not *pay* to be evil. It is an instinct of our heart to believe this. If the world is governed in a moral way, then essentially the Old Testament saints were right in looking for happy results to the good man.

After all, our whole human society is regulated by ourselves on this basis. We make it one function of punishment to deter from breaking the law. There may be an element of retribution in our legal punishment, to assert the offended majesty of the law, but as a social function I am not sure but that the chief idea in our punishments is preventive. We remember the judge's dictum when he passed the sentence of capital punishment on a horse stealer: "You are to be hanged, not for stealing horses but that horses may not be stolen." It is arguable, of course, that extreme punishments do not serve their purpose, but that is only a matter of degree and does not touch the real issue. It is perhaps arguable also that we are wrong in basing our punishments on such grounds, and that we should think more of a possible redemptive purpose in punishment rather than a preventive. But, as a matter of fact, one function of punishment from the point of view of society is undoubtedly to deter others, "lest the righteous put forth their hands unto iniquity." Society seeks to protect itself and to keep its members from undue temptation.

Ideally, Ruskin may be right in holding that justice is not meant to be either corrective or preventive, but vindictive. If we looked upon it as entirely preventive, then it would be merely a matter of expediency and not of principle. It would be to hang a man as a scarecrow and not as a malefactor. If punishment were looked upon merely as a device to protect society, to frighten other people from committing the same faults, it would be a purely selfish scheme which would deserve failure. And, as a matter of fact, being largely looked on in that light it does fail. For we often find that habitual criminals look on it as a fair game, a fight between themselves and society as to who shall get the better of it. Surely our punitive system should consider the reformation of the offender before even the protection of society and the vindication of outraged law.

The failure of our laws here only suggests that we need deeper sanctions for morality than external ones, such as that "honesty is the best policy." Even if facts did prove that it does not pay to do evil, it would not be a sufficient ground for true morality. It would be a kind of prudence. A man cannot be called a good man in any real sense unless his life is regulated by principles within. A man is not really righteous until he would not put forth his hand to iniquity whatever the consequences. Even although the moral world seemed topsy-turvy, he has that within him which refuses to let him be moved. Hope of reward and fear of punishment are motives on a low plane. They are probably necessary in the education of the race and of the individual, but they are at best only rudimentary morality. They are like leading strings to teach a child to walk, or like stakes to support a young tree, taken away when the tree becomes self-sufficient. The child has not learned to walk till he can do without the leading strings. The tree may be helped by the stakes at first, but they are not part of its life, and it would be a sickly plant if it could not do without them. Our laws may have to appeal to some extent to the motive of prudence, but a man cannot be called good if he merely refrains from evil from fear of the policeman. Before what he does, or abstains from doing, can be called moral, it must correspond to an inward judgment of right. It must be more than blind obedience to a rule, and more than a decision on the ground of what is likely to pay best. If we ruled our conduct only so as to keep out of prison, it would be a misuse of language to call it goodness. The true root of duty is inward conformity to conscience, conformity to a standard set up in a man's own soul.

History and experience teach us to distinguish between the inward and the outward in this whole matter. Indeed, the scheme of life seems designed to lead us from the outward to the inward. For it is not self-evident that honesty is always the best policy in the outward sense. Wrong has often been on the throne and right on the scaffold. With Browning, we may hold from experience that it is wiser being good than bad and safer being meek than fierce; but that can only be when we put a deeper meaning into what is wise and what is safe. Certainly there is no security for true morals till we would choose to be good and meek, quite apart from the fact that they were the wiser and safer course from a worldly point of view. Our Lord did pronounce blessing even upon those persecuted for righteousness' sake, but it was not because it paid as a policy, or rather it was because it did pay essentially and eternally. The pure in heart are blessed; for they see God. It is not a matter of rewards and punishments in the ordinary sense, though nothing can alter the fact that there *are* rewards and punishments, and the chief of these are not things added from the outside, but in themselves.

The reward of being good is goodness. The reward of virtue is itself. A good man shall be satisfied from himself. The punishment of sinning is sin. The final good or evil consists not in having, but in being. The deepest punishment of hatred is to have the hating heart that fills the mind with hateful thoughts. Evil brings its own stain and sting. The moral world in which we live is designed this way. Our life is run on these lines, so that we, after these Christian years, accept the Psalmist's principle with only a deeper undercurrent of meaning. "Do good," he prayed, "unto those that be good"—and we believe it. *Good to the good,* for which he prayed, is indeed a principle rooted in our hearts. The sceptre of wickedness shall not rest, cannot rest, upon the lot of the righteous. When the righteous see it to be so, are sure that it must be so, can they be tempted to put forth their hands unto iniquity?

"Good to the good" we feel to be reasonable and necessary. It ought to be so, say our instincts. It ought to be so, say our minds looking calmly on the facts. It will be so, say our best desires. It will be so, say our hearts, moved with doubt and troubled with many present appearances. It is so already, says faith. It ought to be so—it will be so—it is so, says faith, seeing deeply into the heart of things. The world is built that way. "That the righteous should be as the wicked that be far from Thee, O God." Faith will never believe it. It knows that to trust in the Lord is to be as the immovable hill, and is to be surrounded by His grace and love as the mountains are round about Jerusalem. Faith brings God in the heart and God in the life, safe within from evil of self, safe without from the evil of the world. It is to be established within and intrenched without, as the holy mount which cannot be moved.

Is this poetry and not fact? Poetry like this *is* fact.

Gaius Glenn Atkins

[1868–   ]

Gaius Glenn Atkins held several leading pastorates in the Congregational Church before becoming Professor of Homiletics and Sociology at Auburn Theological Seminary. He was born at Mount Carmel, Indiana, and received his education at Ohio State University. His preaching and writing have been of great influence. In 1914 he was awarded the Church Peace Union Prize for an essay on International Peace. During the First World War he was director of Foyer du Soldat with the French Army. The following sermon shows his thorough understanding of national and world social conditions, and his deep conviction that the solution of man's problems is to be found in the religion of Jesus.

THE TIMELESS QUEST

And he removed from thence, and digged another well: and for that they strove not; and he called the name of it Rehoboth; and he said, For now the Lord hath made room for us, and we shall be fruitful in the land. GENESIS 26:22.

THIS text is a sentence or two from an ancient story of disputed upland pastures, nomad peoples living in black tents, quarrelsome clans, and flocks and herds feeding over the hillsides and needing, above all else, water. It is the story of a little fighting and doubtless much more noisy

arguing over water rights, a show of valor, protest, and competition between swarthy folk in a sunlit land, where there was never water enough
and where a well was a thing to be bequeathed by a father to his son to
be treasured as a great possession or, if necessary, to be fought over.

But there is a gleam through it all of something vaster. The wells
themselves were only pits to catch and hold the wash of winter rains,
hard to dig in rocky soil with poor tools, but indispensable to life then
and symbols still of more enduring supplies for more inescapable needs.
You may read for yourselves the vivid account and what came of it all.
Let us think together of that last well, Rehoboth, which put an end
to all their quarrels, and haunts us still with the lovely suggestion of
its name, the well of "room enough." It is a marvelous well, that well of
"room enough," and the quest for it was already old when the herdsmen
of Isaac and Gerar strove together. The earliest and most inevitable form
which the quest took was the quest for more land, a place in the sun.

There is in the Luxembourg galleries a picture of almost dramatic
vividness. A little procession passes across the foreground, a procession
of skin-clad, long-haired men, masterful with their spears for staves,
striding alongside ox-drawn carts the very creaking of whose wheels you
can hear, and the carts themselves loaded with rough household gear and
women and children sitting wearily upon their pitiful possessions.

The land they were leaving was nearly as empty as the lands they were
seeking. They were migrating not because they were crowded in fact
but because they were pressed in spirit, subject to some strong impulse
and dimly anticipated need. We call it now land hunger; but it was
something far more imponderable than that: it was the first projection
against the skyline of history of the demand of the human spirit for more
room. The migratory procession has never ceased from that day to this.
Our humanity has always been on the trek; we have left nothing unexplored, nothing unsubdued.

Along with room enough in land possession we have always been
driven, and are driven still, by the quest for room enough in economic
resources. The herdsmen of Isaac and Gerar were not the first who fought
over water rights nor the last either.

We have contended for the hinterlands from which rivers are drained
and for the rivers themselves. We have wanted water to drink, water for
irrigation, and water for our trade routes. In our quest for room enough
we have been after coal and iron and oil, desperately eager for the raw
materials out of which the structure of our economic wealth is built, and
by the strange coincidences of history we are ourselves living in a time
when all these forms of competition which have been so long in action
have reached their crisis.

There is no longer anywhere unoccupied, unpossessed, unchallenged room enough either in the ownership of land, the possession of raw material, or sovereignty over the trade routes of earth and air and sky. The frontiers are gone.

The bitter reason of it all is that we are carrying on this costly and often tragic competition for economic room enough in a world whose potential economic spaciousness is beyond the reach of the most grandiose imagination. We have not even begun to touch our economic resources; there is room enough in the world to grow bread for every hungry child; there is stuff enough in the world to build warm and gracious homes for everyone shivering in the cold and labor enough to build it. There is room enough, if we know how to use it, to take every man who has a mind and two hands and make him a useful and contented part of the commonwealth, to make every loving heart and every tender impulse part of our human treasure if we only knew how.

Our first great trouble is that we are seeking a "well of room enough" down the wrong road. We shall never reach it through heartless competition or selfish monopoly or stupid self-aggrandizement. There is never room enough for the strong to trample, the wise to scheme, the capable to push the weak aside, and the questing to take no thought for any but themselves. There is not room enough down that road: the only road down which there is room enough is the road of wise sharing, of intelligent coöperation, of the general assumption of the burdens and perplexities of humanity as our common human problem and the disposal of them in the spirit of Jesus Christ.

The angel on the tower of this church looks across to four buildings which are themselves symbolic of the regions in which our quest for room enough can actually find no frontiers, and we ourselves make our adventurous migrations at the cost of no one else. They have walls, but their walls are built only to shelter what in itself acknowledges no walls. The first of them is the College of the City of Detroit, and the towers above it have their message. "There is always room enough," they say, "in the kingdom of the mind. You shall reach no frontiers in your quest for truth and knowledge."

The herdsmen of Isaac and Gerar thought the Syrian stars beneath which they quarreled were lights hung in a ceiling so near that if you built a tall enough tower you could storm the sky. Now the heavens have opened up and back into unimaginable spaces; we have made the stars tell us the secret of their composition, we have heard in reverence the music of their movement in their ordered orbits, and every new telescope reveals a range beyond the range of the already seen. There is always room enough for the astronomer as he searches the sky. There is room enough in the very dust beneath our feet for the life work of a chemist, and he will leave the dust still unexplored. There is room enough in every science for the tireless action of a mind which finds life all too short. There is room enough in every craft for a lifetime of labor, discipline, and happy skill.

The second building toward which the angel looks is the Library. And who can ever be imprisoned as long as he has a book to read? Every book is a window or a road or a comrade; it is a way into history, into the poet's singing vision. It is a road into the inexhaustible drama of the human spirit. If we should carry our quest for more room into the unexhausted possibilities of our intellectual life, our horizons will widen toward the stars.

The angel on the tower looks toward Symphony Hall, and there is always more room in music. Every symphony carries us out into a world of audible dream and wonder; it enfranchises our earthborn spirits and makes them free of harmonies and vistas and unsuspected beauties. When we have heard the Unfinished Symphony a score of times there is always in it something new of tenderness or longing to vibrate in the strings of a violin and pluck at our own heartstrings.

There is always room enough in art. The blue and luminous horizons of every Italian picture suggest the endless amplitude of beauty. There is room enough in every old lined face Rembrandt has painted for all the patience and the sorrow, the laughter and the tears of a human soul. There is room enough in the lovely broken fragments of classic art to indicate the frontierless country in which the artist lives and works and into which he guides all those who love his art.

And if you grow tired of marble halls, there is room enough in an April crocus to satisfy the hunger of winterbound spirits, room enough in grasses which begin to live again in green to satisfy our own sense of kinship with all earth-rooted life. There is room enough in sunrise and sunset, there is room enough in the overarching skies. There is even room enough for dreams and longings in the transfigured smoke and mist which give sometimes an unearthly quality to our familiar streets. And if there is not room enough in all such things as these, we may be citizens of a still more spacious order. There is always room enough in goodness. I have known many saints first and last, uncalendared but still saints. They have lived graciously and unselfishly and without any renown at all. But they have always tried to be good, they have always found room enough to be better still.

No one of us has ever reached the frontiers of kindness or found the end of patience or come within sight of the limits of the possibilities of perfection of his own soul. There is room enough in love, God knows, radiant, shining, light-touched spaces. No one has ever been able to say, "If I would, I can love no longer, because I have come to the end of the kingdom of love and there is no longer any room for love." No one has ever spent kindness so opulently as to be able to say, "There is no need for kindness left nor any more room in which to be kind nor any exhausted possibilities in my own kindness."

Ah, there is room enough in the regions of the soul and in our practice of the presence of God and in our growing likeness to Jesus Christ for all the power of us and the passion of us. Our fretted, embattled society will never free itself from bitterness and the poverty and the perplexity of its material struggles until it carries the timeless quest of the human soul for room enough over into its own native land into the quest for an inner wealth of life into friendship, into truth, into beauty, into faith, into fellowship with the unseen and eternal. There is always room enough there.

Theodore Gerald Soares

[1869–   ]

Theodore Gerald Soares was born in England and came to the United States in 1886. He received his education at the University of Minnesota and the University of Chicago. After serving pulpits in the Baptist ministry, he accepted a position as professor in Chicago University's School of Divinity. Since 1930 he has been Professor of Ethics in the California Institute of Technology and minister of the Neighborhood Church in Pasadena. His preaching, lecturing, and writing have made his influence widespread. In Dr. Soares' sermons are found a keen understanding of the problems of science and religion.

SCIENCE AND GOD

FORTUNE during the last year published a series of articles by eminent philosophers on the general outlook for civilization. They all agreed that, while the world could not be saved by science, it could be destroyed by science if the spiritual values of man were not made primary.

Julian Huxley, the eminent biologist, in the December number of *Fortune* makes answer to these philosophers. He says they find science insufficient to meet the needs of man because they do not include psychological science. The cure for an inadequate scientific explanation of the world and of man is simply more science. He insists that we should have a philosophy based upon the scientific method and upon nothing else.

Mr. Huxley elaborates his philosophy in five propositions. First, he accuses the men whom he is answering of being dualists, that is affirming two kinds of reality: God and the world, the soul and the body, the mental and material, the spiritual and the physical. No, says Huxley, there is only one. Whatever stuff the world is made of, whatever reality is,—electrons, charges of electricity, energy, being, whatever it is—it is one and not two. It is not the world and God, but only the world. He says, Isaac Newton made the first great contribution to this view. Before him men believed in some great power that guides the stars in their courses. But no such power is needed; the stars guide themselves, *i. e.,* the properties of attraction keep the whole universe in an ever self-adapting adjustment. If it be objected that life is different from matter, the answer is that when this marvelous stuff or substance or reality, or ultimate thing, that is the one existence, reaches a certain complexity it manifests those characteristics that we call life. "Living matter is composed of the same elements as non-living, and no trace of any special 'vital energy' has been detected. The scientific view is that under the conditions obtaining during the early history of the earth, the particular combination of matter that we call life was formed in the cosmic test tube, and once formed could maintain itself by its power of self-reproduction." Darwin shows that all forms of life could develop from the simplest. So as the stars guide themselves, life evolves itself, and, again, God is not needed.

Huxley's second proposition is that man's values—goodness, beauty, truth, conscience, love, ideals—can also be explained on a purely scientific basis. He here leans heavily upon the psychological investigations of Freud. He reminds us that psychology is a very young science only just beginning its research into human behavior. But he believes that Freud has shown how the higher values of man are just as definitely the products of chemical changes in the human organism as are muscular reactions. We are not to think of a soul and a body but of one organism. They may appear to be two but that is only because we look outward and inward. When I see you I perceive an acting and reacting organism, but I seem different to myself as I think, feel, will, love, hate, hope. There is no real difference, the elements have simply an inner and an outer aspect.

For an illustration of the process of value-growth Huxley uses Freud's theory of the development of conscience. A young child is equipped with the desires and impulses which he has inherited from the long past. If left alone some of these tendencies would work badly for himself and objectionably to his elders. So the parental prohibition comes into play. Conflict results. Multiply this through all the long development of man; let it work in the unconscious mind; let it produce in the deep blind, emotional life the complexes that are bred of frustration; there will emerge the strain between right and wrong, the sense of authority, the experience of conscience and of repentance. Out of these profound emotional stirrings of the complex life of man has come that sense of obligation, which seems like an immaterial endowment. As the stars guide themselves and life evolves itself so conscience and the values develop themselves. No God is needed.

Mr. Huxley recognizes the objection that our values seem to be absolute, truth is truth, right is right. Thus Sperry speaks of the "Ethical Universals," Hocking speaks of absolute truth, we hold before us the idea of "the good." The Freudian answer is that the apparent sureness and certainty of these human values arise from the fact that they have had so long a development in the history of the race and have become deeply rooted in our emotional nature. We have the feeling that right is right and wrong is wrong, and yet in practical life we always settle moral questions on practical grounds, as what works well for the greatest number in the long run, or some such criterion.

The inclusion of values in the scientific explanation is fundamental to Huxley's position. Ultimately, he insists, the whole process of nature is one. The attraction of the planets, the stratification of the rocks, the budding of a flower, the devotion of a lover, the patriotism of a soldier, the sacrifice of a martyr, the earnestness of a scientist—all are operations of the one stuff or substance or energy or whatever the unity is. All is one.

Huxley's third point would be disputed by many. He believes that the world exhibits a real progress. From the amoeba to the scientist he sees a real growth. Bertrand Russell has objected that we do not know what the amoeba thinks about it. But, of course, the point is that the amoeba does not think and a thinking being is an advance over a non-thinking. But Huxley in affirming progress denies purpose. The universe does advance to higher organization but it does not will to advance; indeed it does not know that it advances. There is no God; the world simply has the property to progress, and that is all there is to say about it.

The fourth proposition is that man must cease to look outside of himself for any help. He cannot shift responsibility upon God or any power, for none exists. He must rely purely upon his own achievement. This is not discouraging, says Huxley, but heartening. Man has found out how his world works, he has discovered what he is in himself, and what are his powers. He need not concern himself about a soul to be saved but only about a life to be lived. The beliefs which sustained men in the childhood of the race are no longer needed. There is no God, no miracle, no revelation, no answered prayer. And man no longer needs these. He is now in a position to take care of his own welfare. He understands something of the complex psychological processes which have brought him to his present state. Further study on this same basis will enable him to become more and more capable of self-direction and so to grow into what he feels he ought to be.

The fifth proposition is that the developed human personality is the highest achievement of the universe, at least as far as we know. The process that has been going on for billions of years has issued in a being who can understand the process, who can assume some control of the process. It is a glorious thing to realize that we hold this grand position in the vast universe. What a motive to do our best, to overcome evils, to work for a better world, to plan for that fully developed human personality, which is to be the great achievement of the future.

Such is Huxley's scientific philosophy. He believes that it answers all questions that need to be answered—any others are irrelevant.

So he has eliminated God.

But has not Mr. Huxley failed to take the one further step that all his argument requires? We may accept all his positive statements though the Freudian psychology may need some modifications, but has he any justification for his negative conclusions? Let us examine the five propositions.

Yes, there is only one reality, not two, not many. But what kind of stuff, substance, energy, reality, or whatever, is Huxley defining? It must be very wonderful, for it can guide itself, develop itself, become life out of non-life, mind out of non-mind. But that is what we mean by God.

Secondly, what kind of stuff or reality can become a mother's love, and a scholar's devotion, and an artist's genius, and a good man's duty? Suppose that most of the Freudian explanation is correct, still what kind of elemental reality is it that through the long conflict process of the human life on earth has issued in these values? You must judge a process by its results. The Sistine Madonna is only paint. But if it had painted itself the paint would have been Raphael. Let us say that the Sermon on the Mount is explicable by the long human process of man's developing emotional nature, from ancient taboos, through varied experience, all going back to chemical reactions of blood and nerves and glands. Still it is the compelling word that calls us to be our best; it is the selfless human ideal. The process that can produce such result is what we mean by God. We live in a world that could issue in Jesus. Such a world is God.

Mr. Huxley's third point is wonderful in its affirmation but extraordinary in its negation. There is real progress but there is no purpose. The progress happens but it was not intended. What kind of world is it that of its own inner nature and character can progress? That is what we mean by the will of God.

The fourth proposition is that man can expect no help from outside. Humanity is alone. Rickenbacker, floating in your tiny boat in the Pacific, your dying companion in your arms, do not pray, for there is no help from the outside. But there is help from the inside. There is the whole universe of which you are a part to help you. The cosmic process that seems so pitiless as the cold ocean dashes over you is warm, earnest and full of sympathy in those searching planes that are scanning every mile of sea to find you. The answer to your prayer is in those millions who are sending the planes, calling for your rescue, in that mother and wife that will not lose their faith and hope. What kind of stuff or energy or reality is it that has issued in a combination of science, sympathy, effort, faith, that will find you floating out there, hungry and thirsty and cold? It is God. Not a God outside the world, but God "in whom we live, and move, and have our being."

What a bold statement is Mr. Huxley's fifth point. It reminds us of Tennyson's "Heir of all the ages, in the foremost files of time." The developed human personality, "the highest and richest product of the cosmic process." What kind of process could issue in man; and not man as he is but man as he may be? Such a process is what we mean by God.

Mr. Huxley, let us try a hypothesis. That is not unscientific if we test the hypothesis adequately. Let us suppose that the process which produced personality, is itself personal, and that when it produced personality, it meant to do so, and that between the cosmic and the human personalities there can be communion, understanding, love; what would be the test of such a faith? There would be a "peace that passeth all understanding"; there might even be such a sense of union that a man could say, "I and my Father are one"; there would be an inner courage that could express itself, "I can do all things through Christ that strengtheneth me"; there would be a real motive for carrying on the great evolutionary process, not alone but fortified by cosmic might, "The Father worketh hitherto, and I work." The religious experience validates the Christian philosophy.

And allow another hypothesis. Suppose the cosmic personality, having willed the human personality, is concerned not only with the species but with the individual and should out of its marvelous resources find the possibility of a continuing human personality beyond the experience of death; what would be the test of such a faith? There would be serenity, there would be confidence that the future of the race was worth striving for, there would be a scaffolding for our ethics that would make moral achievement a hope and a joy: "Wherefore be ye steadfast, unmovable, always abounding in the work of the Lord, forasmuch as ye know that your labor is not in vain in the Lord." The religious experience validates the Christian philosophy.

Mr. Huxley is justified in his main contention that religion cannot claim any territory of human experience as its own private domain which science must never enter. If it is human experience then it is a matter of nerves and glands and chemical reactions. Science may not yet be able to describe and predict emotional behavior, but there is no prohibition of investigation. Let science and the approved scientific techniques have fullest opportunity. The day is past when religion was afraid that the secrets of its values might be discovered. If religion belongs only in those areas into which science has not yet gone it would have a poor outlook indeed.

When a man as part of the world process asks, How does it work? he is a scientist; when he asks, What does it mean? he is a philosopher; when he asks, Does it care for me? he is religious. It is the same man, it is the same world, only the questions are different.

When Mr. Huxley finds the obligation of moral progress in man's capacity for self development, he has perhaps made a scientific philosophy, but he cannot stop there, he must ask what kind of universe produces obligation, indeed he is "not far from the Kingdom of Heaven."

John A. Ryan

[1869–   ]

John A. Ryan was born on a farm in Minnesota. He was educated at St. Thomas Seminary, St. Paul, and was ordained in 1898 as a Roman Catholic priest. After doing graduate work at the Catholic University in Washington, D. C., he was appointed in 1915 Professor of Moral Theology and Industrial Ethics at that university. He has labored unstintingly to bring about a better understanding of the meaning of Christianity in world relations, and has spoken and written extensively on this subject. The following sermon appeared as a chapter in his book Declining Liberty.

CHRISTIAN PRINCIPLES OF WAR AND PEACE

Blessed are the peacemakers; for they shall be called the sons of God.
MATTHEW 5:8.

CHRISTIAN principles would make peace secure and war impossible. For Catholics this is a truism. We recommend it unceasingly to statesmen and peoples. Not infrequently, however, our manner of stating this proposition suggests the inference that we expect Christian principles to operate automatically. We seem to attribute to the phrase, "Christian principles," something like the intrinsic efficacy which the magician pretends to ascribe to his words of incantation. We speak as though a formal profession of Christian principles in the abstract would of itself bring in a reign of peace.

Two conditions are prerequisite to the efficacious working of Christian principles in the promotion of international peace. The first is specific and detailed application of the principles; the second is such long-continued inculcation that they will have become imbedded in man's emotional as well as his intellectual nature. The general principles must be brought down from the lofty abstract regions of the mind and made a part of the individual's practical thinking; and they must become an integral element in his training, a part of that mental furniture which is readily available for use in everyday life.

It is not an easy or a simple task to apply the moral principles of Christianity to international affairs. There must be both individual instruction and political instruction. Under the first head the religious teacher must declare, expound, interpret, illustrate and make concrete Christ's commandment of love and the divine precept of justice. This teaching must be imparted to all groups and classes; in theological seminaries, in colleges and schools; in the pulpit and in catechetical instruction; in religious books and periodicals. The individual must be taught a right attitude of mind toward all foreigners. It is not enough to declare that "every human being is my neighbor." The obligations which are implicit in this phrase must be made explicit. They must be set forth in detail with regard to foreign races and nations. And this doctrine should be repeated and reiterated. Effective teaching and adequate assimilation depend largely upon the simple process of repetition. The duties of patriotism must be expounded in a more restrained and balanced way than that which has been followed heretofore. Men must be taught that it is not "sweet and becoming to die for one's country" if one's country is fighting for that which is unjust. Without denying or weakening the sentiment of national patriotism, we can set forth that wider and higher patriotism which takes in all the peoples of the earth. And we should bring about a profound shifting of emphasis in explaining the conditions which justify war. Instead of laying stress upon the lawfulness of engaging in war, we should clearly and continuously point out that all the conditions which are necessary to make war morally lawful have rarely existed together in history. We should strive to concentrate attention upon the obligation of preventing war through negotiation and conciliation, rather than upon its lawfulness.

The mental attitude of the people must likewise be changed and reformed with regard to the possibility of establishing permanent peace. One of the greatest obstacles to peace has always been the lazy assumption that wars must come, that there will always be war while men are men. So long as this pessimism prevails, the majority of persons will not assert themselves in the cause of peace. World peace is largely, if not mainly, a matter of human faith. If the majority of people believe that peace can be established and secured, peace will be established and secured. Therefore, we must strive to make the people think peace and talk peace. We must incessantly declare the feasibility of a reign of peace until this idea and this faith become a dominating and effective element in the habitual thinking of the average man and woman. To be sure, no human being knows whether war can be forever banished from the earth. Only God knows. What we do know is that war may be made more and more remote through human action aided by the grace of God. To make war remote, to push it into the indefinite future, is a practical and a sufficient program.

So much for the specific application of right principles with regard to individuals. Were this achieved to the extent that is readily possible, it would not be sufficient. It must be supplemented by effective political action. In its final stage the process of attaining world peace must be carried through by states and governments. In that field also Christian principles must find specific and detailed application.

A fundamental method is adequate preaching of the principles of international morality. The grossly immoral doctrine that states are above the moral law is not so frequently uttered or defended today as it was before the Great War. Nevertheless, it is still implicitly or explicitly accepted and acted upon by statesmen in more than one country. Even where it is not held, there is need of outspoken and frequent declaration of the truth that nations, as well as individuals, are subject to the moral law, particularly to the precepts of justice and charity.

Besides the general preaching of the doctrine that political and international actions are governed by the moral law, its precepts must be applied to particular events, policies and proposals. Moral teaching of this sort must be addressed not only to the people but in an especial manner to statesmen. This is, indeed, a difficult task. It is not easy to determine how far contemporary international actions or policies are contrary to either justice or charity. Even when the moral aspect of the situation is clear, the question may arise whether religious teachers are not bound to remain silent from motives of Christian prudence.

Whatever we may think about the past, we can see some duties fairly clear in the present. All the leading states of the world are morally bound to labor earnestly for the establishment of peace. The methods which seem likely to promote the attainment of this end should command the active interest and approval of all religious authorities. With entire propriety we can urge the people to study deeply and faithfully all the positive proposals that have been brought forward in recent years for the prevention of war. These are the League of Nations, the World Court, the outlawry of war, compulsory international arbitration and universal disarmament. One or more of these methods do not appeal to all of us, but that is to be expected. All of them are deserving of study and consideration and the ideals underlying them are in harmony with the principles of Christianity.

Indeed, the Catholics of the world, both the clergy and the laity, have received specific and authoritative guidance concerning practical measures for the establishment of peace. In his address to the belligerents, August 1, 1917, Pope Benedict XV proposed that:

Moral right be substituted for the material force of arms in the reciprocal dealings of nations; the nations enter upon a just agreement for the simultaneous and reciprocal reduction of armaments; armed force be replaced by "the noble and peaceful institution of arbitration," with the provision that penalties be imposed upon any state which should refuse either to submit a national question to such a tribunal, or to accept the arbitral decision.

In his letter to the American people on the last day of 1918, the same Pontiff expressed a fervent desire for an international organization which "by abolishing conscription will reduce armaments; by establishing international tribunals will eliminate or settle disputes; and by placing peace on a solid foundation will guarantee to all independence and equality of rights."

Any Catholic who opposes any of these things on grounds of selfish nationalism or international hatred is out of harmony with the mind of the Holy See. To be sure, a good Catholic is justified in rejecting any or all of these proposals and institutions, if he honestly thinks that they are or would be harmful to legitimate national welfare or to any other important legitimate cause or interest. But he should take this stand only after careful and impartial consideration and after he has cleared his mind of all jingoism and all hatred of foreign nations. In a word, he should examine the whole situation in the light of objective evidence and in the spirit of Christian charity which knows neither Jew nor Gentile, neither barbarian nor Greek.

James Moffatt

[1870-   ]

Dr. James Moffatt is recognized throughout the world as the author of a new translation of the Bible. He was born at Glasgow, Scotland, and was educated at the Academy, University, and Free Church College of Glasgow. During his college years he won many honors for his ability in the field of classical languages, and he has held many famous chairs at leading universities in Scotland and England. Dr. Moffatt's sermons show his profound scholarship and his mastery of the more subtle meanings of Biblical texts.

SOUGHT AND SEEKING

I have gone astray like a lost sheep; seek Thy servant; for I do not forget Thy commandments. PSALM 119:176.

THAT is the last word of a long psalm, a very long psalm. And what a strange last word it is! You expect something by way of a climax or a crescendo. Most of the psalms end upon a clear, ringing note of assurance and confidence, or leave us in a rapture. They may begin low, but they commonly rise and close upon higher ground. Whereas this psalm seems to die away in a wistful, humble cry of confession: "I have gone astray like a lost sheep."

A strange ending, and yet one that sounds very honest. It is the pleading of a man who is trying to tell the truth about himself, neither extenuating nor exaggerating the facts. He does not minimise what he has done. Yet neither does he make himself out to be worse than he really is. And sometimes people do that. Exaggeration is one of the vices of our religious vocabulary, for we are constantly tempted to use swollen language about our souls and perhaps unconsciously to overstate things. To hear some folk talk, for example, about a person who has gone wrong, one would imagine that they had never been tempted at all. They speak of the scandal from such a lofty height of superior virtue that they convey the impression of living far above the common risks and frailties of human nature. Others, again, may accuse themselves of all manner of evil in a heat of self-reproach; they charge themselves loudly, till, as we listen, we feel that they cannot surely be as bad as they make out. This is, no doubt, a nobler habit than the other. Still, however generous and faithful, it is apt to become unreal; and we ought to be real, honest, and accurate in speaking of ourselves to God or to our fellow-men. There is always something impressive and convincing about a man who does not spare himself but who at the same time does not try to paint himself blacker than he really is. "I have gone astray," says the psalmist; "I've been stupid, I've got myself into a wrong position, I'm in danger." He blames nobody else for his plight. He is too honest to talk of circumstances, but owns up frankly to his personal responsibility for having got off the right track. But then he is not content to remain where he is. "Seek Thy servant," he adds at once, "for I do not forget Thy commandments." Conscience tells him that he is meant to be under the orders of God instead of obeying his own impulses or following the crowd. I have forgotten myself, he means, but I have not quite forgotten the true end of life; I have still some sense of the will of God and some desire to regain the straight road.

Such is the right view to take of our faults: without being lax, we ought to take them quietly; we must not allow ourselves to be overwhelmed, or to imagine that everything is lost. No one who is flippant or superficial would say, "I have gone astray like a lost sheep." But there is no use in being cast down, as though we had dropped too far for recovery. The first instinct ought to be that our lives are still within reach of God. "Seek Thy servant." When a lapse comes, when we have given way to some temptation, and failed badly, there should be an instant sense that we are out of our right place. We belong to God; we have no business to be where we are; we have landed ourselves in a false position by yielding to our lower impulses. If we did not remember who we are and whom we promised to serve, there would be no dissatisfaction at all. But there is. And as we feel a grievance against ourselves for having sunk to a lower level, it is a positive encouragement; for it means that our faults and failures have not yet stifled the sense of life's true end and aim. "I do not forget Thy commandments."

> Oh, we're sunk enough here, God knows,
> But not quite so sunk that moments,
> Sure though seldom, are denied us,
> When the spirit's true endowments
> Stand out clearly from its false ones,
> And apprise it if pursuing
> Or the right way or the wrong way
> To its triumph or undoing.

Perhaps most people tend to take their faults far too lightly nowadays. There is a reaction against the stress on sin which characterised the religion of the last generation in its evangelical aspect. The emphasis has shifted. Indeed if we look farther back, one striking contrast emerges between our modern age and the period which we call the Middle Ages. On the whole mediæval folk, so far as they were religious, were preoccupied with sin and strangely indifferent to suffering; they seem to have been much more sensitive to offences against God than to the pain endured by their fellow-creatures. Nowadays it is the opposite. The modern conscience is extremely sensitive to pain, even sensitive to the point of sentimentalism, but it is not nearly so alive to sin. The present age is by no means so callous to certain forms of suffering in the world as the Middle Ages often were, but it has nothing like the acute consciousness of sin as sin. The average person to-day is not greatly cast down by faults and failings, not sobered when he goes wrong, not moved to be thoughtful and penitent.

Yet, on the other hand, some are still deeply moved. Generalisations are misleading things, and under the surface of life to-day there are still a number of people who secretly are almost crushed by the sense of their unsteadiness, and apt to be depressed by their breakdowns, till they may feel that it is little use for them to try to be religious any longer, when the will seems so easily twisted to evil and bent to lower things. Some of you may feel this, or may know some who are in this desperate position, either through some sharp, definite failure, or through the slow accumulation of things which have silted up like sand and covered the nobler aspirations of the past. It is the position in which one feels that one has taken such liberties with oneself in the body or in the spirit that one has departed from the living God. For some reason or another the clean mind, the honest heart, the straight discipline of the religious life, are practically memories; and one wakens suddenly to the sense of this. A moment of insight arrives, when in a flash the contrast between what we are and what we were meant to be stands out before our startled eyes. It is not a morbid mood, not to be pooh-poohed as an unhealthy feeling. But neither are we to yield to it as final.

The true word for us in such a mood is the word of this old psalmist, who plainly was facing just such an experience. Instantly he turns from his faults to God. "Seek Thy servant," he cries, "for I do not forget Thy commandments." You see, it is not only that we desire to get back, but that there is One who seeks to have us back. It is something to be conscious that, in spite of what has happened, we still remember the true end of life. But it is more, it is everything, to feel that our wistful desire to regain the right track is only the echo of God's desire to have us back. We are His sheep, His servants.

This is what Jesus came to do and comes to do, to "go after that which is lost till He finds it." That curious twinge of conscience, that uneasiness of mind after you have committed a fault, that sense of inward shame, that self-reproach, that restless feeling—that is God stirring you up! It means that you are not being left to yourself. The Lord to whom you belong is seeking you out till He brings you to your right mind again. He will not let you go. He needs you in His service still. Life does not leave you face to face with your past, your weak, bad past. No, no! Even in that far-off age the psalmist knew better than to imagine such a thing. And now that Jesus has come, we should know better still. There is One coming in search of us, to put us back into our right place in His service and fellowship. "Seek Thy servant," is our cry, when we are moved to the depths. And the answer from the heights of heaven is this: "As a shepherd seeketh out his flock in the day that he is among his sheep that are scattered abroad, so will I seek out My sheep; I will seek that which is lost, and will bind up that which is broken, saith the Lord God."

Such is the promise and power of the Lord for you and for me, in our faulty, unsteady lives, so forgetful of His orders, so easily swerving from His care and control. We make slips, pretty bad slips. We give way to temptation. We are wilful, stupid creatures; we fail deplorably. Well, but are we not living in a year of the Lord, and in a world full of forgiveness, where He is ever following up His people to set them right again and to restore them? "Seek Thy servant!" Lord, Thou knowest we are poor servants, and sometimes not servants of Thy will at all. But we are meant to be, and, despite all that has happened, we mean to be.

So it comes to this. It is a real thing, this failure of yours, this shameful collapse, a fault not to be hidden or ignored. Yes, but this is real too, the seeking Lord, the Lord coming to you at once and never ceasing till He finds you and has you back in His service. He misses you, as well as you miss Him. If you wish one of the shortest and most hopeful prayers of penitence, say to yourself, or rather say to God, "I have gone astray like a lost sheep—a silly creature; seek Thy servant, for I do not quite forget Thy commandments." I think that is one of the best pillow-texts in the Bible. You can rest on it with an honest and good conscience, and waken to-morrow morning better able to keep straight and to be more obedient.

Edward Scribner Ames

[1870–   ]

Edward Scribner Ames became pastor of Chicago's University Church of the Disciples of Christ in 1900, and has remained in that pulpit throughout his career. In 1918 he joined the faculty of Chicago University as a teacher of philosophy. He has achieved recognition for his work in group psychology and its application to religion, and his Psychology of Religious Experience *is an outstanding book in that field. Dr. Ames was born in Wisconsin. He was educated at Drake University and at Yale Divinity School. The sermon given here is typical of the simple, direct, and stimulating style of Dr. Ames' preaching.*

THE FAR HORIZON

I will lift up mine eyes unto the hills, from whence cometh my help.
PSALM 121:1.

WE LIVE in a period which cultivates the enjoyment of nature more widely and more eagerly than any recent time. It may be due to the fact that we so largely live in cities and therefore seek change from the pavements and the brick walls, from the noise and the smoke. It may be because we have studied nature more carefully and with better helps so that we see with larger understanding her landscapes and living forms, her atomic energies and her vast galaxies of stars. Nature's mysteries lead us out of ourselves into immense and incalculable realities. They astound and challenge us. They humble and awe us. They destroy man's conceit of his importance and reduce him to an infinitesimal element, vanishing after a swift, short hour of time. In the infinities of space and time the cares and troubles which beset him seem to fall away like unremembered pulse beats. Such contemplation of nature may remove the strain of self-consciousness and relax nerves tense with anxious thoughts. It is healing and releasing like the vision of all vast, impersonal things—the ocean, the sky and the stars.

It is, however, the exceptional individual who can be long content with the companionship of nature alone. All but the very few crave also the presence of the living mind and heart and the touch of a friendly hand. It is usually a kindness to visit a friend whom accident or sickness has long withdrawn from his ordinary associations. He is glad to get news of his habitual world, to hear of the little incidents of labor and recreation, of neighborhood life and enterprise, of love and work, which make up the story of the passing drama. None of us can know how vital this life of other people is to us until we are withdrawn from it. Only then do we realize how much the accustomed greetings of our neighbors, morning and evening, and the conversations woven into the day's work have come to mean to us. There is no punishment for men so severe as solitary confinement, and there is scarcely a pleasure greater than that of free and hearty converse with old friends.

And this human society is more than a means of recreation. It is essential to sanity and moral health. Men constantly measure themselves by the judgments of their fellows. As children need sympathetic spectators to enjoy their block houses, their songs, their drawings, their creations in the sand or clay, so adults have their friendly auditors, their censors and their impartial witnesses. Our minds are hesitant and tentative about their deepest thoughts until they are made vocal and get confirmed by some competent and understanding souls. Even those rugged prophets who break with their day and generation make their appeal to an inner circle of sympathizing spirits or to a more distant, future jury of their peers. Authors are eager to have their manuscripts read by selected friends before they are given to the public. All copy is edited before printing and in effect censored before publication. Scientific men work in groups and schools, artists have associations, athletes belong to clubs, business men unite in partnerships and corporations, reformers create leagues, all men participate with their fellows to gain objectivity and verification for their thoughts and to furnish stability and guidance for the common will. In such companies of friends every participant shares a larger life. He becomes a member of an order which outruns his personal power and extends beyond his life. There is a mystical quality in such an experience which is generated by the very association of kindred minds in an ideal venture. Where two or three are met together in the name of the divine, there the divine is present in the midst of them.

Man lifts up his eyes unto the hills and finds quiet and strength; but in the horizon which the hills enable him to see he seeks the signs of his human kind. For it is in neighborliness and in the social sympathy of men like himself that he finds the longer ranges of vision and hope. And through the common aspirations of his fellows he rises to the contemplation of the divine. An American traveling in Europe is struck by the spires which ascend so high above the levels of the dwellings, as if the very structure of the towns illustrated the fact that out of the associated life of men there is an outreaching for the divine. The cathedrals and temples are witnesses to the need for something vaster and eternal. They stand above the lower levels of life like sentinels of a heavenly world. Through them man's spirit ascends to its noblest heights and surveys its widest prospect. It is in his religion that man feels himself secure above the tides of time and the storms of fate. At her altars he leaves all the dross, all the littleness of his nature. By her ministration he becomes free of his burden of guilt and fear, feels himself united again with the world's great heart of love, and beholds the far horizon of the spiritual world.

Nature is not always friendly and beautiful; human friendships sometimes waver and fail; but the divine love flows unwearied and undiminished. Nowhere is all this better illustrated than in the life of Christ himself. He loved the hills of His native Galilee. No more touching picture is preserved in the record of His life than in the simple statement that He went into the mountain alone to pray. But He did not remain. Presently He sought again the company of His disciples. He wanted them to watch with Him. He craved their comradeship and the sustaining warmth of their faith. But they were not strong enough to bear Him up. They fell asleep, they grew hungry and faint, they became confused when danger appeared. One of them at last betrayed Him, another denied Him with curses, and the rest fled. He alone remained calm and unresisting. But His refuge was in the thought of God. From God would come legions of angels if He summoned them. In God He could see beyond the tumult and the night and behold the far horizon where His triumph was secure.

After all, these horizons of our life are within the natural experience of men. They are within the power of the imagination and this is capable of cultivation. Men working at their desks occasionally turn their eyes to the window and let their thoughts run beyond the walls which shut them in. Or they close their eyes in a moment of reverie and escape into some distant scene of the past or into a gilded hope of the future. And this power of the imagination is not merely a means of escape; it may be made an instrument for setting the day's work in the light of wider relations and deeper meanings. More than ever before men realize the marvelous delicacy and elaborateness of the patterns of life they are weaving. And that realization fills them with a new measure of reverence and of hope. Their souls are tremulous with the knowledge of the share in His creation which God allots them.

This sense of the far horizons of life, and the habit of turning to them for refreshment and strength, belong supremely to the religious way of life. For religion includes this practice of seeing the immediate and the commonplace under the form of eternity.

> All shapes and sounds have something which is not
> Of them; a spirit broods amid the grass;
> Vague outlines of the Everlasting Thought
> Lie in the melting shadows as they pass;
> The touch of an eternal presence thrills
> The fringes of the sunsets and the hills.

Francis John McConnell

[1871-   ]

Francis John McConnell was born in Trinway, Ohio. He early became aware of the social injustices in American industrial life, and has devoted himself to preaching the social gospel of Christianity and to working for a better understanding of its place by the church. He is regarded today as one of the foremost of Methodism's leaders, and as a force in the religious life of the United States. The following sermon expresses his deep understanding of the mission of the prophet in the pulpit, and defines the work of the true prophet.

PROPHETIC LEADERSHIP

God who at sundry times and in divers manners spake in time past unto the fathers by the prophets. HEBREWS 1:1.

THERE are two rather well-marked types of leadership in the warfare for the establishment of the kingdom of God on earth. There is first the man who excels in what may be called a worthy form of popular leadership. This man gathers up what is stirring in the highest ranges of the popular thinking of a time and gives it clear and convincing statement. We may thus think of the popular religious leader as the one who somehow senses the unformed or half-formed conceptions moving in the higher spiritual realms of an age and puts those conceptions into such utterance that his voice becomes genuinely the voice of the time.

Important as this leader is, however, there is another even more important—namely, the prophet. For the prophet labours not at expressing the ideas of the people at a particular moment, but at shaping their thought and at putting content into it. He is not concerned so much with what the people are thinking as with what they ought to think. His utterances may at first be greeted with howls of derision rather than with shouts of applause. By the very fact of repetition, however, and repetition many times repeated, he makes the people familiar with his message, so that at last they admit it as something to be taken into account. The people may never acknowledge or become conscious of their debt to the prophet, but he has been influential in moulding their thinking, nevertheless.

The prophets of the Old Testament so proclaimed their ideals concerning God and man as to make them matters of current discussion and conflict in the great crises of Israel's history. They did indeed announce principles valid for all time. They were men of the future, not in that they predicted the course of future events, but in that they uttered ideas in the language of a given day and with reference to the needs of that day. The first step toward understanding prophetic utterance is to find what it meant to its first hearers.

It is urged against the prophet, whenever he appears, that he should come with some constructive suggestion as to how to remedy the evils which he denounces. It is avowed with wearisome frequency that the prophets are too often negative in their message. They merely tell us what is wrong. This criticism can be rightly urged against some whose message is critical and nothing else. I am thinking of the prophet, however, as one who is speaking in the name of a divinely human ideal. Like Amos, he sets God's righteousness over against the actual statesmanship of the nations of his day, or like Isaiah, he puts the universality of God's care for the nations over against the one hundred per cent patriotism of the Jews, or like Hosea, he places the divine tenderness over against current popular cruelty and callousness. The prophet judges shortcomings in the light of a lofty ideal and does not point out faults merely in the temper of a fault-finder. Now it is the task of the prophet to keep the ideal on high. His first concern is for the ideal. If he takes his eyes off the ideal for the sake of making all manner of practical adjustments in human society, he may dull the keenness of his vision of the ideal itself.

It is altogether aside from the mark for some upholder of an established order in theology, or in social or national or racial relationships, to tell us that the prophets of the Church should keep silent until they can make practical suggestions as to how to improve the conditions which they condemn. There is admittedly a sense in which the reorganization of society in its detailed working-out has to be left to technical experts— to social engineers, to legislators, to judges, in short, to men proficient in the physical and social sciences. If, however, these experts are not to be the masters of society themselves but the servants of society, it is entirely in order for the prophet to tell them that they must conform to Christian ideals of human and divine values, even if the detailed adjustment of the order of society to meet the divine ideals must be left to their technical skill. In a democracy like ours, it is especially important for us to draw distinction between the ideal toward which society is to move and the detailed mapping out of the steps of that movement toward the ideal. One of the temptations peculiar to our society arises out of the likelihood that the scientific expert, whose work is so important for our welfare, will lose the power to see life steadily and to see it whole, and will become obsessed with the all-importance of his own specialty.

Again it is often urged against the prophet that his voice becomes sharper and harsher with the passage of the years. Strange as it may sound this is as it should be. The farther on we move toward the fulfilment of the Christian ideal for society, the clearer becomes the contradiction between that ideal and any given state of society. The more sensitive become the faculties of men to the presence of the evils which thwart the highest development of their fellows, the more uncompromising becomes their speech. It may not be a pleasant prospect which stretches out before us, but we may as well remind ourselves that the farther we move forward, the more disturbing is likely to be the voice of a prophet. Back in earlier times, when there was much more of heavy and deadening human suffering than there is to-day, the vision of the keenest souls could not avoid being dulled to some of the more refined forms of human distress. With the lifting of these grosser burdens, the finer perceptions as to what the human ideal means get their chance and come out into expression. The sensitive fibre then of the prophetic spirit shows itself in a type of expression that becomes progressively responsive to the demands of the best for men.

Finally, objection is now and again urged that the prophet ought to seek better balance in his utterance. We more and more lay stress on poise and what we call sanity as the marks of Christian understanding. There is considerable confusion in this objection. It is no outstanding sign of sanity to use a balanced statement when the truth calls for a marked emphasis on some one phase of moral value. There is not much suggestion of harmony in the clangour of an alarm bell, but if the ringer of the bell is announcing the onsweep of a conflagration or a flood, he is the sanest man among his fellows, and he is acting in the way that shows the soundest poise. Of old we were reminded of the folly of those who cry "Peace, peace" when there is no peace. In the days when prophecy counted for so much in the life of Israel, the prophets who prophesied smooth things and spoke in soft and pleasant accents became suspected at once. Here again all comes back to the inherent worth of the message itself. If the popular mind is far gone in indifference toward the Christian values, the prophet can hardly be called a prophet unless he is willing to cry out harshly and fiercely. Balance of mind shows itself quite as truly in desperate effort to bring about a true balance as in an effort to steady an existing order which may violate the first principles of moral values. If we were to run back through the course of human history and, in the light of our after-knowledge, pick out the few men in the world-crises who seem now to have known exactly what they were doing, and to have shown the soundest moral understanding, we should have to choose, for the most part, those whom we now call by the name of prophet, but whom their contemporaries probably called fools.

It is an article of our Christian faith that the Church on earth is a militant body. If that Church is to be militant as a body of Christ, it must be militant as its founder was militant. It must hold without yielding to the ideals of Christ. It must not raise too much question as to what will be the cost to dogmas and institutions of attempting to put those ideals into practice. For actual shortcomings in carrying out the ideals, the Church may well seek charity and forgiveness, but the Church cannot be a Church of the prophets if there is any trace of lack of loyalty to the Christian ideal itself—or if, paradoxical as it may sound, the realization of that ideal does not seem to be farther off the more eagerly we press on toward it. In a word, it is the task of the prophet never to let us feel that we have already "attained." A satisfied prophet is a contradiction in terms. The prophet is the perpetual reminder that there is no discharge in the warfare of the spirit.

Arthur John Gossip

[1873-   ]

Dr. Arthur John Gossip is Professor of Christian Ethics at Trinity College, Glasgow, and at Glasgow University. Born in Edinburgh and educated at

Edinburgh University and at New College, Edinburgh, he entered the Free Church of Scotland ministry in 1893. His preaching, writing, and lecturing have given him wide influence throughout the English-speaking world. The following sermon is one of Dr. Gossip's best because it displays his ability to develop a simple idea into a powerful piece of pulpit art. It has been read by thousands seeking strength and consolation, and is first on the shelves of many ministers.

HOW TO FACE LIFE WITH STEADY EYES

God is a shelter and stronghold for us; we shall find Him very near; therefore we never fear. PSALM 46:1, 2.

THERE was consternation in Jerusalem. For days ugly rumours had been blowing in on every wind, at first loftily discredited, for, of course, God would work for His people against these heathen dogs, but growing more and more detailed and uncomfortably circumstantial every hour. And then the first panting refugees arrived, with hideous stories, exaggerated no doubt by their panic, of what was happening below the horizon yonder. And by and by the roads were blocked by fleeing folk.

And among it all a man moved calm, and cool, and unafraid. Why? Life had taught him to know God, and he trusted Him absolutely even then. "Aren't you forgetting God?" he asked the scared and shuddering groups. And yet when did He ever fail us? How often He has found a way when to our fathers there seemed no way, and they had sat down, hopeless and helpless, and feeling this, then, is the end. How often in our history a door has opened in a dead blank wall, where certainly there was no door. How they had searched and groped for it, and there was none. But always, even though flustered and confused they overlooked Him, God was very near. And is He not the same God still? And for us also He will manage somehow. Even yet He may save us. Who can tell? If He does, it will be like Him. And the man's heart obviously clings to it that in some way He will. That seems the whole point of the Psalm. And if He does not, then He will give us grace to see things through. For this is not the end; and this dear land of ours, scorched, blackened, charred, will yet know spring and green and loveliness again. To us, too, God is very near, and we shall find it so. For his part, he already felt Him there, and every now and then turned to look up into His face with a child's utter confidence.

That is one of the differences that religion makes. It keeps one cool and brave when others falter, enables one to look out upon life with all its hazards and its threatening possibilities, even to live through the grimmest of these, when for us too they have become dreadfully real, with a bigness and a courage that make other folk look small and peevish, cowardly and mean. The power to do that, to remain so unperturbed in trying days when things go wrong, to face the difficulties and the disappointments that life brings with pulses beating quietly and a heart that can see this through with honour, to be cool and undismayed when others whimper and break down, is one of the gifts that Christ explicitly promises, one of the natural outcomes, so He assumes, of fellowship with Him. I haven't much to leave you, He said with a smile; but there is one thing I can give that no one else can, something that will keep you always steady, that will lift you clean above anxiety and worry—better than that, that will make you a rallying-point at which others who had grown frightened and lost heart, suddenly sure of God again, and themselves bigger and better and braver because they have chanced on you, will turn and face, with stout hearts, what had beaten them, and win. "Peace I leave with you, My peace give I unto you," the very strength of My own soul, the very calm of My own spirit, the very secret that has kept Me steadfast among all My difficulties and temptations. I have done it because I have always known that I am not alone, but that the Father is with Me. And you too can count with confidence on this, that whatever befalls you, you will find Him very near, that He will never forget and never fail, but will always be there where you have need of Him. And being sure of this you can go on to face life valiantly.

Such serenity of mind is a great gift. For here are we set down in this dangerous world, so frail, so vulnerable, with these sensitive hearts of ours so easily wounded, and with dear ones always lying open to how many perils always there, and always leaping out on somebody; and our turn too must come of parting and of heartache and of pain, perhaps of a long agony of suffering to be met with hands clenched tight and lips kept resolutely shut, lest a cry break from us, and "only this to hope for, more of pain, and doubt if we can bear it to the end"; and some day, some most certain day, the cold rush of the waters of death about our feet plucking them from us, and the fading out of all the kindly things with which we are familiar, and the setting forth into the unknown all alone.

How irreligious people manage I don't know; and yet I do. It is because they are far more religious than they think. This generation, largely non-churchgoing, and with Bibles left unread, is still living upon the rumours of the faith blown to it from its fathers' time; and when the crashing billows of life buffet and toss them helplessly to and fro, then, unconsciously, their hands clutch of themselves at the spars and broken pieces of the faith of other days still floating on the waters of their minds, and only because desperately they keep hold of them is it that they are borne to land, saved by the faith that they ignore.

And surely it is true that if only we would soak our mind in that steady sense of God's presence and God's love and God's sufficiency, we would have come on the real cure for worry and anxiety and fear. We cannot tell what lies before us, but we do know this, that every foot of the whole way God will be very near.

And to begin with, that means this, that there will be much happiness before us. For He is lavish with it, heaps it up beyond all reason, so it often seems to us as we look at our rich possessions, and then at our deservings or rather at our lack of them. Paul could not understand God's generosity at all; and Christ says that He often wondered we were not continually staggered by it. And is it not a shame that we speak of the will of God in resigned voices as of something grey and bleak that we must brace ourselves to bear. All that we have worth having is God's will for us. He willed us into being. He willed this adorable earth; He willed this fascinating life that He has planned and worked out for us, crowding it with vivid interests; He willed to give us Jesus Christ. "This is the will of God, even your sanctification," that you grow like Christ. That is His dream for us, and He will never rest until for us and in us that best of all bests comes true. Where God is, there will be much happiness. So much, perhaps, that we will need to be upon our guard. For if adversity can sour, prosperity can ruin. And somehow in the sunshine it is very easy to miss God, to feel no need of Him, to forget about Him, to become flippant and light and giddy. But I will be there quite near to you, He says. Even if you forget, I will burst in on you somehow; even if you lose step with Me, I will recall Myself to your remembrance; even if you do get drawn away from Me, I will not leave nor fail you. You can count upon Me. That, then, is sure.

And, because we are human, sooner or later there is bound to be sorrow, and all those solemn things that we like to put out of mind, and perhaps wisely on the whole. For Henley was probably right in his savage answer to Whyte's glorious sermon on "forefancying your death-bed," that "there is nothing of which a brave and healthy man thinks less." "To-day," said Rainy, "I have a committee, to-morrow I preach, one day I shall have to die. Well, we must try to do each duty as it comes as well as we can."

Still, when they do come knocking at our door we may think God has forgotten us. Ah, but that is impossible! Never dream that! That wild night on the lake, with the boat burying itself in the great seas slapping over it, and the wind a mad hurricane already, and rising every moment; the disciples knew it could not last. If only Christ were here, they thought. Why had He failed them, just when their need had leapt on them, and struck them down like this? And then—"What's that?" they whispered, clutching at each other fearfully. And their wet, tired faces suddenly grown white, they looked at one another. A spirit! It is death then, and there goes the sign of it! But Peter, who was peering out into the darkness, gave a sudden laugh of happiness. "It is the Lord," he cried; "it is the Lord!" How did he know? I think he had been watching for Him, had been sure that He would come, that He would never leave them face to face with death without finding some way of reaching them. And he was right. And if you also think sometimes that He has left you —well, He hasn't. Always you will find Him very near, never so near as when you need Him most.

And days may come when you, it may be, will lose touch with Christ, grow hard and cold and dead as any stone, impervious to all that He can do, unimpressed even by the Cross; when you will stand and stare at it and feel no thrill at all; will hear His voice, and know it is His voice, and say "I won't"; will know what He requires of you, and refuse flatly; will tire of home and fling away into a far country; will go mad, Christ says. Then, at least, you must lose Him. No! For even then and even there He will be very near. As Augustine heard God declaring, "You couldn't have sought Me, if you had not already found Me." And you too will come to yourself again, the madness will clear from your brain, home-sickness for God will spring up within you, nauseating you of the poor nothings with which you had tried to fill His place within your heart. And why will all that happen? Only because even in the far country you have not escaped from God. But there too He has followed you, and even there is very near.

Or, again, some time or other there is death to face. Well, there was once a Persian poet who dreamed that the Judgment Day had come. Everywhere there were panic and confusion, and people rushing to and fro, praying the rocks to fall on them, the hills to cover them. Yet his own pulses he found beat quite normally and his heart felt no fear. "God," he said, "who has led me thus far will doubtless lead me still further," and waited unafraid. "When thou passest through the waters I will be with you." God's promise is still there, still very near.

And the beyond? There was a psalmist long ago who looked for a long time far out into the dark, and saw as little as we do. But of this he was sure, that we can never fall out of God's presence. "If I ascend up into heaven, behold Thou art there. Yea, even if I make my bed in the dark, horrible beyond, behold Thou art there"—even there, very near. And where God is, there are sympathy and love and care and goodness even toward the worst. For our death cannot change His nature, nor make Him whom we have found so marvellously kind suddenly grow hard and cruel and implacable. This God whom we have tried and proved and know will be our God for ever and ever. He will guide us even unto death—aye, and far past it, for as long as we have any being anywhere.

Stephen S. Wise

[1874-   ]

Dr. Stephen S. Wise is descended from a long line of Jewish rabbis in Budapest. He came to the United States in 1875, and received his education in the public schools of New York City, at the College of the City of New York, and at Columbia University. Prepared for the rabbinate, he held his first pastorate at the Madison Avenue Synagogue in New York. In 1907 Dr. Wise founded the Free Synagogue in that city and has been its pastor ever since. Notable among Dr. Wise's activities has been his work as a leader of the Zionist movement in the United States. He founded the American Jewish Congress, and is president of the Jewish Institute of Religion. His influence both in Jewish and non-Jewish circles has been worldwide.

WHAT IS AN AMERICAN?

LET ME ANSWER the question, What is an American? by asking and answering yet another—What Americanism is not. Americanism is not a matter of birth and ancestry, for the American is self-made, not born. Americanism, being ever in the making, is of present content and not of ancient context; is not a birthright-privilege, but a lifelong responsibility. America is not a form or type of government, for, save in its utter essentials, the American Government might change and America yet remain unchanged.

Is it needful to insist that America is not a geographical or territorial name, seeing that the littlest child understands that America is other and more than a place? America is not a place, not a region, not a locality. America is an atmosphere, an ideal, a vision as yet unfulfilled.

Americanism, then, is an ideal, and an American is one who lives by and for that ideal—the dwelling together of men and women under laws of their own framing, with leadership of their own choosing, each free to pursue the ends of life as he sees them, and bound solely by the necessity of ever-present concern for the well-being of all. The basis of the ideal of Americanism is the duty of each to all and the responsibility of all to each. The method of the democracy of America is the rule or self-rule of all and its end the welfare of all.

I call America a religion, for are not the bases, the principles of religion and democracy, one—"religion the principle, politics the application"? Was not the liberator of Italy unerring when he declared that the law of equality between soul and soul lies at the root of every great belief linking man to God? The writer is one of millions of foreign-born

Americans to whom America is the priceless possession of their souls, who love America as sanctuary and sanctity alike, to whom America is enshrined by the side of the altar of the soul's faith in the Highest, fulfilling in very truth the prophecy of a latter-day prophet, "for God and people."

No man is an American who does not place America first, before himself. He must serve America: America must not serve him. No man is an American who is not possessed of a genuinely democratic faith—that is, trust in the people and such devotion to the commonwealth as sets the benefit of all above the advantage of one or some. He who holds democracy to be the rule of the mob is not a democrat, whether his forbears came to Massachusetts in 1620 or he to New York in 1910. American is he who counts "democracy the rule of the many with standards" and strives as one to make it so. He is no American who is a democrat on parade. American is he who is democratic—genuinely, profoundly, passionately.

Two types of Americanization have obtained, the one mechanical and the other spiritual. Mechanical is that Americanization which involves nothing more than setting foot on American soil by a foreigner, his subsequent application for and attainment of citizenship, and adopting the outer manners of America. A decade or more ago, it came to be felt as a result of various causes that the immigrant required protection from those ready to prey upon him. Moreover, it was feared that Americanization, still of vague and elusive content, was not coming swiftly enough and that the processes must be accelerated. Insight and statesmanship lay back of this conviction, but, alas, these were insufficiently touched by the grace of humility. Wherefore the "Americanizers" proceeded in many cases to place their special brand of Americanism upon the immigrant market. Had these humbly said, "Let us, whether Americans of earlier or later growth, together seek after the American ideal," the newer or newest Americans might have been moved. But there was something repellant in the mechanical aspect of these facilitated and accelerated processes of Americanization, which therefore failed to fire the imagination of the immigrant.

Moreover—and this is not only parenthetical—some of the folk in the background, and sometimes in the foreground, of the Americanization movement represented or seemed to represent the very things which the immigrants believed America was not or ought not to be. The movement fell into the hands of—in any event was subsidized by—folk who seemed to the immigrant peoples to be American counterparts of or approximations to the feudal-minded lords of the lands whence the emigrants had fled.

Thus in large measure the Americanization movement began. On the educational side, its insistence upon education for the adult as well as the youthful immigrant, the campaign was beyond praise, and admirable were the measures of protection devised to shield the immigrant from despoilers and debauchers. None the less the movement lacked a fine perception of the inmost meaning of the quest, whose end is Americanism. The foreigner can not be Americanized through calculated effort on the part of those who play with the task as a social pastime rather than cherish it as a religious passion.

America demands not of the immigrant that he be oblivious of the past as his starting-point, but that his soul be fixed upon the goal which is America. I can speak here with the authority of life-long relation to one phase of the problem. As a Jew and Jewish teacher, I have seen it become more certain with the years that the Jew, who chooses to believe or affects to believe that Americanism demands of him a complete break with his racial and religious past, is likely to become an American of feeble faith and infirm will. Disloyalty does not breed loyalty. The finest service to the future may be expected of him, who reverences, even magnifies, the past.

If we would really Americanize the foreigner, we must help him to maintain, and enable America to assimilate, the best things of the spirit that he brings with him from the European world. We must help the foreigner to understand that Americanization need not imply vandalism touching the finest things of the old life. Americanization does not imply repudiation of Europe. We dare not lose sight of the reverence we owe to the civilizations which lie back of many of the immigrants who come to this land. Strange and uncouth they may seem to us, but among them are the children of great and abiding civilizations, and let no man be disesteemed merely because he is unlike ourselves. To Americanize is not to proselytize. American fair play would guarantee to every man the right to worship God according to his own convictions and not according to the persuasions or prejudices of his neighbor. There is a fusing which results in confusion, and there is no reason why peoples and races and faiths of the world should here surrender and abandon all their individuality for the more or less arbitrary purpose of achieving a new racial amalgam.

I urge this lest adoptive or foreign-born Americans be frightened into timid and spineless acquiescence in the policy of insistence upon American uniformity. Uniformity is never the equivalent of unity though often a mask to hide its absence. "Uniformity is the curse of democracy; diversity its ideal." It can not be repeated too often that Americanization is an inward and not an outward process, not base and servile imitation of things external, but free and generous emulation of the inmost soul of America, not simulation of the false but assimilation of the true America. The invertebrate surrender of which I have spoken would mean that adoptive Americans understand they dare not be themselves. In truth, they are not asked to deny and efface themselves. They are neither naked souls nor ragged beggars entering for the first time into a precious heritage but bearing sacred heritages with them, coming in many cases into the possibility of a great future out of the certainty of a mighty past. Ask of the foreign-born American all that it doth become a man to give. Who dares ask or give more is none—for the surrender of one's soul's integrity is suicide.

And this America of ours, its making *by* us from day to day, its reshaping *of* us from hour to hour—how daring an enterprise, how ennobling a hope, to give ourselves for America and to give America to the world! Not America for Americans, but Americans for America and America for all the world.

Howard Chandler Robbins

[1876–   ]

Born in Philadelphia, Pennsylvania, and educated at Yale, Princeton Theological Seminary, and the Episcopal Theological School, Howard Chandler Robbins was ordained in the Episcopal church in 1904. His career has included many noted pastorates throughout the East, among them the deanship of the Cathedral of St. John the Divine, New York City. From the pastorate he went to the General Theological Seminary as Professor of Pastoral Theology. Rain upon the Mown Grass is one of a series of sermons delivered by Dr. Robbins before the vast congregation of the Cathedral of St. John the Divine, and is a fine example of his poetic literary style.

RAIN UPON THE MOWN GRASS

He shall come down like rain upon the mown grass: as showers that water the earth. PSALM 72:6.

RAIN coming down upon new-mown hay and drenching it is anything but a blessing, as every farmer knows. But the Psalmist knew that, too, and this is not at all what he had in mind. He was using the word grass poetically. He did not mean by it the crop which had been reaped and harvested. He meant the ground from which it had been taken. After the mowing, the meadow lies brown and bare, parched by the sun and unproductive, the very picture of exhaustion and inertia, and so it will continue to lie until something happens. If there is to be fruitfulness again, if there is to be production, if the meadow is to put forth new growth and be clothed again with verdure, then there must come first of all a great refreshing. Rain must come down upon it, and showers that water the earth.

That is the metaphor in which, ages ago, a Hebrew poet set forth his advent hope, his expectation of the coming of the Messiah. He was a patriot, and like all patriots, he was looking forward to the coming of a righteous king who should bring his land deliverance. But his thought went deep, and anticipated the nature of that deliverance. Israel lay brown and bare, a land reaped and denuded by the scythe of war. If there was to be new life, if there was to be new vitality, if there was to be new power of production, the Messiah must bring these things. His coming must be like the great recuperative powers of nature. He must come to his people with life-giving power, silently, genially, graciously, a great refreshment. Other poets and prophets of his day were looking forward to the coming of a warrior Messiah, a conqueror, one who should avenge their wrongs and break in pieces their oppressors. This man's hope went deeper. This man's realization of what was needed went deeper. Israel needed deliverance from enemies; true enough, but Israel needed far more than that. The land was exhausted, not only by war, but by the output of passion which accompanies war. Its strength was drained. Its vitality was depleted. It needed a Saviour, a deliverer, a giver of new life. Let the Messiah come so to his people—that was what the Psalmist prayed. Let him come down like rain upon the mown grass, as showers that water the earth.

Rain upon the mown grass. How quiet the simile is! It takes our thoughts into the silent world of nature, with its orderly processes, its gradual changes, and its slow, patient, inevitable maturities. There is something solemnizing and restful in this quietness of nature, something that for our soul's growth and good we need to take into our consciousness. Read Sedgwick's *Pro Vita Monastica,* that beautiful, earnest plea, not for monasticism—the world will not be likely to turn again to that in the old way—but for what monasticism stood for, time for the things of the spirit in the midst of our too busy life, times of seclusion, of isolation, of meditation and the culture of our souls.

We, with our little comings and goings, are so full of speech, so anxious to explain, so afraid of being misunderstood, so ready to give an account of ourselves to anyone who has the patience to listen, that we become insensitive to activities which are conducted without noise and voluble explanation.

And all the while, behind these little volubilities of ours, there lie great cosmic silences in which our lives are set and out of which they take their meaning. Nature is not talkative. Nature speaks only to him who has ears to hear, and to him she speaks in syllables so simple and so majestic that he must enlarge his mind in order to receive her meaning. In silence she bade the planets swing in their vast orbits around the sun. Only to the prepared heart of Newton she breathed a word of the tremendous law by which they are held to their course. In the silence of inscrutable strength and purpose, the processes of nature go on to-day. The sun puts forth its strength and gathers waters from the sea; the clouds are formed, the wind carries them, and somewhere the earth is visited, the springs are replenished, the parched land is visited by rain. But we are not consulted about all this, nor reasoned with, nor provided with explanations. Nature waits, and by and by a Galileo arises to interpret her ways to men; a Francis of Assisi to sing his Canticle of the Sun; or a Coleridge to watch the sun rise from the valley of Chamonix to hear "earth with her thousand voices" praising God.

If the silences of nature are solemn, how much more solemn and full of meaning are silences of God! That Lord of all being, throned afar, that Alpha and Omega from Whom life and thought proceed and in Whom they end, is in no haste to vindicate His ways to men. Why has He given us life? What would He have us do? Does He care for us? Why does He permit evil in the world? Why does He allow the innocent to suffer? Up to His heaven go our prayers, our complaints, our beseechings, our stormy importunings, and over and over again it seems as though no God were listening; as though all the prayers of all the ages were falling away into illimitable space. Wrong doing goes apparently unpunished. Right doing does not save men from pain, from weariness, from mental confusion, from bereavement. We speak, and God answers us by silence. And yet, there are men who have interpreted the silences of God. As Newton and Bacon and Darwin have had ears for the silences of nature, so the prophets have had ears for the silences of God. They have read His utterances in the quiet voice of conscience. They have witnessed long-delayed rewards and retributions. They have learned not to doubt that He has care for His people.

In silence life discloses to us its most precious secrets. A time comes when we emerge from childhood into grave, responsible manhood and womanhood. We eat of the tree of the knowledge of good and evil. We assume the burden that makes character, the burden of accountability for our good and evil deeds. What we say, what we think, what we do, what we are, matters. At times our eyes are open, and we have a glimpse of things under the aspect of eternity, and we see that the moral issues of life matter supremely, that they affect, for good or ill, the eternal destinies of our souls. But this knowledge is not borne in upon us in a moment. We cannot put our fingers upon any point in our lives and say, On that side of the line I was a child; on this side I became a man. Very gradually, very quietly, without tumult or shouting, life initiates us into the first of its great mysteries, the mystery of conscience. Daniel Webster said that two things filled him with awe: the stars in heaven, and the eternal accountability of his soul.

As with the initiation into conscience, so it is with the initiation into fellowship. We are brought into contact with other people. The child world of father, mother, brothers, and sisters expands indefinitely, and we find ourselves in a great complex of relationships, men in a world of men. Some repel us, and we avoid them. To some we are indifferent; our lives do not meet nor our sympathies interlock. But there are others who attract us, and we are drawn to them by gravitations of the spirit as real and quite as mysterious as the laws which govern motion in the physical world. We seek them out, we draw near to them, and still more near in blessed quest of fellowship. If we win their answering love, it is our coronation to have won it. If death takes them from us, we walk softly in bitterness of soul. More and more, as years go by, we learn to find in these human relationships the final meanings and values of human life. More and more we learn to believe with Robert Browning that

> . . . life, with all it holds of joy or woe,
> Is just our chance of the prize of learning love;
> What love might be, hath been indeed, and is.

And yet, this does not come about perceptibly. There is something withheld, something mysterious, something altogether secret and sacred in these initiations into fellowship. Alongside of the ordinary and obvious currents of life, hidden currents have been tending in directions of which we have not been aware. Love is a given thing, and it is given in silence. It comes down upon our lives like rain upon the mown grass: as showers that water the earth.

It was so that Jesus, God's ineffable gift to humanity, made his entrance into the world. Like rain upon the mown grass he came, and as showers that water the earth. One cannot read St. Luke's account of the coming of the Blessed One without seeing behind the wonder and the mystery the supreme naturalness of it all. God's way of giving His Son was like all God's ways of giving, like nature's ways of giving, like life's ways of giving; how the oldest and sweetest of our Christmas carols make less of the amazing difference than of the exquisite resemblance! The babe whose coming divided history as with a sword of light was a babe of flesh and blood, born of a woman, wrapped in swaddling clothes, laid in a manger. The infancy was like that of other babes; the innocent, questioning childhood was like theirs. The life that followed was like that of other men, so far as its outward circumstances were concerned. Jesus grew in grace and wisdom, as other men have grown. Jesus was tempted, and resisted temptation, and grew strong. He was subjected to life's painful disciplines of opposition, bereavement, disappointment: "though he were a Son, yet learned he obedience by the things which he suffered." Jesus brought into ordinary human life the life of the country and the city, the field and the street, the crowded life of manifold interests and relationships such as you and I are living, a perfect truthfulness, a perfect charity, a perfect courage, a perfect trust in God. Is this a strange thing? Is not this the kind of life all men were meant to live? But we, as we try to examine ourselves, as we scan our lives, as we weigh them in great balances of duty and find them wanting, we know the difference between that divine life and our own. We know that Jesus did what no one else has done: that he lived a life of perfect and atoning goodness which like the rain from heaven has satisfied our thirst for an ideal. God is nowhere more Godlike than in His silences, in His reserves, in the manner of His self-revelation. He will not compel our allegiance with thunderbolts. He will not woo our love in whirlwinds. Generation after generation of doubters search heaven for a sign, and lo, no sign is given them but that of a life in their midst so natural, so divinely human, that they lose sight of its unapproachable uniqueness and exclaim, "Is not this the carpenter's son, and are not his brethren with us"? By the mystery of the Holy Incarnation, hid from the wise and prudent, revealed so winsomely, so willingly, to the lowly and the poor in spirit, the good Lord delivers His children.

The prophet Elijah stood upon Mount Sinai and awaited the vision of the divine majesty. "And behold, the Lord passed by, and a great and strong wind rent the mountains, and brake in pieces the rocks before the Lord; but the Lord was not in the wind: and after the wind an earthquake; but the Lord was not in the earthquake: and after the earthquake a fire; but the Lord was not in the fire: and after the fire a voice of gentle stillness." And in that voice Elijah heard his God. That is the Old Testament foreshadowing of the coming of the Messiah. Not in the culture of Athens, not in the pomp of Nineveh, not in the majesty of Rome, but in humble little Bethlehem the Christ Child first appears. A night like other nights, but henceforth unlike them all. A cave like others in the limestone rocks, but sixty generations have paid their homage there. A young Jewish mother, like other mothers, but all generations shall call her blessed. A babe like other babes, weak, innocent, helpless, wrapped in swaddling clothes and lying in a manger, but men will hail him as the Desire of Nations, the Light of the World, the Word made flesh and dwelling among them, full of grace and truth. Is it hard to believe? The shepherds did not find it so. The children do not find it so. Saints, apostles, prophets, teachers, martyrs, the great succession of the faithful through the ages, these have not found it so. And we, if with all our hearts we turn to him, we shall not find it so.

Agnes Maude Royden

[1876–   ]

Youngest daughter of Sir Thomas Royden, 1st Bart., of Frankby Hall, Birkenhead, England, Agnes Maude Royden was educated at Cheltenham Ladies' College and Lady Margaret Hall, Oxford. She has been active in social work and has identified herself with many organizations seeking to better slum conditions. From 1917 to 1920 she was assistant preacher at City Temple, London. She is a speaker of great force and power, and a writer of many books dealing with religion, women's rights, and social problems. This sermon demonstrates her great ability in presenting ideas clearly and effectively.

THE TRUSTWORTHINESS OF GOD

The Father of lights, with whom is no variableness, neither shadow cast by turning. JAMES 1:17.

THE saints have believed in the trustworthiness of God, "with whom is no variableness, neither shadow cast by turning"; the world has never believed it. Only now and then have men caught a glimpse of the great truth that God is changeless and that His changelessness is our peace.

For the most part we have both believed and hoped that God might be capricious. We know of no man so good that we should wish him never in any particular to change, and, making God in our own image, we hope that, good though He be, we shall persuade Him—as a sincere and eloquent pleader might persuade one of us—to be a little better, to change His mind. We wish He might be at times more merciful, more full of compassion to us when we think we need it most; or more relentless and less pitiful to our enemies, who, we fear, may be besieging His throne of grace with their impious and unwarrantable petitions at the very hour of our own prayers.

We should, then, find it easy to believe both that God is unchanging and that His unchangingness is not terrible or relentless, but merciful. We should by now be finding it difficult to believe anything else. How could God, who is One, be changeless in a material universe and capricious elsewhere? Why do we still try by prayer to change the mind of God, and, when we fail, speak of "resigning ourselves to His inscrutable will"? Christ taught us not to be "resigned" to the will of God, but actively to carry it out. Even in the Old Testament we are called upon to understand God—"Come now, let us reason together, said the Lord God"; to stand upon our feet—"Son of man, stand upon thy feet, and I will speak to thee." How strange that in the twentieth century people should still be found to sing "Thy will be done" as a sort of refrain or chorus to verses containing a list of frightful misfortunes, each of which, it is implied, must be "endured" as coming from the hand of God; when the words used ("Thy will be done") were uttered by our Lord Himself as a promise that where the will of God is done, there the kingdom of God is established, so as to make a heaven on earth.

Christ appeals to His disciples continually to understand His teaching —not to be resigned to His inscrutable will. He told His hearers that those who failed to live by His teaching were foolish—not that they were wicked.

Where is the law written down that we may learn it and obey it? The Ten Commandments? Surely this is not all! They do not satisfy us, neither do they give us that power over life and over ourselves that we so long for and so worship in Christ. These codes of law, lofty though they be, solve nothing for us. They are dead things. They do not help in their own fulfilment; they only condemn our failure. "All these have I obeyed from my youth up: what lack I yet?"

We lack Christ. The law is nothing to us until it is lived. The Ten Commandments solve no mystery of life, pain, or perplexity for us. Christ superseded them with a law which is love and of which love is the only fulfilment. He lived this law of Love among men, bore suffering as ourselves; and we beheld His glory, the glory as of the only begotten Son of the Father, full of grace and truth.

Laws are not enough for us. We want a life to show them in action and in power. We want to see the One who proclaims the law live in perfect obedience to that law without once seeking to break, evade, or suspend it; and we want to see that, in fact, what He said was true—that such obedience is power, such service perfect freedom.

We must try to enter into Christ's mind. We must seek the meaning behind His words. How could we do this unless we had a life to illustrate the law? How could He trust us to do it if He Himself had written a book? We should have sat down to read the book and get the law by rote! Now we must both read the books His followers wrote and try to understand the spirit of the Man of whom they were written.

Christ, the great Master of life, moved among men as a conqueror. For myself, I believe that He both healed the sick and raised the dead, calmed the storm and rose on Easter Sunday from the grave; but even for those to whom these are mere fairy-tales there remains the supreme miracle of the life of Christ—the change He made in the hearts of men. In a short life of from thirty to thirty-three or -four years, this man of lowly birth, without wealth or influence or powerful backing, so changed the history of the world that we date now every event in its history by its distance in time from His coming. "Before—or after—Christ"—such is the dating of all our records. Christ cut the history of the world in half.

And this He did by no use of force or of wealth; neither the fear of armies nor of magic entered into His appeal. He achieved all by love. The precepts of conduct which, in cold words, sound either fantastic or unmanly, He made real and glorious by His own life. He gave to all who asked and He lacked nothing. He met hatred with love and unbelief with an authority which owed nothing to astonishing feats of magic. He never defended Himself, and we see in Him the bravest of the brave. He took the sword out of the hand of His friend and went like a lamb to the slaughter, and we cry in admiration, "Behold the Man!"

It is useless to argue that Christ's laws can never be carried out, for He carried them out Himself; to protest that they are inconsistent with themselves, for the utter consistency of Christ silences the protest on our lips; useless to complain that they are unmanly, for no man ever was so gloriously and perfectly a Man.

It is only when we see how patience and courtesy and "non-resistance" look in Jesus Christ that we realise how empty is the mere commandment —how powerless without the living Example. This only deepens for us our knowledge and belief in Christ's assurance that God is Love. To turn the other cheek! To endure all things, to believe all things! How pitiful it sounds in the ears of the noble, sagacious, and courageous pagan! But when he sees all these in Christ, can he despise them any more? They may seem too high for him—they cannot seem too low for him. They may be set aside as too hard—they can never again be utterly despised.

And so it happens that nearly all men have loved Jesus, though not all worship Him. If God is Love, it is more important to love than to believe, for it is only love which has power to create us in its own image. God is Love.

Here, again, life is based on universal, immutable law. Not Eloi alone, four thousand and four years before Christ, created man in his own image, but Love (which is God) always and everywhere does this. We become, by irresistible compelling, like what we love. This is true of the least as of the greatest. So, loving Christ, we learn to live as He lived and to obey the laws which He obeyed. Law is no longer a dead and empty thing, serving only to condemn us for our failure to keep it: it is a living power, enabling us to obey.

Thus Christ was the Word of God, creative and creating in God's image according to His words. "And the Word was made flesh, and dwelt among us, (and we beheld His glory, the glory as of the only begotten Son of the Father,) full of grace and truth."

William Edwin Orchard

[1877-   ]

After his education under private tutors and at Westminster College, Cambridge, Dr. William Edwin Orchard was ordained at Enfield in 1904. His logical mind and his gift for language soon made him popular as a preacher and sought after by those troubled with religious doubts. He has had a great influence on religious thinking in England, and his numerous books on theological problems are widely read. This sermon reveals Dr. Orchard's ability to build up a clear and logical argument and to carry the listener along to his conclusions.

GOD'S PURPOSE FOR MAN

I shrank not from declaring unto you the whole counsel of God. ACTS 20:27.

GREATER than the material world, on which he depends for a foothold, the organic world, on which he depends for food, and the animal world, which has contributed towards his physical frame, man is nevertheless created as an imperfect being, because he is created capable of further development. Here he is differentiated from another type of being, namely, the angelic order. Although created perfect, spiritual beings of pure, unhindered intelligence, capable of beholding the glory of God, at which they are thrilled to inexhaustible and ceaseless praise, and although higher than man in power, the angels are destined to be outstripped by him in nature, and indeed are only created in order to serve man by their material and spiritual ministrations.

Man is created a little lower than the angels, unable to behold God as He is, but only indirectly, or through some condescending theophany; but he is possessed of a craving to see the face of God, to be like Him, and to enter into personal and spiritual union with Him. It is this end, higher than that which any angel can attain or even desire, which necessitated man being created imperfect and unfinished; for ultimate, personal union with God could only be possible with man's own decision. Man is therefore made in a condition in which his destiny can be slowly disclosed to him; slowly it must be, lest its ultimate height should seem for him too high, and he should at once refuse it as impossible. While he is given a soul that desires God and can never be satisfied with anything else, he is given powers of decision concerning himself which are absolute, and can be made irrevocable when he has reached a sufficient knowledge to know all the consequences of such a decision. He is given a body, not to clog this process, but in order to temper the revelation as he can receive it; his physical senses providing a veil against the exceeding brightness of the glory of God, which at last he is to behold and will be invited to share. Further, his body, by its constitution, prevents him from descending to a lower stage, and so becoming unaware of God's purpose; the cravings of the body being themselves unsatisfiable, and so bringing into relief the higher satisfactions of the soul as the only final satisfactions even for the body. The animals, whose evolution may have contributed to his physical constitution, remain to remind him of his own difference from them, and the disaster that would overtake him if, possessing these cravings, he were to sink to an animal level; the beasts warning him against the dangers of falling, the angels setting a standard beyond which he himself may rise.

Sin has involved the whole creation; this not only through the mental blindness and weakened will of man, but in the purpose to which man is now directing his life according to his own will. To make nature serve him was the original intention; man also has been given almost unlimited powers of improving nature, and of making new combinations of natural forces that otherwise would never have come into existence; but at the same time he can pervert these powers to selfishness and destruction. The very working of the external world may have been rendered less perfect by the conflict between the good and the evil angels, so that all kinds of natural catastrophes happen which may have formed no part of the original plan. The animal world also shares in the fall; partly through the influence of the evil spirits, and partly through man's bad example, their instincts are perverted to cruelty by preying upon one another, and development now takes monstrous forms and produces unbalanced multiplication. Worse than this is the increasing temptation to sin provided by sinful example, by man's bringing into existence a diseased and perverted posterity, and above all, the cruelty, both mental and physical, which he is constantly perpetrating upon his fellows; until it is possible for man to look back upon the history of the world and see in it such deluge of blood and tears that he goes on to make this a count against the goodness of the Creator, curses God for His own gift of freedom, and wishes that he had never existed, thus bringing upon himself a further hopelessness and the depression of despair.

The terrible story is not yet ended, the awful conflict between good and evil is not yet decided nor, so far as this earth is concerned, is it predictable; nevertheless, not only was all this foreseen by God, but the Eternal purpose is still maintained, because God is able to use all that has happened as the very means by which that purpose can be attained. Although the fall need not have happened, the fact that it was not only possible, but foreseen, was woven into His Eternal plan, the very fall being used of God to drive man beyond the state of his original innocence, in which he had communion with God, and making him desire something further still, namely, that which the Eternal Son has always had with the Eternal Father, a union of perfect love.

The Incarnation of the Son of God opens more to man than was originally possible to him as created; for not only can man now see God in the Incarnate Son, and enjoy that communion to which Christ freely invites all men, even the most sinful, but He teaches men how they may become like God. This is, however, what man does not altogether want; therefore the appearance of the Son of God in our midst has a most extraordinary result, precipitates a great conflict, and forces sin to disclose its real nature.

All man's sins have wakened in him a certain consciousness of guilt and a certain reaction of remorse; but this final sin of crucifying the Son of God produces in his own nature an immense reaction, as murder of any kind always does, and opens the way to repentance. But by accepting the Cross, and by His Resurrection, Christ shows man that He absolutely forgives this chiefest of sins, and therefore all man's lesser sins; but He also shows that Love cannot be destroyed. The result is that when anyone recognises and admits that he has really crucified the Son of God, and goes on to recognise that the Son of God was willing to be crucified for him, by this accepted sacrifice the nature of God, which is love, stands revealed, and man's own nature is so drawn to that, that he can hardly forbear loving such love. If this love, which springs up quite naturally, is yielded to, it is bound to carry the soul farther, and at length unite it to Jesus Christ in such a close, personal and spiritual way that it makes the soul a member of Christ's Body, and by that means introduces that soul into a corporate communion which makes possible its entrance into the interior life of Deity, bestowing upon it all the love, all the glory, and all the joy which Christ eternally has with the Father.

This redemption flows out to embrace all humanity.

A sufficient vision of God will be granted to all men with or without their consent; but to remain regarding that vision, or to hide away from it, must be their decision. Communion with God must first be offered to man apart from his choice, but each soul must choose whether that communion shall be consummated in complete and eternal union. No union between the soul and God can be possible without a high degree of consciousness having been reached, and that demands, at least, the full knowledge of what God offers to us, a choice that is absolutely free, and an understanding of what is entailed.

There is no grace that will carry you into the kingdom of heaven without your assent. It may need only a very simple and feeble assent to begin your co-operation, but on that there wait the eternal purpose of God, all the forces of history, and all the grace of Christ. To shirk this decision would mean that you are unwilling to accept the purpose of God, which is that your salvation shall be your own decision; and at every stage of its perfection that decision must be repeated. No doubt there is some critical point at which each soul passes in either direction, never to turn back; where that critical point is no one knows, for some decisions may be reversed. But it is here in this life that the final decision is made; though only beyond this life will it be revealed what that decision has been. For although souls may never have known the Gospel at all, or never have had Christ presented to them in any clear or critical way, there are decisions being made every day that are implicitly decisions of faith or unbelief: decisions that must affect our eternal destiny; and there must come a time when these accumulate, so that direction in one way or the other is finally determined. But as long as one is able to hear the Gospel and understand what it means, the possibility of deciding to accept God's purpose is still open.

Whenever the whole purpose of God is made known to you in such wise that your mind recognises that it is true, then your heart must decide whether it loves that purpose, and the will whether it will accept it; and the moment this is clearly seen and freely accepted, or freely rejected, the decision must be final, because there is nothing else to be said, there is no other motive to appeal to. And yet we can seek to make known the whole counsel of God to every man, in every possible manner, without fear, knowing that the clearer it is made the more likely it will be that the purpose of God will be chosen.

And so I now declare unto you that all things that have ever been exist for your sake, and that existence was granted you in order that you might embrace the eternal purpose of God, which is that you should know, serve, love, and enjoy Him for ever. The acceptance of this will make your life here, despite sin and sorrow, hardship and hindrance, full of joy and power, and, if maintained, will bring you to everlasting bliss in union with God. That will infinitely justify creation; it is the only explanation of existence, the only worthy end of life; it will alone bring satisfaction to your soul; it is the consummation for which humanity was made.

Lynn Harold Hough

[1877–   ]

Dr. Lynn Harold Hough's career has alternated between influential pulpits in the Methodist Episcopal church and teaching. From 1919 to 1920 he was president of Northwestern University. Later he went to Drew Theological Seminary as Professor of Homiletics and Christian Criticism of Life, and in 1934 was made Dean of the Seminary. His writings cover many subjects and have achieved a wide reputation. Dr. Hough was born in Cadiz, Ohio. He received his education at Scio College, Drew Theological Seminary, and New York University. This sermon is a fine interpretation of the life and teachings of Saint Francis of Assisi.

THE VOICE OF SAINT FRANCIS

He being dead yet speaketh. HEBREWS 11:4.

So ARRESTING are the messages which come to us from the Middle Ages. So haunting are its voices. And among them all the most memorable, the one whose clear, lovely quality carries farthest, the one which carries in itself most surely the promise of its own immortality, is the voice of Saint Francis. The year 1182 saw his entrance into the world in the little Italian hill city of Assisi. His father, a wealthy merchant, was away from his home when Francis was born, and on his return insisted that the name Francis should be given to his son. There was a gentle and gracious mother who knew how to be silent and to wait. And there was in the lad himself something of the shrewd sagacity of his father, some sense of the lyric music of life which may have come from his mother, and a spirit all alive with the exhaustless vitality which sometimes makes youth so splendid and so hauntingly beautiful. The young nobles of the city felt the charm of Francis as he grew up and, more because of his gay distinction of spirit and his bubbling happiness than because of the free hand with which he spent the money his father gave him, they became his constant companions. Francis wanted all there was of the joy of life. He loved France. He loved French songs full of grace and beauty and hot impetuous passion. And he tasted of the sweetness of every experience he could make his own. One can scarcely claim for him the white flower of a blameless life. But one can claim that he came to the taste of ashes which indulgence leaves with an honest sense of just what it really means. He wanted to be a great soldier. He lay for months a prisoner after one of the little wars of his period. He wanted to be a great knight. He got no farther than a brilliant equipment. Something was "gnawing at his heart half-hungrily, half-awake." Illness came to him. Long, long thoughts took hold of him. Was he in love? asked chaffing companions when his mind quite left them in the midst of their revels. Yes, he was thinking of a lady more wonderful than any they knew. But how should he tell them of the grace and loveliness of that lady Poverty who was beginning to haunt his dreams?

One day, before the crucifix, the figure of the great sufferer itself seemed to become articulate, and the gay young wastrel, troubled by such deep strange thoughts, suddenly felt that the Son of God himself commanded him to build his church. He took it quite literally at first in the terms of stones and mortar. Francis was never of that company who escape from immediate responsibility by subtle figures of speech. His father was the complacent sire of a bright young knight of extravagance with whom the careless élite of the city kept company. But he was angry, indeed, to see the keen young business man with a touch of dissipation upon his face becoming a dreaming lover of piety, who turned his dreams into hours of labor for ruined churches. The struggle of wills was intense. For all the distinguished gentleness of his manners Francis could be very firm. With a dramatic Latin gesture he gave his very clothes back to the man who looked at him with such hard, cold eyes. Henceforth he would say, "Our heavenly Father." He found himself confronting the fastidious coward in his heart as he met a repulsive leper. He crushed the feeling and followed the leper, a loving friend. He sought lepers out and made every gracious quality of his a gift of vital friendliness to their bitter lives. And so he tasted that personal self-sacrifice which from the outside often seems so bitter and from within is often so full of the sweetness of gracious spiritual joy.

A gifted friend who carries about with him a subtle quality of spiritual understanding and sympathy once wrote to me, "Francis said somewhere that we praise the Saints, and justly so, but we do not realize the cost of sainthood. That is particularly so of Francis himself. His personality is so wildly fascinating because he was a saint of the order of poets, and the glamour of his genius hides from us the fact that he walked the same high, hard path that the humblest saint must walk in order to win his victory." Much of the tale of this inner discipline, of this battle in hours when the vision waned and only a stern steadfast loyalty held the lonely battler to his warfare, is of course hidden away in the heart of Francis himself. But through the singing wonder of his pilgrimage we do now and again hear the breaking voice from that austere and terrible struggle in which Saints are made, and we do catch glimpses of a prayer which repeats the very experience of Gethsemane. There are lovely vines with exquisite flowers and luscious fruit hanging upon the walls of that cathedral of the spirit which Francis built. But the walls themselves are of stone which has been quarried in hours of that agony of spirit when the strength of the soul is born.

Francis was all the while being watched by keen and critical eyes. He bore reproach and scorn with a kind of lyrical happiness. And as men watched him they felt something strange and deep tugging at their hearts. A capable and successful merchant surrendered to the subtle moral and spiritual appeal, sold his possessions for the poor and entered into fellowship with the strange and joyous young knight of Poverty and of Christ. The fellowship grew and by and by Francis, who desired above all things to live a life perfectly conformed to that of Jesus, found that he too had twelve disciples. The glory in his eyes, the telltale splendor of his voice and the bright astonishment of his life captured the mind and conscience of a young Italian girl, and, as the event proved, some central sources of character and power were released when she and those who followed her accepted the way of Francis. Always a loyal son of the Church, he sought the approval of the Pope, and that great personage, Innocent III, gave his favor to what soon became a new order. All about Italy the new happy singing spirit of poverty and service spread and soon the whole continent of Europe felt new winds from heaven blowing in its face. There was nothing too difficult for Francis. He actually made his way into the presence of the Mohammedan ruler against whom a crusade was being conducted. He would have won by love where others would win by war. And he did succeed in winning the astonished interest and respect of the Islamic ruler and was allowed to come away safely leaving strange thoughts of a beautifully loving face and shining eager eyes and a voice full of the tenderness of a great expectation behind him.

The joyous simplicity of the earlier years of the order is a thing which leaves a perfume delicate and lovely in the mind of every reader who understands the tale. But what was a joyous and creative spirit was gradually changed into a powerful, almost military, organization. Perhaps in a measure the change was inevitable. But it fairly broke the heart of Francis. He accepted the decision of his ecclesiastical superiors. But the light of the fellowship of the Little Brothers in their first rapturous days was the brightness for which his own heart ever yearned. At least he himself could be loyal to the dream of a brotherhood of utter simplicity and poverty which left even learning for one face which gave life its every standard, its every hope and its every joy. To him the supreme gladness lay in supreme endurance for the grace of Christ. And when, dying at Assisi, he ordered his poor worn-out body to be placed upon the ground, that sacramental touch of the friendly earth gave the last seal to a life which met every experience in utter simplicity with a naked directness which left no room for the protecting sophistries by which we make easier our lives. Even birds had gladly gathered about him. If they did not understand his words, they did understand his love. And it was more than a symbol when they sang rapturously above the spot where his spirit took flight. He left behind in the Church a powerful organization. He left in the human heart an imperishable dream.

"He being dead yet speaketh." It may seem that Francis can have no message for this modern world. It may seem that he can have no power to capture its imagination and to haunt its dreams. But these strident modern voices are not quite so sure of themselves as once they were. The machines we have made have all too often made slaves of us. The spirit of the living creature has not been able to dominate the wheels. And sometimes we fear that altogether machines have become our foes and not our friends. The new knowledge has taught us how to be so preoccupied with forces and things that we forget the glory of self-sacrifice and the wonder of love. It has taught us how to produce chemicals which would destroy a great city in a few hours; it has not taught us how to live together in friendship and mutual understanding.

So we turn again to Francis, who knew the wonder of appreciation without exclusive possession, who knew the poison which so often lurks at the heart of the word "mine." We turn to the divine and joyous self-forgetfulness which heard the song of life like the sound of many waters in the midst of every experience of tragedy and pain. We turn to Francis, to whom the way of Christ was not like a distant sunlit mountain one could love but one might never climb, but rather an immediate and perpetual opportunity satisfying and glorious.

Henry Sloane Coffin

[1877-   ]

Born in New York City, Henry Sloane Coffin attended Yale College and then went to New College, Edinburgh, and to Marburg for his theological training. In 1900 he graduated from Union Seminary, and five years later became pastor of the Madison Avenue Presbyterian Church, New York City. From 1904 to 1926 he served as Associate Professor of Practical Theology in Union Seminary, and in 1926 was made president of that institution. Dr. Coffin's feeling for art and history, his measured liberalism, intellectual ability and power of exposition, have made his sermons popular on American campuses.

THE MIRAGE BECOMES A POOL

The mirage shall become a pool. ISAIAH 35:7.

ILLUSION seems to be an essential part of the arrangement of life. There is something in certain atmospheric conditions and in the structure of our eyes that renders the sight of a mirage inevitable. But illusion is not identical with delusion. We should not have sight of palms and water on the desert if these did not truly exist somewhere. In life to be disillusioned is not by any means always to be disappointed. On the contrary, the reality to which the illusion has led us frequently proves far more delightful than the vision.

Because God's gifts put man's best dreams to shame.

And if illusion be a normal part of the process of life, we ought to expect it in our religious experience—our life with God.

Let us look together at a few essential Christian convictions. Take our belief in a God who has personal relations with you and me. If we have had any first-hand touch with the Invisible through prayer, if we have looked for guidance, for sympathy, for sustaining friendship, we can not help saying with George Eliot's Silas Marner: "There's dealings with us, there's dealings."

So, with Jesus and all the believers of the Bible, and their followers through the ages, we speak of God as possessing a Heart, a Conscience, a Mind, as being one with whom we have comradeship. But when we turn to examine the universe, if the God we worship is its God we must confess that He makes an impersonal impression on us—as Force in whirling electrons, as adaptable Life in myriad plants and creatures, as Order in this unfailingly regular and dependable scheme of things, as Beauty looking forth upon us in the pomp and splendour of June. It is difficult for us to combine these two conceptions—the God who is Force, Life, Order, Beauty, with the God who is Father of Jesus Christ. Many thoughtful men and women abandon altogether the God with whom one has personal relations, to whom one prays, who forgives and redeems and loves to the uttermost. On the other hand, many devout folk shudder at the scientific view of the universe, denounce it as godless, attempt to have legislatures forbid teachers to impart it to boys and girls, and retire into conceptions of the past, asserting that the God of their ancestors is good enough for them.

Are not both needlessly impoverishing themselves? Why not admit that when we speak of God as personal we employ an inadequate symbol, but the best we have, to express what we have discovered in our intercourse with Him? Why not also grant that these impersonal phrases—Force, Life, Order, Beauty—are likewise imperfect symbols, our most intelligible attempts so far to interpret the sum of things? Both contain illusion; but both lead us on to a supreme Reality. When we trust ourselves to God, found along either line of research, the mirage becomes a pool. "With Thee is the Fountain of Life."

Take our belief in Jesus Christ. If we have really let Him control our attitude toward people, break bad habits, determine our purposes, open up for us His reënforcements, we know that He possesses extraordinary power. He seems the embodiment of moral Force. If we have thought about Him until His character made its impress upon our minds, if we have studied what He was to those who knew Him at the first and what He has meant to His followers ever since, we are on our knees before Him. He is to us the divinest we know. God, if God there be, cannot be better. But historians, investigating the documents which record His career, set His figure before us as a Man of the First Century with many of the ideas of His time, who was pictured by His adherents in terms of their age, some of which mean little to us. To-day as so often before in Christian history there is strife between those who stress the Christ of traditional faith and the Christ of scientific investigation. Men seem compelled to accept either the Jesus of critical research and speak of Him merely as a remarkable man; or to disregard current research as infidelity, and to think of Him in the terms of some venerable creed. Can we not be true both to accurate history and to indubitable Christian experience? When we call Jesus Man, we are using a symbol, and we know very imperfectly yet what man may be. When we call Him God, we know even less what God is. We are doing our best to be just to all the facts which history and faith supply, when we say that He is human and divine—God in Man—One like ourselves who does for us things utterly beyond us.

Or take the hope of immortality, the continuing life with God of all who have begun to live with Him here. Jesus was confident of it. "In my Father's house are many mansions; if it were not so, I would have told you." Of that existence beyond the flaming ramparts of our world we possess not a scrap of information which would pass as reliable knowledge. It is easy to ask numberless questions at which we dare not hazard a guess. Most of us have asked them, or heard them asked. It is common to sneer at the static conception of heaven in Christian hymns. But when all is said to discredit this hope, it abides, and under certain circumstances becomes man's dearest possession.

Call our loftiest hopes of the life to come illusions, that does not mean that our anticipations are doomed to be disappointed. On the contrary, if life here has taught us anything through our experiences of our world, of work, of fellow humans, of God, it is that illusions are the means of leading us to realities which eclipse them. As we look toward the unexplored beyond, we say to ourselves: "Eye hath not seen, nor ear heard, neither have entered into the heart of man the things which God hath prepared for them that love Him." We do not take the imagery of John on Patmos or of St. Paul as furnishing exact information of the heavenly country. But experience taught them, as it teaches you and me, that the prime necessities for abundant life are usefulness, companionship, character; and it is these which they set at the centre of their visions: "His servants shall serve Him; and they shall see His face; and His name shall be in their foreheads." "Now abideth faith, hope, love, these three."

Suppose our hymns and prayers be largely symbols of our longings, this is not to say that when for us and ours death comes these shall melt into thin air, and, like an insubstantial pageant faded, leave not a rack behind. We are such stuff as dreams are made on! Our life from childhood, in work and friendship and love and religion, is of imagination all compact. Our experience leads us to expect that in death, as throughout life, for those who are journeying with God, the mirage shall become a pool. The New Jerusalem may be quite other than our social dreams forefancy. But unless we pronounce fallacious all the testimony of generations, who marching through earth on the highway of holiness have found in the thirsty ground springs of water, the ransomed of the Lord shall come with singing into Zion, and everlasting joy shall be upon their heads.

Take this travelling song of faith. Make it of right your own by devoting yourselves, like those for whom it was written, to set up in our world the commonwealth of God, and to take for yourselves in every situation the holiest way—the way of Christ. Cynics will scoff at the forecasts of your faith: admit frankly that with our limited knowledge we must cherish illusions. But do not despise hopes born of faith. Here on your path through an earth which unbelieving souls disparage, and yonder whither sight cannot penetrate, for those who walk in fellowship with God—the mirage shall become a pool.

Harry Emerson Fosdick

[1878-   ]

Dr. Fosdick was born at Buffalo, New York, and received his education at Colgate and at Union Seminary. In 1904 he became pastor of the First Baptist Church of Montclair, New Jersey. In 1915 he was called to the pastorate of the First Presbyterian Church of New York City, and was at the same time appointed Professor of Practical Theology at Union Seminary. Later, in 1926, he was called to the Park Avenue Baptist Church, which, when it moved to Riverside Drive, became one of the great churches of the world. Dr. Fosdick's sermons are masterpieces of pulpit oratory; they have been heard not only by the hundreds who throng the Riverside Church, but by the thousands who listen to him on the radio. His clarity of thought, mastery of phrasing, and simplicity of presentation are well illustrated in the following sermon.

THE BASIS OF MORAL OBLIGATION

LET US approach our thought by noting how many people hold a disheartened attitude toward their religion, as though it were an endeavour after an impossibly ideal life. Say what we will, for example, about the inspiring influence of Jesus, it still remains true that for many he can become an occasion for acute discouragement. To be sure, he is ideal, but look at him! Here we are; there he is. He is a long way up; a chasmed height divides. In consequence, multitudes spend their lives looking wistfully at the religious life through a haze of unreality.

Manifestly, a sharp contrast distinguishes this prevalent attitude from early Christianity. The word "ideal" does not even occur in the New Testament, and the word "ought" as indicating an ideal is used with surprising infrequency. The emphasis of the New Testament is not prevalently upon the ideality of the Christian life. At the beginning the gospel was primarily a message not about what we ought to be but about what we are. "Now *are* we,"—"Now are we the sons of God."

This is the too frequently forgotten approach of the Christian Gospel. It does not start by saying, "You ought, you ought!" It starts by saying, "You are." You are a son of God, and then you ought because you are.

You never can tell what anything ought to do until you know what it is. If an untutored savage from the wilderness could have seen that first commercial dirigible from Europe come over New York City, and if you had asked him what a thing like that ought to do, the untutored savage would have been utterly at a loss. He could not have told you what it ought to do because he would have had no idea what it was. Only when you know what anything is can you tell what it should be expected to do.

At this present juncture of affairs in our generation's moral life, this insistence on founding the "ought" on the "are" is especially pertinent. Many people are making a swift escape from the urgency and cogency of the word "ought." It becomes a stranger to their vocabulary and an alien in their life. It means subjection to a code, they say, subservience to a tradition. "Ought? Who gave this tyrant to rule over us and spoil the free play of our spontaneous desires?" To which some of us would say, "You are quite at liberty to rid yourselves of every shred of moral obligation except that which inevitably arises out of what you are. But there, not simply in the name of religion but of science you will face an unescapable moral responsibility." We *ought* in accordance with what we *are*.

Many people to-day are rightly disturbed about the situation in our American family life and are vehemently protesting in favour of monogamy with strong emphasis upon its obligatory aspects. "It is our duty to be monogamous," they say; "it is our duty to keep the seventh commandment; it is wicked to be sexually unconventional; we ought to hold to the old codes." Upon the other side you will see many youths in impatient rebellion. "The old codes be scrapped!" says the youth; "we will be experimental and adventurous in the sexual realm as elsewhere;

why should the dead hand of an obsolete marriage tradition impede the free exercise of our self-expression?" To which some of us would say, "Let us get down to basic facts. What we ought to do depends on what we are." What are we? If we are polygamous, if that is where the deep secrets of human satisfaction lie, then we ought to act that way. But even history will not support that. Always polygamy has turned out in the end, as in Turkey to-day, to be an excursive by path that has led back to the main road—monogamy. Scholars say that from primitive man on that has been true.

As for your private life, what is it that you would rather have than anything else in the world? You young man or woman, free, unconventional, unfettered by codes, what would you rather have than anything else in the world? Quit pretending! Own up! In your secret love fancies what do you dream of as the greatest possible good? Any normal person can tell. You would like sometime to fall in love with someone who will return your love, so that you two may enter into an intimate relationship which neither of you would want anybody else to invade. You would like to have this relationship publicly recognized in marriage, so that all the world may know that you two belong to each other, and then you would like to have children, so that your love life might flow over into other lives that you have brought into the world. As the years pass and you grow older and the sex life naturally retreats into the background, you would like to have affection there to take its place, a great affection that grows up within the sex relationship and stays after the scaffolding has been taken down. And if life brings you to old age together, you would like to have one die not too long before the other, that there may not be too many years to wait. You would rather have that than anything else in the world.

And all this conservative attitude toward the family is not code, not tradition, not the dead hand of the past. You *are* monogamous, and because you are you *ought*.

If, now, we have our truth fairly afoot, let us come inside ourselves for its crowning application.

"Now are we the sons of God," says the New Testament. Of course, calling us the sons of God, like many another Hebrew-Christian way of putting things, is a metaphor. Put into our western language it means that we are essentially spiritual beings; that the powers that make us personalities with capacities of thought, purpose, and love are not the fortuitous concourse of self-organizing matter, but are the revelation of an eternal Spirit; that we have a divine heritage, a divine nature, and a divine possibility.

Religious people have always maintained that religion is necessary to morality. But they have maintained it in ways that often have made the claim a laughing stock to the intelligent, so that many to-day, in reaction against it, are saying, "We do not need religion to make us good." Old-time defenders of the faith, for example, used to say that unless men believed in the traditional heaven and hell they would not live decently. That will not do! Old defenders of the faith used to say that unless people believed that the moral law was supernaturally handed down, dictated by God, people would not keep it. "Goodness," they said, "requires the weight of supernatural authority." That sort of statement runs off the minds of some of us like water from a roof. Thou shalt not kill; thou shalt not steal; thou shalt not bear false witness; thou shalt not commit adultery—such laws well up out of the necessities of human life, the coherence of society depends upon them, and they do not need to be validated by any theory of supernatural dictation. They are validated by the immediate facts. In consequence, many folk, unable to see any sense in the old ways of claiming that religion is indispensable to morality, are beginning to say that religion has no necessary contribution to make. But it has. It has for this basic reason of which we are speaking. What we ought to do always rests back on what we are. What are we?

What are we, for example, from a frankly irreligious point of view? We are temporary and fortuitous aggregations of self-organizing material elements. We have no spiritual heritage and no spiritual destiny. According to one of the most popular schools of thought to-day what we call our soul is indissolubly associated with our larynx, because we are simply animals that have learned to talk, and all our mental and spiritual aspects were born in our windpipes. As for what we are against the cosmic background, one devotee has recently put it with charming candour. Man, he says, is "a small but boisterous bit of the organic scum that for the time being coats part of the surface of one small planet." That is frank, but on the irreligious basis it is true. We are a small but boisterous bit of organic scum.

One of the most amazing human documents of this generation is Clifford Beers's *A Mind That Found Itself*. Do you remember that story? A sensitive lad, an older brother with epilepsy, the dread terror striking in on the younger boy that he may become an epileptic, too, a terror so dreadful that he does not dare to speak about it to anyone but broods upon it in morbid and melancholy solitude until it begins within his imagination to take on the shape and form of the actual. See him sitting there in the classrooms of Yale University with this freezing horror at his heart: "I am an epileptic." "Doomed to what I then considered a living death," he writes, "I thought of epilepsy, I dreamed epilepsy, until thousands of times during the six years that this disquieting idea persisted, my overwrought imagination seemed to drag me to the very verge of an attack." You remember the consequence—three years in an insane asylum. Yet Clifford Beers has come back again. How close a call it was, however, for he was in the grip of that deep tendency in human nature to become like that which you imagine yourself to be!

Who, then, can overestimate what the Christian doctrine means, that we are the sons of God? Say it to yourself. Make it the rallying cry of your life. You are a son of God, and because you are, you ought.

You young man or woman here, trying to live as though you were not a child of God, you cannot permanently go on happily living on a lie.

Finally, the positive and constructive truth about this matter is that living out from and up to what you really are is the radiant and powerful motive for goodness. Some of these modern cults, like Christian Science and New Thought, have rather badly put it over on us of the old-line churches. There was, I fear, an undue streak of Puritanism in our Protestant tradition and one consequence is that a great deal of our Protestant preaching has at its centre the word "ought." You ought, you ought—duty, responsibility, obligation—you ought! And suddenly these new cults rose up and began saying, "You *are!* You are well; realize it. You are divine; live up to it. You are a son of God; act it. You *are!*" They were taking in earnest that deep tendency in human nature to become like that which one imagines himself to be. To be sure, I have plenty of disagreements with these modern cults, some of them very serious, but never let your disagreement blind you to the sound stuff that makes them float.

The basic element in the Christian Gospel is the doctrine about what we are. Say it to yourselves: "I am a son of God." Make it the rallying cry of your lives: "I am a son of God." Put it at the centre of your habitual thinking and your daily living: "I am a son of God." Live out from it and up to it. Claim your heritage. It is health and peace and moral driving power, and you young people in particular, living in a generation when there are so many cheap ideas of what we are, turn from them as you would from the black plague. You are a son of God—and because you are, you ought.

John Haynes Holmes

[1879-   ]

Born in Philadelphia and educated at Harvard University, John Haynes Holmes was ordained in the Unitarian ministry in 1904. In 1907 he was called to the Church of the Messiah, New York City, which he reorganized in 1917

*as the Community Church. From this pulpit he has exerted a great influence
upon the more liberal elements in the American church. He has consistently
attacked inequality and injustice, and in his sermons has sought to make clear
the implications of the social gospel. This sermon is a fine example of Dr.
Holmes' intellectual perception and spiritual depth, and reveals his profound
religious conviction.*

WHAT DOES IT MEAN TO LOVE GOD?

If a man say, I love God, and hateth his brother, he is a liar; for he that
loveth not his brother whom he hath seen, cannot love God whom he hath
not seen. I JOHN 4:20.

IN THIS passage we find several important statements. First of all, it is
declared that the love of man and the love of God are two entirely different things, to be distinguished one from the other in our thought.
Secondly, it is declared that the love of man is the primary obligation of
the soul, and that the love of God lies beyond, and is conditioned by,
the love of man. Lastly, and most important of all, from our present
point of view at least, it is intimated that the love of God transcends
and thus surpasses the love of man, by reason of the fact that to love
our brother is to love what we have seen, but to love God is to love
what we have not seen. It is this third and last point which we must
notice. The love of God, as distinguished from what we ordinarily accept
and understand as the love of man, signifies the love of the invisible.
It is the reaching out of our souls toward that which lies beyond
the apprehension of our physical senses—the dedication of our lives to
what we cannot know, but, in the absence of all knowledge, may "faintly
trust." It is akin to faith, so nobly described in the book of Hebrews as
"the substance of things not seen." It is what Tennyson so wonderfully
unfolded, in the opening lines of his "In Memoriam"—

> Strong Son of God, immortal Love
> Whom we, *that have not seen thy face,*
> By faith, and faith alone embrace,
> Believing where we cannot prove.

There have always been a few men to whom the invisible, as it presents
itself in space, has had an irresistible attraction. They have cared nothing
for the seen and the known, and everything for the unseen and the unknown. One such man was Christopher Columbus, the discoverer of
America. How could this Genoese voyager be satisfied with sailing the
familiar trade routes of the Mediterranean, or even coasting along the
less familiar shores of Spain and France, when beyond him, to the west,
there stretched the vast expanse of the Atlantic, on which no ship in

living memory had sailed? What lay beyond that horizon? Where would he arrive, if he steered steadfastly toward the setting sun? What lands were hidden in that realm which was invisible only because no man had yet dared to see? This western skyline of the Atlantic became a passion with Columbus. Its breezes called him, as the voice of Jehovah called Moses unto Sinai. To cross that line, and see what lay beyond, became the purpose of his life. He lived for nothing else, cared for nothing else. To this one quest he gave his all, and made it therefore his religion. In other words, he loved the invisible, in so far as this invisible was to be found beyond that western verge of rolling sea; and shall we not say that, in this love of the invisible, he loved God?

More important, however, than our relations with geographical space and cosmic space, are our relations with the men and women who populate this globe. Most of us are tribal creatures; we are interested only in those persons whom we can see and feel and know—the members of our family, the citizens of our town, our associates in business or in pleasure. The people who for any reason live beyond the borders of our experience, the multitudes whom we cannot or do not see and therefore do not know, to these we are usually as indifferent as we are on occasion hostile. We have no concern for the man who belongs to another social class, lives in another section of the city, or is a member of an alien race or nation. We have not imagination enough to understand the aspirations of these people, or to sympathize with their difficulties and sufferings. If we think of them at all, it is usually to fear them or hate them, because they live in a different manner, use a different language, are loyal to different principles and ideas, from ourselves.

Every now and then, however, there appears a man whose human interests cannot be confined within the borders of his particular family or tribe. He loves men just because they are men. Barriers of sea and land, distinctions of race or creed or nationality, do not touch in the remotest degree the affections of his heart. If men are ignorant or unfortunate in any way, if they are bearing burdens or stumbling beneath oppressions, then immediately he is their brother in suffering, and especially their comrade in the struggle for deliverance. Men who are invisible, in other words, are as real and precious as those who are visible, especially if they have need of human sympathy.

It should be obvious that this clue of the invisible is leading us to some definite answers to the question as to what it means to love God "whom (we) have not seen." Taking this "invisible," first of all, as it appears in the realm of space, we found it suggested that a man loves God when he moves beyond the fixed horizon of his little world, and launches out upon some adventure of the soul, a quest of truth, or a quest of service and compassion for the outcast and unfortunate among his fellow-men. Secondly, taking this "invisible" as it appears in the realm of time, we found that a man may be said to love God when he emancipates himself from the bondage of past and present, and reaches forth into the future of a better world, and gives himself unstintingly not to the preservation of what has been and now is, but to the creation or fulfillment of what may and ought to be. But not yet have we sounded the depths of our problem, for there is another and more fundamental realm where the invisible appears—that realm, lying altogether outside the borders of time and space, which we call, for lack of a better word, perhaps, the realm of the *spirit*.

A man if he be in the true sense of the word a man, lives only incidentally and occasionally in the material realm. At bottom, of course, he is an animal in the sense that, as a condition of survival, he must respond to certain physical appetites and needs. But no man who is really a man is content to exist on this low plane of animal experience. Just to the extent that he is a man and not an animal, he finds himself concerned primarily with certain things which never enter into the life of the animal at all. What these things are, it is difficult to say. They seem to belong not to the outer world which we can see and touch, but to a mysterious inner world which is quite beyond our reach. They relate themselves not to any functional sensations of the body, but to certain extraordinary processes of the soul which we call thought and emotion. In themselves they are imponderable, intangible, invisible—as unreal and baffling as the wind which "bloweth where it listeth, and thou hearest the sound thereof, but knowest not whence it cometh or whither it goeth." Their invisible quality is what is perhaps most distinctive of these things which characterize the man as contrasted with the animal. How often in life do we see a man who deliberately ignores or defies those things which make up the whole sum and substance of the animal's existence?

Now, it is these realities, which are thus so distinctive of human beings, which constitute what we mean by the things of the spirit. They are those forces of the inner life of man which are so unreal that they can be seen by no microscope and measured by no balances, and yet so real that men will surrender for them food, shelter, comfort, ease, everything that the world can give. The true man will go bankrupt rather than break his word or violate his conscience. He will starve rather than forsake his ideal or betray his love. He will die, on the battlefield or on the scaffold, rather than desert the cause to which he has pledged his faith. Regulus, the Roman, went back to a death of hideous torture in Carthage, rather than break his promise to his captors. Socrates chose deliberately to drink the hemlock, rather than escape through violation of the laws which he had sworn as a citizen to uphold. Jesus faced Calvary, and the ending of his work in tragic failure, rather than take up arms against those who came in arms against him. These, and thousands like them in every age, have been like Moses who chose "rather to suffer affliction with the people of God than to enjoy the pleasures of sin for a season." These afflictions were real in every material sense, but more real were virtue, honor, faith, righteousness, love. These things, invisible to every eye but the mind's eye, belong to the spirit and not to the flesh. Their rewards are "the fruits of the spirit," of which the animal is so unconscious and the unworthy man so contemptuous. But to the true man they are the only reality, and life a perpetual dedication to their service. It is this which we mean by the life of the spirit, and this also, I must believe, which we mean by the life of "him who is invisible." To love not the flesh but the spirit, this is to love God. For "God," said the Nazarene, "is spirit, and they that worship him must worship him in spirit and in truth."

Albert Wentworth Palmer

[1879-   ]

Born at Kansas City, Missouri, and educated at the University of California and Yale Divinity School, Albert Wentworth Palmer has served leading churches in this country as well as the Central Union Church, Honolulu. During the First World War he was with the Army Y.M.C.A. in Europe. From the pastorate he went to the presidency of the Chicago Theological Seminary. The sermon given here reveals Dr. Palmer's liberal point of view and his simple but forceful way of presenting modern problems and dealing with the common man.

RUNNING AWAY FROM LIFE

Jonah rose up to flee unto Tarshish from the presence of the Lord. JONAH 1:3.
If I take the wings of the morning and dwell in the uttermost parts of the sea, even there shall thy hand lead me and thy right hand shall hold me. PSALM 139:9.

EVER since the days of Jonah men have tried to run away from life, and have found that it can't be done. And ever since the days of the Psalmist spiritually-minded men have learned that life, wherever lived, is not apart from the care and help of God. The prodigal son does not always come home to find the Father's house. Sometimes, even in the far country, he lifts up his eyes from feeding the swine and finds his Father there.

The most extreme and dramatic way of running away from life is by committing suicide. Far be it from me, as a minister who has shared the intimate sorrows of many families, to speak harshly of those who have chosen this door of exit from a life of trouble. Suicide, like divorce, needs to be understood rather than denounced. It is a tragic revelation of a troubled and discordant mind even as divorce is of an unloving home. Back of both these tragedies lie deeper problems—how to create a joyous home and how to insure a unified and harmonious soul. Sometimes suicide comes because of physical breakdown—a wholesome outdoor life might have forestalled it. Sometimes, of course, it comes from entire mental irresponsibility. Again it may be due to the overwhelming of balanced judgment by a sudden mental crisis which the victim attempted to bear alone—when a few words of counsel from a friend would have shown a way out. No wonder a Salvation Army barracks in a desperate slum once put up this notice: "Before committing suicide please consult the adjutant!" If people whose mental burdens seem overwhelming would just consult somebody—the minister or the policeman or even the elevator boy—they would find that no situation is so bad but that there is some honorable way out, and strength from God to take that way.

The newspapers seem to indicate a recent epidemic of suicides. I say "seem," for one learns to distrust newspapers as accurate gauges of reality. They play up what they are interested in or what they arbitrarily consider news, so that one can never be sure just how much their report of current life has been colored by conscious or unconscious propaganda. Possibly a scientific study would reveal no sudden change in the number that for various reasons take their own lives.

And yet it must be admitted that there is much in the current philosophy of life to promote rather than prevent a policy of self-destruction. The college student to-day, for example, meets much that is unsettling. Some of his teachers seem to have no very clear-cut standards of right and wrong, beyond a feeling that some actions are not "nice" or "pretty." A mechanistic interpretation of the universe seems to leave out the spiritual values of life as a mere unimportant by-product to be either ignored or apologized for. Mechanistic psychology knows no soul and is hardly conscious of consciousness, let alone of any hope of immortality. There are no bugle calls to heroic action in the dawn of life sounded by this materialistic subpersonal philosophy. It would not be surprising if youth cried out to such a life when—

> "Fear and faith alike are flown;
> Lonely I come, and I depart alone
> And know it not where nor unto whom I go;
> But that thou cans't not follow me I know."

There is something more to life than mechanistic impersonal behavior—that life is a task with value and with meaning.

If youth fails to gather such an interpretation of life and feels wearied and disgusted to be merely a cog in a great world machine, let the Church share with the college its due part of the blame. For while the classroom has seemed to teach a mere barren mechanicalism, the Church has too often made its message deal with issues long outgrown and phrased in terms meaningless or powerless to modern youth. A conception of God and a philosophy of life which can use and translate or, when necessary, effectively challenge the scientific thought-forms of our age is what the age demands. A religion which accepts science as far as it goes and then goes on to insist upon the supreme importance of the further realities of moral idealism, beauty, love, and personal devotion, is what youth needs. It is for the Church to set up banners in the dawn, to call attention to the spiritual values in life, what Canon Streeter calls the quality of life after science has reported all it can on things, which, after all, have to do only with quantity. Youth will not run away from a life filled with spiritual meaning, life which contains real tasks not to be lightly laid aside.

But there are other ways of running away from life. In this cushioned and upholstered age we try to run away from physical hardship and exertion. So many things are done for us that it seems quite delightful until we find that we are losing our teeth and our health for lack of hard work! And so we go back to our gymnasiums and masseurs and, more pleasantly, to long outdoor camping expeditions because, after all, we cannot run away from life in its elemental demand of facing hardship and physical exertion.

Political and social responsibilities are similarly unescapable. You are too busy to run for office? You really must get off the grand jury? You can't be expected to take part in politics, not even in your own precinct club? You are not even to be depended on to vote? Well and good. But listen! When disease runs riot in the slum district because of the corrupt inefficiency which has flourished in some Board of Health because of your indifference, and that disease spreads to your pleasant suburb—what then? Here is a criminal bred by the corrupt politics and unspeakable jail and criminal court conditions which you did nothing to prevent—when that criminal meets you in some dark shadow and shoots you down or someone dear to you, perhaps the question will arise whether we can ever successfully run away from our civic responsibilities.

People all about us are trying to ignore their moral responsibilities and pass them by. "We won't count this one," they say with Rip Van Winkle to each daring sin. But just when they think they are "beyond

good and evil" the tether of the moral law brings them up with a
sharp jerk.

> "I said 'Good-by' to my conscience,
> 'Good-by, forever and aye';
> And conscience forthwith departed
> And returned not from that day.

> "I said 'Return' to my conscience,
> 'For I long to see thy face';
> But conscience replied, 'I cannot—
> Remorse sits in my place!' "

So, if there were time, I might point out it is with religion also. It
seems easy to run away from religion. We are too busy, too practical
to bother. It seems rather troublesome with its fussy details of church
attendance, Bible reading, prayer, grace before meat, Sabbath observance,
Sunday schools, and all the rest. Why not chuck it overboard and get
on very well without it? And then, just as we seem to have banished it
successfully, sunset making the western sky all glorious, or the birth of
a child and a bit of helpless humanity in our arms, or a death and
the strange peace on a countenance well loved and forever still, breaks
in upon our complacency and tells us that religion can never be evaded.

Let me call your attention to the greatness of Jesus in that he never
ran away from life! He heard the summons of John the Baptist and
answered it by his self-dedication at the Jordan—"Suffer it to be so
now: for thus it becometh us to fulfill all righteousness." It is the first
utterance of his active ministry, and what a bugle call to face life through!
And so he goes on. In the wilderness, at the well curb in Samaria, with
the hungry multitude, in the streets of Jericho, on the steep relentless
road up to Jerusalem, amid the money changers, before Pilate, on Calvary's hill he evaded nothing—he never ran away from life. Matthew
Arnold said of Sophocles: "He saw life steadily and saw it whole." But
of Jesus may be written also: "He faced all life unfalteringly and saw it
through."

A. Eustace Haydon

[1880–   ]

*Dr. A. Eustace Haydon was born at Brampton, Ontario, and educated at
McMaster University in Toronto, and at the University of Chicago. He became
an ordained Baptist minister in 1913. After holding several important pulpits,
he went to the University of Chicago as teacher in the department of Com-*

parative Religion, and has been head of this department since 1921. From this position of leadership, Haydon has exerted considerable influence upon the more liberal tendencies in American religion, especially the work of the Humanists. The following sermon is a statement of his liberal position and an attempt to define clearly the ideals which have motivated the Humanistic movement.

THE HUMANIST RELIGIOUS IDEAL

IN THESE days of the religious sciences, if one is to interpret religions at all he must do it in terms of our human, planetary quest. To gather the history of religions of the planet into a single sentence, one might say that it has been all, all the long labor of it, the effort of human groups to wring from their environing, natural world a satisfying life. It has been the unconquerable thrust of the spirit of man for realization, for the good and complete life. There are some who delight to picture that brave battle of the ages as dark tragedy. It has been rather an epic.

In our solar system, with its thousands of millions of miles of span, our little planet is almost lost in solitude; yet astronomers tell us that the solar system is merely a point of light in the vast deeps of the stars; that in those illimitable spaces are stars so far away that light from them reaches us only after thousands of years. And beyond our universe are others, universe beyond universe, until the mind reels, staggering into those unimaginable paths of eternity. Yet here on this tiny, little lost world, forgotten by the timeless stars, man has been bravely battling for life, trying by coöperative effort to build a home, a satisfying, beautiful home for the Children of Earth, striving, in spite of crushing defeats, to entrench his values in a none too friendly world.

The religions of the world tell the story and they tell almost the same story in outline. They show how man's ideal of the good life slowly enlarged from the effort to realize satisfaction of merely physical desires to aspiration for higher spiritual qualities. Man came to value friendship, joy, beauty, love and loyalty more than mere material things. They show that man's crude early efforts to understand environing powers rose by stages until high philosophical concepts of ultimate reality emerged. They show how man's naïve technique of control, by magical forms and ceremonies, gave way to better understanding and at last to science, a nobler method of mastery in the service of the spiritual ideal. Through all the religions of the world we trace the story. Defeat dogged the footsteps of every human group down all the weary way. Man did not have the knowledge or the tools necessary to master the planet. He did not know how to control nature. He did not understand human nature. He had no means to harness material things to the spiritual ideal. In some religions men turned from the actual world to find reality behind it; in some, the ideal was projected into the divine guarantor who was trusted to provide it beyond this troubled life. Even though broken and beaten man clung to his dream. The glory of the human is that the spirit of man refused to be ultimately defeated; each new generation of the human family, heir to the endless struggle, snatched up the standard to set it farther in the face of chaos and the uncertain future. Underneath all, always, was the basic thing—the need of living. The shaping force of religions was this desire of human beings to live and to live in the fullest way. The fundamentals of religions are not in ideas, nor in ceremonies or institutions or forms. The true fundamentals are those human relationships in which men find joy or despair, happiness or sorrow, defeat or the thrill of victory, the expression of mind and will, the joy of creative work or bondage, the sense of futility or the honor of service well done. The urge for satisfying human relationships is the shaping and controlling factor in the development of religions. This demand for full and joyous living breaks old shackles of idea or custom and broadens religion out into new exfoliations of thought and ideal.

Today, in all the religions of the world, old bonds are being broken under the pressure of the forces of the modern world. Men everywhere see the history and future of humanity in a new light. The history of religions reveals to modern thinkers the drama of the past. The history of morals, of law, of institutions shows that each of these is rooted in the service of human living. Even human nature itself is seen to be what it is because of man's effort to adjust himself to the natural and social environment. Human nature is intimately related to the unfolding and transformation of the planet itself. More important, for the modern world, men see that new scientific insight and power have created instruments of civilization which have broken down all the old separations of the planet, broken the barriers which kept peoples apart in safe aloofness and so bound the whole world together that the problems of every little state in remote hinterlands are the problems of all mankind. It is a new world. The religions of the peoples must needs feel the pulse of the new life.

Since the world now has a common science, common problems, the realization has dawned that the religious ideal must be one. If we are to find, in the modern world, the way of life which will yield joy and beauty and creative power; if the age-old quest of historic religions is to find embodiment today it must be an effort to realize the good life as a united humanity. It must involve not one group, nor one race, nor one nation but gather into its service the coöperative energies of the whole human family.

In the approach to that task they have many assets denied to the prophets of religion in the past. The tools of science, the enlarged vision of science and the scientific attitude and method make a vast difference in program and in thought. It is possible now to think of the solidarity of mankind. It is possible to see all ideas and institutions of the past as relative to life situations now outgrown and to take an attitude of appreciation toward them while deliberately refusing any longer to be bound by them. It is possible to expect assent to the demand that human life today shall be allowed to formulate its own world view in the light of modern knowledge, to project an ideal of religion for this age and to embody the ideal in vital forms suitable to the enlarged aspiration and needs of the new world. This emancipation from eternal truth and sacrosanct institution is a great gain for the creative religious life.

Another element which enters into the actual background of the modern religious ideal is the experience of the western world with the creations of science. We have seen science become a Frankenstein monster. We have seen the creative power of science get so completely out of human control as to menace the citadel of civilization. We have seen machines threaten to destroy the very spiritual values man has achieved in his long toil of the ages.

The problem of religion then is clear. Science must be humanized. As a united humanity we must formulate our religious ideal in terms of a reorganization of the social structure of the world so that all scientific knowledge and the resulting economic power shall be bound to the service of the shared life of the race.

This new religious hope carries in the heart of it the old quest of the ages. As our fathers sought the satisfying life thousands of years ago so we still seek, but the vista of vision is wider and the problems more appalling. We seek the elimination of evil, not an explanation of it. We can no longer sit idly by, lulled by the anaesthetic of faith, while the evils of a maladjusted social order overwhelm millions of our fellows, while those who come smiling into life with high hopes go down defeated and crushed to futile death. The modern religious ideal must guarantee to the children of men a free opportunity for full life, the values of personality, the satisfaction of being creative factors in a worthwhile world, the thrill of responsibility of sharing in a real way in the making of a progressively better culture, the joy not only of sharing the values of the past, the hopes of the present but also of creating, in thought and act, elements to enrich the future heritage of man. A united humanity, served by scientific knowledge, master of material things, organized about an ideal of a shared life which will make possible the opportunity for satisfying living to every individual soul—this is the religious goal to which the old religions of the world are moving.

The quest of the good life today is seen to involve the harnessing of all resources to the service of spiritual values. There does not seem to be any reason why the remediable evils should mar the lives of men, least of all war or the possibility of war. There seems to be no reason why we should condemn millions of the sons of men to hopelessness and despair, to poverty and vice and crime when we know that these things are the product of social conditions which may be remedied. Some social philosophers have said that 95 per cent of all the evils men suffer are the result of faulty social organization. The religious ideal seems a challenge to the creation of a free coöperating democracy of splendid individuals, who, sharing the common heritage, will at the same time accept responsibility and find joy in serving and beautifying the common life. Too long we have been blundering, groping in the shadows. We can no longer neglect the use of the knowledge we possess. The vision became insistent. No longer may we comfort ourselves by saying that it has always been so, that man is not equal to the task, that human nature is weak and instinct with selfishness. The first maxim of social science denies it. Today religion has come to full consciousness of its planetary task. Today over all the world, religious leaders are rallying the peoples to try once more to realize the ancient ideal of a brotherhood of man on earth, to build, before the fall of the final doom, a glorious era of spiritual culture shared by all men.

It may be a daring dream. World-weary philosophers of the ancient religions gave up the hope; world-denying saints sought the ideal in another world; sage theologians put their trust in God and despaired of the powers of man; practical men, laughing at the religious vision, deliberately mould the world to their will. The time has come to actualize the religious ideal by the united energies of mankind directed by creative intelligence. Never before in the history of the religions did men see the task so clearly. Never before in human history did they have in their hands the scientific tools they now possess. Never before did they have the eyes of science to see and analyze the problems as they can now do. Never before was it possible to control material resources as it is now possible. Never before was it possible to gather human energies about a task as it is now possible to organize them. Never before in the history of the world did the outstanding leaders of the great religions see the religious task and ideal through the same eyes and in the same terms as they do today. It may be that the future may realize the dream and lure that glorious music out of life which has eluded and escaped the toiling children of men through the long centuries of the past. Religious men will at least enlist for one more effort to make spiritual values dominant in human civilization, to embody in world organization the religion of humanity.

Joseph Fort Newton

[1876-   ]

Born in Decatur, Texas, Joseph Fort Newton was ordained in the Baptist ministry in 1893. Since that date he has served as pastor of the City Temple, London, the Universalist Church of the Divine Paternity, New York City, the Memorial Church of St. Paul, Overbrook, Philadelphia, and the Church of St. Luke and The Epiphany, Philadelphia. Before going to St. Paul's, he entered the ministry of the Episcopal church. His career as a writer and lecturer has made him famous throughout the Christian world, and his books have had a wide circulation both in the United States and England. A deeply religious man with great poetic imagination, Dr. Newton has worked constantly for a better understanding among the various religious groups in the world. The following sermon is illustrative of this endeavor and shows his great catholicity of spirit.

MY CHRIST

All things were created by Him, and for Him. Christ in you, the hope of glory. COLOSSIANS 1:16, 27.

EACH MAN has his own need, and that need, whatever it may be, is his point of contact with Christ. It is enough to have met Christ, if your heart is going out to Him in faith and desire. There is no one way where all must go, where none can wander and all must know—no, there are many gates to the City of God.

From this you will perceive my reason for speaking of Him as My Christ—even mine. For some what follows may seem to be a series of wild words, but it is not. Instead, it is a calm understatement of the reality of Christ as life, and time, and trial, and struggle have given me to see it. Blessed, or cursed, with an intellect critical, analytical, of ultra-conservative cast and habit of thought, tinged by a temperament which, if it had its way, would make this world dismal and dun-coloured—it is surely significant that a mind so made up finds itself, midway in this mortal life, a devoted lover of Christ and a humble student of the great mystics. Never will the day fade from my memory when the prologue of the Gospel of John became, for me, the profoundest philosophy on earth. Not as an argument but as a vision of the ultimate reality taking human form and speaking the truth of things. Let me tell you a little of what that vision means, if so that we may see where our paths have crossed and whither we are going. Studying Christ is like looking at a sunrise: each man who looks is filled with the beauty and glory of it, but the splendour is undiminished. Over all its ineffable wonder falls, subduing the mind, softening the heart, and exalting the life.

First of all, my Christ is a real fact of history—no phantom whose life is a poem in the writing of which all humanity collaborated. That is a pretty fancy but not a fact. There have been many efforts to show that Jesus was a myth, a human life imagined, a drama; but they fall flat. No. He lived on earth "the human life of God," having a place in history and a date in time. What that means to you it is not given to me to know, but it means much to me. It means that we follow no dim wisp of dreams, but a real person who walked among men on this old earth. Whatever else Jesus was, He was a man—sweetly, richly, vividly human; and His divinity was revealed through His humanity. He stands nearest to us by His humanness, His limitations of knowledge, His weariness. That is why His words, once spoken, have never ceased to speak. That is why when you hear them it is like a voice in your own heart—like your mother waking you in the morning with a kiss in the days that come not back.

But my Christ is more than a person: He is a personality; that is, a person with some force behind it, having its sources in the Unseen. Recall His power to attract persons, and the way in which men who saw Him suddenly rose and wanted to follow Him. That is ever the mark of personality. Then, too, His words bear an impress and aspect so unique and characteristic that they are living witnesses for Him. But He is more than a personality, He is a growing power in history, too. While He lived everything seemed to be against Him, but He was not dismayed. Just when His work commenced, the forces of evil gathered and He had to die. Yet He took that early and tragic death and made of it the very path by which to reach the heart of man. With Love alone He won His way, until to-day He is nearer, it oft seems, than when He walked in Galilee.

Nor is this to mistake an illusive feeling of the heart for reality. It is a fact of history that Christ is the great spiritual dynamic of the world—a force to be reckoned with by him who would estimate the spiritual possessions of mankind. How is it that the personality of Christ persists and keeps pace with the ages? How can such a thing be? There are many explanations, but they do not explain. Some talk of the Christ-ideal, but without a living Reality behind it that ideal would long ago have faded. No; stripped of all sentiment and looked at in the cool light of critical fact, Christ is no mere ideal, but a living Presence and force in the world to-day. Let me offer a suggestion—that the Spirit that is behind history, in it and over it, and the Spirit that we call Christ, are one and the same; else why is He our eternal contemporary, in defiance of time, distance, and death?

And not only of history, but of nature, too, with her order now luminous and dark, now glorious and terrible. Christ is not an exotic, not an alien force coming from without, but the flower of the long process of evolution, revealing, in His fragrance and fruit, the spirit and meaning of the whole. That was my reason for saying that a man of science, if he will look back from Christ as from a high watch-tower, will see that He is the final act of nature, as He is the central figure of history. And looking forward, the light within Him of the new heavens and the new earth is the grandest of all prophecies. Hovering above all our wronged and troubled earth is His vision of the kingdom of heaven—the one unifying vision of the life of man, giving it coherence and a promise of ordered advance out of chaos. He has made it real, and He will yet make it come true for us. As an unveiling of what lies at the heart of this dark world, He answers all my questions, and satisfies my heart utterly.

Of course, it is one thing to accept this as a philosophy and another thing to lay it to heart, love it, live in the light of it, and think in the glow of its revealing splendour. For me Christ is not simply a Fact in time, or a Force in history, but also, and much more, a Friend—and in this sense He becomes more to me as my feet journey farther inland on the isthmus of life. For many faith is less easy as life becomes more real; but when I come to Him with deep questionings, a hush falls over me, and I know that He is questioning me. In that silence, far sweeter than any music, is my rest. Then it is that my heart burns within me along the way, and His words, always wonderful in their depth and surprise, come home to me with a vivid beauty that is not of earth, leaving a still singing in my soul—as if He were speaking them to me for the first time.

Therefore, my Christ, while deeply and tenderly human, out-tops humanity, and has no peer among the sons of man. He is the Divine Reality, so far as we can know it or need to know it. That is why He satisfies all types and conditions of minds, and why they find in Him a tie of fellowship; all one in their littleness, one, also, in their joy—His grace as manifold as human need is diverse. No mere mortal could thus satisfy, much less cleanse, this "little, infinite thing—the human soul." When men put theories aside and listen to His voice, they hear the Eternal calling them in words the sweetest, the profoundest, and the most simple ever moulded by human lips. So it is with me at least, and I feel that it will be so with any man who will let his heart have its way.

My only hope for the future of the race, and the ultimate reign of purity and justice, is in Christ. Everything else may fail—but He will not fail. There is something in His gentle, persistent spirit as inevitable, and ultimately as irresistible, as the movements of the natural order. Often enough the Church has failed, by folly or default, but He has come to the rescue with His reviving and reclaiming wonder. This is His world, and He will yet have His way with it. Of old, men fought against Him and put Him to death, but it was futile. They were not done with Him when they left Him hanging on the cross. In the crisis of individual souls, in the strange vicissitudes of history, over and over again, when it seemed that men had done with Him, "then came Jesus, the doors being barred, and stood in the midst." And there He stands to-day, a challenge to the heart and conscience of mankind. No earthly barrier can hinder His presence in the lives of men or the story of nations. He rolls away the great stones from all sepulchres and takes new forms and assumes new glories as the ages go by—the same yesterday, to-day, and forever. He is the Divine Life. He must increase. And His victory is as sure as the flow of the tides and the march of the stars.

Willard L. Sperry

[1882–   ]

Dr. Willard L. Sperry was born in Peabody, Massachusetts, and received his education at Olivet College. He also attended Oxford University, England, as a Rhodes scholar. Upon his return to America he soon gained recognition as a preacher, and in 1922 was chosen Dean of the Theological School at Harvard University. Dr. Sperry is considered one of the most penetrating interpreters of our present religious situation. His sermons show a deep spiritual understanding, as well as wide scholarship and literary skill.

THE RIVER OF LIFE

All the rivers run into the sea; unto the place from whence the rivers come, thither they return again. Ecclesiastes 1:7.

Every man of us comes to the moment when he stands gazing thoughtfully at the moving and mysterious river of life. He hears the plaintive song of human perplexity coming over its tides,

"The river of life! Nobody knows
Whence it comes or whither it goes."

Careless men, thoughtless men, are content to float upon its surface for a little while without asking to know its origins and its destiny. But thoughtful men become Seekers of Rivers. Some inner compulsion forces them to try to map out the river system of human nature and human society. They wish to know where life begins and where it ends, and it is the business of education and religion to further them in their quest.

It is unnecessary to remind you that the obvious and conventional method of trying to discover what life means is to follow life to its sources and to interpret it in the terms of its origins. Would you know what human nature and character are? Go back into the hinterland of instinct and animal behaviour. Would you know what states and churches and kindred human institutions mean? Read the truth of them in the folk-ways of aborigines, the movements of the herd, the organization of the hunting pack. Read biology, anthropology, and the newer psychology. These disciplines will reduce man to his simplest and lowest terms, and ridding him of all that is irrelevant and accidental, will tell you the truth about him.

The up-stream country which is discovered to you by these sciences with the backward look is a wild and forbidding place. The farther you go into this world of human beginnings the more savage the scene becomes. All around you is heard from half-human throats "the yelp of the beast." Religious creeds, codes of decent morality, all the stuff of modern faith and conduct, disappear in irrational and brutal customs of aborigines who seem unable to distinguish between truth and falsehood, right and wrong. Back of all the mountains on which beatitudes and decalogues were preached you come upon a naked savage kneeling in a panic of fright before a basalt rock, or upon a wild tribe celebrating in lascivious orgies the fertility of nature. In the place of moral heroes and martyrs for truth's sake you have a lewd and cruel being, who spent his life hunting, idling, gnawing bones, lusting, and fighting. This, says the remorseless science which has led you thus far, is what man resolves himself into when you factor out the irrational and irrelevant decencies which constitute that disease known as civilization. This is the original truth of man: this is the permanent and important truth of man. As man has been, so he is and shall be. Man was ever a fighter and a satyr, so one fight and one fling more.

In so far as I have tried to sketch boldly and with strong colours, but I hope not unfairly, a situation in which many of us find ourselves in this generation I have raised the question, "What has religion to say to all this?"

Religion has three things to say.

First: Any religion which is to command the respect of thinking men will not deny or prohibit the right of sober science to discover what man came from.

There is a timid and cowardly faith abroad which goes about wringing its hands with apprehension whenever any explorer of these matters turns his face to the dark backward and abysm of time from which we came. They say that it is dangerous to faith to go too far and to stay too long in that fever-cursed jungle of primeval things.

Those statements were prompted by doubt rather than faith, and witness to fear rather than conviction. With that temper no religion that is worthy the name or that is to endure, can stop to parley. If that is religion, then many of us must choose irreligion. It is precisely because we do not believe that religion requires any such temper that, in the name of religion, we will go anywhere with any honest man who is trying to find the true answer to a valid question.

Second: None of these sciences with the backward look ever takes away the ultimate mystery of life. The greatest scientists know this best, and are uniformly modest men. "The vulgar belief," says Sir Arthur Thomson, "that science has explained everything is a hopeless misunderstanding."

All human thinking is compelled at last to give a name to the primitive residual Mystery that remains when we have done our best to understand life and the world. Instinct, Electricity, the Ether—these are names which have been given to aspects of the infinite Mystery. We know no more what they mean or all that they mean than we know what we mean when we say, "God." Science gets on with its work by naming the mystery, by giving it a notation in the hard equation of life. But science has not yet succeeded in eliminating the unknowns from that equation.

Third: Religion says that although life has a backward look it has also a forward look, and that when you are trying to find out the truth of human life, the look ahead is on the whole more important and revealing than the look back. A man's hopes and plans and purposes are probably a better definition of his true self than his memories. This is as true of the race as of the individual.

William James used to say, as a sober psychologist, "Origins prove nothing." He was thinking of the power of the human mind and will to direct life to ends which often give the lie to origins. To the statement, worn threadbare, that you cannot change human nature, one of William James's successors in his department answers, "It is human nature to change itself."

If this were not so, how are we to account for facts which we see all about us? Your picture of the savage frenzy of primeval religious orgies will account for many of the dark rites which Livingstone must have overseen in the African jungle, but there is one item in that landscape which your theory of religion as the survival of magic does not explain, and that is David Livingstone himself. In the end you must give some account of how and why there came to be a man like that, one who, in the words of that slab in the nave of Westminster Abbey, laid down his life for his friends, that he might explore the undiscovered secrets and abolish the desolating slave trade of central Africa, that open sore of his world.

Your theory that all morality reduces itself to the permutations and combinations of the instinct of self-preservation, and that every act of unselfishness is simply selfishness in conscious or an unconscious disguise, is an insult to the memory of those men who years ago courted and wed death in a hospital in Cuba to prove a bold hypothesis as to the transmission of yellow fever.

Your dogma that fear is the motive power of religion and ethics is a slander upon the life and death of Mallory, the master at Charterhouse, and Irvine, the Oxford blue, who elected "to go all out" on the summit of Mount Everest.

Without denying anything that truth-seekers find and truth-tellers say about the unpromising beginnings of human life, its already demonstrated facts are beyond those origins and often strangely and nobly different from them. For there is another truth to be told, and that is this,

> "thou hast great allies,
> Thy friends are exultations, agonies,
> And love, and man's unconquerable mind."

The goal toward which our steady minds and strong wills are set is, therefore, far more the truth of us than our unlovely and unpromising origins. These sources cannot be denied and up to a point they condition our adventure, but they do not wholly define it or determine it. All through the New Testament there is this forward look as the substance of the Christian life. Paul was willing to forget the things that were behind, not because they were untrue, but because they were inadequate. He set his face to run the race that was before him, which had as its goal his high calling in Christ Jesus. He would have said, in our day, what Matheson, the blind preacher and poet, said, that he had never come up with Jesus, modern as he was.

So it is that John Stuart Mill, in giving a rule for life, gave also a definition of life for those who call themselves Christians: he could find no better rule for living than this—so to live that Christ might approve of one's motives. But that definition will be found only by those who believe that the truth of life lies in what is before them even more than in what is behind them.

Daniel A. Poling

[1884–   ]

Daniel A. Poling has been active in the work of the Christian Endeavor Society all over the world, and in the prohibition movement in the United

States. In 1912 he was the candidate for governor of Ohio on the Prohibition ticket, and in 1916 he was temporary chairman of the Prohibition National Convention. He was born at Portland, Oregon, and educated at Dallas College, Lafayette Seminary, and Ohio University. He holds several honorary degrees and has written and lectured on many subjects. What Men Need Most is typical of his style and his plain but forceful pulpit technique.

WHAT MEN NEED MOST

Sir, we would see Jesus. JOHN 12:21.

FOR the maintenance of physical life there are four absolute necessities, —oxygen, water, food and sleep.

But if life is to be more and better than bare existence, there are other necessities; if life is to be well-rounded, fruitful and happy, we must have more than bread to live by. The lowliest brute breathes, drinks, eats and sleeps, and remains a brute.

On our physical side we will do well to consider the claims of exercise, especially we of the office and bank, who have a tendency to waist extension rather than chest expansion. Now and then one finds the exception to the rule. I have known a man of eighty who was hale and hearty in spite of the fact that habitually he never walked when he could ride, and who slept with his windows tightly closed. Such an exception proves the rule for most of us, however.

Rest and recreation are necessities, too. From the fierce clamours of our cities we must periodically find relief, or become nervous wrecks, and, worse, nerve mannikins. We need to place another emphasis upon recreation and make it in our vacation season, in our holiday, however short, a *re*-creation. Unless we do, we will find ourselves dreaming of times when we will turn aside to enjoy a well-earned relaxation, and play, but coming into an early old age, a premature decrepitude, with our dreams unrealised.

But perhaps our order has been inverted. To place an emphasis upon rest and recreation implies that work has a large and fundamental place in the scheme of life. Is it not an absolute necessity to generous, worthwhile living? Pity the person without a task, a task worth giving body and heart to. The electrical wizard Steinmetz was credited with saying, a little while ago, that presently electricity would be so applied as to make possible doing the menial, the drudgery tasks of society, in four hours out of twenty-four, leaving for us all, twenty in which to find repose and enjoyment. Even with such a programme, such a division of time, the world would be far from an ideal society unless our minds and souls had been schooled to appreciate and rightly use the time.

Ah, and how friends have become a necessity,—an absolute necessity in my life! Who would live without them? And could we? Unconsciously we lean upon them; they are part of our unexposed, innermost being, —true friends, I mean, deeply true, vastly intimate, friends who are not questioned and could not be. With such a friend I stood one evening by the open grave of another friend, and later when I spoke of our infrequent visits, our irregular letters, our wide separations, he replied, "Yes, and how great a thing it is to possess a friendship that does not stand at last upon even its most delightful forms, that does not depend upon pen or contact or speech!"

Again, life needs to-day, needs imperatively, a great ambition. Woe is the man who never hears a high call, in whose ears never sounds a mighty shout of challenge. Woe is such a man, for his character has in it a fatal defect; something,—something vital, has been left out. A great English mountain-climber on being asked why he took the risks involved in climbing Mt. Blanc, replied, "Because Mt. Blanc is there." When I read of each fresh attempt to swim the English Channel, I find something elemental stirring within my own breast.

Do I hear you say, "A useless waste of time and energy"? Well, nearly so, I grant, but at least an indication of the fact that the divine fire burns and needs only to be given a better torch. Another follows the same gleam to find an elusive disease germ and isolate it. Youth, with the passion of it in his blood, dedicates his life to a great cause; becomes a Gough, or John G. Woolley of prohibition, a Lovejoy or Garrison of emancipation; a Lincoln of patriotism.

Ah, and the distraught times in which we live wait on men and women to hear high ambition's call to-day. The East Side of Jacob Riis is crying for his spiritual descendants. A thousand cities of this continent alone need as many Hull Houses, and the terrifying war clouds which stand again along the horizon of Europe remind us that we have done little enough to keep our promise; that we have scarcely inconvenienced ourselves to strengthen society against the bloody-mawed monster of armed conflict. What a generation for the soul of ardent, generous, Jehovah-led youth to come upon! Here is the new impossible to be dared; here is the new earth waiting for new-born men and women to give it birth.

We have come quite naturally now to what man needs most—to his supreme necessity. Is it health? No. Is it water? No, it is not. Is it food? No. Is it sleep? No, it is none of these nor is it all of them. Nor is it rest, recreation, friends, work, ambition; nor is it the divine fire of an overwhelming compulsion. What does man need most?

But first we must know two things about man,—these two things. Where does he come from—what is he? And where is he going—what is he to be? There are certain living creatures which die when their physical environment is changed; in these species tragedy follows tragedy, until a careful study has been made of the creature itself, and until the fundamental things about its life are known, its peculiar needs supplied.

Thus it is with man. Give him breath and bread, drink and repose, —all of these,—but give him nothing more, and he will die, for man has come from God, and his destiny is heaven-born. His soul is restless until it rests in Him: all of the physical necessities, however abundantly supplied, are not enough. And so, after he has tested every other, man comes at last, as came the Greeks of the text, with the importunate request, "Sir, we would see Jesus." We would see Jesus, not the disciples, nor the high priest, but Jesus. Sir, we would see Jesus: We would see Jesus, for He alone can forgive our sins, cover them with the divine alchemy of His forgetfulness, until the corrosion of our blighting remorse is arrested. We would see Jesus, for He alone can satisfy our insatiate thirst; He alone can give us peace. We would see Jesus,—Jesus of the well, who cries, "Whosoever shall drink of this water shall thirst again; but whosoever shall drink of the water that I shall give him shall never thirst, for the water that I shall give him shall be in him a well of water springing up into eternal life." We would see Jesus and know His companionship, for earthly friends, however true, must fail us in the end; the father stands upon the threshold of the innermost chamber of his child's suffering, and struggles to enter, but cannot; the mother bends low over the fevered brow of her now unconscious darling, and with travail of soul beats against the inexorable provision that places a limit upon her ministry. Ah, we would see Jesus, for He crosses the threshold, he takes captivity captive, and with Him there is no, "Thus far shalt thou come and no farther." Out to the end of the world He goes with us; brother to every human woe is He; healer of the last agony; comforter of the deepest sorrow, and captain of our salvation. The importunate cry of the text is the voice of every language; it is the voice of the multitude surging about these ancient foundations, the multitude that all unknowing passes by. Somehow these must be led to find Him.

"We would see Jesus." Men and women, do you hear it? It is a supplication and a challenge,—a supplication and a challenge to the church first of all. One winter Sunday night at the close of an evangelistic service, in response to a special invitation, a man in one of the rear pews of a great church raised his hand. Later, while in a personal conference with the minister, he confessed his sins to his Maker, called upon the name of his Saviour, and found forgiveness and peace. His first words, as he rose from his knees, will remain with that preacher so long as he lives. O Church of God, hear them; these were the words, spoken not in bitterness, but in great surprise,—"How does it happen that for twenty years, because I promised my mother, I have been going to at least one church service every week, sometimes Catholic, sometimes Protestant, and last Sunday night was the first time I was ever given a chance to get to the foot of the Cross?" Sir, we would see Jesus!

That cry sounds like a wail of death above the ravished cities of the Near East where so-called Christian nations have signed the terms of Mahomet the bloody. "We would see Jesus. We have seen the statesmen and the warriors; we have heard their promises, and in a delirium of joy have shouted the praises of those we acclaimed as our emancipators, only to find that again we had been deceived. Now we, a broken remnant, in hospitals and refugee camps, in orphanages and secluded mountain fastnesses,—we would see Jesus."

This is the cry of every division in our complicated society. I hear it in the coal conferences and in steel—We would see Jesus! and see Jesus it is or know again the hardship of strike and of lockout; see Jesus and find the Jesus way, or fail, fail and face again the empty furnace of the poor and the bitterness of industrial strife.

Here is a programme in idealism,—and only such a programme has even the promise of success. All others have already and absolutely failed. Here is a programme in idealism founded upon the Decalogue and illumined by the light that lighteth every man coming into the world: a programme in idealism that declares its ultimatums in terms like these: "Thou shalt not kill; thou shalt not covet; thou shalt not steal; thou shalt not bear false witness;" and that trumpets its great summation, "Thou shalt love the Lord thy God with all thy heart, and thy neighbour as thyself."

Only one thing remains to be said. Those who came seeking Jesus in the story of the text, sought an introduction from those who knew Him. The supreme business of the Christian Church is the introducing of men and women and society to Jesus Christ. But only those who know Him themselves are competent to introduce others to Him.

It is the cry of a dying world: Sir, we would see Jesus. My friends, are we, we of the church, prepared to answer that cry?

William Leroy Stidger

[1885-   ]

Dr. William Leroy Stidger is widely known through his radio sermons and his many books dealing with religion. He was born at Moundsville, West Virginia, and was educated at Allegheny College, Brown University, and Boston University. Since his ordination in the ministry of the Methodist Episcopal

*church in 1914 he has been a national leader in Methodism. The sermon given
here is a fine example of the evangelistic character of Dr. Stidger's preaching,
and reveals his mastery of the dramatic.*

LORD JESUS CHRIST—REALITY!

Jesus Christ the same, yesterday, to-day and forever! HEBREWS 13:8.
From everlasting to everlasting Thou art God! PSALMS 90:2.

JOHN MUIR describes the beautiful snow-banners which in winter play
around El Capitan; great, flimsy banners of the beaten snow, pounded
to white dust against old granite mountainsides, which fling themselves
into the winds out across the valley in beautiful display.

He also describes the mists that rise from the tumbling waterfalls of
the Yosemite and fling themselves against the granite cliffs of El Capitan.

These snow-banners and these mists of the valley are but the breath
of a passing whim of nature—beautiful, but a breath—while El Capitan
is reality. So all of life's experiences are but mists against a granite cliff
compared with the experience of knowing Jesus Christ the great Reality!

I have stood on the Pacific Ocean's shore after a storm, and have
watched the white foam scudding along the beach in great drifts as high
as a man until they broke themselves to pieces on the rocky coast. I have
looked upon these masses of drifting foam, and then have turned to look
at the old cedars of Lebanon on the Monterey Drive, and the rocky cliffs,
until I have known that, compared with that flimsy sea foam, when I
looked upon the cedars, gnarled and twisted with the storms of many
centuries, and the white cliffs, that I was looking upon such Reality as
Jesus Christ is amid the changing things of human life.

I have stood on the slopes of gigantic Mount Shasta and have gathered
to my heart's content the great, tall, beautiful Shasta lilies which grow
in abundance on the slopes of this hoary-headed giant. I have carried
those lilies to camp, and they have beautified my room and perfumed
the air, but in the morning they have been gone. But when I looked out,
there stood old Shasta, as it has stood for untold eons, sentinel of silence
and stability, for all time. And as I have looked upon this contrast, I
have known that all earthly things compared with the changeless Christ
were like the lilies of the field that bloom on Shasta's slopes; and that
the one unchanging thing is the changeless Christ in a changing world.

> Reality, Reality,
> Lord, Jesus Christ, Thou art to me!

And my soul is satisfied and I stand secure. Amid the changing currents
my ship sails serenely forward to its goal.

Compared with David, Isaiah, and Job, Christ seems real. These others seem so far away. They seem to be parts of some great drama. They seem to walk and talk in some far-away time and land. They are like misty characters in a dream, and they do not seem near and dear to the human heart as does Jesus.

None of these is a character that one has a feeling that he could snuggle up to, and talk with, and hold close to his heart. They are beautiful, and they are worthy, but they seem misty and unreal, while Jesus Christ, of all the biblical characters, seems to be the great Reality.

In fact, the entire Old Testament seems unreal compared with the New Testament. This is not accounted for by the mere fact that the Old Testament is older in time than the New. There is something more subtle than that. It is a feeling. It is a sense of far-awayness and unreality that we have about the Old Testament. The New Testament seems to belong to us. It is Reality.

There is something more direct in the parables of Jesus than the Oriental symbolism of the Old Testament. There is something more real in the story of the birth of Jesus than in the symbolic story of the birth of the earth. The symbolism of the Old Testament is not so real as the directness of the miracles, the parables, the walking up and down the earth of Jesus and His little band of disciples.

Jesus lived and walked, and talked and suffered, and died on a cross, and went into a tomb and rose again, and there is a sense of reality about it all that we do not feel about the far-off events of the Old Testament.

And when we analyze what it all means, what thing there is about the New Testament which gives it this touch of reality, we must admit that it is the central figure of the New Testament.

For untold centuries there have been bitter theological controversies. When we are in the midst of them, as we are now, we have a sense of regret and wish that we did not have to go through them, but history has proved that they are but great birth pangs; and that out of the travail of all such controversies has come some great truth, some forward movement of the Church toward God.

There was that great controversy over Transubstantiation in the early Church. It was a question as to whether the actual body and blood of Jesus was changed by the touch of a priest. It was a bitter conflict. The church of that day believed that when a priest's hand touched the wafer it became by a mysterious process an actual part of the body of Christ. We smile at such a conception to-day, but it was a bitter battle while it lasted—and, indeed, it is not over even yet.

This will serve as an illustration of the age-old controversies which have raged through the church world for untold centuries over such theological matters as the Fall of Man, Infantile Damnation, and Inherent Sin. The church of another day believed that every child which was not baptized would be burned up in an everlasting fire of brimstone and hate.

To-day we are in the midst of such a controversy over the literal interpretation of the Bible. We have the raging battle between so-called Fundamentalists and Modernists.

We also have our denominational differences, and they are many. We have certain Baptists believing that immersion is absolutely necessary; we have the extreme Lutherans who will have no communion with even the rest of the Protestant world. We have bitterness and unkindness. We also have the controversy over the Virgin Birth of Jesus Christ, and that has raged for many centuries.

But I talk to-day of the Reality of Christ. The mere fact that He stands out as a great Reality above all controversies, all denominational differences, all bitternesses, is the great miracle of all time.

I shall never forget that beautiful sunset evening on top of the Mount of Olives, when I stood with Catholic Bishop Gallagher of Detroit. We had come upon each other by mere chance. We had been in Detroit for five years in political battles and church projects. We had never met each other. I introduced myself. He said, "Dr. Stidger, I have always wanted to know you. I have read so much about you." I returned the compliment.

We stood alone on that hill looking down upon Jerusalem in that glorious sunset behind the Gate Beautiful through which Jesus had gone on Palm Sunday. We looked down upon Gethsemane. We looked across at Calvary. Then I said to the fatherly old Catholic Bishop, "If there was ever a spot on the earth where we ought to have everything in common it is here, is it not?"

The lonely old man put his arms about me and said, "Yes, we stand on common ground here, my boy! We surely do!"

And why not?

We have our controversial differences, we have our ecclesiastical disputes, we have our theological battles, but surely all of us can agree on the divine Reality of Jesus the Christ.

> Reality, Reality,
> Lord, Jesus Christ, Thou art to me!

In a constantly changing world there is ever the changeless Christ, the great Reality of all human life.

"Jesus Christ, the same yesterday, to-day, and forever!"

Ivan Lee Holt

[1886–   ]

Ivan Lee Holt was born in DeWitte, Arkansas. He studied at Vanderbilt University, the University of Chicago, and at several centers of European learning. In 1909 he was ordained in the Southern Methodist ministry, and began a series of preaching assignments which quickly brought him to the attention of the entire church. From 1915 to 1918 he was Professor of Old Testament Literature at Southern Methodist University in Dallas, Texas. In the sermon given here Dr. Holt's wide scholarship and fine use of the language of the pulpit are displayed.

THE POWER OF THE INNER LIFE

And when they were past the first and the second guard they came unto the iron gate that leadeth into the city; which opened to them of its own accord; and they went out. ACTS 12:10.

MEN have long dreamed of Utopias. In the days of the Hebrew monarchy great prophets of that race looked forward to a Messiah's coming: a highway would stretch across the desert on which the captives might return from distant Babylon; the desert itself would rejoice and blossom as a rose; the ransomed of Jehovah would obtain gladness and joy; and sorrow and sighing would flee away. Through the Christian centuries there has been a keen anticipation of Christ's coming to establish a reign of justice and mercy in human hearts. Groups of Christians crowded the highways of the world on the night of December 31 in the year 500, in the year 1000, in the year 1500, and at other times, ready to meet Christ and join with him in the overthrow of the mighty Babylon of evil, and in the establishment of a kingdom of joy. Another group has sought with consecration and zeal to bring in the kingdom of Heaven, convinced that Christ has not left this world or its people and that He must reign until He has put all enemies under His feet; these Christians are sure that He will give to all whose hearts are open the gift of more abundant life here and hereafter.

At the close of the War of the Roses in England the people were impoverished and the land desolate. Hearts were heavy when Sir Thomas More dreamed of Utopia, in a distant island of the sea. Here the economic problems of production and distribution were solved; men learned to live together as brothers, and the less favored groups were the care of all the favored; men learned new standards of value, and they were perfectly happy. In another period of confusion Francis Bacon pictured the ideal society in his New Atlantis. Centuries before, Plato had given a glowing description of the mythical kingdom of Atlantis which had been engulfed by the sea. Bacon found the principal institution of the New Atlantis a great university whose investigators went to the ends of the earth in search of knowledge. As wisdom grew happiness increased and wiser men became ever better men.

It is in periods of distress that men with burdened hearts and souls dream of Utopias—Utopias that lie a long way off in time or place. Our own generation has read the prophecies of Bellamy and Wells, and has felt the thrill of human brotherhood.

We ought to face the future with assurance, but each of us longs for the fruit of his work and sacrifice. We would like to usher in the Kingdom and live in the Utopia. If it is to be a million years in coming we can never know its joys. The problem is the same as the prophets of Israel faced. Should the Messiah come and establish His kingdom, what of the faithful through the generations who have long since died? Is there no word of cheer for us, who wait, save only that the work is worth the doing? Fortunately, there is.

A follower of Jesus heard Him speak often of the Kingdom, and remembered a thrilling phrase, "The Kingdom of Heaven is within you." Men would seek it here and there, look for its signs in the heavens, only to find it in their own hearts. Peter preached this "Kingdom within," and was imprisoned. About him were the thick walls of a Roman prison; in front of him were its iron gates. He had no physical strength to break down walls or open gates, but one day he "came unto the iron gate that leadeth into the city, and it opened of its own accord, and he went out." There was a strength within before which iron gates opened of their own accord, and the prisoner walked out into the liberty and joy of the city.

There are prison walls that shut in the mind, and the soul, and the spirit. A wall around a human mind is a misfortune. One is in doubt; the churches are torn by dissensions; a conflict between religion and science disturbs; the average religious man feels like a straggler along the highway, following in the wake of a defeated or victorious army, scarcely knowing what the fight has been or will be. Where will he turn for answer to his question? What attitude will lead to satisfaction? To every one distressed in mind Jesus says, "Follow the truth; the spirit of truth will lead you unto all truth." The man who is concerned to "Ask, and seek, and knock" in his search for truth will find the prison gates of the mind opening of their own accord.

A wall around a human soul is a tragedy. One is a prisoner of sin! The word sin is not a popular one to-day; we prefer to substitute foible, or mistake, or slip. But two things are apparent to every student of human conduct. The principal reason for our failure to establish a perfect society is the fact that we are dealing with such imperfect men. "We can never make an A-1 Society out of C-3 men." In all our discussions of covenants and agreements it becomes more and more apparent that men must be redeemed from selfishness and sin. In the second place, ethical instruction and beautiful mottoes will never bring redemption. There is a mighty passion for war, a passion for greed, a passion for lust; only a mightier passion can redeem, a passion for God as Savior! To every sinful man Jesus offers the water of righteousness, the bread of life, the release from sin. "And if I be lifted up I will draw all men unto me."

A wall around a human spirit is a calamity. As in every generation man to-day wants to know whether the universe is friendly. There are so many sorrows in one's life and so many tragic injustices that God seems often to have left His universe. Man turns to his religion and is impatient when his questions are not answered. "It is not the principal function of religion to answer questions," says Principal Jacks. Its function is rather to give a man courage to go on in the face of perplexities. Hear Jesus urge, "Be of good cheer, I have overcome the world." "Let not your heart be troubled; believe in God." "The Father knoweth." In every trying personal experience Jesus points a way out and insists that a man may know the kingdom within, and experience such strength of soul that prison bars slip back, and prison gates open of their own accord. How many there are who have found it so! How many have learned the power of the inner life!

Peer Gynt goes out in the world seeking adventure and happiness. After years of wandering he returns home to find the happiness he had sought afar. Maeterlinck sends children out to seek the bluebird of happiness under the guidance of a fairy. They go to the past and then to the distant future; finally they return to find the bluebird in their own home, where he had been all the time. Emerson once wrote, "Though you travel the world over to find the beautiful, you must carry it with you or you will find it not."

"The Kingdom of Heaven is within you." "And when they came unto the iron gate that leadeth into the city it opened to them of its own accord and they went out."

Curtis W. Reese

[1887–   ]

Curtis W. Reese has been a leader of the liberal movement in modern religion. His interest in labor relations led him to take an active part in reform

*movements. He was born in Madison County, North Carolina, and was edu-
cated at Mars Hill College, Southern Baptist Theological Seminary, and Ewing
College. He was ordained as a Baptist minister in 1918. His sermon here is one
of a series which attempts to state the Humanist faith, and shows clearly how
Dr. Reese turned to Humanism because of his concern over labor and social
problems.*

THE FAITH OF HUMANISM

THERE is a large element of faith in all religion. Buddhism has faith in the
inexorable laws of Karma; Mohammedanism in the unyielding will of
Allah; Confucianism in the moral nature of Heaven; Christianity in the
love of God; and Humanism in man as the measure of values.

There is a large element of faith in all philosophy. Idealists have faith
in eternal values; Realists in the objective reality of facts; Naturalists in
an inner survival urge; and Pragmatists in the workableness of truth.

There is a large measure of faith in all science. Faith in the orderliness
of nature and in man's mind to comprehend it makes science possible.
There could be no science if we began with chaos on the part of the universe and incompetency on the part of man.

There is a large element of faith in all human relations. The foundations of government, the warp and woof of economic relations, and especially the very structure of the home, partake in large measure of the
nature of faith.

Hypotheses, postulates, and assumptions in their proper realm are com-
parable to faith in the realm of religion. In this way I speak of the faith
of Humanism.

Competent philosophers, scientists, and even theologians, regard working assumptions as tentative. They constantly check for error; they diligently gather new data and re-examine the old generalizations in the light
of the new facts. They welcome criticism and verification from competent
persons. Their faith is consciously experimental. And it is thus with the
faith of the Humanist.

Humanism aims to comprehend man in his total setting; to know him
as a child of the cosmos, as the individual member of the human group,
and as the parent of civilizations yet to be. It sets as its definite goal,
not knowledge for its own sake but knowledge as a means to the enrich-
ment of human life. Here it attacks its problems with evangelical fervor
and summons to its cause all knowledge, all faith, all hope, and all love.

Let us sketch the faith of Humanism in broad outline and see what
it has to offer.

In the first place, Humanism has faith in the trustworthiness of the
scientific spirit and method; viz., freedom of inquiry and controlled experiment. Fundamentalism is skeptical of science; Modernism merely

flirts with science; but Humanism says that, while science may give us inadequate knowledge, it gives all we have and we must make the most of it. Upon science and the legitimate inferences from its established facts we are dependent for our knowledge of the nature of the universe, of the evolution of life, and of man's prowess and possibilities. And how stimulating yet sobering it is to contemplate the universe of modern science!

With the destruction of the old cosmologies went many a man's sense of being at home in the universe. For vast multitudes the very foundations of the deep were shaken. The ships of the mighty went down, and only the skiffs of the tough-minded remained afloat. Hence the first task of any religion today is to face with utter frankness the cosmic situation that confronts the modern mind; to marshal such evidence as modern science reveals, examine and evaluate it, and determine to what extent it upholds human hopes.

The revelations of science have given us not a smaller but a bigger universe; not a simpler but a more complex universe; not a poorer but a richer universe.

Coming nearer home, consider the evidence of geological knowledge. Scientific authorities estimate that life has been on this globe a thousand million years and that the age of the earth itself is some small multiple of a thousand million. They show how age after age this whirling globe has picked up stray matter; brought forth the germ of life; and how life has been fruitful and multiplied manifold, producing species of wondrous complexity and marvellous intelligence.

In a most impressive way, the late Jenkins Lloyd Jones once vividly outlined a scale of the vast epochs of the world's history. Borrowing the suggestion and a part of Dr. Jones' collection of facts, I have laid out the creative periods on a scale of one hundred units. On this scale, it takes fifty units to represent the growth of the earth in what Haeckel styled the "tangled forest" period, during which the only vegetation was in the water and the only animals the skulless creatures of the sea. We add thirty-three and one-half units for the period in which ferns appeared on land and fishes in the deep; eleven units for the period in which pines and reptiles appeared; four units for the period when the mammals appeared and the young were brought forth alive and the period of infancy prolonged—the period of leafed forests, of birds and animals. Bringing the scale up to the present time, we add one and one-half units to represent the modern period during which man has appeared and has begun to assume his responsibility in the creative process.

In man, then, is the fruitage of what Aristotle called "the inner perfecting principle," of what Lamarck called "the slow wishing of the animals," of what Darwin called "natural selection." In him is the fruitage of age-long mother love, paternal care, and communal life; of an age-long struggle to liberate the fore limbs, to swing hands on flexible wrists, and to develop the throat to the point of speech.

Man is fortunate in that he is the heir of ages past; he is promising in that he is the parent of ages yet to be.

In the second place, Humanism has faith in the capacity of man increasingly to understand the universe and his place in it.

It is true that we do not know very much about any one of the many things that call from the depths of the atom, or from the immensities of space. We do not know what life is, nor how a bit of protoplasm carries within it the potentialities that subsequent development proves to be there.

But however inadequate may be man's capacity to understand the universe, there is no other vessel of information. There is no valid oracle of knowledge. There is no verified revelation of reality. There is no yoga-short-cut to wisdom. Man by means of his own science must unravel the skein of existence if he would weave the fabric of knowledge.

Admitting our lack of information, it is still true that man has demonstrated his capacity to understand with increasing accuracy and clearness the nature of his world and of his relation to it.

In the third place, Humanism has faith in the ability of man increasingly to achieve the possibilities inherent in the nature of man and the universe.

In his control of nature's modes of operation, man is skillful and masterful. As an everyday affair he makes power that was once thought to dwell only among the clouds, and to be the exclusive possession of the gods. From the depths of the earth he brings forth riches untold. The physical world is beginning to do man's bidding. Not less wonderful is man's understanding of psychological laws. We are beginning to know how to predict and compel results. We now know that within certain limits public opinion and public conscience are subject to human control.

As man learns more and more about nature's processes—both physical and psychological—he learns that human intelligence is a co-worker with nature.

In his origination and development of moral ideas, man is wise and far-seeing. As man has needed moral ideas for his advancement, he has achieved them. Moral ideas have never been handed down from heaven in systematized code, though such has been thought to be the origin of both the Hammurabic and the Mosaic codes. When man needed the moral idea of private property, he achieved it; then he who took that which belonged to another became a thief. When man needed the moral idea of communal property, he achieved it; then he who thrived by monopoly became a social parasite. When man needed the moral idea of the sacredness of human life, he achieved it; then he who killed another became a murderer. Man achieves his moral ideas; and when he gets done with them he replaces them with more and better ones.

In his creation of spiritual values, man is hopeful and prophetic. Man achieves his spiritual values because he feels the need for them. He feels that he wants to secure more power in the pursuit of the good life. Hence, he has followed teachers who have proclaimed the more abundant life; he has made religions, and has evolved magic and prayer. Out of the inexhaustible soul of man, in response to his needs, have come forth gods and devils, angels and demons, heavens and hells. These man has made at his will and destroyed when he would. Other values innumerable has he brought out of the depths of his being, personified and sent them forth to battle in his behalf. These spiritual creations of man are so real that they die hard. Aye, they refuse to die until put to death by some greater spiritual creation.

But man's past achievements are only preparatory. They have merely opened his eyes to the greater possibilities of the future. In his power to dream dreams and to see visions, man is potentially the creator of nobler things yet to be.

Humanism holds that the religion that would be useful in this new day must be neither individualistic nor socialistic, but mutualistic. It must seek to weave the best personal values into a noble social order. It cannot preach a gospel that is purely personal nor one that is purely social; it must preach a gospel that will help to balance personal and social impulses to the end that individual man shall experience within himself the harmony of his impulses, and mankind be organized for the harmonious development of all the races of the world. Such a religion is now finding expression here and there among all churches and all religions, and in the lives of many who are not associated with any religious movement.

Humanism is bringing into the light of day a religion of, by, and for the whole man and the whole world.

Ralph W. Sockman

[1889–   ]

Dr. Ralph W. Sockman has the distinction of having held only one pulpit during his entire ministry—Christ Church, Park Avenue, New York City. Dr. Sockman was born at Mount Vernon, Ohio, and was educated at Ohio Wesleyan, Columbia University, and the Union Theological Seminary. He has enjoyed great popularity as a public speaker, and has made many addresses at colleges and over the radio. He is represented here by a sermon preached in the pulpit of the Madison Avenue Methodist Episcopal Church which was the name of Dr. Sockman's church before it moved to Park Avenue.

PREJUDICE

PREJUDICE is a sin which every one denounces and almost no one seriously confesses. It is difficult to dislodge from the human mind because the possessor does not think he has it and does not think it dangerous if he has. Prejudiced persons do not come crying to be saved from their bigotry. It is this self-deception and self-satisfaction which help to make prejudice so baffling.

Sins of the mind can be so much more subtly dangerous than sins of the body. These latter, like lust or intemperance, usually leave their open marks and thereby are likely to induce a sense of shame and a spirit of repentance. But mental sins, such as prejudice or pride, beget no bodily brakes which serve to check their progress. For this reason Jesus had a harder time with them than with the manifest vices of the outcasts and the derelicts. In the presence of Jesus' purity the Magdalenes grew repentant; in the atmosphere of Jesus' honesty the publicans grew conscientious; but the prejudiced minds of the respectable Pharisees only grew the harder. After the Master had tried vainly to soften them with the warmth of his love and to pierce them with the shafts of his ridicule, he said to them bluntly, "The publicans and harlots go into the Kingdom of God before you."

Hence, while prejudice is not one of those colorful and picturesque sins against which we can arouse a popular crusading attack because it does not put its possessors in the gutter or in prison, it is nevertheless one of the most stubborn and sinister.

That blind unreason which shutters the mind against the light of logic and refuses to look facts in the face—that is prejudice. That cold predisposition which closes the heart against the approaches of affection and cruelly judges before it hears the defence—that is prejudice. That vampire of the mind which flies about in the darkness of ignorance and sucks the blood of ruddy hopes and healthy enterprises—that is prejudice. That smouldering dislike of the different which can flame up into a rage of hatred against our pioneers, our saints, and our saviours—that is prejudice. Among the sins of men there is none which has more heavily hindered our progress.

Whence come these prejudices of ours? It would seem at times, out of nothing. As was said by one of its victims:

"Prejudice, like the spider, makes everywhere its home and lives where there seems nothing to live on." But when we look more closely we can discover some materials out of which these spidery prejudices are woven.

In the first place, some of our prejudices have come by social inheritance. It has been said that we are tattooed with the beliefs of our tribe while we are yet in our cradles. At a surprisingly early age we take on the unreasoned likes and dislikes of our families and our communities. A discriminating lady in a New Jersey suburb was telling recently of her little eight year old daughter's first manifestation of race prejudice. The small girl came home from school one day, dropping the remark that she did not like a certain playmate. The mother at once sensed the fact that here was the beginning of race discrimination for the schoolmate had a Jewish name. The wise mother, thinking she would scotch the evil idea in its very inception, tried to explain that the Jewish people had just as much to be proud of as any other race. She ended by saying, "Why, don't you know that Jesus was a Jew?" The tiny girl pondered that a moment and then replied, "Well—anyway—God was an American."

Here was an illustration of the way a prejudice can precede the stage of reason. Many of our dislikes developed in that hazy half-vision of childhood before the clear light of reason dawned, and when we have become men we have not put away the childish things. It is highly important that we should watch the juncture of the older and younger generations in order to prevent the child from catching the prejudices of the parent. We should try to keep the sour grapes which the fathers have eaten from setting "the children's teeth on edge."

A second source of prejudice is ignorance. We often dislike because we do not know. We prejudge on partial knowledge. In earlier days when means of communication and social interchange were few, some of the prejudice due to ignorance may have been excusable. But now that nations, races and religions have been brought within range of acquaintanceship such old prejudices can no longer be pardoned.

And certainly it would be supposed that our Hebrew and Christian religions with their doctrine of divine fatherhood would bring us to a human brotherhood. But it is humiliating to confess that religious bodies have frequently been fomenters of prejudice. Recently leading liberal members of the Jewish, Roman Catholic and Protestant faiths have been meeting in discussion groups seeking a better understanding between these three great religious organizations. At those round tables it was brought out that despite all our public protestation of friendship there is given little opportunity to the membership of any one religious body to know the facts about the others. What the average Protestant church member, for instance, knows about Judaism or Roman Catholicism is gleaned from the literature of his own church rather than from the writings of the other groups. And very often, it must be admitted, we take our supposed information from anonymous and irresponsible sources. In the absence of authentic inside knowledge regarding other religious faiths, all sorts of rumors and misinformation rise to poison and prejudice the minds.

Yes, with all our printing presses and travel, with all our schools and churches, much prejudice due to ignorance still persists. We need more full information to free us from the narrowness of half-truths. But we need something more than mere facts. We must have imagination enough to put ourselves in the other fellow's place and see how the facts look to him as well as to us. That is, if I am to be fair-minded toward the member of some other faith, I must try to imagine how I should feel if I had been reared in his religious environment. If I am to be fair-minded toward the member of some other race, I must try to think how life would look to me if my skin were of his color. It takes imagination as well as information to free us from the prejudices of ignorance. And it takes also consecration to cement our information and imagination together into concrete enduring fairmindedness. Facts, no matter how well understood, do not guarantee the formula of fair and brotherly conduct. There must be the will to follow where the facts lead, cost what it may. Only thus can we escape from our imprisoning caves of ignorant prejudice.

A third source of prejudice is fear. Fear is at the root of more unfair dislikes than we commonly realize. Take, for instance, that prejudice against foreigners which is so common among uncultured Americans, leading to vulgar epithets like "dago" and "chink." How much of that aversion could be traced back to the fear that these foreign immigrants might take away our jobs or lower our standards of living! Or consider the hostility to the people of different color. I have spent a recent week in the Southland receiving again the gracious hospitality of that region, and I have been once more reminded that racial bitterness is largely confined to the lower classes and is due more to fear of economic rivalry than to race differences. Or turn to our religious groups. Is their hostility to one another due to their differences of creed or rather to the fear, conscious or unconscious, that the other might secure too much control of the social and governmental institutions?

Whenever any group, religious, racial or national, fears its prestige or security threatened by another group—there you have fertile ground for prejudice. And there you have also the host of pernicious propagandists seeking to cultivate those seeds of fear and hostility. Among the curses of contemporary life are those persons who play upon the fears of others. One of the needs of our time is to rid society of these professional writers, secretaries and agitators who make a living rousing the prejudices of people by playing up their fear of other groups.

When we thus see from what sordid materials of tradition, ignorance and fear our spiders' webs of prejudice are woven, we feel a springtime urge for a mental house-cleaning. We desire to be open-minded. We wish to be purged of the stigma of unfair thinking as well as unfair playing. We would be tolerant. But tolerance as a mere passive attitude of non-interference is not enough. The word "tolerate" often connotes condescension. A man frequently says "I tolerate—, but," and then follows the tell-tale confession of dislike. Religious tolerance may be a long sea mile from religious brotherhood. A policy of hands off as between races, nations, sects, or persons is not an adequate program for the removal of prejudice.

Passive tolerance must be supplemented by active and frequent conference. When two individuals or groups come together to talk over their differences, a process of mental approach begins which resembles a hot rally in tennis. By making a first gesture toward understanding, one participant forces the other to shift his position, however slightly, to receive it. By this interchange of ideas each works closer to the separating net, provided a sportsmanlike temper is preserved on both sides. Thus the method of friendly conference can be made to help mightily in translating mere tolerance into real brotherhood. Along this line more progress has been made during the last five years than in the preceding fifty.

But good as it is, the act of conferring together is not enough. In overcoming prejudice working together is even more effective than talking together. Still fresh in our minds are those fraternal feelings begotten by war-time cooperation between religious and racial groups. When men are bearing the same burdens and sharing the same sufferings they discover that the divisions of sect or race do not reach down to the heart.

No more conspicuous illustration of the power of cooperation in conquering prejudice could be cited than that of Lincoln's treatment of Stanton. During the presidential campaign, Edwin M. Stanton is reported to have spoken of the rail splitter from Illinois as "a low cunning clown." His aversion to Lincoln continued vocal through the early period of the latter's administration. The reports of his attitude were carried to the White House. Natural human emotions would seem to have prompted the president to resentment. But Lincoln did not add to his own burdens by bearing personal grudges. He might then have merely tolerated Stanton in contemptuous silence, or he might have been magnanimous enough to call in his critic for a conference. Lincoln, however, went further. He appointed Stanton to his cabinet. A few years later when the martyred leader lay dead, it was Stanton who stood by his bedside and said, "There lies the greatest ruler of men the world has ever seen."

It was cooperation plus conference which broke down that barrier of personal prejudice. It was the same combination which served so quickly to cement the south and the north after the now almost-forgotten civil war. And only thus can we bring a Christ-like spirit of brotherhood into our own communities.

Geoffrey A. Studdert Kennedy

The son of a vicar of a poor parish in Leeds, England, Geoffrey A. Studdert Kennedy was educated at the Leeds Grammar School and Trinity College, Dublin. After his ordination, he returned to work with his father in the slums of Leeds. In 1914 he was appointed Vicar of St. Paul's, Worcester, a very poor parish of some 3,000 communicants. This background and experience gave him a deep sense of social needs and enlisted him in the cause of the poor and underprivileged, a cause reflected in much that Dr. Kennedy has written and spoken. As chaplain during World War I, he was awarded the Military Cross in 1917. His burning social consciousness and compassion for the less fortunate are revealed in the sermon given here.

BREAD, WORK, AND LOVE

Give us this day our daily bread. MATTHEW 6:11.
But My Father giveth you the true Bread. JOHN 6:32.

ARE you afraid of poverty? I am. I have been all my life. I think that if we are honest with ourselves, most of us would confess to a fear of poverty. It is, next perhaps to the fear of death, the most prevalent and powerful of all the fears that haunt and hurt the lives of men and women in the world. Fear has always played a leading part in human life, and the fear of poverty is an ancient enemy. All down the ages men have struggled against it, and human history may well be viewed as the story of that struggle, a tragic and terrible story. Life, when you strip off the trimmings, is nothing but the struggle for bread.

Now, that seems to be a mean and sordid view of life, and we are tempted to turn from it, and dismiss it with disgust. And yet, if we are honest and courageous in our thought, we cannot help acknowledging that there is much truth in it, and without honesty and courage there is no hope of salvation either for our bodies or our souls.

When we think of ourselves, you and I, and of our daily lives, there is nothing which in reality influences our thoughts and actions so much as the way in which we earn our living, struggle for our daily bread. For many, perhaps for most of us here, the struggle is in part disguised. We are not conscious of struggling with or against anybody else. We apply for, or are chosen for, a job, and we do it. We may do it for the most part without thinking of what we are to get out of it. It is our duty, and we may find much joy in it. We are paid for our work, but we do not work only, or even mainly, for our pay. We do not consciously struggle for bread. And yet there are facts behind our consciousness. If we lost the job, if the pay were delayed or cut in half, we should become vividly conscious of it. We should be, as we say, brought up against realities. We should become conscious of daily bread.

You applied for and got that job, and you were very pleased. You felt at peace with all the world. You got it. Somebody else did not. But he got something else. Perhaps he did. Perhaps he did not. He may be searching still. You were not conscious of cutting the other out. You did not want to cut him out. But you did. There was a struggle for bread. Sometimes even in these days you can see the struggle, naked and without disguise, if you go and stand outside the dock gates at Liverpool and see the foreman come out to get men for a ship's unloading. There is a crowd of men always. More men than jobs. God only knows upon what principle or system they are selected. But watch the faces of those who are not successful, and you see the struggle for bread, naked, and in its nakedness pitiful. Naked or decently disguised, the struggle goes on. It always has gone on. All over the world. Throughout all time. Man with man, tribe with tribe, class with class, nation with nation, there always has been, there is now the struggle for bread, and behind it driving, goading, wounding, the fear of poverty.

How are we to reconcile this age-long and world-wide struggle for bread with the picture of our Father's love which is the essence of the Gospel of Jesus Christ? Is the world a home or a battlefield? Is life a struggle or a gift? Is the Gospel picture itself just a golden garment of make-believe with which pious hands have sought to hide the ugliness of the struggle for bread? Must we, if we be honest, tear that garment away and be content to look upon the naked fact? That is a question which, in a thousand different forms, presents itself to Christians of to-day. Can we face the facts of life and still believe in our Father? God does not give us bread. We have to struggle for it. We must either earn it or steal it; there is no third alternative. If a man will not work, neither shall he eat. That is the law of life. Those who strive to evade that law are thieves. There are the sick, the aged and infirm, and the children, and to them we feel it is right that we should give their daily bread.

But there is something degraded and degrading about giving bread to those who ought to earn it. There is something wrong about begging. Giving away money, or bread for which money stands, is one of the most difficult and dangerous things in the world to do. Even when a brother begs for what he ought to earn, a man might very well hesitate for fear of doing harm. There are men and women we would like to help, and we know they need it, but we dare not offer to give. They are what we call proud. They have a strong conviction that they ought to earn. God does not give us bread. There never was a harvest on the earth until men learned to work together. Men may hunt and kill alone, but they must sow and reap together. It was work that taught us love. That is the other side of the picture. Men have learned to love each other by working together for bread. There is, and there has been, a struggle for bread, but the struggle never made the bread; it has always meant work, and work is the author of love. Husband and wife were first of all workmates. They came together to work for their children, and by working learned to love. The family was a working unit, and is a working unit still.

For thousands of years it was the chief working unit. All labour centred round the home, and the only love there was on earth was found within the home. Men loved their own kith and kin, but outside that narrow circle the world was full of enemies. But slowly the working unit widened as men learned to trade with and work with their neighbours. Then neighour-love began. It grew very slowly. Men were suspicious of one another and afraid. They distrusted strangers and did not willingly combine. Often they fought one another bitterly before they settled down to work together. But always as they worked together love and friendship grew. And as the working unit widened, wealth increased and the harvest was more plentiful. For the more men work together, the richer the harvest grows. Love is the real source of wealth. It has not been a smooth and easy process this; it has been checked and broken a million times. It is checked and broken still. The old hatreds and suspicions, the old fear of strangers and dislike of foreigners, persist and constantly tend to break the wider working unit up or prevent us making it. But in spite of apparently insurmountable obstacles the majestic process persists. The working unit widens, and with it grows the sweep of neighbour-love. God's plan and purpose for the world are being wrought out through work. He has taken a great step forward in these latter days. The working unit has, with almost dramatic suddenness, widened out until, for the first time in history, it includes the entire world. The harvest for which you meet to render thanks at this Festival of Harvest is the harvest of the world.

But a few years back a summer such as we have had would have set the ghost of famine walking through our villages and towns. But our harvest-fields are wider now, and we reap from all the world. God has spoken and decreed that from henceforth all men and women, east, west, north, and south, over the length and breadth of the earth, should be workmates, and by working together learn to love. It is in some ways a terrible decree, because we are not ready for it. Our old habits and inherited ways of thought die hard. We still want to be independent and work away at our own little plot. We will try to conquer one another, and pretend that we do not need one another. We break out into squabbles and fights, and the feet of warring armies trample down the golden corn and lay waste the smiling summer lands. We still are savages at heart, suspicious, mistrustful, stubborn, and very much afraid. We wave our flags and beat our drums, and threaten one another at home and abroad. We organise ourselves into independent cliques, classes, and nations, and stand up for our rights. On the surface it would seem as though God's decree were causing more hatred than love. But all this fretting and fuming is vain. God has spoken, and we shall be one. Slowly and painfully, but surely too, we are learning our lesson, the lesson of universal love.

Those who see at the root of all man's life the struggle for bread are, I believe, right in their facts, but wrong in the meaning they give to the facts. They do not overrate the importance of the economic factor in human evolution, but they do misinterpret it. They do not understand the meaning of bread. They think of bread in terms of struggle, whereas it should be thought of in terms of work, and then of love. They think bread means war, when in truth it means peace.

It is with our eyes fixed upon the future that we pray, "Give us this day our daily bread"—not merely that we may be fed, but that the Father's name may be hallowed, His Kingdom come, His will be done on earth as it is in heaven. It is with our eyes fixed upon the future that we stretch out our hands and take into them a piece of Bread, which, because in loving fellowship we have offered it up as all bread should be offered up, means Christ, and helps to make that meaning part of the very substance of our souls. For the Kingdom of God comes not by sword or strife, nor yet by sitting still, but as men learn to will and work together in ever-widening fellowship and in the spirit of Him who came not to be ministered unto, but to minister—who is the true meaning of Bread.

Frederick W. Norwood

Frederick W. Norwood was born in Australia. He attained tremendous popularity among the soldiers when he served as chaplain in France during World War I. After the war he was called to London to succeed Dr. Joseph Fort Newton as pastor of the London City Temple. Here he quickly became one of the great preachers of the present generation. In 1922 he spent one summer in the United States as exchange preacher at the Broadway Tabernacle

Church, New York City, and was given the degree of Doctor of Divinity by Ursinus College. Dr. Norwood's sermons are intensely vital, and his pulpit manner is exceedingly human and unconventional.

RECIPROCAL FAITH

Many believed in his name . . . but Jesus did not commit himself unto them. JOHN 2:23, 24.

"BUT JESUS." That disjunctive is dislocating, startling, arresting! We had thought that He wanted people to believe in Him; we had been told that the reason He did these signs was that they might believe in Him. Why then, when they did believe in Him, did He fail to respond? Have they not said in our ears until we were weary of hearing, "Only believe"? But there seems to have been a difficulty upon His side; they believed, but He did not respond. "But Jesus!" The disjunctive arrests the reverent mind, sets it thinking, probing back even to the original tongue itself, and then we discover that the same word in the Greek is rendered differently in our English translation. The same word that means "belief" is also translated "commit."

"Many believed in him . . . but Jesus did not commit himself unto them."

Our translators, in seeking to find a word which would make the meaning clear to English ears, have probably to some extent obscured the sense. They might have got nearer to the mark if they had said, "Many believed in Him, but Jesus did not believe in them."

Belief then is a reciprocal thing after all. It takes two to make a Christian—myself and Jesus. If I believe in Him, and He does not believe in me, am I a Christian? How futile it has been for us to put all the emphasis upon our side of believing. Belief is a reciprocal thing. We have overemphasized the value of the creed, yet nothing has been more often demonstrated than the fact that correctness in creed is not necessarily the same thing as correctness in spirit. One would trust a Christian with one's life, but one would not necessarily trust the merely orthodox. The creed is our side of faith, but there is another side, and faith is not consummated until the two meet. That is a fact of human experience.

What I believe depends upon a good many things. It depends to a great extent upon the way in which I have been brought up. It depends also upon the cleanness with which certain things have been explained, upon the nature of the experiences through which I have passed in life, and also upon my own reaction to those factors, so that what I believe depends not upon myself alone. It is not impossible that there are some folk who have been brought up in a wrong way, to whom things have never been explained, whose experiences have been very adverse, and yet Jesus might believe in them, though they did not believe in Him.

In that great parable, which He told, of the end of all things, the parable of the sheep and the goats, as we call it, you remember He represented Himself as saying, "Blessed are ye," and some of those to whom He spoke said, "Lord, when saw we thee?" They did not know Him, they had never met Him, but He said, "Inasmuch as ye did it unto these, ye did it unto me." They did not believe in Him, but He believed in them. I venture to think that there are many people in this world who do not believe in Jesus, who never heard His name, who have not had the possibility of believing, but He may believe in them; and if one has to separate the two, surely that is the greater thing after all.

As we study the life of the Master, in His dealings with men, does it not seem to you that the chief factor in their salvation was not so much their belief in Him as His belief in them?

"Simon," said He, the first day that Peter came to Him, "thou shalt be called a rock." Simon Peter was anything but a rock, the days came again and again when that element of instability in his character allowed him to be swept off his feet and threatened to engulf him, but I can imagine Peter pulling himself up and saying, "He said I was a rock," and a rock he became at last.

Thomas was not very successful as a believer; he was not built that way; he could not help himself; he had to ask questions, and often enough he found his problems insoluble. But Jesus believed in Thomas, and one day revealed Himself in a special manner to him. Jesus knew what we discover as we study the life of Thomas, that perplexed as he was mentally, he was very loyal personally. It was Thomas who said, when they tried in vain to restrain Jesus from going down amongst the Jews for fear He might be stoned, "Let us go with him, that we may die with him." Thomas was not very clear in his theological beliefs, but he was very loyal in his personal trust, and Jesus believed in Thomas.

Jesus believed in Zaccheus; I do not know why,—I cannot find anything about Zaccheus that makes me disposed to believe in him, except that Jesus did. He was chief of the publicans, and the publicans were a bad lot, but Jesus believed in Zaccheus, and Zaccheus came down from his tree into the midst of the hostile crowd and said:

"Lord, the half of my goods I give to the poor; and if I have wrongfully exacted aught from any man, I restore fourfold."

Jesus believed in Zaccheus, and Zaccheus accordingly believed in both Jesus and himself.

Jesus believed in Mary Magdalene; I do not know why. There is not much in her life to inspire confidence, but Jesus believed in her, and Mary Magdalene became pure and beautiful because of His belief.

Jesus believed in the woman of Samaria; I can hardly tell why. To me she seems ignorant, vulgar, curious, as well as immoral, but He believed in her, and the woman responded to His belief and became a naïve evangelist.

It was the same in His pictorial teaching. Jesus believed in the publican in the Temple; whether he was a real character or not I do not know, but he was typical. Jesus believed in the publican who only smote his breast and said, "God, be merciful to me a sinner." He did not seem to believe overmuch in the Pharisee, though the odds are all in his favour. He had performed all his religious duties, he fasted twice in the week, he gave alms; there appears to be little wrong in the Pharisee, but Jesus did not believe in him much. He did believe in the publican, and somehow our hearts go out to the publican and not to the Pharisee.

Jesus believed in the younger brother in that parable of the Prodigal Son; I do not know why; there does not seem much indication that he was worth believing in. Thoughtless, selfish, grasping, riotous, careless. I have seen lots of prodigals like that; God knows they are pitiful people; they have such a way of drifting back again to the hog-troughs. One would find it easier to believe in the elder brother, who had never done anything palpably wrong, but had been a loyal son and a faithful worker all the days of his life. But Jesus believed in the younger one, and the world's sympathy goes in the same direction. You feel somehow there was that in him, in spite of his weaknesses, which made him superior to the elder brother. It was the belief of Jesus in them that transformed men more than their belief in Him.

And surely it is the same to-day. It is not so much what I believe, for I have been taught many things, as you have, and have had certain influences playing upon me all the time, as you have. It is not so much what we believe; that is half of the problem; but the real value lies in the response that comes to us from that in which we believe. In other words, a Christian is not a man who holds on to Jesus by a mere intellectual effort; a Christian is a man or woman in whom the Spirit of Jesus becomes manifest. Jesus may become manifest in a man or woman whose mental knowledge concerning Him is very vague and imperfect indeed.

We build churches, preach sermons, try different religious methods, like children playing with their building blocks. The great worker upon the hearts of men is the invisible silent Spirit, and only He knows how He transmutes that external meaningless belief into the character that merits confidence. We pay too much attention to the merely doctrinal side of our creed. I do not minimize its value, it makes all the difference to have a clear and pure teaching, but it is only half of the mystery after all. It is not so much whether I believe in God as whether God believes in me. I am not a Christian because I think it most probable that Jesus of Nazareth was the Son of God; I am a Christian rather if Jesus of Nazareth could have trusted me—can indeed trust me now.

In this City Temple one always has the consciousness that there are folk who gather from Sunday to Sunday, but who have little definite creedal belief. I want to say to you, "The essence of true Christianity is being worthy of the trust of Jesus Christ." Suppose that the great eternal Spirit in this world is a Spirit like that of Christ. Suppose that the last question that shall be asked of us, when life is over, and the greater light has dawned, shall be asked in the Spirit of Jesus of Nazareth, will not the supreme thing be whether we have so lived as to have deserved His trust? You have your difficulties, but can you go away determined to try to live so that Jesus Christ would have trusted you, would have rested His cause in your hands, and believed that, in spite of all your weaknesses or your failings, you would remain loyal and carry through at last?

Let us try to live so that Jesus might reasonably believe in us. They whom Jesus could have believed in are usually those in whom others believe. When sufficient time has passed, we forget the idiosyncrasies of their belief and remember just THAT!

George A. Buttrick

[1892–   ]

Dr. George A. Buttrick was born at Seaham Harbor, England. After completing his education at Victoria University, Manchester, and Lancashire Independent Seminary, he came to the United States and began a highly successful preaching career. In 1921 he was called to the pulpit of the old First Church, Buffalo, where he so distinguished himself that he was invited to succeed Dr. Henry Sloane Coffin at the Madison Avenue Church, New York City, in 1927. He is regarded as one of the outstanding pulpit orators in the country, and his sermons never fail to attract large audiences. This sermon is an Easter message, vivid and profound, with a power born of deep faith and conviction.

THE GOSPEL OF IMMORTALITY

If a man die, shall he live again? Job 14:14.
. . . the appearing of our Savior, Jesus Christ, who abolished death, and brought life and immortality to light. II Timothy 1:10.

"If a man die"—the question old as death itself and as new as the newest grave! But what a strange way to ask it: "*If* a man die." There is no "if" about death. The "grim reaper" whets his scythe on the day we are born, and soon or late the scythe will cut us down. That is one of the few prophecies we may indulge with certainty concerning this uncertain thing called life.

Since man *must* die, shall he live again? There is nobody into whose field of affection that "reaper" has not come. One moment your friend was there—light in the eyes, speech on the lips, energy in the hands, a warm and living spirit; the next moment—gone. In that fraction of a second what has happened? Everything is as before—eyes, lips, hands—but everything is different. Nothing has been lost except—your loved one! Then are souls blown out like candles? Are those terrible and familiar words of Shakespeare the whole truth and nothing but the truth?—

> Tomorrow and tomorrow and tomorrow,
> Creeps in this petty pace from day to day,
> To the last syllable of recorded time:
> And all our yesterdays have lighted fools
> The way to dusty death. Out, out, brief candle!
> Life's but a walking shadow; a poor player,
> That struts and frets his hour upon the stage,
> And then is heard no more: It is a tale
> Told by an idiot, full of sound and fury,
> Signifying nothing.

The first of these texts asks the inevitable question. Notice the second text: It speaks of Jesus as bringing immortality to light. Immortality, that is to say, was in human life before he came, but it was encompassed by shadows and doubts. He brought it into the daylight so that every one might see it. Immortality was like a seed and Jesus was like the sun. He drew the seed from its dark prison and made it blossom gloriously. We may fasten, then, on this truth first: Immortality has always been in human life. There is eternity in our nature.

Age after age the instinct for immortality endures. Flames cannot scorch it, nor floods drown it, nor bayonets pierce it, nor sorrow conquer it.

In other realms of life instincts are not deceptive. By some sure intuition the birds fly south before the first touch of winter has come. An instinct is their only compass, but it does not play them false:

> I go to prove my soul.
> I see my way as birds their trackless way—
> I shall arrive. What time, what circuit first,
> I ask not: but unless God send his hail,

> Or blinding fireballs, sleet, or stifling snow,
> In some time, his good time, I shall arrive:
> He guides me and the bird.

Likewise, immortality is in our conscience. Have you ever heard a man say, as I once heard a man say in bitter indignation for a wrong done to his child, "If there isn't a hell, there ought to be." It is the voice of conscience, and conscience also says: "If there isn't a heaven, there ought to be." There are too many wrongs unrighted for this to be the only world.

Again, immortality is in our affections. What true affection has ever been content to die? Say of some loved one lost to you that the loss is total and irretrievable, and even as you say the words your spirit will shudder. That shudder is prophetic of eternity. Love will not believe that love is nothing but ashes and tears.

Once more, immortality is in our sense of God. The feeling for God was in the world before Jesus came. I am speaking now not of the mind's assent to the proposition that God exists.

Those who have known God cannot think of him as one who would blow out personality as though it were a cheap candle. They cannot think of God as having power to make children capable of longing for immortality yet without power to give them the immortality for which they long, for in that case Death would be the real God and our so-called "God" would be a tinpot monarch ruling by sufferance. Nor can they deem it possible (these who have known God) that he has mocked his children with the dream of eternity, for then he would be not God but a devil with creatures far nobler than he. I am appealing now directly to the religious experience of the race. It is not less valid (it is more valid, I think) than any other kind of experience. The highest religious insight of mankind has not been able to think of God as either a half-God ruling over a vast graveyard or a devil-God mocking his children with false hopes. The saints ever have said: "O taste and see that the Lord is good," "his loving-kindness is better than life," "Yea, though I walk through the valley of the shadow of death, I will fear no evil." They have faced denials as Frederick H. W. Myers faced them:

> Whoso has felt the Spirit of the Highest,
> Cannot confound him, or doubt him, or deny;
> Yea, with one voice, O world, tho' thou deniest,
> Stand thou on that side, for on this stand I.

We are urging the truth that immortality has always been embedded in human life. It has stirred only fitfully, perhaps, but it has never been destroyed. It is in our instincts, our conscience, our love, our sense of God. Death is a cold and stubborn fact. Its stillness is terrifying to the eyes, its silence to the ears, it unresponsiveness to the hands. But which will you believe—your eyes or your conscience, your ears or your heart, your hands or your sense of God? The issue narrows to that question.

To that question—and Jesus! The facts concerning Jesus are that he lived and died and rose again. He lived—as no competent student denies. He died. Nobody need doubt that fact. It is reflected in the utter despair of his disciples. "We trusted this had been he who should have redeemed Israel" . . . but he was not what they had hoped. Such was their mood. Their Messiah, their King, had ended not on a throne but (irony of ironies) on a cross. They remained, the bedraggled survivors of a broken cause. Oh, well, they would know better than to trust the next dreamer. "I go a-fishing," said Peter. Back to the old tasks, sadder but wiser men! Jesus died. Then what happened? Suddenly this same Peter is facing the foes of Jesus with reckless courage. Listen to him as he speaks to them: "Jesus of Nazareth . . . him ye have taken, and by wicked hands have crucified and slain. Whom God hath raised up, having loosed the bonds of death, because it was not possible that death could hold him!"

What had happened? We must concentrate on the primary and central fact. The rolling away of a stone is not primary. The manner in which the tomb was robbed of its corpse is not the primary fact. The problem of the resurrection appearances of Jesus is perplexing and important, but not primary. This is the primary fact: As it might have been on Good Friday the disciples of Jesus were downcast in tragic loss, and as it might have been on Easter Sunday they were thrilling with victory. Why did these cowering men suddenly rise from their bemoanings and with light on their faces fairly spring on the world with the message of a living Saviour for whom they were willing to suffer any persecution? Read the New Testament, and see if there are any "In Memoriam" tendencies in it. It is filled with the sense of the abiding, empowering presence of Jesus. Why?

Delusion, suggests somebody. Oh, no! Figs do not grow on thistles, and the fervor that quickened a dead world did not grow on the stalk of a delusion. The noble army of martyrs did not embrace death by faggot and sword for the sake of a delusion. Churches named after this crucified Jesus did not spring up like flowers in a wilderness all because of a delusion. Our hymn books are not crammed with devotion to a living Jesus because the best men and women for two thousand years have fed on the ashes of a delusion. Mighty events demand a commensurate cause. There is only one commensurate cause and Peter proclaimed it: "Whom God hath raised up, having loosed the bonds of death, for it was not possible that death could hold him."

He has brought life and immortality to light. It was in our conscience, but our conscience was sadly blemished. It was in our love, but our love at best was selfish. It was in our sense of God, but our sense of God was dim. Then he came. He was all conscience—a holiness passionately pure; he was all love—a compassion self-forgetting even unto death; he was all sense of God—walking in God as in an atmosphere, vital with God as a pulse is vital within the blood. We must reverently honor his own claim: "I and my Father are one." The immortality which has stirred fitfully within our shadowy humanity shone radiant in him: "He brought it to light." What had he to do with death? How is it conceivable that a few chemical changes in his flesh could extinguish his soul? "It was not possible that death could hold him."

I beg you: Take your faith out of the subjunctive mood. Do not say, "If Christ be risen." Put it in the indicative mood. Say with a conviction born of him, born of the deathless quality of his soul, born of the experience of his living power through the Christian years: "Now is Christ risen from the dead." Trust your loved ones to his care. Trust yourselves to him by trying to live his life. So shall you have immortality—not as an argument but as a life, not as a theory but as his presence! "Thanks be to God who giveth us the victory through our Lord Jesus Christ."

Abba Hillel Silver

[1893-   ]

Educated in the public schools of New York City, at the University of Cincinnati, and the Hebrew Union College, Abba Hillel Silver has become one of America's most brilliant Jewish preachers. His picturesque style of speaking and his gift for leadership among his people led to his being called in 1917 to the rabbinate of the Temple of Cleveland, one of the country's largest synagogues. He is a member of several influential Jewish bodies and has played a major role in Jewish education in this country. The following sermon glows with the light of idealism noticeable throughout the history of the Jewish people.

THE VISION SPLENDID

Choose you this day whom you will serve. JOSHUA 24:15.

WE ARE told in sacred lore, that when their hours of study were over, and the wise men left the halls of the Academy, they departed from one another with the following quaint and beautiful blessing: "Mayest thou behold thy world during thy lifetime, but may thine end be in Life Eternal, and thy hopes, may they endure throughout all generations." On New Year's Day, we too take leave, not from one another, but from the old year, and from all that it held for us of good and evil, of gain and loss; and I know of no more seemly benediction which we can bestow upon one another at this hour, than this selfsame prayer of the Rabbis.

If I were to bless you this day, between the dark and the dawn of the New Year, with the choicest gift in the treasure-house of God, I could think of none more rare and precious than this. It is threefold benison, each part segment of a perfect whole: "Mayest thou behold thy world during thy lifetime." Is there anything more complete than this? To see our whole world while we live! The world of our desires and the world of our hopes! To win every goal, to taste every fruit, to slake every thirst at the fountain of success. What a generous benediction this is! Surely this is what we pray for on this, our Holy Day. "Grant us life, long life; grant us health, happiness, prosperity, peace. Let us not die ere the last mile of our journey is covered and the last beautiful scene glimpsed. Permit us to see our whole world while we live."

And how thoroughly human a prayer it is! What man is there who would wish to close the fascinating book of life before the last chapter is read and the last page is turned and the story is fully told! Unless he be of those who have suffered much, whose eyes have been darkened by unutterable sorrow, and from whose hearts anguish has drained all love of life. We all wish to live, to see all, to know all, to taste all, to have all. The world is so resplendent with the works of God and the works of man, with the beauty that dwells in the earth and in the habitations of the children of earth. Our souls are hungry for this earth beauty and this life beauty, for all the wonder and grace which are in existence. How very human then is this prayer, and how truly it voices our deepmost longings. And yet, somehow, the wise men of old, who uttered this valediction, keenly felt its incompleteness, for they hastened to supplement it: "But may thine end be in Life Eternal, and thy hopes, may they endure throughout all generations." On the face of it, a paradox! If one could see his whole world in his lifetime, why should his end be in life eternal? If one could realize all his cherished hopes here and now, why should they be extended throughout all subsequent generations?

But the Rabbis, who saw life steadily, felt this wish to be inadequate, because unattainable. They knew that no man can see his whole world in his lifetime, nor realize his high hopes in his generation. But they also knew of a world which every man could realize in his lifetime, and of a hope which every man could see fulfilled. In the eyes of the Rabbis there were two worlds; the world of our wishes and desires, and the world which these same wishes and desires create for us and in us. The world of our dreams and hopes, and the world which these dreams and hopes surround us with. In a sense every man builds his own world. Every man constructs his own world, his universe of wish and desire, the far-flung constellation of passionate cravings and longings, whose fiery center is self. The worlds of no two men are alike. Some build their world of clay, of carnal wishes and coarse desires. It is narrow, never extending beyond the reach of the senses. Others fashion their dream-empires of finer stuff, of the needs of the mind and soul as well as of the body. Theirs is a larger estate, reaching out through spiritual roads into distant worlds. Still others, who are caught up by some vision and touched by some inspiration, shape their worlds out of ineffable beauties, transcendent and measureless to man.

And each builder would like to see his dream-world come true in his lifetime. But God, the Master Builder, who has his own plan and his own architectural design, has so ordered his Universe, that none shall see his world fully realized in his lifetime, and that the finer and subtler the stuff the dream-world is made of, the more difficult shall it be of attainment. Even the clay-world is hard to attain. Low desires and earthly cupidity, even when satisfied, leave ashes in the mouth. Each fulfilled desire incites to others, stronger and more impetuous. "The sea hath bounds, but deep desire hath none."

Difficult as the clay-world is of attainment, even more difficult is the dream-world which some men wish to see fulfilled in their lifetime—the world which is not circumscribed by the ordinary wants of life, the world fashioned out of the silver sheen of ideals and the gold of aspiration, the world patterned after the similitude of God's own perfection. The man who, conscious of his high estate, fashions such a world, and who, by his dreams, would lengthen the road between himself and the beast, and shorten the road between himself and God, the man who projects a wish-world of justice and peace, an empire of knowledge and love, of truth and beauty, that man will never see his world fulfilled in his lifetime. Such wish-worlds are eternities in the making. No single hand can effect them, no single generation can encompass them. Such dreams lead the dreamer, not to the goal of consummation, but to the pit and the dungeon, the rack and the cross, and all the miserable artifices of a world afraid of his dreams. Such dreams lead the dreamer along the dolorous road of frustration and loneliness, to death.

Many illustrations come to our mind when we think of this. Let us but choose two—an ancient and a modern one. Moses, a leader of men, built for himself a dream-world of heroic design—to liberate a people from the yoke of bondage—to give it a law and a land—to fashion it into a priest-people and to send it forth a messenger of a new revelation and a new covenant. Did he see his world come true? On the top of Mount Nebo, he died a lonely and a world-wearied man, his tired eyes straining to catch a glimpse of the land of his unfulfilled promise. He freed the people. He broke the chains of their body. He could not break the chains of their soul. He gave them freedom, they enslaved themselves. He gave them a law, they flouted it. He gave them a hope, they destroyed it. Where was his world?

And what became of the dream-world of that modern dreamer—Woodrow Wilson? Somewhere in the Capital of our land, there lived for two years a broken old man, alone with his memories, ruminating among the ruins of his shattered dream-world. He had visioned mankind healed and redeemed, made one in peace and freedom. He failed. During the early years of the great world struggle he sought to maintain neutrality. He failed. He gave his life blood to establish a covenant of peoples to enforce peace. He failed. He hoped for peace without victory, and failed. He hoped for peace with victory, and failed. He hoped that justice and comity would follow the Pentecost of calamity, and behold, violence and hatred everywhere. Did he see his world in his lifetime? He died even as his dreams died.

Our ancient sages knew the sorry plight of such world builders. They therefore added to their benediction this phrase: "But may thine end be in Life Eternal, and thy hopes, may they endure throughout all generations." The end is not here—cannot, should not, be here. A world which a man can achieve in his lifetime is unworthy of him—unworthy of the reach of his imagination, the chivalry of his spirit, the hardihood of his faith. Only such tasks and ambitions are worthy of us as lay bare the finitude of our bodies and the infinitude of our souls, the impotence of flesh and the omnipotence of spirit, the brevity of our days and the eternity of our dreams. Blessed is the man whose dream outlives him! Blessed is the man who is strong enough to see himself grow old and powerless while his ideal remains young and green. For then, old age assumes a dignity which compensates for our infirmities. The flame of life may burn low, but the holy incense of our visions will rise inextinguishable from the undefiled altars of our ageless souls.

The world, then, of dreams and ideals which man creates for himself, cannot be, should not be, achieved in his lifetime. But the Rabbis knew of another world which they believed every man *could* and *should* achieve in his lifetime. It is the world created for man by his own ideals. It is built up of mental and spiritual reactions to those ideals, out of enthusiasms and exaltations which these very ideals and loyalties create within him. For the ideals of man give to his life a definite content and a definite scope which are his real world. This, then, was the meaning of the Rabbis: "May your life be blessed with the vision of a world so beautiful that it will crowd your life with beauty, even though the vision cannot be fulfilled in your lifetime. Life may deny you the world of achievement, it cannot deny you the world of poetry and romance and the rich savor of living which the very presence of the vision within you will create for you." Therein does the spiritual differ from the physical. The physical must be owned or consumed to be enjoyed, but we need not own or consume or realize our ideals in order to enjoy them. We enjoy them in the quest, and struggle for them, in our devotion to them.

Such is the potency of ideals. They give us a whole realm of celestial beauty in which to live, even while these ideals are passing through the tragic stages of denial and frustration which lead to their ultimate transfiguration. And such ideals are within the reach of all men. One need not to be learned, or highborn, or opulent, to have them. They are more precious than gold—and yet the pauper may have them for the asking. Some men have vast estates, but they are lost in waste and weeds. Others have a few square feet in front of their little homes, but love plants a flower-bed there and a tree, and behold, there is beauty and the dream of perfection.

The cobbler at his lathe may have an ideal of high artisanship. He will see the charm of his work during his lifetime. The day-laborer who is conscious of the indispensable character of his work, the merchant who is faithful to his standards of service, the employer who finds in his office a challenge to unselfishness, the professional man who regards his calling as a consecration, all of them have a dream-world which will outlive them, but one which will abundantly bless them throughout their lifetime.

These ideals are near at hand. You need not ascend mountains to find them. They have no habitation. They are everywhere. They are not only near, they are seeking us. Halevi, the mystic poet of the Middle Ages, exclaimed: "I have sought thy nearness, with my whole heart have I called upon thee, but when I went forth to find thee, I found that thou hadst been seeking me." Our ideal is seeking us. Open your eyes, it is here, in your home, in the multitudinous acts of mutual love and sacrifice, in the exalted experience of friendship, in shop, store and office, in your community, in social work, in civic work, in religious work, in the humblest and highest task it is there.

"Behold, I have set before thee this day, Life and the Good, Death and the Evil. Choose thou Life!" Amen.

Fulton John Sheen

[1895–   ]

Dr. Fulton John Sheen, an outstanding Catholic preacher and leader, was born in Illinois and received his education at the Catholic University of America, at the University of Louvain, and at Rome. He was ordained priest in 1919 and in 1926 became a member of the faculty of the Catholic University of America. As a teacher of theology and philosophy, as a guest preacher in many of the leading Catholic churches of America including Saint Patrick's Cathedral, New York City, and as a speaker over the radio, Dr. Sheen's influence has been great among both Catholics and non-Catholics.

THE CHRISTIAN ORDER AND EDUCATION

THERE ARE THREE points we should like to make in today's sermon. First, it is a sound American principle that democracy cannot function without religion and morality. Secondly, American democracy is not making provision for religion and morality. Hence, thirdly, the necessity of restoring religious education in order to preserve democracy.

First, democracy cannot survive without religion and morality.

The second paragraph of the Declaration of Independence is at the same time a Declaration of Dependence, for it states that our rights have come to us from God, and therefore are "unalienable." If our rights come to us from God, as rays come from the sun, does it not follow that only on condition that we preserve our dependence on God will we preserve our independence from tyranny? A negative support is given to this thesis by the totalitarian systems, for it is universally true that where religion is most persecuted, there is man most tyrannized.

This intrinsic connection between democracy and religion is part of the American tradition.

As George Washington the founder of our country said: "Of all the dispositions and habits which lead to political prosperity, religion and morality are indispensable supports. In vain would that man claim the tribute of patriotism who should labor to subvert these great pillars of human happiness . . ."

In the year 1928, Calvin Coolidge stated: "Unless our people are thoroughly instructed in the great truths of religion, they are not fitted to understand our institutions, or to provide them with adequate support."

President Roosevelt said in 1940: ". . . Practical steps should be taken to make available to children and youth through education the resources of religion as an important factor in the democratic way of life and in the development of personal and social integrity."

We have now come to our second point, namely, democracy is not at the present time making provision in education for religion and morality. About the only group modern education really caters to is the group that neither practices nor believes in any religion.

In order that this fact may be developed without provoking any prejudices we shall quote only Protestants and Jews in testimony of its truth.

On December 29, 1940, Mr. Walter Lippmann, addressing the American Association for the Advancement of Science stated: ". . . Modern education is based on a denial that it is necessary, or useful, or desirable for the schools and colleges to continue to transmit from generation to generation the religious and classical culture of the Western world."

Professor Hutchins of the University of Chicago, in June 1940, stated: "In order to believe in democracy we must believe that there is a difference between truth and falsity, good and bad, right and wrong, and that truth, goodness, and right are objective (not subjective) standards, even though they cannot be verified experimentally. Are we prepared to defend these principles? Of course we are not. For forty years and more our intellectual leaders have been telling us that they are not true . . ."

The White House Conference of 1940 stated that of the thirty million children in the United States between the ages of five and seventeen, sixteen million received no religious education whatsoever. When you take out of this sixteen million those who are being educated by the Catholic Church, at its own expense, the proportion becomes more staggering still. It was this growing irreligious element, consisting of those who are devoid of all training in religion and morality, that prompted President Roosevelt in 1940 to say: "We are concerned about the children who are outside the reach of religious influences and are denied help in attaining faith in an ordered universe, and in the Fatherhood of God."

Nicholas Murray Butler of Columbia University commenting upon the fact that the pagan element alone in our population is given the benefit of our tax money stated: "Even the formal prayer that opens each session of the United States Senate and each session of the House of Representatives, and which accompanies each inauguration of the President of the United States, would not be permitted in a tax supported school."

As regards the higher seats of learning, such as colleges and universities, very few of them have retained religion as an integral part of education. Columbia University, for example, was established in 1753 with the chief objective to "teach and to engage children to know God in Jesus Christ." An investigation made some years ago revealed that same college had reduced the number of students believing in God from one in five at entrance, to one in twenty at graduation.

If this condition of ignoring religion and morality existed in less important matters it would have been remedied long ago. If, for example, it had been discovered that the geography of Russia was left out of our schools, how quickly it would be inserted. Why is nothing done about that which our tradition says is the indispensable condition of democracy?

This brings us to our third point—the necessity of restoring religious education in order to preserve democracy. Just as Christian principles demand that democracy be extended economically, so as to give both capital and labor a share in the profits, management, and ownership of industry, so too the Christian Order demands that education be made more democratic by widening its influence so that it satisfies not only the atheist, but also the believer in God. For that reason those interested in the preservation of democracy have suggested that some assistance be given to those who are aiding it by teaching religion. As Professor Hutchins has stated it clearly: "The States may, if they choose, assist pupils to attend the schools of their choice. Since we want all American children to get as good an education as they can, since we know that some children will not voluntarily attend public schools, and since we are not prepared to compel them to do so, it is in the public interest to give States permission to use Federal grants to help them to go to the schools they will attend and to make these schools as good as possible."

What possible objection could there be given in a democracy to equal opportunities for education along religious and cultural lines? The first objection urged is that education should be "neutral"—and "neutral," in this sense, means that religion should not be taught. This is a fallacy. The fact is that there is no such thing as neutral education, that is an education without morality and religion.

Religion and morality are not related to education like raisins to a cake, but as a soul to a body. There can be a cake without raisins, but there cannot be a man without a soul. If education does not inculcate a moral outlook, it will inculcate a materialist or a Communist or a Nazi outlook. Neutrality is absolutely impossible in education. By the mere fact that religious and moral training is neglected, non-religious, non-moral—and in consequence anti-religious, anti-moral—ideology is developed. Religion is either included or excluded in education. Hence a school from which religion is excluded, is bound to become irreligious.

The old notion of "no indoctrination of religion" really meant "indoctrination of doubt and unbelief."

To say we want an education without dogmas is to assert a dogma—the false dogma that man has no soul, no supra-temporal purpose, no other goal than to make money, wed, and die. Without religion and morality there is no philosophy of life, and therefore no proper understanding of the man to be educated. After all, what is the use of living as human beings if we do not know the purpose of being human? Those who are given a so-called "neutral" education have *no reason* for being anything other than anti-social, or of using society for their own personal ends. The only way this egotistic impulse in man can be combatted is by a renewal of his nature from above. This rebirth by God's grace enables man to be a member of society without losing his personal dignity. There is no disputing the necessity of controlling selfish tendencies. All education admits this. The choice is in whether the State will control it by its omnipotence, or whether man will control himself with the aid of God's omnipotence. The whole of civilized man is today confronted with this question: "To whom do you belong?" Education will give the answer.

A second objection against extending democracy in education to those who believe in God and morality, is that America was founded on the principle of the separation of the Church and the State. This is absolutely true and we have no desire to change this principle. But our country was not founded on the principle of the separation of religion and the State. Our Founding Fathers intended that no particular religion should be the national religion, but they never intended that the State should be devoid of religion. It never entered their minds that we would grow up to be an irreligious nation, nor did they ever think that education would be divorced from religion and morality. This is evident from the fact that no signer of the Declaration of Independence was educated in a non-religious school. For a century the United States did not have a President who was educated in a non-religious school. It is true that the First Amendment of the Constitution forbade the establishment of any religion as a national religion. This was because there was an established religion in ten of the thirteen colonies: The Congregational religion in three; the Episcopalian in seven. But the same amendment ordered that Congress should make no laws prohibiting the free exercise of religion.

In the Northwest Ordinance of 1787, our Government insisted that "schools and the means of education shall forever be encouraged," because "religion, morality, and knowledge" are necessary to good government and the happiness of mankind.

Nor is the insinuation true that religious schools are not American schools. A Lutheran school which teaches religion, or a Baptist school which teaches religion, or a Catholic school which teaches religion, even though they are maintained at the expense of these religious groups, are public schools.

Why is it more important now than at any other time to restore religion and morality to education? Because we are entering into a new era of history wherein the grave threat to man's freedom is from the Omnipotent State. Once a nation ceases to believe it begins to obey. As William Penn warned: "Men must be governed by God or they will be ruled by tyrants." The choice before the world is this: Truth or Power, that is, either live by God's Truth or exist under State Power. We are coming into the days of Omnipotence where we will live under the Omnipotence of God or squirm under the Omnipotence of Power.

When Hitler came into power in 1933, the first to capitulate were the professors, and the one force which has never capitulated is religion, as the Catholic bishops and Pastor Niemoeller bear witness. It was the professors who allowed the independent administration of the universities to be abolished, the universities offering no objections to State elected "Rektoren" and "Dekane" who were forced upon them. It was a bitter disappointment for all who considered the German universities the defenders of right and justice; but when one considers that specialization had been carried so far, and a unified philosophy of life so universally abandoned, there was no one idea around which they could rally.

Given a crisis in any country in the world in which totalitarianism in any form threatens the liberty of its citizens, and the first to capitulate will be the non-religious educators. How could it be otherwise, for without a faith, how could they oppose a faith? It will be only those schools which give a moral and religious training which will challenge the right of the State to dominate the soul of man.

That is why the safeguard of American democracy and freedom is in the extension of religious and moral training, and not in its suppression through excessive burdens. There is no reason in the world why any school in the United States which teaches religion and morality should be penalized for being patriotic, or why it should bear all the expenses for giving to the nation the two supports without which, as Washington told us, a nation cannot endure.

It is not fair, it is not democratic, to cater only to the non-religious in education. A child who goes to a religious school may walk on streets maintained by public funds, but in many instances may not ride to school in a bus operated at public expense. The State will build a chapel for citizens when they get into a penitentiary; how about building a few schools to prevent them through moral discipline from getting into a penitentiary? We are preparing an army of ten million men to defend Christian liberty and justice on the battlefields. Shall we not tell them something about that Christian liberty before we give them a gun? A government "of the people, for the people, and by the people," should respect the will of those who believe in religion and morality, even though they be in the minority—for democracy is not the custodian of majority privileges, but the preserver of minority rights.

Would it not be a good idea for America to cease talking about the right to worship, and to begin talking about the duty to worship? For 150 years we have been celebrating our Bill of Rights. How about celebrating our Bill of Duties? The first ten amendments to the Constitution are our Bill of Rights; the Ten Commandments of God are our Bill of Duties.

God grant that America will not be blind to its duties to God Who has given us our rights; that parents will realize that when God made each of their children, He made a crown for each in heaven, and that a vacant crown is their unfulfilled responsibility and their severe judgment; that children will harken to the call of Him Who said: "Suffer the little children to come unto Me, . . . For such is the Kingdom of Heaven" (Mark 10:14). Given another generation of Godless education and we will have tyranny; given religion and morality in education and we will be the most potent government influence for peace in the world. Then shall America be great. And we will love it not because it is great; it will be great because we will love it in the name of God—and that makes anything great.

Some time ago a Nazi soldier in occupied France took his French wife into a hospital. Seeing a crucifix on the wall, he ordered the nun to take it down. She refused! He ordered her again saying that he did not want his child ever to look upon the image of Christ. The nun took it down under threat. The father's wish was fulfilled to the letter. The child was born blind.

God grant that we may never deny to our children the right to gaze upon the image of the Saviour of the World.

Allan Knight Chalmers

[1897–   ]

Dr. Allan Knight Chalmers was born at Cleveland, Ohio, and was educated at Johns Hopkins University and Yale Divinity School. During World War I he served for ten months with the Foyers of the French Army and, after the armistice, was for a brief period in the Motor Transport Corps of the American Army. This experience caused him to give up his ambition to become a professor of history and turned him to plans for entering the ministry. In 1920 he became assistant to the minister of the Dwight Place Congregational Church, New Haven, Connecticut, and later he was called to the Broadway Tabernacle, New York City, to succeed the distinguished Charles E. Jefferson. Dr. Chalmers' simple style, together with his keen imagination and deep religious understanding, are illustrated in the following sermon, typical of his Sunday morning services at the Tabernacle.

THE MIRRORS OF GOD

By this shall all men know that ye are my disciples, if ye show love one to another. JOHN 13:35.

THERE is a little booklet of Principal Jacks of Oxford called "The Lost Radiance of the Christian Religion." I want to use it for an atmospheric prelude to our thought this morning. He develops in his own way the theme that man is a being of vast potentialities and that the world is a storehouse of inexhaustible riches. I read you but one sentence from that book. He speaks of those "who adopt the phrases distinctive of the Gospel but miss the radiant energy that transfigures their meaning and makes them effectual; so that in the long run their Christianity reduces itself to the pursuit of moral excellence under a system of inviolable law like the religion of the Book of Deuteronomy." The book is worth having around if for nothing else than to read some such sentence occasionally, and to see its title standing out on one's shelves,—"The Lost Radiance of the Christian Religion."

My thought will lie in a somewhat different direction. With that as background in our thoughts I am going to talk to you about—Christ. I must confess that it is necessary to take a long mental breath before dealing with the central personality of our faith. We are so queer in our loyalties about him. I hope you noticed the preposition which I used. We argue about him, his theological and metaphysical being. Was he or wasn't he? Did he or didn't he? As men argue about the geology of Genesis, so we have worried about the biology of Christ. We have lost his dynamic.

If you will turn your minds back to a scene occurring just after the Last Supper, you will find yourself in a garden near Jerusalem. Mary stands there weeping. She has just visited the tomb and the body of Jesus is not there. Unable to see through her tears, she says to a figure standing by, "They have taken away my Lord and I know not where they have laid him." Jesus asks her gently why she cries. Mary, still not recognizing him, tells again of the lost presence of Jesus. He says one word,—her name,—"Mary!"; and Mary, her eyes cleared by the firm quietness, recognizes him and says, "Master!"

Am I doing any violence to that scene by drawing from it a parable of life? I do not want to. It does seem, however, that we have pictured there our thoughts of Christ in the present age. No theme is of more perennial interest. He is still being headlined in the papers. Philosophers from their studies, scientists from their laboratories, historians in their research, change our views about him sometimes and sometimes wreck them. The intensity of work, the pursuit of pleasure, these things have taken him away and we can no longer find him in the places where once he was. Those most rigid in their so-called faith in Christ seem sometimes the most bitter and un-Christlike in the way they live; refusing fellowship to all those who do not accept their particular doctrine about him,—about Him, mark you, who said in desperation to his followers one day, "Not every man who says unto me, Lord, Lord, but he that doeth the will of my Father."

I disagree most heartily with those who say that a controversy about Christ is a good thing for the Church, that it rallies men to a cause, that it gives them a standard around which to gather. If we have to fight about him to be Christians we have certainly reversed his spirit. Christianity is living, not loyalty to a belief. "By this shall all men know that ye are my disciples, if ye show love one to another."

From somewhere back in my mind there echoes a curious controversy about angels. The ancient theologians used to argue about how many angels could stand on the point of a pin, trying to reconcile religious faith with the world they knew. How we laugh to think about it. But we are told today that there is a universe of electrons within that same pin point. The seemingly foolish argument is in the present day an interesting scientific problem. "You see," some simple souls say, "it was not as silly as it sounded. A legion of angels *might* have danced upon a pin point."

That change in point of view is obviously not important. Pins are still the same. The essential thing about a pin is in its use. Be they angels or electrons that dance at its point, be it a matter of religious faith or a matter of scientific belief, will it hold, will it do its job? That is the point about the pin point which concerns us.

Likewise, the essential thing about Christ is not his virgin birth or any other doctrine that seeks to explain him. It is whether you have seen him so clearly that the radiance of your life draws other men unto him as a longing and a goal.

In rightly dividing our thought, I want to give you two flashes of light which shone from the life of Jesus in the three years of his earthly ministry and which give us a clew to the radiance of that dynamic spirit.

He was unique, first of all, in his peculiar relationship with God. He knew Him as never man did. Does the tremendous revolution in men's thought of God which Jesus brought, ever occur to you? It is natural for us to think of God as "our Father which art in Heaven." That was a radical heresy in Jesus' time. God was king, ruler, judge, avenger, creator, before. Men trembled in His presence.

You remember when the Children of Israel were transporting from one place of their wandering to another, the sacred Ark of the Covenant, the holy container of the Most High, which must be handled only in reverence by the priests, Uzzah, a common man, a cart driver, walked beside the Ark, and when it tipped perilously on the rough road, he put up his hand to steady it, and God, so the account gives us to understand, struck him dead. "Do you mean to say," the inference would be, "that I, God, cannot take care of my own? I told you not to touch the Ark. Die!" That was a natural interpretation in those times,—a proud, powerful, fearful God.

And then, "Our Father," "Like as a father pitieth his children," "God so loved the world." Jesus took that idea which had been hinted at in esoteric minds and fascinated the thought of common men with it. It is difficult for us to appreciate what that idea meant for Palestine. That the royal God of large affairs, to Whom a thousand years was but as a day, could have time for the humblest of His subjects was a Rip Van Winkle experience in the thinking of men.

We must try to keep fresh in our minds the spiritual brilliance of that revelation. Christ was constantly elaborating God to men. The prodigal's father watching and waiting until the son builds within himself by the experience of life that resolve to come back, even as a servant in his father's house, is so familiar that we miss its significance.

Jesus revealed God so that men through the centuries have been fascinated with his interpretation. It troubles men because it ought to be and is not. He takes a "far-off divine event" out of the realm of a comfortable spiritual idealism and puts it upon our desk pads under the heading, "What to do today."

The revelation of God the Father is not all of God, we know. How can the finite compass the infinite? It is an idea, however, big enough and true enough to call forth all the power of a man's personality. What is in the infinite no man knows, but this stretches man's finite to what is for him an infinite experience. Until we have come closer to filling out that conception of God, the Father, in the common life of man, it is enough for us to try to live it.

He made us feel that obligation. "He spake as never man spake." He showed a new conception of God. He lived in harmony with that God's character, so that he could say with truth, "He that hath seen me hath seen the Father." God was in and through him. He was truly the Son of God.

Not only did Jesus give man a different revelation of God, in like manner he also revealed man to men so that man still longs for the making of men into that Christlike revelation of what man might be. Business men, statesmen, leaders of all branches of men's thought and action say, somewhat helplessly, to be sure, but they say it, that it is in the degree in which men accept Christ's man's standard that the world will be saved.

He believed that men (any man) could become the sons of God; that the brotherhood of man, an essential corollary to the fatherhood of God, was possible, and called men to try it.

One cannot read the story of Jesus in the Gospels, one cannot look upon the pages of history, without realizing the transforming effect of his illumined spirit. Men have needed that radiant quality, the inspiration of one who knows where he is going and is not afraid to go ahead against opposition. The fellowship of Jesus has made weak men strong and strong men heroes.

It makes no difference to me how you determine Christ theologically. I care only that you catch the radiance of his life. As we get closer to the real Jesus, this person of unselfish devotion to the cause of progressive righteousness, we find our lives becoming worth something in the world.

Jesus has never been pictured except in imagination. The only way we can judge what he did look like is to see his reflection in the lives of people. Men look into our lives for the traces of his vanished presence. You and I are the mirrors of God.

Index